A World Engraved

A World Engraved

Archaeology of the Swift Creek Culture

Edited by
Mark Williams and Daniel T. Elliott

The University of Alabama Press
Tuscaloosa and London

Copyright © 1998
The University of Alabama Press
Tuscaloosa, Alabama 35487-0380
All rights reserved
Manufactured in the United States of America

∞

The paper on which this book is printed meets the minimum requirements
of American National Standard for Information Science–Permanence of
Paper for Printed Library Materials, ANSI Z39.48-1984.

Library of Congress Cataloging-in-Publication Data

A world engraved : archaeology of the Swift Creek culture / edited by
Mark Williams and Daniel T. Elliott.
p. cm.
Includes bibliographical references (p. 301) and index.
ISBN 0–8173–0912–8 (paper meets minimum requirements)
1. Swift Creek Site (Ga.) 2. Indians of North
America—Georgia—Antiquities. 3. Indians of North
America—Southern States—Antiquities. 4. Indian pottery—Southern
States. 5. Excavations (Archaeology)—Southern States. 6. Southern
States—Antiquities. I. Williams, Mark, 1948 Aug. 1– II. Elliott,
Daniel T., 1954–
E78.G3 W67 1998
975'.01—ddc21
98–9001

British Library Cataloguing-in-Publication Data available

Contents

Figures and Tables

Figures

Tables

Preface

Perhaps the best carvers of wood in prehistoric North America lived in the southern Appalachian region of the United States between 1400 and 1800 years ago. These Native Americans, certainly represented by many different unknown ethnic groups, have come to be known to archaeologists as the Swift Creek people. Unfortunately, and certainly ironically, not a single wood carving from these people has survived the ravages of time and been preserved to the twentieth century. All that we know of their magnificent wood-carving tradition comes from the images of carved wooden paddles that were impressed into the wet clay walls of their ceramic vessels. These pots, when fired, preserved a decorative art style that is timeless in its beauty and evocative of a different and fascinating way of seeing the world.

The first recognition of this Swift Creek pottery as a distinct and special ware occurred in 1936 near Macon, Georgia. Archaeological excavations took place on a small Indian mound near the banks of Swift Creek, an obscure little stream just northeast of Macon. The excavations there were a small part of a major depression-era archaeological project designed to put people back to work in simple government-sponsored projects. The pottery from this site was immediately recognized by Arthur R. Kelly, who was in charge of the excavations, as unique and distinct from the pottery of any other site excavated in the central Georgia area.

Over the next fifty years research on the Swift Creek culture progressed slowly at best. Occasionally another site would be tested, and eventually the geographic range for this pottery was better understood. Some progress was also made on dating the Swift Creek sites. In all this time, however, there were no detailed or extended attempts to summarize what had been collectively learned about these sites and the people who produced them. It was with this in mind that the Lamar Institute decided to conduct a small conference in the spring of 1993 with two explicit goals. The first goal was to summarize the history of our knowledge of Swift Creek, and the second was to bring together the full range of Swift Creek scholars to present new problems and directions for what we might term *Swift Creek studies*. This volume is the result of that conference.

The Lamar Institute Swift Creek Conference took place on May 28 and 29, 1993, at Ocmulgee National Monument in Macon, Georgia. The detailed conversations of the conference were taped, transcribed, and recently published by the Lamar Institute for those who wish additional details about Swift Creek. The attendees at the conference included the following archaeologists: David Anderson, Keith Ashley, Judy Bense, Dave Davis, Dan Elliott, Rita Elliott, Ricardo Fernandez-Sardine, Jennifer Freer, David Hally, Bennie Keel, Teresa Paglione, Dan Penton, David Phelps, Rebecca Saunders, Betty Smith, Don Smith, Frankie Snow, Karl Steinen, Keith Stephenson, James Stoltman, Mark Williams, Dean Wood, and Jack Wynn. Additional attendees at parts of the conference included Ann Coolidge, Sylvia Flowers, David Smith, Ford Smith, Michelle Smith, and John Wilson. The chapters of Alan Marsh (Chapter 2) and Betty Smith (Chapter 8) were not written explicitly for the conference but are included here because of their importance and relevance. The chapter by Jones, Penton, and Tesar (Chapter 13) grew from a paper presented by Penton at the conference. All of the other chapters are revised versions of papers presented at the conference.

We thank Ocmulgee National Monument, superintendent John Bundy, and Sylvia Flowers for the use of their Discovery Room and help with the meeting. We thank Rita Elliott for taping the proceedings, the Macon Coliseum for the loan of tables, and the Department of Anthropology, University of Georgia, for the loan of film equipment.

The first two chapters of this volume provide a historical background for modern Swift Creek studies. Following these chapters, we have chosen a simple geographical model to sequence Chapters 3 through 14 from north to south within the Swift Creek region. The specific range of subjects of these chapters is widely varied and we applaud this variety. Swift Creek archaeology is still a youthful inquiry. The final chapter, authored by David Anderson, provides a summary of our knowledge of this important archaeological culture to the present day. The attendees and supporters of the 1993 conference clearly believe, as we do, that Swift Creek was a special archaeological culture and that knowledge of it should be shared and nourished. We hope this book is just the beginning of serious future Swift Creek studies.

A World Engraved

Swift Creek Research
History and Observations

Mark Williams and Daniel T. Elliott

The Swift Creek period in Georgia and the surrounding states is recognized almost exclusively by the distinct pottery associated with the period from approximately A.D. 100 to A.D. 750. The earliest recorded illustrations of what we now know as Swift Creek Complicated Stamped pottery were presented almost 70 years before the type was formally recognized, however. In 1873 Charles C. Jones illustrated at least one sherd of this type in his classic volume *Antiquities of the Southern Indians* (Jones 1873:21, plate XXIX). He did not recognize them as distinct from the other stamped sherds he illustrated, most of which were much more recent in date.

Additional Swift Creek sherds were illustrated in 1903 by William Holmes in his summary volume of the Indian ceramics of the eastern United States (Holmes 1903). Again, he had no idea how old they were and did not recognize them as distinct from other paddle-stamped ceramics from the Deep South. Both of these studies were conducted before the value of ceramics as a dating tool was recognized. Further, relatively little was made of Swift Creek ceramics before this century because they were virtually absent from the multitude of mounds that were opened in the nineteenth century: Swift Creek pottery is not burial pottery. The peripatetic Clarence B. Moore found and illustrated a few sherds of Swift Creek Complicated Stamped pottery from Florida burial mounds in two of his northwestern Florida publications (Moore 1902a:470, 472, 1918:525, 565).

Although Margaret Ashley presented a credible analysis of Mississippian period stamped pottery from the northwestern Georgia Etowah site in her 1932 paper, there were no Swift Creek sherds in her collections from there, nor have any been found at Etowah since then (Ashley 1932). Indeed, this particular stamped pottery was unrecognized as a separate type by all researchers until the landmark study of Arthur R. Kelly of the excavations at Macon, Georgia, published in 1938. For the first time systematic excavations on a large scale included a site that had this material in profusion. This site was the Swift Creek mound (Kelly 1938). The chapter by Alan Marsh in the present collection (Chapter 2) discusses some of the logistical aspects of its excavation in 1936 and 1937.

This mound was approximately 3 meters high when excavated and had been plowed for many years. Kelly and his wife, Rowena, were reportedly fascinated by the beautiful complicated stamped ceramics found there in abundance. Although he devoted fewer than two pages of his sixty-eight-page report to the description of the excavations, he spent nearly twenty pages discussing the pottery found there. In fact, he devoted more effort to discussing Swift Creek than any other aspect of the Macon Works Progress Administration project, including even the main Macon Plateau site. Further, the Swift Creek site was the only piece of the eight-year massive excavations at Macon that he completed as a site report in his later life. Clearly, it is with Kelly's excavations at Swift Creek that the substance of this book really begins.

Although Kelly presented one small photographic plate of the remarkable Swift Creek pottery in his 1938 report, it was not until the following year that a formal type definition was written and presented by Jesse Jennings and Charles Fairbanks (1939b). Their description was the lead definition in the second newsletter (March 1939) of the then newly constituted Southeastern Archaeological Conference. In addition to the formal description of the type, two plates of sherd drawings by James Jackson, illustrator with the Macon project, were included. As Jennings and Fairbanks noted in their description, the Swift Creek material was similar to material from the Tennessee River valley in northeastern Alabama described by William Haag in the first newsletter (February 1939) that Haag had named Pickwick Complicated Stamped (Haag 1939b). The Pickwick material was tempered with crushed limestone rather than sand and had a more restricted range of designs. The similarity is undeniable, however, and Pickwick still represents the northwestern limit of what is now universally called Swift Creek pottery.

On the Georgia coast, Joseph Caldwell and Antonio Waring recognized the presence of Swift Creek–like pottery there and named this relatively rare variant Brewton Hill Complicated Stamped in the fifth newsletter of the Southeastern Archaeological Conference, published in August 1939 (Caldwell and Waring 1939). In the report of the excavations at the famous Irene site near Savannah, Caldwell and McCann expanded briefly on the presence of Swift Creek on the Georgia coast, particularly in association with late Deptford materials (Caldwell and McCann 1941:51).

In the period immediately before World War II, Charles Fairbanks, who was still working out of the Macon area, visited the huge Kolomoki site in Early County, Georgia. He was somewhat surprised to discover that the majority of ceramics at the site were of the Swift Creek style. This was surprising because the 18-meter-high mound there was assumed to date, along with the presumed village, to the later Mississippian period. Fairbanks quickly realized and stated that perhaps this was not the case (Fairbanks 1941).

Swift Creek pottery was recognized in eastern Tennessee by Thomas Lewis and Madeline Kneberg in their 1946 publication on the Hiwassee Island sites. In this invaluable report based on their 1937–1939 excavations, they documented and illustrated materials that, while rare at the site, are clearly recognizable as Swift Creek (Lewis and Kneberg 1946:84–85, plates 45 and 46).

Charles Fairbanks completed his classic paper *Creek and Pre-Creek* in 1947, although it was not published until 1952 in the Fay-Cooper Cole Memorial volume edited by James B. Griffin (Fairbanks 1952). In this paper, Fairbanks provided one of the first good summaries of the Swift Creek archaeological culture, albeit mainly from a central Georgia slant, and it should be required reading for anyone interested in the subject.

In the summer of 1940, Gordon Willey conducted an archaeological survey of northwestern Florida that, coupled with his exhaustive analysis of collections made before then by other researchers in the area, led, after the war, to his 1949 publication *The Archaeology of the Florida Gulf Coast* (Willey 1949). Few volumes in any area of the southeastern United States have so thoroughly organized, summarized, and detailed the local archaeological knowledge as did this report. Willey had been heavily involved in the Macon work from 1936 through 1938 and was as familiar with Swift Creek materials as any archaeologist. In 1936, for example, he had excavated the Stubbs mound site south of Macon, which had a significant Swift Creek component

(Williams 1975). In addition, his work at the Cowart's Landing site further acquainted him with the Swift Creek material (Willey 1939). When he began his work in Florida he quickly recognized the presence of a significant amount of Swift Creek pottery there as well, and he observed that the complicated Swift Creek pottery was virtually always found in association with a wide variety of plain, incised, and punctated pottery that had not been present in central Georgia. He named these sherds the Santa Rosa series. Thus he was led to call this distinctive combination of ceramic styles the Santa Rosa–Swift Creek material, and the name has stuck in Florida to the present. The chapters in this collection by Judith Bense (Chapter 14) and by Calvin Jones, Dan Penton, and Louis Tesar (Chapter 13) discuss aspects of this Florida Swift Creek material. In addition, the chapter by Keith Ashley in this volume (Chapter 12) overviews the Swift Creek material from northeastern Florida, an area that was not surveyed by Willey.

From 1948 through 1951, excavations were directed at the Kolomoki site by William Sears, then of the University of Georgia. These excavations were reported by him in a series of four publications between 1951 and 1956 (Adams 1956; Sears 1951a, 1951b, 1953, 1956). All of the excavations were conducted to provide better information about the site because it was being developed as a state park. Although it had been acquired by Georgia in 1935, little knowledge of it existed beyond Fairbanks's information that the site contained Swift Creek pottery. With Sears's excavations at the site one of the longest-running, and now resolved, controversies about Swift Creek began. Sears saw the Swift Creek materials at Kolomoki as distinct from Swift Creek as it was understood at that time, and he named the materials and their associated time period for the site itself. His interpretation of the sequence of cultures at the site, however, made in the absence of clear stratigraphic information at the site, was at odds with that of many other archaeologists. He now has acknowledged his misinterpretation in the article *Mea Culpa* (Sears 1992), and the issue is at rest. Chapter 11 herein by Karl Steinen views Kolomoki in a larger social setting.

Although Kolomoki did not yield clear stratigraphic data, two sites excavated in the lower Chattahoochee River valley to the west of Kolomoki did. As part of the Lake Seminole excavations conducted by the University of Georgia in 1949–1951, Joseph Caldwell excavated Fairchild's Landing and Hare's Landing, both of which produced stratified Swift Creek to

Weeden Island period deposits. Had these sites been adequately reported in the early 1950s, their unambiguous data would have stemmed the controversy immediately.

As part of the same project just mentioned, Ripley Bullen excavated six additional sites in the Lake Seminole basin in the summer of 1953. His report of these sites was completed in 1954 but was not published until 1958 (Bullen 1958). In this report he illustrated Early and Late Swift Creek material from several of the sites and reported the first radiocarbon date for Swift Creek—A.D. 350.

Work conducted in 1940 and 1941 was belatedly published in a 1960 report by Steve Wimberly on the pottery from several excavations in the Mobile Bay vicinity of southern Alabama. Wimberly's report showed that clear and obvious Swift Creek pottery was in use at least this far west on the Gulf Coast (Wimberly 1960:figure 41). This was associated with Santa Rosa pottery, and Wimberly named it Porter. The Swift Creek pottery was very low in frequency at these Mobile Bay sites, however.

By the mid-1950s the geographic distribution of Swift Creek was fairly clear to all researchers, and its association in time with the Hopewell phenomenon of Ohio was becoming clearer (Figure 1-1). The latter idea was further developed by Caldwell in his doctoral dissertation completed in 1957 at the University of Chicago (Caldwell 1958). In this he took a wide-ranging, large-scale look at the relationships of many local archaeological cultures, particularly from a Georgia perspective, through time and space. Swift Creek was a part of his discussions, and it became a critical part of his South Appalachian tradition. Studies of this sort are vital, but the actual amount of local data necessary is enormous. Indeed, in retrospect his study suffers from a lack of adequate site data. However, this desire to understand archaeological cultures from a large-scale perspective must remain an important impetus for our research.

Swift Creek's assumed connection to and contemporaneity with the Hopewell Interaction Sphere, as Caldwell soon named it, were made much clearer by the excavations at Mandeville, a small two-mound site on the eastern side of the Chattahoochee River. Excavated prior to construction of the Walter F. George Reservoir, Mandeville showed unmistakable contacts with Hopewell. There were human figurines, panpipes, cut mica, and a wide variety of other burial items that were known to be part of the Hopewell trade.

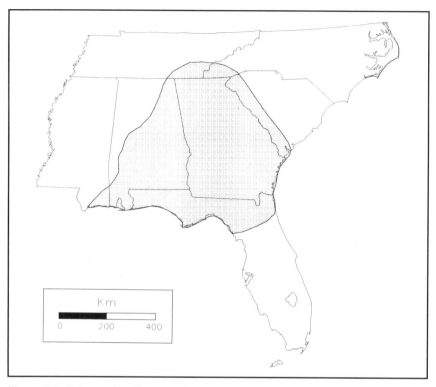

Figure 1-1. Primary distribution of sites with Swift Creek ceramics.

Further, the site contained large quantities of Swift Creek pottery. The work was led nominally by Arthur Kelly, but most of the actual direction was provided by James Kellar and Edward McMichael (Kellar, Kelly, and McMichael 1962). Betty Smith conducted her dissertation research on this important site and continues to be fascinated with it as demonstrated by her exploratory chapter in this volume (Chapter 8).

Robert Wauchope, who conducted research in Georgia for a short period in the late 1930s, provided the next step forward for the study of Swift Creek. While teaching at the University of Georgia he conducted a survey of many sites in northern Georgia and excavated at some of the sites he located. Although he left the state in late 1940 and never conducted research in this part of the South again, he did eventually write a report on his survey. In 1966 his *Archaeological Survey of Northern Georgia with a Test of Some*

Cultural Hypotheses was published—482 pages of fine print accompanied by hundreds of artifact drawings and photographs (Wauchope 1966). This volume immediately became the standard reference for archaeology in the area and to a diminished extent remains so now. It codified information about the various periods in Georgia's archaeological past in much the same way Willey's 1949 volume had done for Florida, and Swift Creek was prominently included in the presentation. The timing of Wauchope's publication was fortuitous with respect to the codifying of Swift Creek, for, as pointed out above, the distribution of it in space and time was by then pretty well established. It was a known archaeological-cultural entity, and most of the current researchers on Swift Creek came of age professionally with the publication of Wauchope's volume. Certainly archaeological survey in northern Georgia has yielded many more sites since Wauchope's time. The chapters by Dan Elliott (Chapter 3) and by Dave Chase (Chapter 5) in this volume sift through the vast amount of data from this large region. Mark Williams and Jennifer Freer (Chapter 4) examine the patterns of distribution of Swift Creek mound centers in northern Georgia and discuss their functions from a new perspective.

Although Kelly and his wife, Rowena, had initiated studies of the designs on Swift Creek pottery in the late 1930s, and most other researchers had made simple observations about the designs, no systematic work on them was done before Bettye Broyles's work published in the late 1960s (Broyles 1968). In her brief article she related how she began in 1959 to transcribe the fragmentary designs from individual sherds into complete paddle designs and catalog them. The data for her work came from four sites on the middle Chattahoochee River watershed. She presented eighty-three complete design drawings in her article and discovered many of the techniques later amplified and expanded on and presented by Frankie Snow and Keith Stephenson in this volume (Chapters 6 and 7). The drawings also led indirectly to the works of Rebecca Saunders (Chapter 10) and James Stoltman and Frankie Snow (Chapter 9) presented in this volume. Broyles's work provided the inspiration for all later work on Swift Creek designs. A few of her published illustrations are reproduced here in Figure 1-2.

Arthur Kelly, working with Betty Smith, did finally write a site report on the Swift Creek site at Macon in 1975, just four years before his death (Kelly and Smith 1975). By the time of its completion there were few sur-

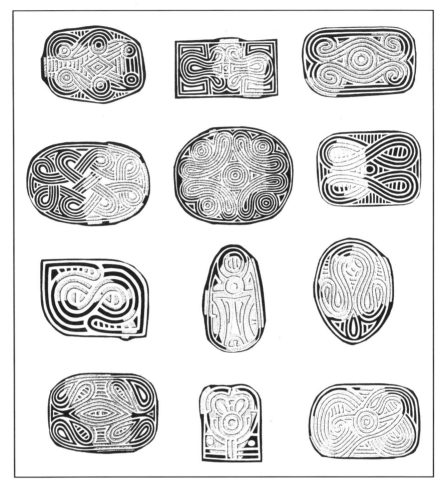

Figure 1-2. Selected Swift Creek designs drawn by Bettye Broyles (1968).

prises for anyone, since the work there had been conducted thirty-nine years prior to the report. Swift Creek had become established as a vital and curious link in the long line of archaeological cultures that marked the past in Georgia and the surrounding states.

The vast majority of other Swift Creek archaeological work from the late 1960s to the 1990s consists of descriptions of individual site excavations and occasional summaries similar to this one (Cook 1979; Fish and Jefferies 1978; Reitz and Quitmyer 1988; Schnell 1975; Wayne 1987). We will not

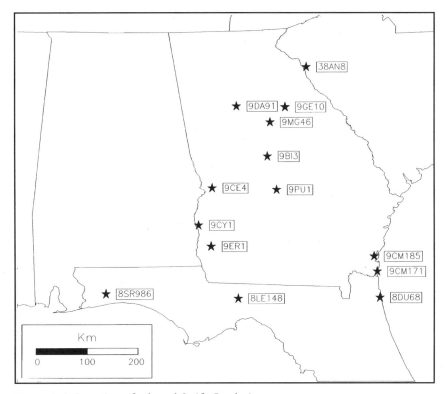

Figure 1-3. Location of selected Swift Creek sites.

detail any of that here since much of it is discussed in the context of the individual chapters in this collection. Before presenting the chapters, however, we wish to make a few general observations about Swift Creek here in addition to those David Anderson makes in Chapter 15.

Observations

Figure 1-1 presents the estimated distribution of sites with Swift Creek pottery in Georgia and the surrounding states as presently known. Figure 1-3 presents the locations of the major sites discussed here and in the chapters that follow. We must begin with the simple and perhaps painful truth that, beyond the pottery, there is little that distinguishes the Swift Creek archaeological culture from many other Middle Woodland archaeological cultures in the eastern United States. Having admitted this, the unique and intriguing Swift Creek pottery may yet be able to teach us some things about the culture itself. First, the most obvious thing we have learned from the pottery is that these people were excellent wood carvers. Such a tradition of detailed wood carving would not, in our opinion, have been born in and limited to the carving of paddles for stamping pottery. We imagine the Swift Creek world as one in which almost everything made of wood had carving placed upon it. Spoons, weapons, handles of all sorts, boxes, and even the wall posts and timbers of houses might have been elaborately carved. Our thoughts here are of the elaborate carvings from the cultures of the northwest coast of the United States or of Polynesia. The decoration of the paddles for the pottery may actually have been a very minor part of the multimedia on which they practiced their carving. More direct evidence for our suggestion of the importance of wood carving in the Swift Creek period may lie buried in some undiscovered peat bog or swamp in southern Georgia or northern Florida. Until such evidence is discovered, we certainly admit the speculative nature of this suggestion.

The second area of our comments involves the designs themselves. Most archaeologists now believe that these designs had some meaning—that they symbolized ideas that were presumably important to the people. It seems likely that the pottery was not the most important locus of these symbols, and there is no reason not to suppose that these same symbols were also painted on a wide variety of items, woven into baskets, and even tattooed onto their bodies. It may have been that these important symbols were put on the pottery via the carved paddles as an afterthought. We just cannot see pottery as the primary platform for the expression of important symbols. Pottery after all is a humdrum part of the lives of most people and concern for its decoration is low compared to decoration of the body, clothing, and the home. Our point is that just because we do not have these things preserved for the Swift Creek archaeological culture we should not overestimate the impact of the pottery, even with their complex stamped designs, in the lives of these people.

Having said this, however, what little we can learn about their symbolic world we must learn from the pottery. Frankie Snow makes the case, as did Bettye Broyles, for many of the designs being highly abstracted images of plants and animals. If this is true, we suggest in jest that we should perhaps look for some undiscovered species of hallucinogenic frog or mushroom whose distribution coincides with the Swift Creek area. We believe the most important aspect of Snow's work with the designs, however, concerns their distribution in space, based on the paddle identities. Although there seems to be plenty of room for more research in this area, one important thing is clear. These designs were not unique to individual tiny areas but were used in larger regional contexts. This tells us something important about the social interactions in the area—to wit, these contacts were signaling social unity on the regional scale, rather than social distinctiveness on the local scale. In other words, the local people were not walling themselves off but actively reaching out to the outside world. In the jargon of today, they were networking. They likely were exchanging information just as much as they were moving items of trade. Indeed, we would suggest that it might profit us to look at the entire Hopewell Interaction Sphere as more of an information exchange network rather than a "trading network."

This open system outlook seems different to us from those of the Early and Late Woodland periods in which the societies in Georgia are, we believe, perhaps better interpreted as closed local systems. If this is true in some measurable or meaningful manner, the most obvious question to ask would be why? Under what economic, social, political, or religious conditions does open networking flourish? What was the real value to local people who desired to be connected to the Woodland Information Super Highway? Perhaps, by analogy with what is happening with many people in America now with the advent of the World Wide Web, wherein the *idea* of the accessibility to imagined infinite information is more important to people than the information itself. There was a sort of greed for the connection rather than a need for the connection.

As for Swift Creek itself, we are certainly delighted that all these chapters have been written and presented as evidence that research into the Middle Woodland in the Deep South is in good hands. Arthur Kelly was satisfied to have begun the book on Swift Creek. It remains for us and the future to continue literally to write the pages of that book. We hope this volume is a positive effort in that direction.

Swift Creek Site Excavations
The Works Progress Administration and Black Labor

Alan Marsh

On March 4, 1933, as Franklin D. Roosevelt took the presidential oath, the country was in the midst of a great depression. The banking system was in collapse, the economy was in shambles, and 25 percent of the labor force was unemployed. The nation turned its eyes to the new president in search of leadership and hope. People anxiously waited to see whether the "New Deal for the American people," which he had promised in his Democratic National Convention acceptance speech in 1932, would become reality. They did not have to wait long. During the first "hundred days" of office Roosevelt launched relief and recovery programs that would aid millions of people over the remainder of the decade.

The hope of a new deal, however, was not shared by everyone in 1933. In a political system administered by white males, it seemed highly unlikely that work relief and racial reforms would be undertaken to remedy the plight of blacks, particularly black women. Under President Roosevelt's initial New Deal programs this proved to be the case. The National Recovery Administration (NRA), created in June 1933, soon became known as the "Negro Run Around" and the Agricultural Adjustment Administration invited discrimination by allowing white landowners to dominate county committees (Graham and Wander 1985:281).

After 1934 blacks began to benefit more from the New Deal. Factors that accounted for this change were the growing number of black voters and intellectuals and politicians who advanced the notion of racial justice. First

Lady Eleanor Roosevelt was a vocal spokesperson for the rights of blacks and prominently associated herself with black organizations and leaders. Harold Ickes, Secretary of the Interior, ended segregation in the Interior Department lunchroom and is credited with employing blacks as consultants or special assistants.

The advocates of social reform in the federal government, however, could not overturn the prejudices embedded throughout the country and particularly the South: they would have had to change a way of life and a philosophy that was entrenched in the culture of the region. The New Deal did make some inroads for blacks, but within the framework of existing white guidelines.

One of Roosevelt's New Deal programs that employed blacks, including black women, was the Works Progress Administration (WPA). Although much has been written about the WPA, little has been written about the African-Americans who comprised its work force and the significant work that they accomplished. An examination of events relating to archaeological excavations at Ocmulgee National Monument during the 1930s, in particular a WPA project for black women, illustrates the attitudes and concerns that local sponsors had about such a project and how the work had far-reaching results in the field of archaeology.

On May 6, 1935, President Roosevelt created the WPA and named as its director Harry L. Hopkins. Also in May Executive Order 7046 was signed, which mandated that "all those qualified by training and experience to be assigned to work projects shall not be discriminated against on any grounds whatsoever" (Sitkoff 1978:69). WPA projects, however, were proposed and supervised at the local level and, especially in the South, the local level in many cases was not friendly to blacks. Many of the blacks who found employment found themselves on "beautification projects" planting flowers and landscaping. Few were able to gain supervisory positions on WPA projects. Of the more than 10,000 WPA supervisors in the South, eleven were black (Sitkoff 1978:49).

In Georgia, black WPA workers were not welcomed by state officials. One official stated that "there will be no Negros pushing wheelbarrows and boys driving trucks getting 40 cents an hour when the good white men and white women working the fields alongside these roads can hardly earn 40 cents a day" (Sitkoff 1978:49). This attitude was reflected in the pay scale among workers despite federal guidelines. The average monthly relief check for whites in Atlanta was $32.66, whereas blacks received $19.29 (Sitkoff 1978:49). Racial problems were not limited to pay. The state administrator for WPA, Miss Gay Shepperson, was criticized by some because blacks and whites were forced to go down the same hallway to get to separate restrooms in the Fulton County Relief Office (Holmes 1975:106).

The issue of black versus white labor was also present in middle Georgia. During December of 1933 archaeological excavations were begun at the site of several Indian mounds in Macon in an area known as the Ocmulgee Old Fields. The project consisted of 205 white males employed under the auspices of the Civil Works Administration. This was followed by other programs such as the Public Works Administration and Federal Emergency Relief Administration. In 1934 the area was authorized to become a national monument, pending acquisition of the land by the public and its donation to the federal government. The National Park Service then had a vested interest in the Ocmulgee mounds and worked with local officials to acquire a WPA project at the site. Efforts were successful and in 1935 white WPA workers were added to the roster. With more than 500 people working at the site it was one of the largest archaeological projects in the nation. All of the workers were white and most were male.

The question of whether to use black labor at Ocmulgee was discussed in 1935 by local civic leaders, National Park Service officials, and politicians. In October of that year Verne Chartelain, acting assistant director of the National Park Service, wrote to one of the principal local organizers of the excavations, Charles C. Harrold, and asked whether any public buildings were available nearby for a camp for 200 blacks (Chartelain 1935). He stated that the Park Service's request for a camp at Ocmulgee had repeatedly been turned down because new camp buildings were apparently necessary (this possibly referred to a Civilian Conservation Corps [CCC] camp). One week later General Walter A. Harris, local attorney and instigator of the excavations, wrote National Park Service Acting Director Demaray and warned him about the possible danger of locating a black camp at Ocmulgee. The letter also complained that Arthur R. Kelly (supervisor of the excavations at Ocmulgee and in surrounding areas since 1933) and his assistants could no longer live on WPA wages (Harris 1935). Concerns echoed sentiments found at the state level; there should be no competition by employing blacks along with whites on New Deal programs in Georgia.

The National Park Service found that other people were concerned with bringing a black camp to Ocmulgee when it asked the Macon Historical Society to sponsor the camp. The Society, instrumental in the land-acquisition efforts for the park, was also cautious about involvement with such a camp. On October 30, 1935, Herbert Kahler, acting custodian (superintendent) for the Park Service at Ocmulgee, sent a telegram to the director of the National Park Service stating that "because of local conditions, the Macon Historical Society does not desire to sponsor a colored camp but will cooperate if placed on the property by the National Park Service" (Kahler 1935a).

The following month Kahler again wrote the director of the Park Service. This time he stated that a CCC camp was wanted at Ocmulgee as well as an Emergency Conservation Works camp for black people. He feared though that the "pay difference of $2.50 per month would cause trouble, the two races wouldn't work together, and the colored boys would run riot in town" (Kahler 1935b). Kahler suggested that the black men be used at the Lamar tract, approximately 5 kilometers below the main dig. He also advised the director that during a conference between Congressman Carl Vinson and Maconites Charles Harrold and Walter Harris it was decided that a black camp would be accepted and that the Park Service was to request one at once (Kelly and Smith 1975:iii).

Despite the new willingness to accept a CCC camp for blacks, it was almost two more years before a CCC camp came to Ocmulgee, and then it was all white. The groundwork was laid, however, and a project that employed blacks began the following year under the direction of the WPA. The size, location, and composition of the labor force illustrated that organizers were still approaching the idea with a great deal of caution.

The new WPA project was begun in March 1936 and employed between thirty and forty black women (Figure 2-1). The workers conducted excavations but did not work with other New Deal laborers at the main project. They found themselves at the Swift Creek site, about 5 kilometers downriver from the main excavations and not far from the Lamar site, which Herbert Kahler had proposed as the site for a black work program in 1935. The women served as an archaeological field crew under Arthur R. Kelly. Hugh

Figure 2-1. Excavation crew for Swift Creek site.

Hanna was unit supervisor; Joseph Tamplin, engineer; Joseph Coke, photographer; and James Jackson, artist-illustrator (McIntyre 1939:24).

The crew itself was acquired locally by the WPA. Documentation is not clear as to why the project turned out to be for black women, but local officials may still have been afraid that black men would "run riot in town." In contrast, attitudes toward black women were much different. Lucy McIntyre, field supervisor for the WPA in Savannah, wrote this account of black women employed on the excavations of the Irene mound near Savannah: "[F]rom the standpoint of archaeology they have proven careful, docile, efficient workers, especially suited to this type of work. By temperament they are undisturbed by monotonous routine and opposed to hurry and bustle; by training they are docile, accustomed to unquestioning obedience; while by religion they have a great respect for the abodes of the dead" (McIntyre 1939).

When the work began at Swift Creek, the site, in eastern Bibb County, comprised two mounds and a village area situated in a cultivated field. Using shovels and trowels, workers dug test trenches and carefully and methodically uncovered the story of the ancient inhabitants of the site. Emma Walker, one of the women on the Swift Creek crew, recalled in later years that her task with a shovel was to remove a layer of dirt "so thin you could see the shovel underneath it" (Walker and Watson 1991). Work was tedious, but fruitful, and more than 2,000 artifacts were recorded in the find books that were kept. Artifacts from the site showed occupation of the area during the Archaic, Woodland, and Mississippian periods (from circa 9000 B.C. to A.D. 1100).

One of the most important discoveries, however, was evidence of a culture of people who used carved wooden paddles to produce elaborate designs on their clay pots. The newly defined culture was named after its type site: Swift Creek. Since its initial discovery by the black women of the WPA, evidence of the Swift Creek culture has been found throughout Georgia and into Florida.

Work by the WPA women continued until the winter of 1937. At the termination of excavations about three-fifths of Mound A was standing, and project supervisors were hopeful that future excavations would yield more knowledge about this new archaeological culture. Unfortunately, during World War II, the Swift Creek site was used by nearby Camp Wheeler, an infantry training center, as an ammunition dump. Dirt from the mounds was used to cover the ammunition and trenches were dug through the village area to bury garbage.

The work by the Swift Creek crew might have seemed trivial compared with the much larger project taking place at the same time on the nearby Macon Plateau site. However, the importance of the Swift Creek excavations should not be overlooked. They added to our knowledge of the country's prehistory, and Swift Creek is the type site for the culture that bears its name. It also demonstrated to the people during that portion of our history that blacks could be employed as an effective and efficient archaeological force.

The termination of the WPA program at Swift Creek was also the termination of the use of black workers on the Ocmulgee excavations. Thousands of laborers were employed on New Deal programs at Ocmulgee between 1933 and 1942, but this group of about forty women comprised the only blacks involved in the work. This reflected the national picture as well. Between 1935 and 1941, only about 3 percent of all WPA workers were black women (Jones 1985:217).

Some scholars have argued that funds from the WPA and other New Deal programs were used to reinforce traditional class, racial, and sexual divisions. It is true that most black crews were segregated and women did not work with men. What is important to note is that blacks *were* employed by New Deal programs, and a new level of service was opened up to them, such as the excavations at Swift Creek. While they did not work alongside whites at most sites, they performed the same tasks. In the depression era of the 1930s, having a job and earning money was the primary concern to workers, however. Emma Walker remembered earning $16.50 every two weeks while employed by the WPA at Swift Creek. For a widow with two children the WPA project was a blessing (Walker and Watson 1991). The New Deal presented a new beginning. Racial justice and equality were still a long way off, but some of the first steps were made during the 1930s with projects like the Swift Creek excavations.

The Northern and Eastern Expression of Swift Creek Culture
Settlement in the Tennessee and Savannah River Valleys

Daniel T. Elliott

The Swift Creek type site, located on Swift Creek in Bibb County in central Georgia, was excavated in 1936 and 1937 (Kelly and Smith 1975). By 1939 the usual range of the Swift Creek Complicated Stamped ceramic type was listed as "Georgia, northwest Florida, perhaps north into the Tennessee Valley" (Haag 1939b). The pottery was seen as older than Macon Plateau and Lamar and approximately contemporaneous with Stallings Island fiber-tempered and Deptford check-stamped wares. Obviously the temporal placement of Swift Creek has been significantly refined since 1939, but the geographic range data are little improved.

The core area of Swift Creek culture has traditionally been considered by archaeologists to be central Georgia, although few studies of the range and settlement distribution of Swift Creek sites on a regional scale have been attempted (McMichael 1960). The core area is assumed in this chapter to include the Alabama, Apalachicola, and Altamaha river systems.

This study is an attempt to define partially the Swift Creek phenomenon by focusing on its northern and eastern peripheral manifestations. Basic settlement and contextual data on approximately seventy-five sites containing Swift Creek pottery located on the periphery are presented. The study focuses primarily on the Tennessee and Savannah river drainage basins but also examines sites with Swift Creek attributes even more remote from the core area.

Swift Creek pottery is found in at least five southeastern states, so a settlement study documenting all known instances of its occurrence would be a major undertaking. In many cases, the presence or absence of Swift Creek pottery can only be determined by hands-on examination of the artifacts from a site. This study relies primarily on published reports that identify Swift Creek components, supplemented by a partial review of state archaeological site files in Tennessee, South Carolina, and Georgia.

In a previous settlement study of Swift Creek in northern Georgia, Rudolph (1985, 1986) reviewed the Georgia Archaeological Site File for counties north of the Fall Line and identified 211 Swift Creek sites; she considered most of these to be of Late Swift Creek age. As Rudolph (1986) noted, the temporal position of Swift Creek in northern Georgia is confused. Wauchope (1966) and others (Rodeffer et al. 1979; Taylor and Smith 1978) place Swift Creek in the Middle Woodland period, whereas others (Garrow 1975; Rudolph 1986) consider it to be Late Woodland. Anderson (1985:45–47) places Swift Creek Complicated Stamped in a Middle and Late Woodland context (dating from A.D. 200 to 800) for the Piedmont and the upper Savannah River region, although his placement is based on a precious few radiocarbon dates. Anderson and Joseph (1988:231–32) conclude that Swift Creek was not present in the upper Savannah River (Russell Reservoir region) until the Late Woodland period (circa 1500–1000 B.P.). At the mouth of the Savannah and in adjacent coastal areas, however, Anderson and Joseph (1988:231–32) equate Swift Creek with Deptford Complicated Stamped as defined by DePratter (1991), and they propose a date range of A.D. 100 to 600 for the inner Coastal Plain and Fall Line areas. Although most of the Swift Creek sites in northern Georgia are considered Late Swift Creek, Williams considers mound construction at the Little River and Fortson mounds to be from the Early Swift Creek period, on the basis of ceramic rim-form analysis (Williams 1992; Williams and Shapiro 1990).

Although other researchers have focused on analysis of Swift Creek design elements in their studies (Rudolph 1986; Snow 1975), the goal of this study is more rudimentary. It seeks to answer the question, where is Swift Creek, and where is it not? While simplistic in purpose, these assembled data are necessary for any intelligent study of the subject matter. A wealth of information on Swift Creek exists, but it is widely scattered in published form, unpublished manuscripts, and site files and hidden in artifact collections at museum repositories scattered across the eastern coast. This study attempts to bring these dispersed data together. Only after sites with Swift Creek research potential are identified can more sophisticated studies of Swift Creek society be developed. From a settlement studies perspective, at this writing we are in the first stage of systematic archaeological research on Swift Creek culture.

Swift Creek in the Tennessee River Watershed

Swift Creek is generally seen as a minor occurrence in eastern Tennessee during Middle Woodland times (Chapman 1973:58). Nowhere in Tennessee is Swift Creek pottery found in any quantity (Jefferson Chapman, pers. comm.). A closely related ware, Pickwick Complicated Stamped, was defined in Pickwick Basin (Haag 1939a:1–2; Webb and DeJarnette 1942). Swift Creek design motifs appear on Pickwick limestone-tempered sherds, and, in many instances, temper may be the only distinction. Pickwick pottery is generally associated with the Middle Woodland period in Tennessee and Alabama; however, the problem with the Pickwick ceramic type is that it includes nearly all complicated stamped sherds on limestone-tempered paste and researchers have lumped together curvilinear and rectilinear motifs that may cover the period from Swift Creek to Etowah times. Pickwick Complicated Stamped pottery is a minority ware in Middle Woodland assemblages on the Tennessee River and no single site has large quantities, and because of this it has received little attention by scholars in the region.

Swift Creek pottery has been found in the headwaters of the Tennessee River on very few sites. Keel (1976) found Swift Creek sherds as a trade ware in the Connestee phase at Garden Creek Mound 2 in North Carolina. Southerlin (Bobby Southerlin, pers. comm.) reported finding minor amounts of Swift Creek Complicated Stamped pottery mixed with sherds from the Connestee series at the Connestee site (31TV1). Other Swift Creek sites in North Carolina are known from Transylvania County near Brevard (Wayne Roberts, pers. comm.) and from Swain County. David Moore recently excavated a palisaded Napier village near Cullowee, but no Swift Creek component was identified. Moore suspects that as many as a dozen sites in the North Carolina mountains may have Swift Creek pottery, although a tally is presently unavailable (David Moore, pers. comm.).

Two sites, and possibly a third, in the Little Tennessee River basin have yielded Swift Creek pottery. At Icehouse Bottom on the Little Tennessee River, forty-nine Swift Creek Complicated Stamped (early) sherds were interpreted as trade ware (Chapman 1973:57–58). Most were in Levels 2 and 3 and had mixed Woodland provenience. An A.D. 439 ± 75 weighted average date (based on six dates) was obtained for the Connestee phase occupation at Icehouse Bottom.

The Patrick site, 40MR40, also on the Little Tennessee, had a Middle Woodland Connestee and Candy Creek phase component, including some pottery that should be considered Swift Creek. This material was confined to the plow zone and a few features (Schroedl 1978:86). One radiocarbon date was obtained for the Middle Woodland occupation (A.D. 520 ± 155, GX5246). The Pickwick pottery sample consisted of 577 sherds (of which 20 percent also had quartz temper). Some illustrated examples include Swift Creek motifs. The Middle Woodland sample included twenty-four rectilinear and 264 curvilinear designs (Schroedl 1978:93). Of these, 196 quartz-tempered complicated stamped sherds bore design motifs similar to those of Swift Creek and Napier Complicated Stamped ceramics. The plow zone assemblage included forty-seven rectilinear, sixty-three curvilinear, and eighty-six undifferentiated complicated stamped sherds. Also at Patrick were 183 unidentified sand-tempered complicated stamped sherds: fourteen with Napier-like designs and thirty-four with Swift Creek curvilinear designs, including several illustrated examples (Schroedl 1978:100).

One other site on the Little Tennessee River, Martin Farm, also contained possible evidence of Swift Creek ceramics. Pickwick Curvilinear Complicated Stamped pottery occurred as a minority ware at Martin Farm, as did unidentified sand-tempered complicated stamped sherds (Schroedl et al. 1985:169).

Chickamauga Lake, on the Tennessee and Hiwassee rivers, produced eleven sites containing Swift Creek pottery and twenty-five containing Pickwick pottery. The Pickwick pottery sites may include other components such as Woodstock or Napier, however. This is the greatest concentration of occurrence of Swift Creek wares in the Tennessee Valley. Chickamauga Dam may represent the northwestern boundary of the general occurrence of Swift Creek sand-tempered pottery, because downstream from that point it is replaced by the Pickwick series, with the notable exceptions of the Pinson mound site and Russell Cave.

Works Progress Administration (WPA) excavations in the Chickamauga Reservoir yielded Swift Creek pottery at five sites. The greatest amount of Swift Creek pottery was recovered from the Candy Creek site, 17BY14, located at the confluence of Candy Creek and the Hiwassee River, where sixty-two Pickwick Complicated Stamped sherds, twenty-two Swift Creek–style complicated stamped sherds, and five Napier Complicated Stamped sherds were found (Lewis n.d.). Lewis and Kneberg defined the Candy Creek focus as containing minor amounts of complicated stamped wares that closely resemble the Swift Creek type of central Georgia, suggesting that these people were receiving pottery "if not the stamping paddles themselves, from that source" (Lewis and Kneberg 1941:33). Swift Creek appears late in the Candy Creek occupation. Although no site report was produced for the Candy Creek site, Lewis and Kneberg describe the occupation there as semisedentary with no evidence for substantial houses, although the midden accumulation was almost a meter thick in places. Faunal preservation on the site was poor and there was no evidence for use of shellfish. Houses were closely grouped and there were numerous cooking and storage pits, some of which were used for tightly flexed burials (Lewis and Kneberg 1941).

The Ocoee site, a village site upstream from the Candy Creek site at the confluence of Ocoee Creek and the Hiwassee River, yielded a minority representation of 190 Pickwick, twenty-one Swift Creek, and two Napier Complicated Stamped sherds. Limited excavations were conducted on this site, but they have not been reported.

The Davis site (4HA2 and 6HA2), a substructure mound and village located on the Tennessee River near Chickamauga Dam, yielded 171 Pickwick, nine Swift Creek, and fourteen other sand-tempered complicated stamped sherds (Lewis n.d.). Extensive excavations were conducted at the Davis site, but they have not been reported.

Swift Creek and Pickwick sherds are illustrated from Hiwassee Island, 40MG31, at the confluence of the Hiwassee and Tennessee Rivers, which Lewis and Kneberg consider part of the Hamilton component (Lewis and Kneberg 1946:plates 46 and 47). Hiwassee Island contained many burial mounds, shell heaps, and a large substructure mound, but none of the mounds is attributed to Swift Creek people. On the basis of the narrow lands and grooves in the design motifs, they probably represent a Late Swift Creek occupation at Hiwassee Island. Lewis and Kneberg also illustrated a number of Swift Creek sherds attributed to eastern Tennessee, but no detailed provenience is available. Hiwassee Island yielded eleven Pickwick, nine Swift Creek, and two Napier Complicated Stamped sherds (Lewis and Kneberg 1946:88). The Swift Creek pottery finds illustrated in the Hiwassee Island report include folded rims, but no notched rims, and they probably date to Late Swift Creek times.

A recent shoreline survey of Chickamauga Reservoir yielded Swift Creek from eight sites (40MG88, 40MG89, 40MG141, 40MG157, 40MG216, 40RH14, 40RH19, and 40RH66) and Pickwick Complicated Stamped pottery from twenty-three sites (Elliott 1993b). Sites 40MG141, 40MG157, 40RH14, and 40RH19 are located along the Tennessee River. Surface collection at 40RH19, a large site measuring approximately 1600×150 meters on a levee remnant, yielded one Swift Creek sherd. This site was first visited by WPA Surveyor Buckner, who described it as an extensive shell deposit of unknown depth (Elliott 1993b).

Site 40RH14 contains an extensive freshwater shellfish midden along the Tennessee River. This site was not investigated beyond the survey level during the WPA salvage work. Three mounds were reported by WPA Surveyor Buckner in 1936: one was reportedly looted at the time, one could not be found during a 1987 survey, and the third was relocated during a recent survey (Buchner and Childress 1991:84–86). This site also yielded a single Swift Creek sherd.

Sites 40MG157 and 40MG141 are located on levee remnants on Moon Island. The main part of 40MG157 covers an area 250×30 meters, and two Swift Creek sherds were collected from it. This site contains scattered freshwater mussel-shell lenses. Site 40MG141, measuring 100×10 meters, yielded a single Swift Creek sherd (Elliott 1993b).

Sites 40MG88, 40MG89, and 40MG216 are located on the Hiwassee River, whereas the other sites are located on the Tennessee River. Sites 40MG88 and 40MG89 are located in close proximity on levee remnants. Site 40MG88 measures $1,000 \times 40$ meters and yielded a single Late Swift Creek, or Napier, sherd. Site 40MG89 is a smaller site, 175×31 meters, which also produced a single Swift Creek sherd. Site 40MG216 is a large site measuring at least 450 × 90 meters on a levee remnant and it yielded a single Swift Creek sherd. This site also contains an extensive limestone box cemetery (Elliott 1993b).

None of the survey sites yielded more than two Swift Creek sherds from the surface. Nine of the twelve Swift Creek sites in the Chickamauga region also yielded Pickwick Complicated Stamped pottery. The Chickamauga Lake Swift Creek sites are nearly equally split between the Tennessee and Hiwassee river drainages. All of these sites are located along major riverine features including terraces, levees, and islands. No upland Swift Creek sites are known from this region.

Although the Pickwick series continues to occur below Chickamauga Lake on the Tennessee River, Swift Creek trade ware is quite uncommon. Pickwick Complicated Stamped pottery is often found on sites, but nearly always as a minority ware. At 40HA102, a site on the Tennessee River near Chattanooga, a trash pit yielded Napier and Swift Creek Complicated Stamped motifs on limestone-tempered pottery (Council 1989:93). In the Nickajack Reservoir, several sites yielded Pickwick Complicated Stamped pottery in low frequencies (Faulkner and Graham 1965:20, 1966a:49, 1966b:42). These wares were first recognized by Graham (1964:25), who reported Pickwick Complicated Stamped pottery comprised 10.9 percent of the wares during his initial study of Mocassin Bend (Graham 1964). This assemblage included mostly rectilinear designs, but included Swift Creek–like and Napier-like folded rims.

At the Westmoreland Barber site (40MI11), thirty-three sherds, or 1.1 percent of the pottery assemblage, was identified as Pickwick Complicated Stamped. This assemblage contained zoned Swift Creek–like designs. Of five rimsherds found, two were rounded and three were folded. The age of this assemblage was estimated at circa A.D. 200–300, but no radiocarbon dates were obtained. At the Lay site (40MI20), located nearby, fifty-four Pickwick Curvilinear Complicated Stamped sherds were found in the Middle Woodland phase (Faulkner and Graham 1965, 1966a, 1966b).

Pickwick pottery continues into northern Alabama, but no published references to Swift Creek pottery were found for this region except for Russell Cave (Griffin 1974; Walthall 1980). In a review of northern Alabama Copena sites, Pickwick Complicated Stamped pottery was found on sites 1LU65 and 1MG63, but no Swift Creek wares were identified (Cole 1981:363–64).

Far from its zone of occurrence, a modest Swift Creek presence has been identified at the Pinson site, a large multiple Woodland mound complex located near Jackson, Tennessee. Swift Creek Complicated Stamped pottery was recovered from the Duck's Nest sector and from the Mound 14 sector. A radiocarbon date of A.D. 60 ± 380 (UGA 979) was obtained from a feature containing Swift Creek pottery, but this radiocarbon date was discounted by the archaeologist as not of any value (Mainfort 1990:89). Instead, Mainfort considered the Swift Creek presence at Pinson to be contemporary with the Duck's Nest occupation from which several radiocarbon dates were obtained. Again, Mainfort discounted two dates as too recent, A.D. 415 ± 65 (UGA 4681) and A.D. 606 ± 135 (UGA 4910), but he accepted a third date of 125 ± 90 B.C. (UGA 4542) for the occupation (Mainfort 1990). Given the radiocarbon dates returned from the Simpsons Field site discussed in the following section, however, these presumed spurious dates may have some validity (Wood et al. 1986).

Swift Creek pottery also has been identified in Ohio at the Seip and Turner sites and in Indiana at the Mann site (Kellar 1979; Prufer 1968:14; Rein 1974). At the Mann site a surprisingly large collection of Early Swift Creek pottery was found. The absence of Swift Creek pottery on sites in the intervening areas, however, argues for rapid and direct long-distance trade.

Swift Creek in the Savannah River Watershed

The headwaters region of the Savannah River has produced fewer than one-half dozen Swift Creek sites. Tugalo mound (9ST1) contained what Caldwell identified as late Middle Swift Creek ceramics mixed with Etowah pottery in the premound stratum (Williams and Branch 1978:34). A minor amount of sandy-paste Swift Creek pottery (n = 8, of 2,349 Woodland sherds) was found at Tomassee (38OC186), and this was interpreted as possibly representing trade ware in the predominately Connestee component (Smith et al. 1988:61). At Chauga mound and village (38OC1), Swift Creek pottery was "fairly evenly distributed throughout the mound and in the mound outwash elements, as well as in the village" (Kelly and Neitzel 1961:77). Swift Creek pottery (n = 7 Swift Creek Complicated Stamped sherds) was recorded by Thomas Ryan (1971) at a predominately Pisgah site in the Seneca River floodplain (38PN26).

Surveys and excavation on the upper Savannah River identified Swift Creek pottery at fourteen sites in the Richard B. Russell Reservoir project (9EB9, 9EB17, 9EB83, 9EB85, 9EB86, 9EB167, 9EB259, 9EB430, 9EB431, 9EB259, 38AN8, 38AN29, 38AN126, 38AB22) from a sample of more than 600 sites, with a Swift Creek sherd sample of 413; the ensuing Napier wares were represented by 109 sherds (Anderson and Joseph 1988:25, 232; Elliott and Blanton 1985; Goodyear et al. 1983; Hutto 1970; Taylor and Smith 1978:423–28; Thompson and Gardner 1982; Wood et al. 1986:172, 182). Interestingly, 72 percent of the Swift Creek sites in the Russell Reservoir area were located on the western side of the Savannah River watershed.

At Sara's Ridge (38AN29), on a Savannah River levee immediately downstream from Simpsons Field, Swift Creek pottery was found in the plow zone over an area 30 meters in diameter, but no associated features were identified. This occupation may be related to the Simpsons Field occupation (Wood et al. 1986).

The largest representation of Swift Creek in the Russell Reservoir, or in the entire northeastern boundary zone for that matter, was at Simpsons Field (38AN8), where two to three surface concentrations of complicated stamped pottery were defined over an area 175 meters in extent (Wood et al. 1986). A total of sixteen Late Woodland features was excavated including bell-shaped pits, shallow-basin pits, earth ovens, and two burials. Twelve of the Late Woodland features yielded 1,556 sherds. A total of 298 Swift Creek Complicated Stamped sherds was recovered from this site. Napier sherds ($n = 59$) were reportedly associated with the Swift Creek wares and were interpreted as contemporaneous. This component was radiocarbon dated to A.D. 700–1260. Use of the site was described as an intensive, short occupation (Wood et al. 1986). No houses were reported, although Anderson (1985) conjectures that the site contains a ring of posts 8 to 10 meters in diameter that might represent a house. The two burials contained no grave goods. Quartz was the dominant raw material in the Late Woodland features, followed by chert, soapstone, metavolcanics, and sheet mica. Radiocarbon dates for the Simpsons Field Swift Creek occupation were A.D. 630 ± 50; A.D. 720 (Beta 2603); and A.D. 960 ± 50 (Wood et al. 1986:52, 63, 69, 82). These are the only radiocarbon dates for Swift Creek from the eastern or northern margins of this culture. It should be noted that the majority of feature stains at this site were not excavated (Anderson and Joseph 1988:233).

At Gregg Shoals (9EB259) on the Savannah River, curvilinear complicated stamped pottery bearing designs similar to Early Swift Creek and rectilinear complicated stamped pottery bearing designs similar to Late Swift
Creek were reported (Anderson and Joseph 1988:245; Tippitt and Marquardt 1984:chapter 7, 15–17).

At 9EB17 on the Savannah River (Wood et al. 1986), Swift Creek sherds
were found scattered over an area 100 meters in diameter and in one feature
(Feature 13) that also contained sheet mica and a quartz crystal. Despite
exposure of 200 square meters in this area, no other Swift Creek features
were found. Sixty-two Swift Creek sherds were recovered. This component
was classified as an Anderson phase (A.D. 600–750) occupation (Rappleye
and Gardner 1980; Wood et al. 1986:217–18, 236, 240, 242). No Napier
sherds were reported from this site.

Swift Creek pottery and one associated pit feature were reported on the
Harpers Ferry site (38AB22), a levee site on the Savannah River, although
the ceramics were reexamined by later researchers and reclassified as Lamar
(Anderson and Schuldenrein 1985:74; Glander et al. 1981:3–24).

At Ruckers Bottom (9EB91) on the Savannah River, Swift Creek was
represented by thirty-seven sherds, as was Napier, among a total of 34,000
sherds. The Swift Creek sherds were confined to a small area of the site, while
the Napier wares were more widespread (Anderson and Joseph 1988:321).

Swift Creek Curvilinear Complicated Stamped, Napier Rectilinear
Complicated Stamped, and Weeden Island–like incised pottery were reported
from Paris Island North (9EB431 and 9EB430), but no follow-up excavations were undertaken at either site (Thompson and Gardner 1982:94). The
remaining sites in Russell Lake containing Swift Creek wares were not investigated in any detail.

The South Carolina piedmont has received a great deal of survey coverage. Among 2,000 sites located in Sumter National Forest, Swift Creek was
found on only one (38AB354). This site, on Johns Creek in Abbeville County,
contained a small quantity of Late Swift Creek Curvilinear Complicated
Stamped pottery (with folded rims) and one nearby, possibly associated,
low, flat-topped burial mound (38AB355) known as the Ramona mound
(Jim Bates, pers. comm.; Elliott 1984, 1993a). Site 38AB354 is the eastern-
most documented Swift Creek site in the Savannah River system. The age of
Ramona mound is presently unknown, but a small quantity of plain sand-

tempered Woodland ceramics has been recovered from the site. Rodeffer et al. (1979) recorded one identified Swift Creek sherd out of a sample of 135 sherds on site 38GN290 located on the Reedy Creek floodplain near the eastern edge of the Savannah River drainage system.

Fewer than a dozen Swift Creek sites are reported from the central Savannah River region. Ten sites from the Clark Hill Lake region yielded Swift Creek pottery and only in extremely small frequencies. These include site 9WS64, located on Fishing Creek, and 9LC51 and 9LC52, located on a ridge just above the Savannah River floodplain, all in Lincoln County, Georgia, and 9EB529, an upland site on the Broad River, and 9EB524, located in Elbert County, Georgia. The pottery from 9EB524 is probably Late Swift Creek, as evidenced by folded rims (Elliott 1993c).

At Anthony Shoals (9WS51), just upstream from Clark Hill Lake on the Broad River in Wilkes County, Georgia, a sparse scatter of Swift Creek ($n =$ 6) and Napier ($n = 3$) complicated stamped pottery was found in three excavated areas extending over an area of 150 meters (Wood and Smith 1988:50). A small mound was reported by Carl Miller a short distance downstream from the Anthony Shoals site, but it has since been destroyed (Elliott 1993c). Although the age of this mound is unknown, it possibly was associated with the Swift Creek presence at Anthony Shoals.

The Rembert mound and village site, located above the Savannah River/Broad River confluence in Elbert County, Georgia, apparently had a Swift Creek component, although it was not identified by Caldwell (1953). Wauchope (1966:373–74) collected twenty-two sherds from Rembert mound that he identified as Early Swift Creek. These include examples with folded rims, however, arguing for a Late Swift Creek placement. Site 9EB513, the underwater component identified in the vicinity of the Rembert mound site (9EB1), contained three probable Swift Creek Complicated Stamped sherds (Anderson et al. 1992:56).

Swift Creek pottery is reported from the Long Cane Creek shoreline by private collectors (J. Ray Purdy, pers. comm.). My examination of Purdy's collection also revealed a possible Napier or Swift Creek Rectilinear Complicated Stamped component on a village site north of Patterson Creek in South Carolina.

Fortson mound (9WS2) is a flat-topped mound located in the interriverine region of Wilkes County south of Washington, Georgia. The site was

first examined by Arthur R. Kelly in the early 1950s and, recently rediscovered and reexamined by Williams (Elliott and Kowalewski 1989; Williams
1992), is tentatively dated to Early Swift Creek times on the basis of the
presence of notched rims. Folded rims are also present, however, and larger
pottery collections and radiocarbon dates are necessary to pin down the
age of this mound. The associated habitation is small and the site was not a
village.

During the 1890s, Doctor Roland Steiner collected significant amounts
of Swift Creek pottery from an upland village site at the confluence of Kiokee Creek and the Savannah River (USNM Catalog Number 210294).
While this collection has not been completely analyzed, a preliminary examination identified a strong Swift Creek presence in this area. The Swift Creek
pottery from this site includes unmodified, slightly rolled, and slightly folded
rims, with crisp design execution. No notched or scalloped rims were observed, suggesting the site is Late Swift Creek.

Swift Creek pottery was reported as a minority ware from features and
in a midden context from site 9RI88 on the Savannah River near Augusta
(Elliott and Doyon 1981:123). A possible Swift Creek component is also
reported by Phelps from White's mound (9RI4) (T. J. Lattimore collection,
Tulane University, New Orleans, Louisiana).

South of the Fall Line on the Savannah River watershed, Swift Creek
sites are few. Surveys of more than 50,000 acres at the United States Army's
Fort Gordon in the sand hills of Georgia have identified a very few sites
containing rectilinear stamped pottery that may be Late Woodland, but no
definite Swift Creek Curvilinear Complicated Stamped has been identified
among assemblages from a sample of more than 1,400 sites (Chad Braley,
pers. comm.).

Swift Creek sites are extremely rare in the interior Coastal Plain of the
Savannah River system. Swift Creek pottery was not found along Brier Creek
or on the lower Savannah River despite extensive excavations in the region
(Brockington 1971; Elliott and O'Steen 1987; Garrow 1984; Smith 1986).
Single Swift Creek sherds are reported from 9BK24 near the Savannah River
and from 9BK33 (Honerkamp 1983). Despite extensive excavation along
lower Brier Creek by Garrow and Associates, no Swift Creek sites were found
(Elliott and O'Steen 1987; Garrow 1984). Survey of the surrounding uplands yielded only one site with Swift Creek pottery, 9SN37, on an upland

ridge approximately 2.5 kilometers from the Savannah River near the Brier Creek confluence (Elliott 1987). Another possible Swift Creek sherd is reported from the surface in the Theriault locality (9BK67) in Burke County, Georgia, but no sherds have been recovered from excavations in the area (Brockington 1971; Ledbetter 1991; Sassaman 1992). Swift Creek pottery occurs at fewer than eight sites on the Savannah River Plant in Aiken and Barnwell counties, where more than a thousand sites have been located and many thousands of acres have been surveyed. In this region Swift Creek is always an extreme minority ware (Sassaman et al. 1990; Ken Sassaman, pers. comm.). Stoltman (1974) found no Swift Creek pottery at Groton Plantation in Allendale County, and DePratter's more recent research there has found only one Swift Creek sherd from more than 200 sites. Brewton Hill Complicated Stamped and Napier were reported as minority ware from the Bostick site (38HA1), located on a small creek 2 kilometers from the Savannah River near Estill, South Carolina (Stephenson and Brockington 1969:7–8). Despite extensive research in Effingham County, Georgia, no Swift Creek pottery has been recovered in that area (Elliott and Smith 1985; Fish 1976; Smith 1986).

Swift Creek is present in the coastal Savannah area but is not common (Caldwell and Waring 1939; DePratter 1991; Hanson and DePratter 1985; Waring 1968). Fewkes was the first to report a Swift Creek variant ware in the lowest level of the first mound at the Irene site (Fewkes 1938:24). De-Pratter (1991:172–73) redefined Brewton Hill Complicated Stamped as Deptford Complicated Stamped, which he now considers to be the regional expression of Swift Creek. This pottery appears late in the Deptford period (Deptford II, A.D. 300–500). Rims are described as straight, not tapered, and the lips are described as squared or occasionally rounded. The Deptford site (9CH2) and Deptford mound (9CH2a), east of Savannah; Budreau (9CH9), located on White Marsh Island southeast of Savannah; and 9CH19 yielded minor amounts of Deptford Complicated Stamped pottery. These sites should be considered to have probable Swift Creek connections.

Swift Creek in the Santee River Watershed and All Points East

Northward along the coast past the Savannah River watershed in South Carolina, Swift Creek nearly disappears. Despite extensive cultural resource management excavations on the South Carolina coast, Swift Creek has not been reported from that region (Christopher T. Espenshade, pers. comm.; Robert Morgan, pers. comm.; Michael Trinkley, pers. comm.).

Rodeffer et al. (1979:332–34) reported one identified Swift Creek Complicated Stamped sherd in addition to other unidentified complicated stamped sherds at site 38GN260, located near the headwaters of Coronaca Creek in the Saluda River drainage. A substantial Swift Creek site in Greenville County in the foothills of the Blue Ridge Mountains was reported to me by an amateur archaeologist, but it is undocumented (Wesley Breedlove, pers. comm.). No Swift Creek pottery sites are reported from the Camden area, a scene of extensive mound building during later periods. Survey of more than 35,000 acres in the United States Army's Fort Jackson has yielded more than 1,000 archaeological sites, but no Swift Creek pottery. In the Francis Marion National Forest, an area extensively surveyed has produced more than 1,600 sites, and none contains Swift Creek pottery (Robert Morgan, pers. comm.).

The Swift Creek Periphery

At least seventy-five Swift Creek sites have been documented beyond the core area of central Georgia into the Tennessee, Savannah, and Santee watersheds. The Tennessee basin contains at least seventeen sites with Swift Creek wares and a greater number with Pickwick pottery, a closely related series that also includes pottery from later periods. Only four sites have yielded significant amounts of Swift Creek pottery (defined as more than one dozen recognizable Swift Creek sherds)—Icehouse Bottom, Patrick, Ocoee, and Candy Creek—and on these sites Swift Creek is overshadowed by greater frequencies of Pickwick pottery. Below the Chickamauga Dam, Swift Creek is completely replaced by the Pickwick limestone-tempered series, except at the Pinson mound site and Russell Cave. For the most part, the Tennessee River system is the northern boundary of Swift Creek ceramics. Long-distance trade to sites in the core of the Hopewell culture is known, but there appear to be broad expanses in between where Swift Creek pottery is entirely absent.

The Savannah River watershed contains fewer than fifty known Swift Creek sites representing all physiographic zones. Major components of Swift Creek pottery, however (measured by more than a dozen recognizable Swift

Creek potsherds), are present on only nine sites: Tugalo, Chauga, Sara's Ridge, Simpsons Field, Transect 21 (9EB17), Rembert, Fortson Mound, Steiner's Kiokee Creek, and Deptford. Settlement is greatest in the Blue Ridge Mountains and upper Piedmont regions, and no substantial Swift Creek sites have been identified in the interior Coastal Plain. This stands in sharp contrast to the extensive Swift Creek presence in the interior Coastal Plain of the Altamaha drainage (Snow 1977). The Savannah River valley is in essence the eastern boundary of Swift Creek culture.

The majority of Swift Creek settlements on both the Tennessee and Savannah river systems tentatively date to Late Swift Creek times (after A.D. 500). They frequently are found with later Napier design motifs and tend to have plain, folded rims and not the earlier notched varieties. Exceptions exist, however, such as Fortson Mound and Icehouse Bottom. The Early Swift Creek sites that are found on the periphery may be special sites and not domestic sites.

Swift Creek people on the periphery were living in a wide range of physiographic provinces and on a broad array of topographic landforms. This is true for both the Tennessee and Savannah watersheds, but upland Swift Creek settlement is more characteristic of the Savannah River system. On the Tennessee system, Swift Creek and Pickwick pottery samples are almost always minority wares on large multicomponent ceramic sites. As a result, these components have often been lost in the shuffle when these sites were described. Other sites, such as the Candy Creek site, contain significant Swift Creek components, but they have not been fully reported.

While there are mounds on sites in both river systems, Swift Creek mound construction is found only in the Savannah River system. Sites with Swift Creek–era mounds include Fortson and Deptford and, possibly, the Ramona and Rembert mound sites. None of the major Swift Creek Tennessee River sites has Swift Creek mounds, except possibly Pinson, although Swift Creek pottery is found on several sites that have mounds from subsequent times such as Hiwassee Island. This may reflect the ceremonial character of these Swift Creek sites, or it may simply be that mounded villages tended to develop on landforms that were desirable for settlement throughout prehistory. Some Swift Creek pottery is reported from caves and rock shelters in Tennessee and Alabama, while none from such locations is known from the Savannah drainage.

On the Tennessee River the presence of Swift Creek decorative motifs on limestone-tempered paste strongly suggests local manufacture, although the paddles may have been traded. Some sand-tempered Swift Creek pottery may be trade ware, owing to the very different appearance of the paste in site collections, but this needs to be resolved by more rigorous study, because it cannot be determined given the current state of the data. On the Savannah River there are sites containing sufficient quantities of Swift Creek ware to suggest local manufacture, while sites that contain fewer than a dozen Swift Creek sherds argue for trade.

One might expect greater similarity to Hopewellian culture on the Tennessee versus the Savannah drainages because of the geographic proximity to the Hopewell homeland. Chapman (1973) identified Hopewellian connections at Icehouse Bottom in Tennessee and Keel (1976) identified Hopewellian artifacts at Garden Creek in North Carolina, but elsewhere evidence for exchange is absent. No Hopewell material has been reported from the Savannah River system.

Many problems remain in defining the Swift Creek periphery. Desperately needed is a detailed study of the design elements on significant collections of Pickwick Complicated Stamped pottery. For the Tennessee River system, the Candy Creek and Davis sites are prime candidates for study, but there are others. Rudolph (1986) initiated a noteworthy study of Swift Creek design elements in northern Georgia, but what is needed is a merger between her approach and that used by Snow for southern Georgia and Florida (Snow 1975). This study should include Pickwick wares as well.

Absolute dates for Swift Creek occupation are quite rare on the periphery and dating should receive high priority in cultural resource management studies in the region. The available data allow only for crude age separation on these sites. Similarly, data on households, architecture, and subsistence are nearly unknown for Swift Creek sites on the periphery. At present, only a sketchy view of the variety and diversity of Swift Creek sites on the periphery is available. The settlement spectrum includes mounded sites with limited adjacent habitations, multiple clusters of debris that may represent small groups or extended families, smaller pottery scatters that may represent single households, and isolated occurrences of Swift Creek ware that may be the result of trade only. While Swift Creek villages may exist in these areas, the distributional data on Swift Creek ceramics across large village sites necessary to substantiate this are presently unavailable.

Swift Creek, characterized by its distinctive curvilinear complicated stamped design elements, is found across a 1,000-kilometer expanse of southeastern North America as far from the homeland as the Mann site in Indiana. From the type site near Macon, Georgia, which does not necessarily represent the center of this culture, Swift Creek sites are commonly found up to 400 kilometers to the north and 300 kilometers to the east and southeast. Swift Creek sites on the periphery are not abundant, but they are known and are quite varied in content. Social evolution and geo-politics during Swift Creek times were dynamic. Sites on the periphery may provide crucial clues in understanding the developing social complexities that undoubtedly accompanied Swift Creek ceramic art. These symbols probably conveyed powerful ideas, but the mechanisms of this conveyance must await more detailed study.

Shrines of the Prehistoric South
Patterning in Middle Woodland Mound Distribution

Mark Williams and Jennifer Freer Harris

It is often said that archaeological research yields more questions than answers. The 1991 excavations at the Fortson site in Wilkes County, Georgia, provided strong and direct support for this aphorism. The Fortson site (9WS2) is located in the east-central portion of the northern Georgia Piedmont, on a minor drainage some 40 kilometers west of the Savannah River. It had been first discovered and tested in 1950 by Arthur R. Kelly of the University of Georgia, but Kelly, who died in 1979, never wrote a report on his testing. Further, he never recorded the exact location of the site, no field notes are extant, and the site was completely lost for the following thirty-eight years. In 1988, the site was rediscovered through the efforts of Dan Elliott and Steve Kowalewski (Elliott and Kowalewski 1989).

The small collections made by Kelly at the site were examined by Elliott and Kowalewski, by one of us (Mark Williams), by David Hally, and by David Anderson, who was then working on his dissertation on the Mississippian occupation of the Savannah River valley (Anderson 1990). All agreed that while most of the sherds in Kelly's collection dated to the Middle Woodland Swift Creek period, some dated to the Mississippian Lamar and/or Savannah periods. This was not surprising, because there were a number of other mound sites in northern Georgia that had both of these occupations. Indeed, this sort of reoccupation has become recognized as a consistent pattern in the area and eventually should be studied in its own right as an important research question.

We should state that Williams's research interests at the time were centered on the distributions of Mississippian period mound centers in northern Georgia, focusing on the Oconee River valley to the west of the Fortson site (Williams and Shapiro 1987). In that region, it was clear that there was a systematic and evenly spaced growth of mound centers associated with the chiefdoms in the area. The original recognition of this even spacing was made some years earlier by Smith and Kowalewski (Smith and Kowalewski 1980). Williams's work in the valley has shown that the final pattern of Mississippian period mound site distribution resulted from a far more complex sequence of site abandonment and resettlement than had been originally assumed.

David Anderson had conducted similar settlement pattern studies in the Savannah Valley to the east as part of his dissertation research. When the initial Fortson data were examined by Williams, Anderson, Hally, Elliott, and Kowalewski it seemed clear that the Fortson mound was situated at a unique location between known Mississippian mound centers in the Oconee and Savannah valleys. Specifically, it was located halfway between the Shoulderbone site (9HK1) near the eastern edge of the Oconee Valley (Williams 1990) and the Rembert site (9EB1) on the eastern side of the Savannah River (Anderson 1990). The assumption of all involved, then, was that Fortson was the center of a small Mississippian period chiefdom that in some way connected the known centers in both the Oconee and Savannah valleys. This led Williams to direct a brief University of Georgia archaeological field school at the Fortson site during the summer of 1991.

The field school program at Fortson included making a contour map of the mound, shovel testing the area around the mound to determine site size, and placing a single 2-meter excavation square on the edge of the mound in what appeared to be thick midden deposits. This latter technique has been shown to be the most effective technique for defining the Mississippian components at many mound centers (Smith and Williams 1994).

The area immediately around the mound had been recently cleared of trees and ground visibility was excellent. As the excavations and the shovel testing proceeded one pattern became rapidly clear—there was no Mississippian pottery at all on the entire Fortson site! After recovering from the initial shock of this discovery, we hurried back to the lab in Athens to reexamine the sherds from Kelly's excavations. There was a single bag of sherds (UGA

Catalog Number 846) that contained all of the Mississippian material. The catalog entry for this number does list it as being from 9WS2, but the provenience information is written in pencil in a different hand and says "no data on bag." We are now quite confident that this collection did not come from the Fortson site. Probably, no one will ever know where it *did* come from.

Thus with one bad bag of sherds the visions that Williams, Anderson, and others had of the Fortson site's being an important Mississippian center linking the chiefdoms in both the Oconee and Savannah valleys went out the window. The Fortson site was "merely" a Middle Woodland mound center. What now? Then Williams remembered this was not the first time, or even the second time, that this had happened to him. The Lingerlonger site (9GE35) in Greene County, which he had tested in 1986, was another would-be Mississippian mound center that had also turned out to be a Middle Woodland mound site. Also, the Little River site (9MG46), which he had tested in 1984 and 1987, yielded an unexpected Middle Woodland component in addition to its Mississippian component (Williams and Shapiro 1990). Little River has two mounds that date to the Middle Woodland period.

As Williams pondered this, he realized that he knew of another Middle Woodland mound on the main channel of the Oconee River—the Cold Springs site (9GE10) in Greene County. He looked at a map and suddenly realized that these four sites might not have been randomly placed because, with one exception, they were evenly distributed. As aptly stated by Yogi Berra, this was "déjà vu all over again" for him. Here was the same type of pattern he had seen in the distribution of Mississippian mound centers in the Oconee Valley and beyond (now excluding the Fortson site). He had certainly not expected this for the Middle Woodland period.

All of these sites had clear evidence of Early Swift Creek occupation, although the data from Lingerlonger are in need of additional support. Enough of this pattern was present, however, to tempt us to expand the pattern by examining the site data in the Georgia Archaeological Site File in Athens. Some of the sites recorded for this chapter are definitely Early Swift Creek sites, some are small mounds of probable Woodland origin, some are small mounds of unknown period, and some are even rumored mounds. We have intentionally and admittedly cast our net wide at this initial stage of inquiry.

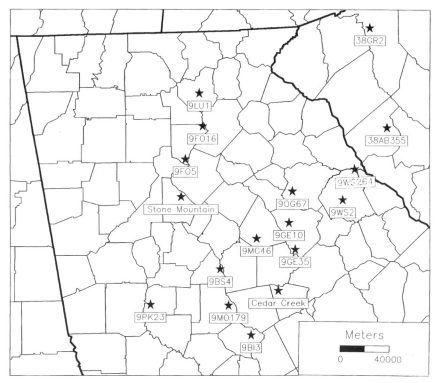

Figure 4-1. Possible Swift Creek shrines in northern Georgia.

Although the data are of variable quality, it appears to us that there is a patterning to the distribution of Middle Woodland mound centers in pied-mont Georgia, continuing into upper South Carolina (Figure 4-1). We have not yet examined data from Alabama, North Carolina, or the Georgia Coastal Plain since this study is preliminary in nature. The next section of this chap-ter presents the site-specific information for those sites included on the map, and the final section of the chapter discusses the distribution of the centers; the implications for economic, social, and political interpretations of these Middle Woodland societies; and the problems with the data. For this chapter, we intentionally limited our search to the Piedmont region east and west of the Oconee Valley in Georgia and have not looked into the Coastal Plain or into Alabama or North Carolina. The pattern in those areas should be ex-amined in the future.

Site Descriptions

The first sites described are in what we consider the core area of our knowledge and are where the pattern was first discerned.

Little River

During the summers of 1984 and 1987 Mark Williams and Gary Shapiro undertook excavations at the Little River site (9MG46) in the southern portion of Morgan County, some 15 kilometers south of Madison, Georgia. The site is located on a broad ridge overlooking Blue Creek, a tiny tributary of Little River. Two of the four earthen mounds and a large portion of the village at this site date to the Early Swift Creek period (Williams and Shapiro 1990). Mound B contained Woodland ceramics and a stone gorget, as well as a burial that may have been disturbed prehistorically. Mound C appears to be a small Swift Creek period garbage mound, although there is a possibility that there is a burial pit deeper in the center of the mound structure. Crystal quartz flakes made up 50 percent of all flakes from the site. This site also contained a late Lamar period Mississippian occupation.

Cold Springs

Two earthen mounds and an occupation area were excavated at the Cold Springs site in Greene County (9GE10). The site is located a few kilometers northwest of Greensboro, Georgia, and was excavated as part of the University of Georgia's Lake Oconee project. Both mounds appeared to have been constructed beginning in the Early Swift Creek period. Mound A was a flat-topped mound approximately 2.5 meters in height and 50 meters in diameter. Mound B, a smaller mound, was apparently constructed as a burial/crematorium mound. Perhaps the most interesting aspect of this site was its low population during occupation. Fish suggests that it was a "largely 'vacant' center, serving an outlying population, and home for a small number of persons among whom may have been caretakers and specialists" (Fish 1978:16). The site had a later Etowah period Mississippian occupation over the Middle Woodland occupation.

Lingerlonger

The Lingerlonger site, 9GE35, was located in 1977 by crews from the University of Georgia working on the Lake Oconee project. It is located on a high, broad ridge overlooking the shoals in this section of the Oconee River valley. A map was made of the site at that time by Paul Webb. The site was revisited in 1986 by Mark Williams as part of a University of Georgia field school. The site was remapped and post-hole tested at that time. The earthen mound there is conical, approximately 3 meters high, and a very broad 40 meters across. No Mississippian material was located at this fairly large earthen mound, and no village deposits were located. It is confidently placed in the Woodland period.

Fortson

As stated in the introduction to this chapter, the Fortson site, 9WS2, is located in Wilkes County, a few kilometers south of Washington, Georgia. It is located a few hundred meters east of a small stream on a broad ridge top. The mound is a fairly large flat-topped earthen mound, some 50 meters in diameter and more than 3 meters high. There is very little evidence of a village associated with the site. There is an outcrop of moderate-sized nodules of limonite in the immediate vicinity of the mound. A report of the 1991 testing at the site has been completed by Williams (Williams 1992). The site is primarily an Early Swift Creek site.

Barrow Creek

In Oglethorpe County Jerald Ledbetter has reported (Jerald Ledbetter, pers. comm.) that a rock mound (9OG67), 5 meters in diameter and 0.5 meter in height, was located in the Barrow Creek Survey Tract. The mound was unfortunately bulldozed in 1987. No cultural material was found in the rock pile although a number of Swift Creek sites were recorded in the immediate surrounding area.

In the area to the east of the core area, the following sites have been located. Some are more certain than others, of course.

Miller's Mound

Miller's Mound (9WS264) is a Woodland mound site on the southeastern side of the Broad River at Anthony Shoals, near the Savannah River. It was first described by Carl Miller, who conducted the survey of the Clark Hill Reservoir, as a circular earthen mound approximately 15 meters in diameter and less than 2 meters in height. No cultural material has been recovered from this site. The Georgia Archaeological Site File provides information on an amateur excavation at the site by C. E. Thompson of Washington, Georgia. He dug an L-shaped trench through the mound and reported a stone slab found at the subsoil level. Attempts to relocate the site during 1992 and 1993 by Dan Elliott and others were not successful. The mound was recently (January 1998) relocated, however, by Chad Braley and South-eastern Archeological Services, Incorporated. It was located a bit further west than anticipated, but clearly is the same site that Carl Miller had found in the late 1940s.

Ramona

The Ramona site was discovered about 1984 by Dan Elliott. Located northeast of Abbeville, South Carolina, site 38AB355 consists of a small conical-shaped earthen mound less than 2 meters high. The only testing of the site was by Elliott and Williams in 1984 and consisted of a simple shovel test on the summit placed in a looters' pit. The site contained no Mississippian sherds. The area around the mound was in pasture at the time of the visit, and it is located a few hundred meters from a small stream with essentially no floodplain.

North Fork Mound/Camp Old Indian Mound

North Fork mound (38GR2) and Camp Old Indian mound (38GR3) are located very near one another just south of the North Saluda Reservoir, north of Greenville, South Carolina, according to the South Carolina Archaeological Site File. They were both discovered early in the twentieth century, and neither has received any formal archaeological excavation.

In the area to the southwest of the core area, a number of sites or suspected sites have been identified. These include the following sites.

Cedar Creek

An 1804 land survey was made between the land belonging to Georgia and the land belonging to the Creek Nation. The survey was conducted by Colonel Benjamin Hawkins. Jerald Ledbetter found the field notes for this survey stored at the University of Georgia's Hargrett Rare Book and Manuscript Library as part of the Telamon Cuyler Collection. The notes describe an archaeological site on Cedar Creek somewhere near the junction of Baldwin, Putnam, and Jones counties. The site is described as "a work of ancient fortification" in the notes. There has been very little survey in this area in recent years. It is included here because this location matches well with the distribution of our other sites. The site description may be referring to a rock mound site, which are plentiful in this area. Clearly, more work is needed in this section of the Oconee Valley.

Swift Creek

The Swift Creek site (9BI3), the type site for all Swift Creek sites, which was first reported by Arthur R. Kelly in 1938 and then again by him and Betty Smith in 1975, was a mound and village site located on Swift Creek in the Ocmulgee River drainage. Located just east of Macon, Georgia, in Bibb County, this site was essentially destroyed during World War II. This occupational mound was approximately conical in shape, approximately 3 meters in height and 35 meters in diameter, and included a surrounding occupation area.

Plant Scherer

In 1977 Fish and Jefferies (1978) undertook excavations at two stone mound sites in Monroe County, Georgia, as part of the Georgia Power Company's Plant Scherer project. Both of these sites (9MO179 and 9MO180) overlook Berry Creek, near the Ocmulgee River, and have scatters of small stone mounds surrounding them. The first site (9MO179) contained three large stone mounds and fifty-two smaller ones. The second site consisted of one large stone mound and ninety-one smaller ones. Although no culturally diagnostic materials were recovered from site 9MO179, and the major mounds were damaged by looting and construction, excavations revealed evidence of some faunal material at the base of Mounds A, B, and C. The large mound at site 9MO180, however, yielded Middle Woodland period artifacts, including a platform pipe, mica, and simple stamped ceramics. Burned human bone was also uncovered at the large mound at site 9MO180, suggesting this was a crematory platform. Neither site 9MO179 nor 9MO180 contained evidence of Woodland habitation. In addition, these sites appear to have served different ceremonial functions inasmuch as there was no evidence for human burial at site 9MO179.

Ward

A search of the Georgia Archaeological Site File provided early sketchy information on a three-mound site located on Major Ward's Plantation in

Butts County (9BS4) near the Ocmulgee River. The Georgia Archaeological Site File information listed a 1939 report by Wauchope in which he described a Dr. Tolefree of Monticello, who excavated some of the mounds and found a "variety of Indian implements." No cultural affinity is known for this mound group, and unfortunately no other information is presently available. Given the lack of apparent Mississippian occupation in this area, and the presence of much Middle Woodland occupation downstream, we list the site here, although more work is admittedly needed on it.

Apple Orchard

Another earthen mound structure less than 2 meters high and about 20 meters in diameter was reported by Ray Crook along the Flint River in Pike County, Georgia. He referred to it as the Apple Orchard site (9PK23), and the mound is now destroyed (Ray Crook, pers. comm.). The western edge of the site is located on the Flint River floodplain. Although no excavations were conducted in his brief visit to the site, Crook reports that a survey of the immediate area produced ceramics of several periods, projectile points, hammer stones, and lithic debris. This site needs further confirmation but might have a Middle Woodland occupation.

To the north, in the upper Piedmont and into the lower edge of the Appalachians, an additional chain of sites is recorded in the Georgia Archaeological Site File. The implications of this northern chain, and the apparent empty area on the down side of the Brevard Fault (the headwater area for the Flint, Ocmulgee, Oconee, and Broad rivers), are currently unknown. This northern chain includes the following sites.

Stone Mountain

Although we have no record of a specific mound, there once was a rock wall around the summit of the massive 800-foot-high rock feature known as Stone Mountain. The now-destroyed wall probably dated to the Middle Woodland period (Smith 1962). Further, the work of David Chase in recent years has revealed the presence of Middle Woodland ceramics in a small rock mound near the base of Stone Mountain (David Chase, pers. comm.). This mound also contained probable cremated human remains. There are a great many additional stone mound sites in this area, many of which are *not* the result of historic Georgia farmers. Stone Mountain itself may have been a magnet for people in Middle Woodland times, just as it is today.

Shakerag

The Shakerag mound site (9FO5/9FO211) is located in Forsyth County on a drainage near Dick Creek and its confluence with the Chattahoochee River. Wauchope (1966) described this as a "small, almost wholly sand-buried mound near the creek bank about .25 miles from the river." There was a sparse scattering of sherds on the site including several Swift Creek sherds. The majority of the ceramics date to the Late Mississippian period, however.

Summerour

The Summerour mound (9FO16) was located on an extensive bottom-land alluvial ridge above the Chattahoochee River. The mound, now destroyed under the Buford Reservoir, was approximately 3 meters in height, 70 meters long, and 45 meters wide. Middle Woodland, Late Woodland, and Early Mississippian ceramics provide culturally diagnostic material for this site. Joe Caldwell excavated a portion of the base of the mound, and the findings have recently been reanalyzed by Tom Pluckhahn (Pluckhahn 1996). Middle Woodland ceramics are common in this region, and there is some possibility that some of the mound dates to this period.

Camp Glisson

In 1954 Arthur R. Kelly and his student Edward Beam excavated a stone mound (9LU1) near Dahlonega, located on Cane Creek (Kelly and Beam 1956). The mound was approximately 10 meters in diameter and 2 meters high. The mound was constructed using tabular stone blocks of exfoliated bedrock material. No evidence of human remains was found at this site, although some faunal material was recovered. Several lithic artifacts were cataloged in the artifact assemblage and were roughly categorized as Archaic period projectile points/knives.

Analysis and Discussion

The pattern discussed here will certainly change in the future. Probably several of the sites or possible sites we have listed will prove not to be a part of the pattern. We do believe, however, that others will turn up that will reinforce the pattern. Attempts must be made to examine the data of additional states to the east and west of the current research area.

The spacing of sites in the Oconee Valley is approximately 29 kilometers.

The spacing of many others is in the range of 29 to 35 kilometers. Hally recently conducted an important study of the distances between Mississippian centers in Georgia and much of the Southeast and concluded that most primary chiefdom centers are between 10 and 30 kilometers apart, whereas complex chiefdoms have administrative centers about 40 kilometers apart (Hally 1993:165). Few would argue that the Middle Woodland societies in question here were organized as chiefdoms, but the spacing between the mounds is curiously similar to the lower of Hally's Mississippian distances. We believe that a very different locational principle was at play in the distribution of the Woodland centers than existed for the Mississippian ones. What that principle might have been is currently unknown to us, however.

Most of the sites have very little midden. This implies that few, if any, people were living at such sites on a permanent basis or that their period of use was very brief. It follows that these sites were nonsecular in nature. The fact that the sites do not appear to be lived on implies that the visitors arrived at and left the site usually on the same day. Such a scenario would be in accord with a closer spacing for sites.

The locations of the known mounds cover a wide variety of topographic and ecological settings, with the tops of broad, high ridges being perhaps the most common. Although some sites are in the floodplains of rivers, most are not. This implies that location with respect to good-quality agricultural land was not an important consideration. The locations of these mounds on higher elevations might mean that many of them have not been submerged under reservoirs and can yet be located and tested.

Studies of the distribution of small Middle Woodland sites that are near the mounds have not yet been undertaken systematically. We believe, however, they are clustered close to the mounds and do not occur randomly over the entire Piedmont. In the case of the Barrow Creek "mound," for example, a systematic surface survey of the surrounding clearcut revealed a group of Swift Creek sites around it. Surveys less than 1.5 kilometers to either side of the Barrow Creek tract, however, produced no Swift Creek sites at all. The same is true of the known settlement patterns surrounding the Cold Springs mound and village, with no Swift Creek sites located outside of the immediate periphery of the site.

What are the functions of the mounds? They typically do not contain the remains of houses. In all likelihood they do contain a few burials and/or cremations. Clearly everyone was not buried in a mound, however. Are the mound burials the burials for chiefs? Are these societies chiefdoms or tribal/big man societies? The sites are not chiefly compounds because few, if any, people actually lived there. We believe that these sites and other Middle Woodland sites such as Rock Eagle (9PM85) might be best described as *shrines*.

The word *shrine* comes from the Latin word *scrinium*, which means "a chest for paper" (OED 1878). In 1385, Chaucer used the word *shrine* to mean "a case or casket for a dead body." In 1526, Tinsdale used the word to mean "a receptacle containing objects of religious veneration." In 1629, John Milton used *shrine* to mean "a place where worship is offered or devotions are paid to a saint or deity." Milton's use is the same as in common parlance to this day. We contend that the word *shrine* used in this manner comes closer to describing the functions of Middle Woodland mound sites than any other word used to date. Indeed, few functional terms have ever been applied to these sites. Shrines are typically thought of as centers for personal ritual, rather than corporate ritual. The material implications for such a pattern are in direct agreement with those recognized from the Georgia Middle Woodland sites discussed in this chapter.

Questions of sociopolitical organization may also concern the evidence for increasing social aggregation and regional integration throughout the Middle Woodland. How does the origin of these shrines relate to the change from constricted, localized settlement in the Early Woodland to the patterns of interregional exchange and interaction that begin in the Middle Woodland? For example, the items made from crystal quartz from the Little River site and the probable items made from limonite at the Fortson site must have been produced for consumption beyond the local level. This suggests an important question about the use of Middle Woodland exotic artifacts in the context of shrine use. We believe that such a perspective might be a productive avenue for guiding new research about Middle Woodland cultures.

Finally, it is interesting to note that many of these sites were reported in the late nineteenth or early twentieth century but were frequently lost or ignored in recent years because they were small and because they were *not* Mississippian period mound centers. It would not surprise us if, on further research, such small mound sites turn out to date to the Middle Woodland period.

Swift Creek
Lineage and Diffusion

David W. Chase

Of all the Woodland archaeological complexes in the North American Southeast, few are more intriguing in terms of origin, geographic extent, and ultimate fate than the prehistoric entity that is known now as Swift Creek. The concept became a part of the literature with its first recognition by Arthur R. Kelly (1938) and with a later and more detailed evaluation by Smith and Kelly (1975).

In reviewing published data on the subject, one cannot overlook references to the several non–Swift Creek archaeological complexes that somehow played a significant role in the shaping of its configuration as a society. These neighboring complexes, I believe, had a very positive impact on their lifeways and their fate. Some of these complexes involve Marksville, Deptford, and, interestingly enough, Hopewell. In its final form, Swift Creek seems to have maintained its closest ties with Weeden Island and possibly Napier archaeological cultures.

Many scholars have added bits and pieces to the Swift Creek scenario over the years since Kelly's type-site findings. This chapter will cite many of those who made significant contributions toward the understanding of the Swift Creek culture largely through its most visible artifact—complicated stamped pottery. This tradition marked, for all practical purposes, the very beginning of Swift Creek and lasted as a ceramic technique until early European-contact times. Through its specific definitive attributes, decorative motifs, and style, southeasternists can now readily identify this pottery. Thanks to Snow (1977) and Broyles (1968) archaeologists now have a better grasp of the issue of paddle carving and tradition exchanges.

Origins of Paddle-Stamped Pottery

Paddle-stamped pottery dates from very early times in North American ceramic prehistory. Blanton (1979:51) describes his Satilla series as containing "relatively thin, simple stamped and check stamped or plain ware tempered with a composite of fibre and sand." He suggests that this ware represents a transition from fiber-tempered to Deptford stamped types. This ceramic type appears in the upper Satilla River basin in southeastern Georgia. Blanton suggests that check-stamped and simple stamped pottery may have had simultaneous beginnings. At any rate, one is inclined to agree that check-stamped and simple stamped finishes represent the earliest examples of paddle stamping.

Walthall (1980:87) indicates that simple stamped fiber-tempered pottery occurs in the Wheeler culture (Broken Pumpkin Creek phase) in the upper Tombigbee drainage area. He gives a temporal position of this ceramic as sometime between 1000 and 800 B.C. This indicates that the tradition, if it diffused from the Georgia Atlantic coast, must have left connecting traces elsewhere through the Tennessee River valley and into the Georgia Piedmont; however, curiously enough, little if any evidence of fiber-tempered pottery is known in Georgia above the Fall Line.

Innumerable sites that produced both check-stamped and simple stamped pottery have been found along the Atlantic coast and westward into the Georgia Coastal Plain. A common taxon for the form has been Mossy Oak Simple Stamped, which Caldwell (1958:35) states is "so far the earliest of the manifestations we consider directly in the Southern Appalachian Tradition." Mossy Oak, with its artifact assemblage containing Archaic lithic material (Fairbanks 1952:286), is projected as a very early paddle-stamped pottery possibly earlier than the check-stamped form emerging in the Deptford cultural arena. Today it is known that all simple stamped pottery is not Mossy Oak. Elliott and Wynn (1991) have defined what appears to be a Late Woodland simple stamped ware from the Vining site excavated in the 1930s and refer to a number of sites elsewhere in Georgia that produced simple stamped pottery that appears to be too late to be classified under the taxon Mossy Oak, which still survives in the literature as an Early Woodland type.

Paddle stamping was not confined to the application of a carved wooden stamp or other decorating instrument. Another technique apparently involved the wrapping of a stamping instrument with woven material and pressing it into the wet clay in the first stages of pottery making. Other forms of fabric impressing involve cord marking and net impressing; both occur prominently from New York southward to Florida. Ceramics made with the use of a fabric-wrapped paddle occur in the early stages of Georgia Woodland development; a good example is Dunlap Fabric Impressed, a basic ceramic of the Kellog phase (Caldwell 1958:23). The technique of wrapping paddles with cord or other fabric may have originated as early as 500 B.C. and subsequently diffused westward into the Tennessee Valley, where it occurs as a limestone-tempered variety of a Dunlap-related type (Heimlich 1952). It further spread into the Tombigbee riverine system where it manifests in the Miller series as Saltillo Fabric Marked, which begins in the Miller I period and disappears finally in Miller III (Jenkins 1982:140–41). The route of diffusion for the type is not presently known; however, a number of sites I explored in coastal-plain Alabama have yielded a sand-tempered fabric-impressed pottery similar in characteristics to both Dunlap and Saltillo.

In defining his South Appalachian Tradition, Caldwell (1958:34) includes the sequences of complicated stamped pottery as seen in the Swift Creek tradition. At the time of that publication, and indeed until the present, no pinpointing of the origin of this style had been postulated. Willey (1949) observes a strong Marksville connection to Early or Santa Rosa Swift Creek especially in the western end of the Florida panhandle. The Marksville period manifests more commonly along the Mississippi and on Louisiana Gulf coastal sites, although ceramics of the period are known to extend farther east. Santa Rosa Complicated Stamped pottery appears to become more common as one follows the coast eastward. Indeed, this point is reinforced by Greenwell (1984:141), who refers to sites on the Mississippi Gulf Coast as containing Marksville–Santa Rosa period ceramics but indicates that "the Swift Creek complex is barely represented on the Mississippi Coast." For all practical purposes, Santa Rosa–Swift Creek is little more than the Early Swift Creek defined by Kelly in 1938.

Jenkins indicates that Marksville pottery occurs with Miller I types in eastern Mississippi (Jenkins 1982:69–70). Sherd types illustrated and described by Willey (1949:372–75) for Santa Rosa–Swift Creek include a rocker-stamped type, Santa Rosa Stamped, implying a possible Marksville relationship on decorative grounds.

A number of radiocarbon dates have been cited by Toth for the Marksville period (Toth 1979:190). These suggest a range of from 80 B.C. to A.D. 210, which appears to be acceptable for this period, although Toth regards this as unreliable. He suggests that dates of A.D. 20 to A.D. 210 may be considered to be within the expected range.

In a search for the beginnings of complicated stamped potters, it may be important to mention the recovery of certain unusual stamped types from the Walker Street site (9ME60) (Chase et al. 1994). This is essentially a Cartersville period site featuring check-stamped tetrapodal pottery. Associated with the latter were a number of sherds impressed with a curvilinear design but with the grooves walled off into checks—a sort of curvilinear check-stamped motif. In the Bureau of American Ethnology report the type was described as follows: "A few sherds showed a combination of check stamped and complicated stamped, possibly transitional forms belonging to Willey's New River Complicated Stamped." There is a difference, however, between the curvilinear check-stamped sherds found at the Walker Street site and New River Complicated Stamped (Willey 1949:384). The latter type shows both check-stamped and complicated stamped designs on the surface of the same vessel, whereas in the Walker Street types the checks were in the grooves. Near Montgomery, Alabama, I explored site 1MT108, which did, in fact, contain pottery that was very similar to New River Complicated Stamped and that may be the earliest complicated stamped pottery in that region. The site also contained a good component of the slightly later Cobb Swamp complex, which is related to the Cartersville phase.

I believe the Early Swift Creek Complicated Stamped variety emerged inland at one of three possible areas: (1) near the type site in central Georgia (Kelly 1938), (2) near the Halloca Creek site on the Fort Benning military reservation (Chase 1957), or (3) near site 1BR15 in Barbour County, Alabama, a significant multicomponent mound with ceramic sequences from Cartersville through Ocmulgee Fields complexes and including a component of Early Swift Creek (DeJarnette 1975:95). All of these sites appear to represent an inland version of Early Swift Creek as opposed to the Gulf Coast Santa Rosa period. The Halloca Creek site (9CE4) appears to contain all the ceramic elements present at the type site with many of the Santa Rosa types such as Santa Rosa Stamped omitted. A credible possibility could be in a region embracing two significant sites, Mandeville (Kellar et al. 1962) and Crystal River (Brose 1979a; Sears 1962). This could very well be a likely area to search for the Swift Creek genesis. Goad (1979:243) touches on this factor in discussing the exchange network "of the Santa Rosa–Swift Creek complex [which] may have operated in the following manner: exotic materials such as stone, galena, mica, and copper entered from sources in the Appalachian Mountains, the Great Lakes, and Alabama." Dates have been given by Brose (1979a:148) for Crystal River. The first is A.D. 350 ± 25 and the second is A.D. 530 ± 230. The first of these dates is close to the Mandeville time frame, and exchanges between the two sites cannot be ruled out. Here again Hopewell connections can be seen inasmuch as Hopewell-type artifacts did occur at Crystal River. Considering the probable significance of Crystal River, its burial mound complex, and large size, it could very well embrace the beginnings of the Swift Creek tradition. Sears (1962:6) cites the Yent complex as having Swift Creek Complicated Stamped pots associated with the Yent mound. The Yent site is located along the Florida Gulf Coast just as the coastline begins to bend southward. Smith (1979) views the Crystal River site as being of great significance in what she considers to be an exchange center for specific types of artifacts. Clearly, considering the burial mounds, the two stelae, and the Hopewell-type artifacts, one may conclude that the site must have had an important ceremonial function involving both Swift Creek and Hopewell activities.

Smith (1979:183) states that the period A.D. 250 to A.D. 500 was one in which ties with Santa Rosa–Swift Creek were most pronounced at the Mandeville site. It may be important to note that one premound date (Mound A) is 1840 ± 70 B.P., or A.D. 150. The dated zone contained notched and scalloped rimsherds, both of which denote an Early Swift Creek provenance. Smith states that the bulk of the Swift Creek pottery in Mound A came from Layer III, which yielded a radiocarbon date of 1860 ± 65 B.P., or A.D. 90. This date may be too early considering the sample source (however, one date from the Halloca Creek site was A.D. 60). I am suspicious that the inland sites of Early (as opposed to Santa Rosa) Swift Creek could predate the Gulf Coastal complex, but a good battery of Early Swift Creek dates will have to be obtained to nail this down.

The Mann Site

For some time it was held that Early Swift Creek Complicated Stamped pottery did not manifest much farther north than the type site near Macon,

Georgia. This idea had to be reconsidered with the discovery of the Mann site in southern Indiana (Kellar 1979). This unusual site has quantities of classic Early Swift Creek pottery present in its collections, with all of the classic design elements represented. These include Swift Creek Complicated Stamped, Crooked River Complicated Stamped, and St. Andrews Complicated Stamped. Kellar notes that tetrapodal supports are present but not common. On the other hand he states that 47 percent of the rims are either notched or scalloped, a positive diagnostic Early Swift Creek trait. Associated projectile points include an expanded stemmed base projectile point, which in the local area is called Lowe Flared Base. In the Alabama-Georgia area, the type is known as Bakers Creek (Cambron and Hulse 1964) and appears commonly to be associated with Early Swift Creek ceramics; the types are also associated with Copena points. It is interesting to note that Hopewell-type artifacts were also recovered from the Mann site. These include zoned as well as unzoned rocker-stamped pottery, mica, copper, and galena, as well as stone platform pipes and figurines. Considering the existence of an Early Swift Creek site close to the Hopewell heartland, and the occurrence of Hopewell artifacts together with Early Swift Creek pottery at Mandeville and Crystal River, one is compelled to speculate as to a most important economic relationship between the two peoples. It is curious to note that classic Hopewell pottery does not seem to occur in the southern sites, although exotic artifacts of stone do. Were the latter religious objects transported by practitioners or traders?

The Miner's Creek Site

The Miner's Creek site (9DA91) is located on the northern bank of the South River in southern DeKalb County and was initially explored by Georgia State University students under the direction of Roy S. Dickens, Jr. Mainly because of time constraints, the project was conducted for a short time in the spring and fall of 1976. The fieldwork was applied to the portion of the site being used as a sand quarry and, at the time, the top portion of the site was being bulldozed. Fieldwork consisted mainly of excavating exposed features. In the process, a good Swift Creek component was identified with a great number of complicated stamped sherds recovered.

Sometime afterwards, the DeKalb County Parks and Recreation Department acquired the site for a public park. During the spring of 1988, the county authorized the Greater Atlanta Archaeological Society to resume work on the site. Work began in the spring of that year (Chase 1991). Interest in quartz crystals, galena, and mica is evident at the Miner's Creek site with the finding of a number of these objects together with at least two figurine fragments. Two early dates were recovered for what appeared to be an Early Swift Creek ceramic complex associated with a notched-rim simple stamped ware. One radiocarbon date processed for the complex, which I have named Panola phase, is 1720 ± 90 B.P., or A.D. 230 (Beta 41699). This was from wood charcoal taken from a pit penetrating the floor of Level 6 and would represent the early occupancy of this site by Panola phase people. A second date of 1620 ± 60 B.P., or A.D. 330 (Beta 41700), was obtained for wood charcoal recovered from a post mold from the floor of Level 7. Of some interest are complicated stamped design elements identical to some recovered in the Coastal Plain by Frankie Snow (Frankie Snow, pers. comm.). Fewer than a dozen classic Early Swift Creek Complicated Stamped sherds were recovered. All of these sherds were from the lowest profile levels; however, the dates obtained should be coeval with the Early Swift Creek time frame. The simple stamped rims at Miner's Creek are notched, which has been described by Wauchope (1966:48) on other sites in northern Georgia. Cartersville Simple Stamped, var. Miner's Creek, has lands and grooves that are well pronounced and separated, whereas Mossy Oak Simple Stamped has lines that are very thin and close together and in some cases appear brushed. Both of these types were found in abundance at Miner's Creek.

At Miner's Creek a very few check-stamped sherds were found, which could be described as Cartersville Check Stamped. Those recovered were all at the very base of the profile (Levels 8 and 9) and are, in most cases, heavily mica tempered. A second type of stamped ware I have named Panola Check Stamped consists of a bold check in a diamond, rather than a square, shape. A number of these feature a raised dot in the center of the square. This type was recovered from the Mann site in Indiana (Kellar 1979:103). Butler (1979:155) also comments on this type, referring to "a check stamp with a raised dot in the center of each grid." On the Yearwood site in southern Tennessee, Butler refers to the sample as "a so-called diamond and dot motif." He views the example as a rare variety of southeastern origin, but it is known in Hopewellian contexts. The exact type was found at Miner's Creek and it is regarded as different from the conventional rectilinear stamped sherds in that the checks are diamond shaped.

The Rocker-Stamping Connection in Alabama

Among the cultural connections that were a departure from the definitive Swift Creek inventory on the Florida Gulf Coast were rocker-stamped embellishments. These include both the zoned variety (Alligator Bayou Stamped) and an unzoned rocker-stamped variety, which Willey (1949:376) calls Santa Rosa Stamped. The latter features stamping with a sharp-edged object rocked back and forth to produce a zigzag effect.

During July and August 1974, during exploration of a site (1DS53) on the Hammermill Paper Company lands on the Alabama River south of Selma, a portion of the area designated as Site C was explored. It was situated on a small knoll overlooking the southern bank of Whiteoak Creek about 300 meters east of its confluence with the river. A number of components were detected in the excavation of a small shell midden, and ceramics recovered include both zoned and unzoned rocker-stamped sherds. One of these features a notched rim. Only one small complicated stamped sherd was found that could not be readily identified. In the spring of 1964, a site located near the mouth of Mulberry Creek in Dallas County, Alabama, produced surface-collected artifacts including a number of unzoned rocker-stamped sherds. No excavation ever took place at the site because the Hammermill Company constructed a processing mill there the following year. At that time, the rocker-stamped sherds could not be identified, but they seem to relate to findings of a type from a site (1LO9) in Lowndes County, Alabama, that was located along the western banks of Tensaw Creek, a tributary of the Alabama River. During the exploration of this site (Chase 1966:96) a number of rocker-stamped sherds were recovered in the very upper levels. Some of these feature notched rims in the manner of Early Swift Creek. Bases feature the very small tetrapods also common in the early variety of Swift Creek. At the time, these were named Tensaw Stamped. In the upper Alabama River drainage Tensaw Stamped became the diagnostic artifact for the early Calloway period. Later Calloway pottery lacks the rocker stamping and notched lip treatment, as well as the small nubbin-like tetrapods. Also, later Calloway ceramics often are tempered with generous amounts of crushed muscovite mica.

Dates for both the early and the later Calloway pottery types were obtained from the Harrington site (1MT231) along the Catoma Creek south of Montgomery, Alabama (Chase 1978). The site's exploration was required as a mitigation because the Montgomery Water and Sewer Board planned to build an outfall line that would bisect the site. Tests during the survey of the pipeline right-of-way uncovered a deep midden and sherds of the Calloway period. A number of features were explored during the excavation, and two of these contained carbonized material suitable for dating purposes. The pits were also selected because one appeared to pertain to the early Calloway or Catoma subphase and the other contained sherds of the late Calloway type or Maxwell subphase. The early Calloway pit dated to 1775 ± 55 B.P., or A.D. 175, and the second or late Calloway pit dated to 1400 ± 60 B.P., or A.D. 550. It seems evident that the Calloway phase might very well have Early Swift Creek connections, probably through the Porter complex of the Mobile Bay region. It also seems probable that Calloway is somehow related to similar complexes farther downriver such as ceramics of the Mulberry Creek site and the Whiteoak Creek site. To date, no Early Swift Creek site has been found in Central Alabama.

Later Swift Creek

Willey (1949) and Sears (1951a, 1956) were among the first to discover the almost inseparable relationship between the ceramics of Weeden Island and those of the later Swift Creek period, which I will henceforth refer to as Swift Creek II. The reason for this consistent association is unclear and is undoubtedly complex. Were they one and the same people with two distinct ceramic traditions? If so, where was the place of origin for the complex? When did it emerge? Smith (1979) indicates that Mandeville, an essentially Santa Rosa–Swift Creek site, was abandoned by A.D. 500. The date might serve as a time marker between Early and Late Swift Creek. One is inclined to suspect connection among Marksville, Crystal River, Santa Rosa–Swift Creek, Green Point, and Yent as resulting in the emergence of Swift Creek II–Weeden Island.

Since Sears's work at Kolomoki there have been a number of additions to the literature relating to this interesting complex. A number of authors have addressed the issue of lifeways of the period with a close look at probable social and religious activities (Kirkland 1979; Steinen 1977). Others like Broyles (1968) and Snow (1977) have focused on the paddle stamping as an art form produced by excellent wood-carvers.

Caldwell comments on the gradual changes in ceramic styles and makes reference to a Middle Swift Creek when he states:

> [T]he stamping tools were more carefully carved and impressions better registered. Rims now show a downward fold. From our point of view, Middle Swift Creek pottery is aesthetically better and designs show a nice balance of freedom and restraint. Throughout this style, motifs are overwhelmingly abstract, although the Kellys are inclined to see some naturalistic forms in the earlier period. In Late Swift Creek stamped designs become larger and dies more carelessly carved and applied. The small folded rim increases in size. Briefly, what we seem to have in Central Georgia is the rise, culmination, and part of the decline of a local pottery style. (Caldwell 1958:37)

It would seem that our Panola phase complicated stamped types would fall partly into a Middle Swift Creek category and partly into a later styling although the globular vessels with the ultrabold stamping elements like those pictured in Sears's (1956) final report on Kolomoki are not present. It may be of interest to mention that fragments of two small complicated stamped flat-bottomed cups occur at Miner's Creek, which are similar in some measure to the Kolomoki vessels.

As has already been mentioned, Early Swift Creek is not represented in Alabama except along the Chattahoochee River and even there sites of the period are not common. In central Alabama, several sites have produced forms of Late Swift Creek Complicated Stamped pottery. On at least two sites, 1MT52 and 1MT173, Swift Creek pottery was found in association with late Calloway (Maxwell subphase). At site 1MT231 along Catoma Creek, as has been noted, late Calloway was dated A.D. 550.

Although this could represent an acceptable date for Swift Creek II contacts in the central Alabama region, it should be noted that no Swift Creek

ceramics were recovered at 1MT231. Other late Swift Creek finds have been
made in the Alabama River valley at site 1MT10 north of Montgomery,
a Late Woodland site with a small exposure of Swift Creek Complicated
Stamped pottery of the late type in an isolated part of the site. Because of
its location and lack of other association, it was not regarded as a component
of significance on this site. Cottier (1968, 1979) has recovered evidence of
Late Swift Creek on at least two sites along the Alabama River.

The Calloway phase underwent changes in the ceramics. Vessel walls became thicker, rim forms changed, and tempering was of sand with none of
the mica additives found in the earlier wares. This period, which clearly
sprang from the Calloway tradition, is called the Dead River phase. Four
important sites of the period are known in the Montgomery area and in
Elmore County to the north of the city. Although no Swift Creek pottery
was ever found in association with Dead River types, a number of late
Weeden Island trade sherds were found in direct association. These included
Weeden Island Plain and red filmed, Keith Incised, and Weeden Island Punctate. One Dead River date might be important here and should represent a
time when the Swift Creek tradition no longer was manifest in Central Alabama. This date was recovered from a site detected and tested during the
Montgomery Levee Survey (Nance 1975) and dated a Dead River hillside
dump at 1175 ± 60 B.P., or A.D. 775 (UGA 962).

In the Gainesville basin, Jenkins (1981:145–46) describes two varieties
of Swift Creek Complicated Stamped: Cunningham and Wilkie's Creek.
These may represent very late manifestations of the tradition for the design
elements in both varieties that "consist of concentric circles and parallel
bars" atypical of later Swift Creek styles known in the Georgia Coastal Plain.
If Jenkins's varieties do indeed represent a western expression of the tradition, then I would suspect that the Tombigbee River may be the limit of the
Swift Creek area. Jenkins suggests that the varieties may have been contemporaneous with Miller II or III periods. Miller II dates to A.D. 490 ± 50,
whereas early Miller III dates from A.D. 700 to 900. According to Wimberly
(1960:121), "the geographical range of Swift Creek involves Georgia, Florida, Tennessee, South Carolina, and Clarke County, Alabama." Although
this was a premature assumption at the time, more recent findings indicate
that Wimberly was correct.

The issue of concentric circles as a terminal design element and a probable final expression of the Swift Creek stamping tradition as seen in Alabama invites a close look at the Walnut Creek site south of Troy, Alabama (Brooms 1977:61), where the predominant complicated stamped type of pottery appears with concentric circles or bull's-eyes, yet some of the rim forms are much like those of Lamar Complicated Stamped. Noting this conjunction Brooms states, "the Complicated Stamped sherds appeared much like Lamar Complicated Stamped ceramics in that the stamping overlapped, was carelessly applied, and poorly executed. However, these sherds displayed only the concentric circle design and the common Lamar traits of various curvilinear and rectilinear designs with filfot crosses were absent."

Late Woodland Connections

As the Swift Creek ceramic tradition expanded there appears to have been some overlapping with the Napier ceramic tradition (Caldwell 1958:44). There are sufficient contrasts between the Napier and Swift Creek stamped wares to suggest that two distinct styles are represented in the surface treatment. I suspect the makers of Napier pottery developed their own stamping style. It would seem that the Napier style evolved ultimately into Woodstock, a terminal Woodland complex in northern Georgia. Good dates for a Woodstock site were obtained by Stanyard and Baker (1992) from the Whitehead Farm in western Georgia. One of these, 1178 ± 100 B.P., or A.D. 772, may be one of the earliest Woodstock dates around. Its importance lies in the fact that it is at a level when the later Swift Creek ceramic traditions were on the wane. Woodstock Complicated Stamped, Woodstock Incised, and line-block stamped sherds were recovered. Other dates were obtained from features: one of 1220 ± 90 B.P., corrected to 1165 B.P., or A.D. 785, and another of 980 ± 90 B.P. These dates should be within an acceptable time frame for Woodstock. A continuation of the complicated stamping tradition from Woodstock to Etowah during the Mississippian period is certain.

In eastern Georgia and along the Atlantic coast, a similar persistence of the old tradition in Savannah Complicated Stamped has to be observed (Caldwell and McCann 1941:45). The type contains concentric circles, concentric diamonds, and barred concentric circles or ovals. All of these elements could have been inspired by the Swift Creek styles. Savannah stamped ware was replaced by the Lamar-like Irene filfot stamped ware.

Tennessee River types include Pickwick Complicated Stamped, which, like much of the prehistoric pottery, is limestone tempered. The type is cited by Lewis and Kneberg (1946), Heimlich (1952), Faulkner (1968), and Griffin (1974) and reveals what appears to be a strong representation of a late stamping style; a persistence, perhaps, of a tradition that extends back to some of the earliest pottery in the Southeast.

Conclusion

As in all archaeological research, more questions tend to arise than answers. This brings to mind the interesting investigations by Snow relating to complicated stamped pottery and the paddles that produced the designs (Frankie Snow, pers. comm.). If paddles were traded and impressed designs were made on different vessels at different locations, this could represent an activity involving wood-carving artisans who may have carved paddles for trading. If this were so, this could account for the diffusion of certain motifs to sites hundreds of kilometers apart. Could the floral patterns or zoomorphic designs have religious significance? If so, then perhaps certain paddle types were distributed in a ceremonial context. One is prone to wonder whether, if this is so, then did the apparently special nature of paddle carving persist into other areas and down through time to be shared by post–Swift Creek peoples?

Swift Creek Design Investigations
The Hartford Case

Frankie Snow

Analysis of Swift Creek Complicated Stamped pottery designs might make it possible to understand better than any other prehistoric culture in Georgia the culture of the Swift Creek people of the first millennium A.D. During the past twenty-five years I have attempted to unveil some of their secrets by reconstructing some of these designs and applying this information to archaeological problems. Hundreds of Swift Creek pottery designs recovered from sites over a broad area of south-central Georgia have been reconstructed and studied. It is now possible to (1) improve the method for reconstructing pottery designs, (2) gain a better understanding of fundamental elements of the Swift Creek world view through this art, and (3) recognize signatures in these designs that permit the reconstruction of contemporaneous settlement patterns and social interaction over a very large area.

Potentially, this prehistoric artwork could tell us much about the people who made Swift Creek pottery; it could yield information about these people's world view, magic, religion, and folktales not accessible by other archaeological analyses. This chapter will examine the data from the Hartford site, 9PU1 (Snow and Stephenson 1990), as a case study in the reconstruction and analysis of Swift Creek art in an attempt to gain insight into what these people were thinking. The use of these designs to reconstruct the social relationships between Hartford and other Swift Creek sites will be explored in Chapter 7 in this volume.

It will be shown that Swift Creek design studies can also provide a database for comparing Swift Creek art with other styles such as the art of the contemporary and closely related Weeden Island people and the art of the spatially distant Hopewell and the temporally distant Southern Cult cultures.

Archaeological excavations were conducted at the Hartford site from the fall of 1988 to the spring of 1989. Investigations focused on a Swift Creek structure uncovered in a submound midden that dates from about A.D. 350 to 400. Adjacent to this submound midden was an arcuate distribution of shell middens that related to a slightly later Middle Swift Creek village dating to about A.D. 400 to 450 (Snow and Stephenson 1990).

Swift Creek Art

In contrast to earlier Woodland cultural groups, who used carved wooden paddle stamps bearing simple straight lines (simple stamped) or crosshatched (check stamped) markings, Swift Creek groups created paddles that often bore very complex motifs. Through a tradition of stamping their unfired pottery with these elaborately carved wooden paddles, people of the Swift Creek culture left us with many clues to the wealth of their complex curvi-linear art (Broyles 1968; Snow 1975). These clues remain preserved today on durable fire-hardened fragments of their paddle-stamped pottery. Because a rich artistic tradition of working in wood is suggested by impressions of wooden stamps on their pottery, even more of their wooden artwork has likely suffered total decay brought about by moisture and the acidic soils that are prevalent in the Southeast. It is unfortunate that the abundant fragmen-tary art that remains on Swift Creek Complicated Stamped pottery, even after considerable effort at reconstruction, results in so few complete images of what these people once carved into the original wooden paddle faces. The Hartford site study adds 103 designs or fragments of designs to the Swift Creek paddle design inventory: sixty-six are from the submound midden and the remainder are from the village.

Carefully piecing together the scraps of design information on Swift Creek potsherds that have been recovered from many sites in the lower Ocmulgee Valley has revealed that these prehistoric people had an inclination toward naturalistic representations. A sample of design variety recovered from these sites is illustrated in Figure 6-1. Some of the most abstract designs seem to be cosmological in nature, but many less abstract depictions are rec-ognized as flowers, serpents, birds, insects, and wolf-like and other animal heads, plus human mask-like designs. These designs seem to record a sha-manistic belief. In contrast to the position offered by Knight (1989:206), at least one design combines traits of animals, such as a coiled serpent with a bird-like crest suggestive of a mythological creature. Figure 6-1, *k*, illustrates a Swift Creek Uktena-like motif that has been recovered in south-central Georgia at 9CF28, 9CF3, and 9CF80; it was also recorded more than 160 kilometers away in southwestern Georgia by Bettye Broyles at the Fairchild's Landing site on the Chattahoochee River (Caldwell 1978:figure 13, mo-tif 42).

Aboriginal symbolism in the southeastern United States during the Woodland period has been addressed only occasionally in the archaeological literature. Phelps's (1970) study of incised motifs that are found on pottery associated with Swift Creek ceramics from Florida was one of the earliest attempts to add meaning to Santa Rosa–Swift Creek symbolism. While he failed to deal with symbolism on the paddle-stamped Swift Creek pottery, he was aware of its potential to yield critical insight into the understanding of southeastern symbolism during the Woodland period (Phelps 1970:93). Knight's treatment (Knight 1989; Milanich et al. 1984) of animals depicted on special ceramics or in effigy-pot representations from the McKeithen Weeden Island site, Kolomoki, and various mounds excavated by Clarence B. Moore is relevant to the current discussion of naturalistic Swift Creek stamped designs. For example, some Swift Creek paddle designs seem to portray the same subjects rendered in Weeden Island Incised or in Weeden Island effigy form.

Some Swift Creek designs portray subjects that have parallels in ethno-historic accounts, suggesting that some southeastern Indian beliefs may have been recorded in these designs almost two millennia before they were re-corded ethnographically. It should be noted that during Swift Creek times these special themes were displayed either on secular pottery as stamped im-pressions or on sacred wares as effigies, whereas during Mississippian times these special symbols seem to have been more restricted to a sacred context.

Artwork similar to that present during Swift Creek times may have sur-vived in a different medium as late as the late eighteenth century as suggested

Figure 6-1. Illustration of a variety of designs recovered from many sites in the Lower Ocmulgee River valley. (Copyright © Frankie Snow.)

Key to figure 6-1

(a) Mask-like design with slanting eyes, forehead symbol, and frowning mouth. A Late Swift Creek design (circa A.D. 580).

(b) Mask-like design with unusual mouth element of intersecting lines. A diamond element is on the forehead.

(c) Mask-like design with a double-bar mouth element, a sun symbol on the forehead, and open loops for eyes with possible triangular eye marking beneath.

(d) Unidentified creature consisting of open loop eyes and a frowning mouth element formed by an arch filled with two barred elements that gives it an Olmec look.

(e) Unidentified creature with design pattern remotely similar to *d*. Mouth element seems to be along the bottom of the design, yielding a smiling expression, and the nose element consists of a bar-filled snowshoe.

(f) Unidentified creature with mushroom-shaped nose element.

(g) Dual bird's heads with one rotated 180 degrees below the other. Bulging eyes, a beak, and a crest are on each bird's head.

(h) Possible buzzard heads arranged as in *g*.

(i) Bird in flight suggested by large tear-shaped wing elements on either side of the body. An apparent crest and a blackened area beneath the eye suggest the cardinal.

(j) Plant with arched triangular leaf-like projections, two four-petaled flowers, concentric-circle fruit-like elements, and the sun shining on the plant in the form of the sun symbol at the center of the design field.

(k) Coiled, crested serpent with rattles placed between crest and bird-like beak. This seems to be a precursor of the serpent seen on the more recent rattlesnake gorgets.

(l) Insect depiction possibly representing the thirteen-year cicada, whose periodic emergence is a striking event. Large forward-positioned eyes and figure-8 wing elements are seen. Note the sun symbol at the center of the depiction.

by descriptions by William Bartram of wall paintings on houses in the Creek
Indian town of Attasse:

> The pillars and walls of the houses of the square were decorated with
> various paintings and sculptures; which I suppose to be hieroglyphic,
> and as an historic legendary of political and sacerdotal affairs: but they
> are extremely picturesque or caricature, as men in a variety of attitudes,
> some ludicrous enough, others having the head of some kind of ani-
> mal as those of a duck, turkey, bear, fox, wolf, buck, &c. and again those
> kind of creatures are represented having the human head. (Van Doren
> 1955:361)

Scholars studying symbolism of the so-called Southeastern Ceremonial
Complex often refer to prior Woodland cultures like Hopewell for possible
connections (Galloway 1989). Yet the rich artwork available from the Swift
Creek tradition has basically remained ignored even though it flourished well
within the area later encompassed by the Southeastern Ceremonial Complex.
In the catalog of Swift Creek designs to follow, designs that seem to parallel
later Mississippian artwork are noted.

Archaeologists have commented on the seemingly endless variety of
Swift Creek designs. Certainly there is great freedom evident in Swift Creek
art. However, the degree of variety appears as an illusion analogous to the
untrained ear listening to the incomprehensible chatter of a foreign lan-
guage. Only the syllables can be detected, but once they are recognized as
components of meaningful words, the sound becomes orderly and recognizable. Likewise, as long as analysis is confined only to elements of designs
(Broyles 1968; Saunders 1986a; Sears 1956) and does not encompass the
entire paddle design, the significance of the design will remain incomprehensible, and the wealth of information available on Swift Creek Complicated
Stamped pottery will be limited. Elements of designs such as the double
spiral may have important expression by themselves. They are not just fill
elements used to provide symmetry but should be analyzed as meaningful
units of the more complex paddle motif.

While the pioneering Swift Creek art studies of Bettye Broyles (1968:50–
51) suggested that designs were occasionally copied, this has never been
clearly demonstrated. Ideas or themes are repeatedly depicted, such as the
figure 8 or human mask, but the instances have their own character and

do not appear to be attempts to precisely copy preexisting designs. Subtle changes of a particular design have been recorded that at first glance may give the illusion of a different design. For example, the wood often cracked as the wooden paddle aged as a result of the regular wetting and drying of the wood when the paddle was applied to the wet clay pot. Sometimes the cracks were minute and sometimes they were pronounced, but always they were oriented parallel to the long axis of the paddle. At 9JD8 the unusually clear impression of a Swift Creek motif, an abstract design thought to represent an insect, shows no evidence of a paddle crack, but on an identical design from 9TF15 a crack pattern has developed that demonstrates the aging of a paddle. In another case a design from a complete paddle was resolved; yet later, at another site, sherds bearing this same design were located that had paddle impressions indicating that approximately a third of the paddle face was missing. Although paddles were sometimes extensively damaged, the potter continued to use them. It is even possible that additional lines could be added by carving them into an existing paddle design. There is also evidence that, by Middle Swift Creek times, potters would, apparently in the absence of a wooden paddle, occasionally use complicated stamped potsherds as convenience paddles, because positive and negative impressions of some designs are known (Snow n.d.). For example, the wolf face design (Figure 6-2, *c*) from the Hartford village midden is also found at the Paul Branch site in Coffee County in both the positive and negative forms. Since depressed areas of a design on a potsherd are actually raised areas on the paddle, some elements of a paddle design are fragile and peg-like and are subject to being snapped off of the wooden paddle. These kinds of changes within an individual design are documented, but they do not reflect the prehistoric artisan's attempt to make two or more copies of a design.

In the summary and conclusions to their report *The Swift Creek Site, 9BI3, Macon, Georgia,* Kelly and Smith (1975) recognized that an important study would be an analysis of Swift Creek Complicated Stamped motifs like that begun by Bettye Broyles (1968). It was envisioned that a detailed record of Swift Creek designs had the potential to provide a unique laboratory for studies of cultural contact and interaction during the Middle Woodland period in the Southeast. The ensuing discussion involves that kind of analysis of minute design data that I have accumulated during the past two decades from Swift Creek sites over a large area of southern Georgia (Snow 1975).

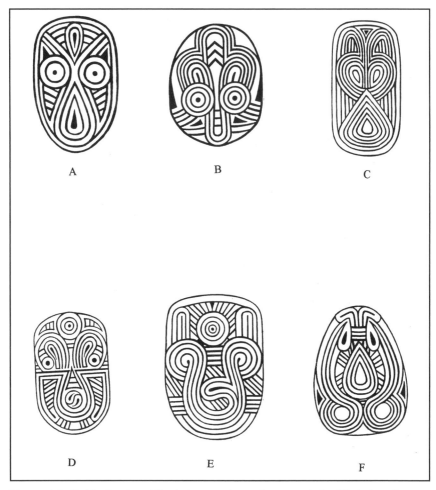

Figure 6-2. Swift Creek paddle designs: *a*, horned-eye mask (owl?) design; *b*, mosquito design; *c*, wolf face design; *d*, spiral-nose mask (bear?) design; *e*, twisted-mouth mask design; *f*, rabbit design. (Copyright © Frankie Snow.)

Design Reconstruction Methods

The following discussion gives a general overview of one method that has been used to recover paddle designs from Swift Creek potsherds. Because overstamping, obliteration, and poorly registered impressions occurred during the pottery-making process, reconstruction of portions of the design occasionally reflects a subjective interpretation of missing or vague data on

Figure 6-3. Earspool mask examples of reconstruction of missing paddle data. (Copyright © Frankie Snow.)

the sherds (see Figure 6-3). No doubt there are errors in reconstruction, especially along the periphery of designs where the paddle impressions are less clearly registered. In a few instances recovery of paddle design data is complete and no reconstruction is necessary and only the interpretation of the design's meaning is subjective. There are instances in which additional sherds have been found to add new information to a reconstructed design previously believed to be complete. In these cases, areas that were guessed at sometimes proved to be correct while others were not. In those latter cases the reconstructions were usually too simplistic. This is because of my tendency to underestimate the artistic complexity of these prehistoric artisans. For example, compare the Swift Creek design on the frontispiece to *An Archaeological Survey of the Ocmulgee Big Bend Region* (Snow 1977) with the same mask-like design located in Figure 6-1, *a*, which has subsequently been updated by additional design data in the forehead area of the mask.

Some researchers have attempted to remove subjectivity in design reconstruction by making images of what is present on the sherds by laying paper over the area of the sherd to be recorded and then pressing an inked roller across that area. This method has resulted in only limited success in design resolution since it also records extraneous marks caused by overstamping, obliteration, tool marks, and paddle slippage. Also, this method fails to bring together design elements from one sherd with additional design elements present on another sherd that was stamped with the same paddle (Shannon 1979; Saunders 1986b). However, the method is useful in that the recovered design fragments can serve as guides to possible design contacts with other geographic areas; for example, similar designs were noted between Swift Creek sites at Kings Bay, where that method was applied, and sites along the lower Ocmulgee River valley. Once these design contacts are suspected, they can be confirmed or rejected only by subsequent sherd-to-sherd comparisons in which it is possible to observe subtle design flaws and paddle crack patterns that serve as signatures for the design being studied.

The method described below, I think, probably achieves high reliability for central portions of a stamp and reasonable accuracy around the periphery and maintains the theme of designs in the reconstructions. For example, if a mask was depicted by the prehistoric artisan, then the reconstructed design will reflect that mask with the possibility of occasional errors near its periphery. For this reason, design contact between sites should not be determined by comparing illustrations. These illustrations should be used only as guides that suggest a possible contact. As stated above, only sherd-to-sherd comparisons should be used to confirm or reject contacts between Swift Creek sites unless the paddle crack pattern or similar detail is also illustrated with the design.

The equipment needed for design reconstruction is simple and readily available. Directional lighting enhances design resolution; therefore, a darkened room with a single light source is a basic requirement. Overhead lighting, particularly a fluorescent source, is least effective. Light from a desktop lamp or light entering the darkened workroom from an adjacent illuminated room maximizes resolution of subtle design information.

Mechanical dividers are needed to transfer design information from the sherds to paper. A pencil, paper, and several erasers, along with lots of time, are also necessary. An innate inclination toward spatial perception is very helpful, though not necessary, and apparently it is not available to everyone.

There are several things one should be aware of that will facilitate design reconstruction. First, understand that all design elements are confined to a design field dictated by the presumed rectangular shape of the paddle head. Closely observe between the raised lines of a design to detect the minute striae that indicate the direction of the wood grain and wood crack pattern.

These are helpful in determining the orientation of the individual design elements in the design field (rectangular paddle head). The wooden paddle crack pattern is oriented parallel to the long axis of the paddle, apparently because that orientation provides maximum strength, though it also may have been easier to carve the wood in that alignment; therefore, any scrap of design data bearing crack marks reveals the orientation of the wood in the design field.

Suspect that the design element that is most frequently registered on the study sherds is centrally located in the design field. This is because of the motor action of the potter attempting to contact the pot with the central portion of the paddle, an area known to sports enthusiasts as the sweet spot. Also, the central area of the design will usually be the most clearly registered area of the paddle design. This is the result of a couple of factors. First, the flat face of the paddle is striking a curved surface of the unfired pot, so unless the potter rocks the stamp on impact with the pot surface such that the paddle face contacts the pot from paddle edge to paddle edge, or unless the vessel surface is not curved but irregular in shape such as in the neck region, geometry dictates that the relief of each line in the design becomes reduced toward the periphery of the impression. Logically, because of the more gradual curvature of large vessel walls, they receive a greater portion of the paddle stamp than do smaller vessels. Second, since the potter shifts position only slightly from one paddle strike to the next, it is usually the peripheral areas of each impression that most frequently become overstamped. While slightly shifting each paddle strike results in thoroughly malleated clay coils across the entire exterior surface of the vessel and coil bonding is maximized, this unfortunately also has a negative impact on the clarity of design impressions. The area of the paddle design least often registered on the pot is the area of the paddle head located nearest the handle. Apparently this derives from constraints related to the potter's motor action.

Since each paddle head has two flat surfaces, it would seem likely that both faces should have been carved. Blank spaces within designs were avoided and it would also seem likely that blank areas of wooden items would have been filled with artwork. Interestingly, even with the possibility of designs being present on both faces of a single paddle, only one example of a Swift Creek vessel bearing two Swift Creek designs is known from thousands of potsherds examined from the Ocmulgee River valley. If the images carved on these paddles represent various aspects of the belief system within the culture, then it may be that strict separation was required to prevent pollution or mixing of opposing ideas. Data suggest that these designs were not only separated at the vessel level but also restricted to separate paddles as well.

Coil bonding was likely the primary purpose of stamping. Pottery decoration was a secondary consideration. If so, this brings up the question of why Swift Creek people bothered to elaborately carve a potter's paddle when coil bonding could be accomplished in other ways. Furthermore, because the laboriously carved design is never entirely registered in any one impression on the vessel, it seems that the complete image of the paddle face on the pottery is not important. Most likely it is the effect produced by overstamping that is recognized as distinctively Swift Creek that was important. It may be that these carved paddles along with other ornate objects with which the Swift Creek people must have surrounded themselves served as visual symbols and reminders when they spoke of their heritage and their intricate belief system.

Naturalistic designs are usually oriented so that the top of the head, in mask-like designs, or the upper parts in plants are toward the distal end of the paddle head. Likewise, lower anatomical parts are placed near the proximal end of the paddle head. A few designs, such as the eye theme illustrated in Figure 6-4, *c,* are rotated ninety degrees from the above examples and may have been properly viewed when the paddle's handle was directed horizontally. Interestingly, orientation of the design on the pottery does not seem to have been important to the potter since figures such as masks are turned a number of directions on a single vessel as the pot is shifted during the stamping process. This, along with obliteration and overstamping, further indicates that the primary reason, but not the only reason, for stamping a vessel was to bond the clay coils.

Since many Swift Creek designs exhibit bilateral symmetry and in some cases quadrilateral symmetry, it is helpful to draw intersecting horizontal and vertical axes on a piece of paper and transfer design data from the pottery to the paper with dividers and use the axes to aid in plotting distances between design elements. As will be seen in the ensuing pages, through this process it is possible to reconstruct partial, and in some cases entire, Swift Creek paddle designs.

With an understanding of helpful clues on design orientation, sorting

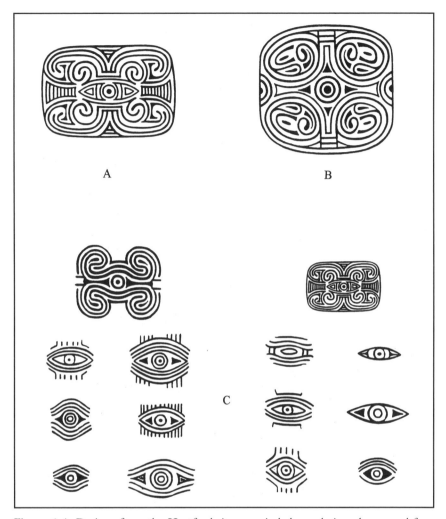

Figure 6-4. Designs from the Hartford site: *a*, spiraled eye design; *b*, sun and four wind birds design; *c*, eye designs and motifs. (Copyright © Frankie Snow.)

through sherds begins in a search for those that appear to derive from one paddle. Locate each sherd that has at least some design information common to other sherds and with luck additional design information will occur on each matching sherd. This serves to link together additional bits of design data that eventually might allow the reconstruction of the entire paddle design.

Subtle design information is enhanced by rotating the study sherd in directional lighting. A darkened room with a single light source provides suitable conditions. Interestingly, optimum design enhancement conditions are likely comparable to those within the darkened aboriginal structure whose remains were excavated at Hartford. Here, the central hearth fire would flicker light across the stamped walls of Swift Creek pottery casting wavering shadows of the seemingly animated stamped designs.

Swift Creek Design: Speculation and Analysis

One hundred three different paddle designs, most of which are fragmentary, are recognized at Hartford. Sixty-six of these designs were found in the submound midden. Many more designs remain unidentified because they are either too fragmentary or too obliterated. Some motifs lack clear impressions, a quality common on Early Swift Creek pottery, and for that reason a large percentage of Early Swift Creek designs remain unresolved.

Interpretations of what the aboriginal artisan intended these paddle designs to represent are highly conjectural. While adventures into this realm may potentially yield much information about these people, faulty interpretations also have great potential to create misinformation about them. Caution is directed to those citing design interpretations since in the past suggested meanings have tended to become accepted fact after being cited a couple of times. It is with some reluctance that these interpretive adventures are undertaken since it is realized that they may be tantamount to wandering through a mine field with considerable potential for one to become anathematized and labeled among those in the crackpot fringe (Thomas 1979:365). Suggested interpretations offered in this chapter are not convictions set in concrete and well-reasoned alternative explanations are solicited. Though it may seem to the contrary, clairvoyance was not part of the interpretive process. Although these interpretations are conjectural, by referring to historical records of aboriginal beliefs, clues are provided as to what may have been intended in times preceding the historical record.

Swift Creek Design Elements

Certain design elements like concentric circles, the eye motif, and the spiral appear to be somewhat formalized symbols of expression that go beyond mere fill elements in a paddle design. It is also these elements that are primary contributors to the curvilinear quality of Swift Creek pottery design, a quality that practically defines the ware. These design elements and their role in the entire paddle design are discussed below.

Ethnographic accounts reveal the way some historic Indians understood their world to have been arranged. For example, the earth was thought to be " . . . a great flat island resting rather precariously on the surface of the waters, suspended from the vault of the sky by four cords attached at each of the cardinal directions . . . it was crosscut by the four cardinal directions . . . " (Hudson 1976:122). Also, it seems that this sky vault may have consisted of a series of concentric stepped levels with the lower levels nearer the Under World and the highest levels nearer the Upper World (Hudson 1976:123). Swift Creek designs illustrated in Figure 6-5 can be examined to see if there are possible fits with this spatial arrangement.

The important concept of how their cosmos was arranged would seem to be a prime subject to be depicted on Swift Creek wooden paddles. On the basis of historic references about the spatial arrangement of the cosmos, several reconstructed Swift Creek designs do seem to be analogous. A basic theme in the cosmology of the historic southeastern Indians is that the earth is divided into quadrants. This concept is represented more than a millennium earlier in the Swift Creek art shown in Figure 6-5 (first two designs on the *left*). Also, it can be seen in Figure 6-5 that this arrangement of circles or squares surrounded by filled quadrants is common in Swift Creek art. Quadrants, which presumably are analogous to the four divisions of the earth, may be depicted as either spirals, loops, squares, or hachured areas in Swift Creek designs.

The sun's daily pass across the sky is another important event described by historic Indians. The concentric circle element, which historically is analogous to either the sun of the Upper World or its earthly representative, fire, is probably the most common design element in Swift Creek art. Its frequent central location in the design field is likely a reflection of its paramount importance. In Figure 6-5, *upper left,* the sun seems to be in the center of the design, represented by a solid dot surrounded by two circles. Lines radiating from the sun symbol divide the entire design into four sections and the long axis formed by two of these lines may also symbolize the daily path of the sun. If this is true, then the lines that form the short axis across the design may signify the sun's seasonal north-south swing across the sky. That these

Figure 6-5. Cosmological designs. (Copyright © Frankie Snow.)

people may have monitored the sun's seasonal position, aided by the spatial arrangement of mounds, has been suggested for the McKeithen and Kolomoki sites (Milanich et al. 1984:91–92, 189–91). A more bold attempt at demonstrating that the spatial arrangement of mounds at the Kolomoki site involved their use in sighting the movement of the sun has also been offered (Hardman and Hardman 1991). In Figure 6-5, *lower left,* the sun symbol is replaced by an eye motif and the quadrants are filled with spirals.

The sun symbol and the eye symbol occur with equal frequency in the submound midden. That the sun and eye symbols are interchangeable design elements may be related to the Choctaw belief that the sun watched down on them with its blazing eye (Hudson 1976:126). Subsequently, a change in the emphasis of these two motifs took place during occupancy of the Hartford village. No eye motifs were recovered from the village, but the concentric circle, the sun motif, persists there.

Historically, southeastern Indians believed the sky vault consisted of a series of steps that were ascended and descended by the sun during its daily pass. Four of the designs illustrated in Figure 6-5 have step-like elements at either end of the design element. They may represent the sun's daily sky track. If the foregoing speculation has any validity then additional parallels might be expected between historic beliefs and Swift Creek symbolism.

Spiraled elements of designs that are components of the larger composite paddle motif may reveal additional information about the message intended on a paddle design. For example, two lines spiraling about each other is a design element that has been observed frequently on designs representing birds in Swift Creek art (Figure 6-1, *third row*) and also on bird effigy ceramics in Weeden Island. On the design in Figure 6-1, *I,* the artisan placed the spiraled motif on the breast of a bird in flight. However, in case one missed the symbolism there, it was repeated in a more bold display as spirally arranged wings in flight. Additionally, the stout beak and the pointed crest of this bird suggest a representation of the cardinal, a bird important in some historic Indian mythologies because of its red color (Mooney 1900:252–54). Possibly even more critical to this bird's identification is the thickened portion under its eye that trails from the beak. It is this throat area of the male cardinal that is black on an otherwise red bird. Historically red and black were significant in that they usually represented opposite ideas: the eastern or rising sun (birth?) and the western or setting sun (death?), respectively. A bear-like creature, and the nose area of one mask-like design (Figure 6-2, *d*), utilized the double-spiral design element. Other designs, mentioned in the preceding paragraph, seem to show the four cardinal directions separating quadrants filled with spirals (the four winds?) and may depict the aboriginal people's mental image of how their world was arranged (see Figure 6-5). Most bird designs have spirals. The elaborate design in Figure 6-4, *b,* seems to show the centrally located sun and in each quadrant a stylized bird bearing a spiral beneath its beak.

In each instance the spiral design element appears to indicate the move-

ment of air or motion and is located at a point where locomotion occurs; for
example, the wings of a bird and legs of a bear. In one case, the spatulate-
shaped nose area of a mask-like design displays the spiral element. In the case
mentioned in the previous paragraph, each quadrant of the cardinal direction design is filled with a spiral whose direction opposes that in the adjacent
quadrant and the spirals seem to portray the wind or a whirlwind. In Mexico
the Zapotec's concept of the pèe (Marcus and Flannery 1978:57–59) may
reflect a similar belief.

In southeastern Indian mythology the wind played an important role in
the creation story in which it was responsible for having blown away the fog
and darkness that enveloped the primordial earth to reveal the land along
with the plants and animals familiar to them (Swanton 1928:110–13). The
twisting or spiraling motion of dust devils may have provided a visible image
of the wind that the aboriginal could easily express with the double-spiral
design element. An Oklahoma Creek named John McGilvry, *Ho-tul-ko-mi-ko,*
was known as Chief of the Whirlwind (Hudson 1976:figure 110).

Other examples of spirals are seen surrounding the important eye motif
in Figure 6-4, *c.* Because of its redundancy the eye motif must have been an
important symbol that could be interpreted as the watchful eye of their God
superimposed above their world. It should be noted that the bear, bird
names, and the wind were important and closely associated titles of clans
that were grouped under the White Clan in some historic tribes of southeastern Indians (Swanton 1928:110–13).

Emerson (1989:67–78) presents an extended discussion of spiral symbolism and offers an alternative to the wind explanation that includes how
birds, serpents, and fertility are represented by rain or water. He borrows
from Phelps's (1970:92–94) interpretations of the spiral in view of its
known meaning in the Mayan glyph system.

Furthermore, Emerson notes how counterclockwise spirals equate with
coiled serpents and the Under World and how clockwise spirals, being in
opposition, indicate things of the Upper World. Although directed at Mississippian symbolism, his ideas may have relevance in Swift Creek iconography. Two examples of crested serpents coiled in a counterclockwise direction
(Figure 6-1, *k*) have been recovered from Swift Creek Complicated Stamped
pottery at other Swift Creek sites in the Ocmulgee Valley (Snow 1975).
While the double spiral occurs as an element in many composite designs, its

importance was further suggested when it was found standing alone as a complete paddle design at the Lind Landing site (9WL7).

Initially it was difficult to understand how one could reconcile the spiral's suggested wind meaning, being proposed here, with its previously acknowledged rain or water symbolism. The wind interpretation is complicated by the natural phenomenon of spiraling water eddy currents. The logical transition from wind to water is suggested as follows: whether it is a weather front passing through, a collapsing thunderhead, a spiraling tornado, or a hurricane, the wind appears to bring the rain. Wind and rain are closely associated meteorological phenomena in the southeastern United States and in the absence of rainfall natural production (fertility) is greatly reduced. The wind's association with fertility or production of food seems to be demonstrated in an Iroquois story about a supernatural being called a Bushy-head (the wind's tendency to dishevel hair may have been the origin of this supernatural's name) that delivers the people vegetables (Fenton 1940:417).

Like the concentric circle element's dual sun/fire meaning, the spiral element obviously also denotes multiple ideas. That the spiral element usually does not occupy the central place in a paddle design may be interpreted as suggesting that its meaning is secondary to that of the often centrally located concentric circle element.

If the spiral does symbolize the rain-bearing wind, then an anomaly or a diametrically opposed idea exists for the wind. An important part of the fire-making process involved blowing the smoldering punk, which resulted in the appearance of a flame. Waring's (1968:50) discussion of the cult-bringers showed that some historic aboriginals regarded the *Hayuyalgi* as winds that fanned the Busk fire. Swanton (1946:423–24) quoted James Adair on the process of fire making in which kindling of the fire involved the use of an unspoiled swan's wing to fan the fire. So, here it can be seen that the wind appears to deliver both fire and water, two antithetical elements of nature and two elements that the people diligently attempted to prevent being polluted by the other.

With the presumed knowledge of the meaning of a few basic design elements it becomes possible to speculate or make observations beyond a simple statement. For example, when a mask-like design with a spiral element on its nose is seen (Figure 6-2, *d*), it indicates that more than another face is depicted. It is possible to speculate that the face includes a movement-of-air symbol or more properly a breath symbol, indicating that the face represents a being, possibly a shaman, who blows on patients as part of the curative process; on a grander scale, the Master of Breath may be indicated.

These interpretations may seem to us strange and sometimes ridiculous, but as Hudson (1976) has pointed out, Indian mythology, at least during historic times, has a subtle orderliness to it that attempts to explain their world. Even with the suggested meaning of the three design elements discussed above an understanding of their intricate symbolism is far from being understood.

Many Swift Creek motifs were recovered from the floor of a Swift Creek submound structure at Hartford. These will be discussed below followed by an examination of Swift Creek art from an adjacent, but slightly later, Swift Creek village.

Hartford Submound Midden Designs

The Swift Creek Complicated Stamped ceramics excavated from the submound midden at Hartford can be used as a case study in design analysis. In the following paragraphs, Swift Creek art and how these designs may reflect Swift Creek beliefs are explored.

The long-nose mask (Figure 6-6, *a*) presents a theme that persisted for several hundred years. Masks with elongated noses have been recorded several times in Swift Creek iconography. The redundant nature of this design suggests that an important theme was depicted. What relationship, if any, it has to the Hopewellian and Mississippian Long-Nose Gods is not known (Hall 1989). Knight reports that one of the most frequently occurring bird species in Weeden Island iconography is the roseate spoonbill (Milanich et al. 1984). One element of Figure 6-6, *a,* does show a long spoon-shaped design suggestive of this bird's bill. The roseate spoonbill may be seen in its simplest and most abstract form in Middle Swift Creek art where three lobes, with the centrally placed invaginated lobe being the nose, suggest this depiction (see Broyles 1968:plate 17, *bottom row*). This design also occurs at the Solomon site in Twiggs County, Georgia.

The horned owl design (Figure 6-6, *b*) is one of several owl-like designs reconstructed from Swift Creek pottery. Provided that this design depicts an owl as suggested, it is another example (see Figure 6-2, *a*) of an animal from

Figure 6-6. Swift Creek paddle designs: *a*, long-nose mask design; *b*, horned owl design; *c*, sun and wind design; *d*, thickened-circle bull's-eye design; *e*, slit-eyed snarling cat design. (Copyright © Frankie Snow.)

the Swift Creek people's world that was recorded during historic times as being indicative of ominous events (Hudson 1976). The occurrence of animal-like designs with sacred implications on complicated stamped pottery in the context of common village midden debris contrasts with their sacred occurrence in mounds, like those at Kolomoki, where these representations appear as ceramic effigies. Sherds bearing this design have a diagonally notched rim typical of Early Swift Creek. However, a faulty radiocarbon date of A.D. 606 ± 74 was obtained from charcoal thought to be associated with sherds of this design. This determination seems to be about 200 years too recent.

The design in Figure 6-6, *c*, is characterized by the use of thickened or solid elements such as the centrally located solid football-shaped element that is a motif often seen on Early Swift Creek pottery (Kelly and Smith 1975). The design also employs other solid elements to form the entire depiction rather than the usual hachured elements. The two triangles and two lobe elements mark the four directions with the triangles likely forming the east-to-west orientation and the two solid lobe elements marking north and south. Two large concentric circle motifs are on the left and right portions of the design and a central area composed of four spiraled elements surrounds the direction markers. If concentric circles are a sun symbol and spirals represent a wind symbol, then an important symbolism can be suggested for this paddle design. Concentric circles (the sun symbol) are placed near the left and right sides of the stamp and the outer rings of the sun symbols are unusual; they are incomplete with solid triangular elements issuing outward from them in the direction of the centrally located solid football-shaped element. Spiraled wind symbols are seen on each side of both solid triangular elements. These design elements can be interpreted to show the sun sending down the wind (somewhat analogous to wind faces on old map cartouches) to clear the fog from the primeval earth. So, it is possible that what is depicted here is, in part, analogous to the genesis or creation scene described in historic southeastern Indian mythology.

The thickened circle bull's-eye design (Figure 6-6, *d*) occurred in the submound midden. This design has also been found at the Swift Creek site (9BI3) in Bibb County and nearby at one of its satellite sites, the Solomon site in Twiggs County. Variability of line thickness is demonstrated.

The slit-eyed snarling cat illustration (Figure 6-6, *e*) is an example of a design having line widths that appear larger than usual for Early Swift Creek. No notched or scalloped rims were found on sherds bearing this design, which further suggests a divergence from Early Swift Creek traits. This is one of several designs from the submound midden whose line widths suggest a trend toward Middle Swift Creek designs. The symbolism of this feline-like design, a symbol of power in Mesoamerica (Webb 1989), is unknown in the Swift Creek context.

The vertical position of sherds that showed the spiraled eye design (Figure 6-4, *a*) in the submound midden was recorded, as were the depths of several other designs. It was thought that if considerable time had elapsed from the point of initial use of the structure until it was no longer used that differences in the superposition of certain designs might be detected. The vertical distribution of this eye design was in the 0- to 10-centimeter level and continued down through the midden to the 50- to 60-centimeter level, which is at the base of the midden. Contrary to the 600-year range variation obtained from three radiocarbon dates, this suggests that the interval of time involved in the deposition of the submound midden is not to be measured in centuries but in decades. Other designs were monitored for possible indications that they might be restricted to a particular level in the midden. The so-called figure 8 has lines bold enough to suggest Middle Swift Creek quality pottery, yet its distribution ranged from the 30- to 40-centimeter level to the bottom of the midden. This suggests either that the initial use of broader design lands began while the typically weaker lands of Early Swift Creek designs were still in use or that considerable mixing took place in the midden.

The sun and four wind birds paddle design (Figure 6-4, *b*) is from the submound midden. It is unusual in that a set of elements resembling a stylized bird's head is couched in an egg-shaped spiral configuration in each quadrant of the depiction. A teardrop-shaped eye is discernible with an arched triangle subtly suggesting the bird's curved beak. The use of a spiral, the wind symbol, beneath the bird's beak is seen on most Swift Creek bird representations, though it may be placed on other parts of the bird. Spirals located beneath the bird's beak may be analogous to extended tongues frequently displayed on various animal and/or human subjects during the Mississippian period. The horseshoe-shaped element beneath the eye may represent a highly stylized bird's claw bared as if in combat (see Hudson 1976:figure 39). This combative attitude may indicate that the falcon is being symbolized. A sun symbol is centrally located on the paddle. If, as suggested, the sun and birds are displayed on this design, two important Upper World representations are combined in the depiction. A faulty reconstruction of this design is partially represented on a potsherd illustrated in the original type description for Swift Creek pottery (Jennings and Fairbanks 1939b:2).

The layout of the sun and four wind birds design is similar to those of eye element designs (Figure 6-4, *c*) and cosmological designs (Figure 6-5). This demonstrates how the eye element and the sun symbol are interchangeable. The spiral or whirl-like elements themselves are arranged so as to vaguely suggest birds' heads and seem to represent the four winds from their respective corners of the earth. Similar spirals have been recorded on the breast of a bird design (Figure 6-1, *I*) recovered from Swift Creek potsherds at Milamo (9WL1) (Kelly 1956).

The eye motif as a component element of the design is a popular theme; it occurs as the main central element on sixteen different Swift Creek designs from the submound midden (Figure 6-4, *c*). The eye occupies a central location in the design field, with one known exception, and is surrounded by spiraled or convoluted fill elements that complete the depiction. Its central position in the design field and its repeated occurrence point to an important symbolism for the eye motif. One unusual eye configuration involves a series of parallel lines with the eye element placed at their center (Figure 6-4, *c*). A conscious effort seems to have been made by the paddle carvers to avoid duplicating existing eye motifs. It is as though their unique eye design was their personal expression of reverence to an important deity. Each artisan may have known all of the other eye variations that existed in a community and was thus able to avoid duplication or else there was an almost endless number of combinations of elements that could produce unique eye motifs.

While several Swift Creek paddle designs have been reconstructed that are human mask or animal face representations, none uses the above eye motif style for that facial feature, though the concentric circle, which sometimes appears to be interchangeable with the eye motif, is used. This would indicate a special meaning for the eye motif reserved, perhaps, for representing an all-seeing, all-knowing deity.

Further, the illustrations in Figure 6-4, *b* and *c*, show that the eye motif is interchangeable with a motif consisting of concentric circles, a motif thought to symbolize the sun. According to Hudson (1976:126), "the Choctaws believed that the Sun watched them with its great blazing Eye, and so long as the Eye was on them they were all right, but if the Eye was not on them they were doomed." Hall (1979:262) comments on how the eye symbol, the sun, and crystals may have been interrelated. In contrast, as mentioned above, the eye element has never been observed as eye depictions on animal or human mask-like designs, but the concentric circle element does frequently appear as an anatomical eye. This may allude to a subtle difference in meaning between these two elements. Additional evidence for a broader symbolism for the concentric circle element is revealed by its use as a forehead symbol on some mask-like designs (Figure 6-1, *c,* and Figure 6-2, *d* and *e*) and its central placement on plants (Figure 6-1, *j*) and insects (Figure 6-1, *l*), where it seems to be more of a badge than an anatomical part of the naturalistic design.

The eye motif is recorded in an Adena mound (Gaitskill) on an engraved clay tablet depicting the hand-eye design (Webb and Snow 1945:95). In later Swift Creek subphases the figure 8 replaces the eye motif as the most common design.

The eye motif maintains a prominent place much later in time when it is portrayed among Southern Cult symbolism. In contrast to the Swift Creek depictions, these later examples of the eye motif are often found on human masks and on animal representations. It seems that worldly creatures are representatives of some deity during the Mississippian period in contrast to a more abstract deity during Swift Creek times. It has been observed that Swift Creek art harbors several design elements that later appear in Southern Cult symbolism (Kelly and Smith 1975).

Were it possible to discover, it would not be too surprising to learn that some Swift Creek dances that took place around the village fire (earthly manifestation of the sun) had choreographed patterns like the spiraled arrangements seen on several sun designs illustrated in this report.

The design illustrated in Figure 6-7, *a,* was recovered from a radiocarbon-dated restorable vessel that was in Test Unit 3 at the 20- to 30-centimeter level in the Hartford submound midden. The design is also known to occur 80 kilometers to the southeast at the Mill Creek site (9CF154) in Cof-

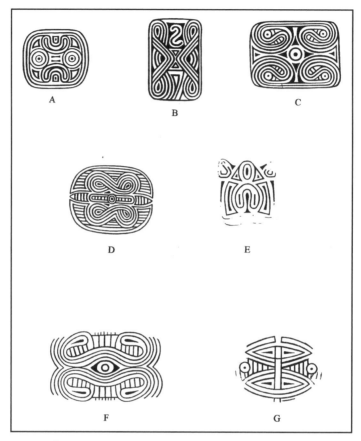

Figure 6-7. Swift Creek paddle designs: *a*, Mill Creek sun design; *b*, cross-eyed S design; *c*, Billy Phillips sun design; *d*, ladder/bull's-eye design; *e*, fertility symbol design; *f*, Little River design; *g*, rectilinear design. (Copyright © Frankie Snow.)

fee County. Large concentric circle elements are visible on either side of a centrally located box that contains two bar elements. Semicircular lobes are seen above and below this box.

The cross-eyed S design (Figure 6-7, *b*) is composed of three intertwining loops on either side of an hourglass-shaped central element. A reversed S is located at one end of the design. Whether the significance of this S is relevant to Hall's (1989:264–66) comments on the S's symbolic representation of the northern-pointing star is not known. Interestingly, the S is located at one end of the design just as the northern-pointing star would appear in the night sky. Further, midway between the intertwining loops on the left and right edges of the design are the elements that give this design the "cross-eyed" part of its name. These crossed eyes may denote the rising and setting sun. A similar arrangement is seen in the design in the upper right corner of Figure 6-5.

The sun symbol is centrally located with four boldly carved triangle direction markers in the design shown in Figure 6-7, *c*. The four quadrants are filled with double spirals that have their opposed lobes differentiated with one lobe being barred and the other having a circled dot element. Several years before the Hartford excavation, Billy Phillips recovered a potsherd bearing this design from another site in Pulaski County.

The ladder/bull's-eye design shown in Figure 6-7, *d*, was recovered from the surface of the submound midden during our first visit to the Hartford site. Subsequently, it was found in five proveniences during the excavations. It was also found at six other sites along a broad stretch of the Ocmulgee Valley. This particular design is illustrated in several reports including *The Swift Creek Site, 9BI3, Macon, Georgia* (Kelly and Smith 1975), *Archaeology of the Florida Gulf Coast* (Willey 1949), *Trend and Tradition in the Prehistory of the Eastern United States* (Caldwell 1958), and *Ocmulgee National Monument, Georgia* (Pope 1956), a booklet published by the National Park Service.

Figure 6-7, *e*, is one of the designs that was most frequently recovered in the submound midden, which suggests that Hartford was the home place for the paddle bearing it. The design is important in its depiction of possible fertility symbols. The horseshoe element (female?) in the lower half of the design is seen with a possible phallic symbol (male?) filling the invagination. Another fragmentary Swift Creek design from 9BH8 also shows the horseshoe element, but in this case it encloses a vulva-like element (Snow 1975:46).

One design fragment (Figure 6-7, *f*) was recovered from several sherds in the submound midden that matches a design in the University of Georgia collection from the Little River site (9MG46) in Morgan County (Williams and Shapiro 1990). This identical design also occurs in Twiggs County at the Solomon site, located southeast of the Swift Creek type site.

The design in Figure 6-7, *g*, demonstrates that, despite most researchers' impressions, considerable rectilinear elements are present in the Swift Creek stamping tradition. No interpretation as to what was intended to be represented on this fragment of a design is offered. However, the double-barred

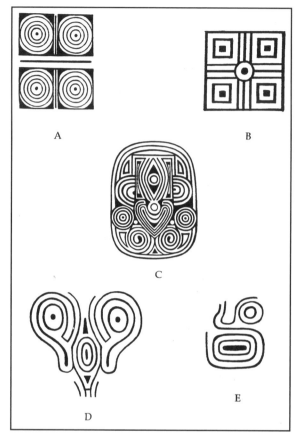

Figure 6-8. Swift Creek paddle designs: *a* and *b*, four-ness designs; *c*, mask with cyclops design; *d* and *e*, barred oval designs. (Copyright © Frankie Snow.)

line passing through the center of diamond-like elements suggests the modified layout of an Etowah motif that dates several centuries later.

Two paddle designs shown in Figure 6-8, *a* and *b*, illustrate the concept of four-ness that is prevalent throughout southeastern Indian ceramic art. Figure 6-8, *b*, is also in the Whatley collection from the Solomon site in Twiggs County. This design appears very similar to a motif commonly found on a much later stamped pottery type called Lamar Square Ground, which is common to the lower section of the Ocmulgee Big Bend region (Snow 1990). Both designs are also illustrated in the find books of Swift Creek motifs recovered from the Swift Creek type site (9BI3) on file at the University of Georgia.

Figure 6-8, *c*, is an example of the excellent caricature that was present in Swift Creek art. This face-like design is reminiscent of some of the art seen on Hopewell bone carvings (Willoughby 1916:plate 6). The design was initially labeled the stacked Vs design because of the pattern that is so pronounced in the central portion of the design field. However, with additional study of the sherds bearing this design something more than Vs was recognized. This design seems to depict a mask with what at first glance appears to be triangular eyes that give it a demonic quality, but these triangular eye-like elements are actually a component of an unusual cyclopean forehead symbol. Anatomical eyes are apparently absent, but placed on the forehead is a vertically oriented symbolic eye, the only known occurrence of this symbol in which it does not occupy the central position in the design field. Though many hours were consumed in the attempted resolution of this design and it is recorded as perceived, the unusual treatment of the eye motif on the forehead evokes the question of error in reconstruction since it does not follow the established formal manner of presenting the eye motif. The usual pattern for presenting the eye is illustrated in Figure 6-4, *c, top*. The mouth is rendered in a clownish manner. While several mask designs have been recorded from Swift Creek pottery, this example is unusual in its detail with ears depicted having large earspools. Masks without eyes are known in historic times. Fenton's study of Iroquois medicine masks recorded twelve mask styles among which is an eyeless mask category (Fenton 1940:411, plate 12).

Design data did not allow for a complete reconstruction of the peripheral areas of this anthropomorphic design. The arch above the forehead and the area beneath the earspools and the mouth are conjectural. However, this conjecture is not made without some basis. For example, because of constraints produced by the corners of the paddle head, the beak-like pendant element below each earspool fits the allotted space. Further, since the beak-like element combines with the earspool to appear as a bird's head and since experience has shown that the spiral often accompanies bird depictions, it is a logical guess that the aboriginal artisan would have chosen spirals to fill the area beneath each beak-like element. By this line of thought the handle portion or proximal area of the paddle design, which is rarely recovered for any design, is reconstructed. If this guess is correct then this mask-like design may be said to represent a shaman since the two bird-like ear ornaments may be buzzards, which, at least historically, represented that occupation. At Kolomoki a human effigy vessel was recovered from Mound D that may represent a similar individual since it bore birds (buzzards?) on each shoulder (Sears 1953:28).

The barred oval is found as a fundamental motif during the Mississippian period; it is also present in Swift Creek symbolism. At the Milamo site (9WL1) it occurs as the central element in one Middle Swift Creek paddle design. Two fragmentary designs from the Hartford submound midden have barred oval elements. One is a bar within an oval (Figure 6-8, *d*) and the other is a bar within a more rectangular element (Figure 6-8, *e*).

The preceding designs were excavated from the submound midden at Hartford and were likely created by the antecedents of the adjacent Hartford village. The slightly later village designs are discussed next.

Hartford Village Design Reconstruction and Speculation

Twenty-eight designs are illustrated from the Middle Swift Creek village at Hartford; most are incomplete. Designs seem to become more elaborate with natural depictions more numerous and more realistic during the Middle Swift Creek period than designs from earlier Swift Creek pottery in the submound midden. In addition to design data recovered from excavated material, design reconstruction took advantage of three extensive surface collections made in the village area by Danny Ray Reed of Oglethorpe, Leon Perry of Tennille, and Keith Gillis of Macon. Those designs that contain some naturalistic qualities are discussed first.

The horned-eye mask (Figure 6-2, *a*) is an example of a naturalistic design representing the face of some unidentified animal, perhaps an owl. Similar depictions have been recorded on several other Swift Creek sites. If design analysis had been confined only to design elements like concentric circles, teardrops, and barred triangles in this paddle design, as has been done in the past, valuable data would have escaped. The more important composite mask-like design would likely have gone unrecognized.

The mosquito design (Figure 6-2, *b*) was recovered from the surface of the village, but the core of its usual distribution on the basis of common occurrence is along the lower Ocmulgee Valley in Wheeler and Jeff Davis counties. A flaw present in the concentric circles of the left eye verifies that the mosquito design recovered from six locations originated from a single paddle. A mosquito is suggested by the presence of what appear to be wings emerging from behind the eyes, a chevron-filled abdomen, and a hachured proboscis. The use of exaggerated concentric circles for eyes is perplexing since this element is usually a sun symbol. The great freedom of expression evident in Swift Creek paddle art may extend to the individual elements that comprise the paddle motif. Thus, the use of the sun symbol may, through some contorted rationalization, be related to the mosquito's perceived ability to see its victims in the darkness of night.

The wolf face design (Figure 6-2, *c*) is another abstract animal design. Whether a wolf or some other animal was intended is unclear in this depiction. Designs with wolf-like features are known from other Swift Creek sites such as Mill Creek (9CF154) and Milamo (9WL1). Furthermore, at 9CF119, a small Swift Creek site located along Paul Branch in Coffee County, a match with the Hartford wolf face design was recorded. In addition, at this site, which is far removed from the main village at Hartford, the reverse or negative of the wolf stamp was also recovered. These negative stamps derive from stamped pottery fragments that were used as convenience paddles in the absence of a wooden paddle (Snow n.d.). It seems that at 9CF119 there was a temporary campsite whose occupants had a vessel stamped with the wolf-designed paddle that resided at the Hartford village site. This vessel broke and a potter at 9CF119 proceeded to construct a replacement vessel but in the absence of the original wolf face paddle chose to use a fragment of the broken wolf face vessel as a convenience stamp.

Historically, at least, the Wolf Clan was one of the fundamental groups in southeastern Indian society. While on a trip through the Creek country that is the present state of Alabama, William Bartram (Van Doren 1955:361) listed the wolf among depictions on walls of the houses at the Atasi square ground. He pointed out that the heads of these animals were represented with human bodies and vice versa.

The spiral-nose mask design (Figure 6-2, *d*) from the Hartford village is an example of long-distance contact. It has also been recovered by a surface collector just below the Lake Seminole Dam at Chattahoochee, Florida. While total design data were lacking on the potsherds, more than 50 percent of the design was present and only the reconstructed configuration of the eyes is questioned. This seems to represent another large-nosed mask with dentition visible at the bottom, a sun symbol on the forehead, and a bulbous or spatulate nose. The unusual spiraled element in the nose area seems basically to indicate motion, on the basis of the previous interpretation of the spiral design element. Its location in the nose area was puzzling until it was realized that what was possibly intended was to symbolize the passage of air through the nasal cavity symbolized by the triangular element located immediately above. What, if any, connection this design has with the Master of Breath is not known. In other Swift Creek designs the location of spirals, as mentioned earlier, implies motion to birds' wings or the movement of air across those wings, and when placed in the quadrants of earth symbols the spirals seem to represent the circular motion of wind, possibly the mythological wind that cleared the fog from the primeval earth.

The twisted-mouth mask design (Figure 6-2, *e*) is in William T. Sander's collection from the Bob Rush site at the University of Georgia and occurs in our collection in the Hartford Middle Swift Creek village. The design may be interpreted as follows: the mouth consists of a lobed element with diagonal lines suggestive of dentition. Above this is a loop that seems to depict the nose. The composite of these two design elements is arranged in a somewhat spiraled configuration. Again, it is possible that breath or the passage of air is being indicated. A conspicuous forehead symbol consists of concentric circles with ear-like projections on either side. A similarly deformed wooden human mask was recovered at the Key Marco site (Gilliland 1975:plate 48).

Sherds bearing a probable rabbit design (Figure 6-2, *f*) are in the Gillis and Perry surface collections from Hartford. Another sherd bearing this design is from our surface collection from the village. When the design is viewed with the circular loops toward the bottom, a rabbit with a large nose, whiskers, two fluffy front paws, and floppy ears seems to be portrayed in front view. However, when viewed with the loops toward the top of the design, this design suggests that an entire owl-like bird is depicted in front view. Since most bird designs display a double-spiral element and none is evident here, the rabbit interpretation is more likely correct. The proper orientation of the design may be determined by observing whether the loops occur more often and are more clearly impressed on the potsherds than the ear-like elements that are located on the opposite end of the design. The tops of naturalistic designs are normally toward the distal end of the paddle, which is an area of the paddle that is usually more often and more clearly impressed on the soft clay of the unfired pot than the area of the design nearest the paddle handle.

The possible importance of the large-nosed rabbit interpretation for this design is made apparent by Hall's discussion of the Great Hare carving in Hopewell Mound 25 and the rabbit's mythological association with the land of the soul in some historic tribal beliefs (Hall 1989:247, 261–64). It seems appropriate that this illusionary design involves the rabbit; the Creek Indians sometimes regarded the rabbit as a trickster (Swanton 1928:145).

A paddle design depicting paired opposite-facing birds in profile is illustrated in Figure 6-9, *a*. Head, body, and tail features are clearly evident. Woodpeckers have rounded sickle-shaped claws useful for grasping the vertical trunks of trees during their climbing search for food. Perhaps the loops placed between each bird's bill and chest represent sickle-shaped claws. A crest, so common on representations of bird heads from this period, is not evident unless the loops in the central element separating the two birds serve to represent that structure. That these paired birds are arranged in opposition is likely significant in reflecting the dualistic belief that permeates southeastern Indian thought, at least the thought of historic southeastern Indians, in which opposite qualities such as good and evil are played against each other. Slight variations between the two birds, such as the absence of a solid teardrop element on the chest of one, prevents them from being mirror images. The importance of these differences cannot be clearly evaluated; however, according to Emerson (1989), directionally opposed spirals may imply opposite meanings. For example, a counterclockwise spiral, the direction that serpents coiled, had Under World implications and clockwise spirals were associated with the Upper World. Incidentally, it is interesting to note a possible similar interpretation of the spiraled ramp of the Lamar mound at Macon. Priests descended the mound in a clockwise direction (from the Upper World?) and villagers ascended the spiraled mound in a counterclockwise direction (from this world?). The lower central portion of the woodpecker design bears a chevron-filled tapered element. The red-bellied woodpecker, the important *dalala* of the Cherokees, is characterized by similar barred tail markings whereas the red-headed woodpecker lacks them. The remainder of

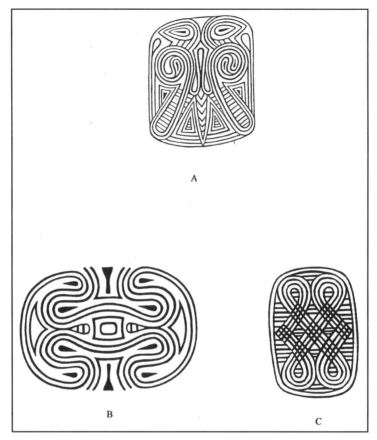

Figure 6-9. Swift Creek paddle designs: *a*, two woodpeckers design; *b*, box-in-center design; *c*, double figure-8 design. (Copyright © Frankie Snow.)

the design seems to represent the spread-out tail section of a bird. Hudson (1976:130) notes that the red-bellied woodpecker was a war symbol, possibly because its red head looks as if it had been scalped.

These woodpecker-like birds bear on their shoulders spiraled symbols that Sears (1956) chose to call wing motifs when they were found incised on effigy vessels at Kolomoki. This spiraled motif is found on another reconstructed complicated stamped bird design at the Milamo site (9WL1) (Figure 6-1, *I;* Broyles 1968:plate 5, *top left*). However, on the latter design, the so-called wing motif is located on the breast of the bird since the bird is depicted with its wings outstretched as if the bird were in flight; interestingly, the spiraled configuration is maintained.

Sears's wing symbol may instead be a wind or air symbol. Indians, during historic times, considered birds to be members of the airy Upper World (Hudson 1976). In fact, a flock of birds taking flight creates a sound comparable to the rushing sound of the wind. Thus, it seems logical that birds would have been closely associated with the wind and might even have been depicted bearing that symbol. If this design portrays red-bellied woodpeckers bearing a symbol for wind then a contradiction or an anomaly is observed. As mentioned above, historic Indians considered this bird to be a symbol of war (Hudson 1976), but, as Swanton (1928) pointed out, the Wind Clan, at least during historic times, was always associated with peace.

Sears further noted that his wing symbol was sometimes incised on vessels that bore no obvious bird features (Sears 1956). The same is true of nonbird designs rendered by the complicated stamp technique. Figure 6-5, *second row, left,* illustrates a design from the Hartford village that contains four spiraled elements arranged about a central concentric circle motif. This is one of several variations of a design that seem to represent a single theme. The general layout comprises four spirals around a central element consisting of a solid dot surrounded by concentric circles and is divided quadrilaterally; this may symbolize the four winds imposed upon a depiction of the world. Spiral elements may have been attempts to illustrate an invisible phenomenon, wind, on the basis of its visible effects such as a whirlwind twisting across the landscape. Note that opposing direction markers for east and west differ from the markers for north and south. A millennium later during the Mississippian period the cross-and-circle motif and the filfot cross were fundamental designs that represented an idea similar to that in this design.

The design recorded in Figure 6-9, *b,* is from Mr. Myers's garden in the Hartford site village and is also recorded from the Westlake site in Twiggs County and the Broxton Creek (9CF3) and Teresa Raceway (9CF100) sites in Coffee County. This distribution spans a distance of 145 kilometers. Very similar design compositions are noted in illustrations by Broyles (1968:plate 13, *third row*).

The double figure-8 design (Figure 6-9, *c*) seems to have connections with the three-lobed twist design from Hartford, though what that relationship is remains unknown. The motif is one of the most common designs on

Figure 6-10. Swift Creek paddle designs: *a*, four-winds design; *b*, sun and earth design; *c*, large-nosed mask design; *d*, sun and ray design. (Copyright © Frankie Snow.)

subsequent Swift Creek sites where it is found modified to a more recognizable figure 8 when occurring either singly or in the double configuration.

A design (Figure 6-10, *b*) from Mill Creek (9CF154) in the Hudson collection has concentric circles centrally located with hachured fill in each quadrant. It may be similar to a design from Hartford (Figure 6-10, *a*). Totally abstract designs such as this often allow for the most bizarre interpretation. However, because its theme seems to be played out in a variety of other renditions (see the four-winds design mentioned above and note a similar design shown by Caldwell [1978:plate 6]), what is being portrayed seems to be an important symbolism. With the mind's eye on the concept of the spatial arrangement of the world as viewed by historic aboriginals, observe one suggestion of a seemingly parallel concept from much earlier in

Swift Creek times. Could it be that the concentric circles centrally located symbolize the sun? Could it also be that the lines forming the longer axis represent the sun's daily sky track? If so, would not the shorter axis denote the sun's seasonal swings north and south suggesting that Swift Creek people recognized a horizon calendar (see Thomas 1979:365)? Is all of this superimposed upon the four divisions of the earth represented by the four hachured elements?

Though incomplete, the large-nosed design in Figure 6-10, *c,* seems to represent another mask-like depiction. A fragment of this face-like design was recovered from a rimsherd found by Keith Gillis on the surface of the village. The partial design is illustrated in a study of Swift Creek designs and distributions published in *Early Georgia* (Snow 1975:figure 6, *c*).

Figure 6-10, *d,* is another example of the southeastern Indian's obsession with four-ness. With the sun symbol in the center, rays extend outward to mark the cardinal directions, which divide the motif into quadrants filled with squares. It is tempting to see the short parallel lines that are bisected by the sun's four cardinal rays as indicating the Indian's imagined levels that the sun traveled above the earth. By constructing the design such that the sun's rays bisect these levels, superpositioning of the sun above the remaining portions of the design is achieved.

Summary

In conclusion, Swift Creek art seems to be most informative about these people and their beliefs. A mass of mounting evidence from reconstructed Swift Creek paddle designs gives some insight into their world view. Interpretations include many of the special animals and symbols such as the eye motif and the circle-and-cross motif noted by Hudson (1976) and others that were part of either the aboriginal belief system or their mythology. When the subjective interpretations of these reconstructed paddle designs, including the sun disk and the four quarters of the earth, coiled serpents, red-bellied woodpeckers, owls, buzzards, a cardinal, a falcon, and a rabbit, are compared with ethnohistorical accounts of aboriginal beliefs, a strong suggestion emerges of an enduring belief system that was in place at least as early as Swift Creek times.

Eventually archaeologists may be able to see that through time this fundamental belief system was elaborated on or modified to meet the needs of an increasingly complex society (Phelps 1970:90). It may be possible eventually to recognize that toward the nascent end of the spectrum there was a Hopewell-like belief system and at the more recent end of this time spectrum there was a highly modified end product recognized as the Southeastern Ceremonial Complex.

Is there an explanation for the similarity between Mesoamerican art and some Swift Creek motifs? Not only are some Swift Creek designs stylistically similar to some from Mesoamerica but also Swift Creek themes of serpents, birds, and the sun and four quarters are paralleled in Mesoamerica. Webb (1989:279–93) discusses the antiquity of the prehistoric conceptual base that is manifested in a redundant set of motifs found throughout the New World. He suggests rather than having Mesoamerican influences pouring into the Southeast that similarities derive from "very basic and ancient ways of conceptualizing and symbolizing significant aspects of reality" and that "these were then subject to functioning and being expressed in similar ways to the extent that the social order of which they were a part had developed similar expressive needs." The ceramic sequence in southern Georgia can be traced back through time from Swift Creek to Deptford then to a transitional semi-fiber-tempered/grit-tempered ware locally known as the Satilla series (Snow 1977) and finally to Late Archaic fiber-tempered wares with the only noticeable bump in evolutionary smoothness being the elaboration in vessel shape during the Swift Creek period. No evidence is known for a major intrusion of an exotic culture. Because of the apparent widespread nature of some motifs, both in time and space, the Swift Creek design study presented here has drawn citations from an extended geographic area and includes ethnographic data from the Iroquois in New England to the Zapotec of the central valley of Mexico. Other than a very ancient source for the roots of both belief systems, no Mayan connection of any sort with their Swift Creek contemporaries in the Southeast is being suggested here.

I have attempted to demonstrate that Swift Creek paddle designs are an important source of cultural information. I hope others will join the effort to exploit this valuable data bank by employing design analysis in future studies.

Swift Creek Designs
A Tool for Monitoring Interaction

Frankie Snow and Keith Stephenson

Unquestionably, the hallmark of Swift Creek material cultural is its elaborately decorated pottery. The highly stylized designs that embellish Swift Creek ceramic ware most certainly served as visual representations of cultural information. As such, this iconography provides archaeologists the opportunity to examine various facets of communication exchange and social interaction. Previous studies of Swift Creek designs have convincingly demonstrated that they are unique stylistic expressions in that no two paddle-carved designs are identical (Broyles 1968; Snow 1975, 1977, 1994). To date several hundred complete and partial designs have been reconstructed from Swift Creek sherds from the lower Ocmulgee River drainage, reinforcing the individualistic nature of these decorative configurations (see Snow, Chapter 6 herein). This database holds the potential to reveal population dynamics in a spatial-temporal context, as well as other social aspects such as group structure and regional interaction.

The conceptual perspective of ceramic design research focuses on the causes, meanings, and functions of style (e.g., Arnold 1984; Conkey and Hastorf 1990; Friedrich 1970; Plog 1978). Although definitions of style in archaeology often vary, most recognize that stylistic forms, such as ceramic designs, are encoded with information. Typically, styles are defined as "visual representations, specific to particular contexts of time and place, that at the least transmit information about the identity of the society that produced the style and about the situation or location where it appears" (Rice 1987:244). Since the mid-1960s, differing approaches in archaeology have been offered regarding stylistic studies of material objects. In early processual analyses, style was viewed as a passive reflection of population affiliations with no intent of communicating overt messages (Deetz 1965; Longacre 1964, 1970; Rice 1987:266; Whallon 1968). Alternatively, style was also assigned an active role in communication whereby socially distinct groups received and acknowledged specific information (Rice 1987:267; Saunders, Chapter 10 herein; Wobst 1977). Ensuing debate led to a more contextual perspective that viewed style as a means for sociopolitical and individual strategies of action (Carr 1995b:154; Hodder 1982a, 1982b). Most recently, Carr (1995a) has developed a rather sophisticated approach to style, which he terms a "unified theory of artifact design." This integrative scheme bridges earlier approaches involving stylistic indicators of social groups by determining the processes that define and maintain these groups and the contextual circumstances under which those processes occur (Carr 1995a:251).

As Schortman and Urban (1992:236) maintain, interregional communication among several societies can be established when stylistic studies indicate the exchange of material goods. Thus, ceramic style analysis offers a means for reconstructing contemporaneous settlement patterns and social interaction networks over a broad area. It is plausible that particular sets of designs, many of which show an inclination toward naturalistic representations, were associated with particular social units (lineages, clans, moieties) of the regional population. Given that this association can be demonstrated along the lines of qualitative and quantitative data, as well as by contextual evidence (e.g., Carr 1995b), the movement of information, goods, or people can be traced spatially. Thus, as we show in the following discussion, the mapping of design contacts between archaeological sites is an initial move toward an explanation of the social and economic dynamics of interacting Swift Creek communities.

In this chapter we explicitly describe and discuss intraregional Swift Creek design contacts with a focus on data obtained from ceramic assemblages recovered during recent salvage excavations at the Hartford site (9PU1) in south-central Georgia. The Hartford site served as a center of primary importance during the latter portion of the Early Swift Creek period and was subsequently occupied during the Middle Swift Creek period although its prominence may have lessened during this time. Although many other design contacts among sites have been recognized in south-central Georgia, the regional significance of Hartford justifies its use as a case study for design contact and interaction interpretations. A summary of the Hartford investigations is in order before we proceed with a discussion of design contacts.

The ceremonial Swift Creek site known as Hartford, which takes its name from the historic community where it is found, is situated in the northern limestone sink region of the Tifton Uplands very near the Fall Line Red Hills physiographic sector of Georgia (Wharton 1978). Located on the eastern side of the Ocmulgee River, the Hartford site occupies a spur ridge overlooking a series of limestone shoals. This narrow section of the river valley provided an ideal fording place for the Uchee Trail, an east-to-west oriented trail that linked aboriginal groups in the Oconee, Ocmulgee, Flint, and Chattahoochee river valleys. This natural ford was also the hub of other aboriginal trails that followed the river (Hodler and Schretter 1986:68). It is quite likely that these trails had great antiquity. This important trail juncture was most likely the major determining factor in the location of the Swift Creek ceremonial center at Hartford, as it linked the site with settlements throughout the region and beyond.

Although the Hartford site had received intermittent archaeological attention beginning in the 1930s, recorded information concerning site occupation, structure, and function was minimal. An account of the archaeological history of Hartford was compiled in detective fashion from early fragmentary sources such as site forms, memorandums, letter reports, accession records, newspaper articles, and personal communications. It is apparent from these records that very little previous work had been conducted at the site. One early description of Hartford indicated that two low mounds were present in the 1930s (Swanton 1939:178). The fill of one mound apparently was used in road construction during a Works Progress Administration project in the late 1930s (Fairbanks 1940). The second mound survived major disturbance until 1988 when it was bulldozed by the landowner in preparation for real estate development. In addition to leveling the mound, the landowner also removed forest cover at the site, exposing a Swift Creek village midden that formed an arc northwest of the mound.

In the wake of this landscaping activity, archaeological investigations were conducted at Hartford during 1988–1989 (Snow and Stephenson 1991). Salvage excavations concentrated primarily on the mound remnants with limited additional work done in the village. Most of the mound fill had been removed down to a premound midden deposit. Excavations in this midden revealed architectural features associated with a large premound structure. The structure is represented by a central refuse pit, four central support posts, a pattern of outer wall posts, small storage pits, and a limestone rubble feature. On the basis of artifactual evidence, the submound structure and village were not contemporaneous. The pottery assemblage from the submound midden dates to the latter portion of the Early Swift Creek period. In comparison, the ceramics from surface collections and three test units in the village midden date to the Middle Swift Creek period. Important to this chapter are the large samples of Swift Creek Complicated Stamped pottery recovered from the submound midden and village midden contexts. The following discussion concerns pottery design contacts and interaction between Hartford and other regional Swift Creek sites.

Caldwell (1964:135–43) has written about a long-distance interregional interaction sphere based on the broad distribution in the eastern United States of a set of artifacts identified as Hopewellian. Through the study of Swift Creek designs, a database has been established that demonstrates that there was also an intensely interconnected set of Swift Creek sites that formed an intraregional interaction sphere in a large part of Georgia. In the ensuing discussion when a design is said to have been recorded on two or more sites, this means, unless otherwise stated, that a common paddle produced the design even though sherds bearing the impression may occur on sites separated by a considerable distance. The confidence that the original and not a copied design is involved is further enhanced when design flaws, paddle crack patterns, or numerous other incidental anomalies are detected in conjunction with a design as it occurs on different sites.

During more than two decades of archaeological survey, a Swift Creek design database has accumulated that establishes a prehistoric interaction involving several hundred instances in which individual design contacts are found among Swift Creek sites in a large area of southern Georgia. This interaction extended from the southeastern corner of the state, with at least five contacts recorded between sites in the Kings Bay area and the lower Ocmulgee region, to the southwestern Georgia area, where six design contacts with the Ocmulgee Valley have been recorded. Within the Ocmulgee drainage more than a hundred design contacts between sites have been recorded.

Through Swift Creek design analysis, it is possible to see evidence of Hartford's interaction with regional Swift Creek sites (Figure 7-1). Almost half of the Swift Creek paddle designs (48 percent) recovered from the two middens at Hartford are known to occur on other sites. Twenty-one of the designs from the Hartford submound midden are recorded on fifteen other sites (Table 7-1), while sixteen designs from the Hartford village are recorded on twenty-four other sites (Table 7-2). It is sometimes possible to suggest the direction of movement for the design. Large numbers of sherds bearing a design from a number of different vessels would be expected on a site where the potter who owned that paddle resided. In contrast, only occasional sherds bearing the same design and often representing but one vessel would be expected at sites that received the design on trade pottery. With the data now available, it seems that more designs at Hartford moved to the site from outlying areas, where their more common occurrence suggests a home place, as opposed to endemic Hartford designs moving outward to satellite sites.

Comparison of the distribution of the earlier Hartford submound designs with the distribution of the later Hartford village designs reveals an interesting pattern. Submound designs from common paddles that occur upstream (sixteen) outnumber those that occur downstream (twelve). This numerical superiority occurs even though the area upstream has received less Swift Creek design study than the extensively surveyed area downstream from Hartford. When the distribution of Hartford village designs common to those from other sites upstream and downstream are plotted, the area downstream has more design contacts (twenty-nine) than the area upstream (six). For the village at Hartford, the largest number of connecting sites (sixteen) occurs downstream. This is compared with only two sites with contacts in the area upstream. Unequal survey may distort the distribution, but it is nevertheless felt that this pattern reflects an expansion of Middle Swift Creek populations downstream into an area little utilized by the Early Swift Creek population.

Another way to test this Swift Creek expansion idea is to determine the site in which a particular design originated. This is done by examining the frequency of sherds bearing the design being studied at each site. As noted earlier, the place of origin of the paddle should be expected to contain multiple occurrences of the design whereas only sporadic single occurrences would be expected in adjacent areas. For example, the ladder/bull's-eye de-

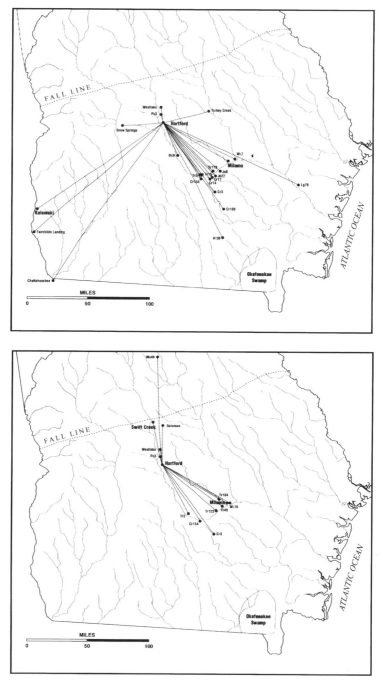

Figure 7-1. Swift Creek design contacts with the Hartford village (top) and with the Hartford mound (bottom).

Table 7-1. Known Design Contacts with the Hartford Submound Midden

#	Design	Contact Sites
1	Four directions	Solomon
2	Enlarged mask	9CF3, Westlake
3	Square of four concentric circles	9BI3
4	Eye	9WL1, Hidden Lakes, 9TF2
5	Little River	Solomon, Little River
6	D	Solomon
7	Horseshoe	9WL26
8	Heart	Solomon
9	Star	9TF104
10	Class A	9TF123
11	Star eyes	9CF154
12	Cross-eyed S	9CF154
13	Restored vessel design	9CF154
14	Thickened circle	Solomon
15	Figure 8	Solomon
16	Four-ness	Solomon
17	Four winds	Solomon
18	Spiral eyes	Solomon
19	No name	Solomon
20	Anthropomorph	9TF49
21	Ladder/bull's-eye	9BI3, Solomon, Westlake, 9PU3, 9WL16, 9TF123

Table 7-2. Known Design Contacts with the Hartford Village

#	Design	Contact Sites
1	Loop eyes 2	9CF154
2	Sun and earth	9PU3, 9WL1, 9JD22, 9CF100
3	Loop eyes 1	Snow Springs, Westlake
4	Bird with square and triangle	9WL1
5	Lobed nose	9CF3
6	Box center	9CF3, 9CF100, Westlake
7	Bold teardrop	9CF3, 9DG9, 9WL1, Turkey Creek
8	Figure 8	Wrighty Harrell
9	Fairchild's/Kolomoki	9TF5, Fairchild's Landing
10	Slant-eyed monster	Westlake
11	Spiral nose	Chattahoochee, Florida
12	Mosquito	9CF154, 9WF1, 9WF7, 9JD8, 9JD22
13	Concentric circle term.	9WL1, 9JD8, Westlake
14	Wolf face	9CF119
15	Two eye-like loops with nose	9WI20
16	Rabbit	9CF154, 9CF14, 9CF17, 9CF100, 9TF15, 9TF5, 9TF119, 9JD8

sign is found in the Hartford submound midden but is also known from four sites upstream and from two sites downstream along the Big Bend. While this design is represented by single sherds at sites downstream, the upstream sites have multiple examples of sherds bearing the design. It therefore seems that the ladder/bull's-eye paddle came from an area between Hartford and Macon and that occasional vessels were exchanged with sites downstream. In contrast, a reverse flow of vessels inward to the subsequent Hartford Middle Swift Creek village is observed. Using the same quantitative logic, several of the designs that are found in the Middle Swift Creek village at Hartford are products of paddles that came from the Ocmulgee Big Bend region. No instances of the most popular Hartford village designs have been recorded in the Big Bend region. These kinds of intersite comparisons are made possible only with large sherd sample sizes, which have been made available as a result of massive site disturbance along the lower Ocmulgee Valley by timber companies.

Clearly, prehistoric Hartford was situated among, and interacted with, a community of villages and small camp sites scattered across Georgia's Coastal Plain. Upstream from Hartford the Shelly, Westlake, Bullard, and Solomon sites and the Swift Creek type site are some important neighbors that were part of this community. For example, the Solomon site, located 55 kilometers northward in Twiggs County, contains at least eleven Swift Creek designs that can be duplicated by identical designs found in the submound midden at the Hartford site. Interestingly, no designs recovered from the Hartford village have been found on the Solomon site. This is another indication that the two middens at Hartford represent different intervals of time. However, that these intervals are close together is suggested by the fact that three other sites are known to have Swift Creek designs found in both Hartford middens. As noted above, the Hartford village has a much stronger design affinity downstream, which is in contrast to the strong upstream orientation of designs from the Hartford submound midden.

Along the lower Ocmulgee River several hundred Swift Creek sites have been recorded, with some having specific design matches with Hartford, especially with the village. One of these, the Milamo site (9WL1), had a direct trail connection following the river with Hartford. Milamo also has five Swift Creek designs that are the product of the same paddles as designs recovered in the Hartford village. While Milamo is primarily a Middle Swift Creek site, a trace of earlier, notched-rim pottery and a few Bakers Creek projectiles were found in the lower portion of the Milamo burial mound (field notes in possession of Frankie Snow). Kelly (1956) points out that Deptford ceramics underlay the Swift Creek village at Milamo thus indicating that a Deptford occupation preceded the Swift Creek occupation.

In addition to the designs from the various sites that match with designs from Hartford, other designs from those same sites are not found at Hartford but have other matches among the sites. Insufficient sampling or chance may create an illusion that Hartford is cut off from these communities during the time that these latter designs were in circulation. For example, two motifs match between Milamo and the Shelly site located near Hartford but were not recovered at Hartford. While this strengthens the concept of a network of interacting communities, it also indicates how much chance is involved in design match discoveries. It also suggests that sites may have been occupied and abandoned periodically.

Historic maps show that Hartford was located at a hub of trails (Hemperley 1989:46–47). It probably functioned as a crossroads in prehistoric times, on the basis of the existence of thirty-four specific Hartford Swift Creek designs that have been recorded sixty-six times on thirty other Swift Creek sites that are distributed across south-central Georgia. One should not assume that each of these thirty sites interacted directly with Hartford, since any design common between Hartford and another site could have resulted from its being distributed by people at a third-party site. Therefore it is conceivable, though unlikely, that people from distant sites with pottery possessing identical paddle designs were ignorant of the others' existence. For example, the rabbit design was found in the Hartford village, but it also occurs on eight other sites located mostly along the lower Ocmulgee River valley. It is likely that at least some of these vessels bearing the rabbit design were distributed to people among the recorded sites who did not directly interact with the population at Hartford. The historic trail that leads from Hartford westward to the Flint River possibly provided another prehistoric route for the movement of Hartford designs. This would have been the most probable route for receiving designs from the west. On the Oconee River, an archaeological survey of the area around Carr's Shoals should recover sites with designs that contact with Hartford since the Uchee Trail led there. Though unconfirmed, a Swift Creek site has been reported near where this historic trail strikes the Oconee. Because Swift Creek designs at Macon-area sites contact with Hartford it is interesting to note that the Lower Creek Trading Path extended from Macon to the Flint River in Crawford County and that Swift Creek potsherds bearing designs that match with Macon and Hartford are known from a Crawford County site.

By the time the structure uncovered in the submound midden at Hartford was occupied, the Mandeville site on the Chattahoochee River had ended its long Swift Creek occupation and the Swift Creek occupation represented in the upper levels of Mound A of the Swift Creek type site at Macon was near its end. Also, by the time the Hartford village was established, the large Kolomoki site was beginning to rise to its forthcoming dominance. The potential was present for design contacts to exist between the Middle Swift Creek sites of the Hartford village and Kolomoki. Several design contacts that are known to exist are discussed below.

Long-distance Swift Creek interactions have also been detected. A turtle design match between the resident Milamo site in Wheeler County and the Kolomoki site 270 kilometers away has been documented (Snow 1982). Was the pot bearing this design moved between the two distant sites or was the paddle moved (see Stoltman and Snow, Chapter 9 herein)? Both scenarios are possible. Though ceramics are fragile and generally thought not to be adapted to the rigors of distant transportation, it should be pointed out that St. Johns pottery, which has a sponge spicule paste not available along the lower Ocmulgee Valley, is occasionally found as a minority ware on Swift Creek sites located here.

Another important design (Kelly and Smith 1975:143, plate 10, *upper right*) that indirectly relates to the Hartford site involves long-distance contact between the Milamo site, the upper levels of Mound A at the Swift Creek type site (9BI3), and the Kolomoki site (9ER1). The area encompassed by these three contact sites includes nearly a fourth of Georgia's Coastal Plain. Sherds bearing this design are the type most often illustrated in the find books from 9BI3, which suggests that the paddle bearing this design resided at the Swift Creek type site near Macon. Only one sherd bearing this design was recovered from Milamo despite the extensive ceramic collection made there. Also, a sherd bearing this design was located at Kolomoki adjacent to Mound A along a steep bank on the western side of the well. Importantly, however, there is an indirect connection for this design with the submound midden at the Hartford site. The design is reported to have occurred in the upper levels of Mound A at the Swift Creek type site along with another design, the ladder/bull's-eye design (Kelly and Smith 1975:143, plate 10, *top center*), which was also found in the submound midden at Hartford. Sherd-to-sherd comparisons between the Swift Creek type site sherd and the suspected Milamo match indicate that the design on both sherds derives from a common paddle. Although the matching sherd from Kolomoki has a micaceous paste, because small mica particles are prevalent in the clays commonly used at Kolomoki, the sherd from the Milamo site contains coarse grit. While micaceous clays are available along the Ocmulgee, the frequency of mica inclusions in Swift Creek pottery there is not as great as that observed at Kolomoki. This suggests that the paddle had moved between Kolomoki and a site from the Ocmulgee Valley. Stoltman's (1989, 1991) petrographic technique of identifying ceramic temper coupled with the design-matching process could determine whether a paddle movement was involved in these long-distance design matches or whether a vessel moved between the two sites (see Chapter 9 herein).

Sears (1951a:8–23), in part, justified creating the Kolomoki complex because of the conceived distinctiveness of that ware from Swift Creek Complicated Stamped pottery found at Macon. Yet, in his final report on Kolomoki (Sears 1956:67, 76, map III), the Kolomoki focus included a broad area from Santa Rosa Sound on the Gulf Coast to the confluence of the Ocmulgee and Oconee rivers. With six Swift Creek design contacts known for Kolomoki and sites along the Ocmulgee, that ceramic difference fades as should the name Kolomoki Complicated Stamped. Recently Sears (1992:66) seems to suggest that maybe Kolomoki Complicated Stamped pottery cannot be separated from Swift Creek. In 1941, Fairbanks, with considerable experience in dealing with Swift Creek at the Macon excavations, did an archaeological site survey of the Kolomoki mound groups in which he clearly described the major occupation as Swift Creek (Fairbanks 1941).

Many designs have been recovered from Hartford that are known to occur on sites upriver near Macon and downstream along the lower reaches of the Ocmulgee. Twenty of these were from the submound midden and fourteen were found in the village area. There are several other designs from the submound midden that strongly suggest contact with Mandeville and the Swift Creek type site, but this has not been confirmed by sherd-to-sherd comparisons. One design bears a wheel-like motif and the other contains nested D-shaped elements (Kellar et al. 1962:345). Even with evidence of considerable interaction between sites, some sites still maintain their individual character on the basis of a preponderance of designs that are not recorded elsewhere.

In conclusion, when a specific design occurs on a number of sites, it can give some insight into regional interaction of Swift Creek people (Snow 1977). Because of the unique quality of individual Swift Creek designs, it is possible to plot spheres of interaction. Settlement patterns can be established from this data that are based on a narrower time interval than is available in most cases. In a few cases, more than one design contact has been recorded between two or more sites. Design distribution may derive from seasonal movement of people, trade between areas, or marriage of people from different Swift Creek centers. Movement of a paddle, and not just transport of a vessel stamped by a particular paddle, may account for some of these design distributions. However, some designs have been tied to their home place; the place where the paddle resided. At the Milamo site (9WL1), for example, the turtle design was found on pottery in many proveniences across the village. This design's ubiquitous occurrence at Milamo, and its presence on adjacent satellite sites, though proportionately less dominant relative to other designs at those sites, identifies Milamo as the place where the turtle paddle resided (Snow 1978). Had this paddle been moved to another site for a time comparable to its stay at Milamo, one might expect to encounter a set of Swift Creek motifs dominated by the turtle design at this second location.

The distribution of Swift Creek designs that has been plotted for the Hartford site is probably a product of a combination of the above-mentioned factors. Hartford's interaction map indicates strongest ties with the area to its southeast (Figure 7-1). This may be a false impression, however, generated by the extensive survey effort along the lower Ocmulgee River (Snow 1977). Additional Swift Creek design information from other areas should give a more accurate map of the Hartford interaction sphere.

Neutron Activation Analysis of Ceramics from Mandeville and Swift Creek

Betty A. Smith

One of the most useful classes of artifacts recovered from prehistoric sites is pottery. Attributes of construction, vessel form, and decoration are used as chronological markers, as defining characteristics of regional or local traditions, and as a means of gauging both intraregional and interregional contact and interaction. The study of pottery begins with the definition of types; in the southeastern United States, one of the first types to be formally defined was Swift Creek Complicated Stamped (Jennings and Fairbanks 1939b).

Swift Creek—say that name to archaeologists, especially those working in Georgia and northwestern Florida, and immediately visions of pottery with curvilinear complicated stamped designs come to mind. Long recognized (Holmes 1903), this pottery type was formally defined as a result of work at the Swift Creek type site (9BI3) near Macon, Georgia (Kelly 1938). In archaeological time, Swift Creek Complicated Stamped pottery spans the Middle and Late Woodland periods. Its geographic distribution centers in south-central and southwestern Georgia and northwestern Florida, but it has been found in other neighboring states and as far away as Ohio and Indiana (in Indiana it is called Mann Complicated Stamped [Rein 1974]). These chronological and geographic settings describe the pottery's archaeological context; but what about the people and the culture of those people who manufactured this beautiful pottery type? Since it is unlikely that only one group of people made all the pottery identified by archaeologists as Swift Creek, how can we go beyond the pottery type to learn about the lifeways of the peoples whose cultural evolution and interaction resulted in the archaeological phenomenon called Swift Creek?

One approach is to use the distribution of the complicated stamped designs to develop hypotheses about cultural processes. Bettye Broyles (1968), on the basis of her reconstruction of Swift Creek designs from several sites (primarily Kolomoki, Fairchild's Landing, Mandeville, and Quartermaster, all in southwestern Georgia), made the following observations:

1. At Fairchild's Landing, one paddle was used to decorate at least nineteen different vessels and another was used to decorate at least fifteen different vessels.

2. At Kolomoki, some Swift Creek designs appear to have been restricted to mound contexts; other designs found in both mound and village contexts were produced from different paddles.

3. Identical Swift Creek designs produced from different paddles were found at Kolomoki and Fairchild's Landing, sites at least 65 kilometers apart.

4. An identical Swift Creek design was noted from a site in Florida (8WA34) and from the Quartermaster site in Georgia, sites 300 kilometers apart.

5. An identical design produced by the same paddle was noted for Fairchild's Landing and Quartermaster (135 kilometers) and for Kolomoki and unspecified sites in Florida (about 160 kilometers).

6. Photographs of ceramics from the Mann site in Indiana appeared to show designs identical to designs from Mandeville and Halloca Creek.

Broyles made no reference to designs shared by Mandeville and Kolomoki even though these two sites are less than 40 kilometers apart. The apparent absence of shared designs may well reflect the chronological separation of these sites; the Mandeville, Halloca Creek, and Mann sites are all Middle Woodland sites while Kolomoki, Fairchild's Landing, and Quartermaster are Late Woodland. Her observations from Kolomoki suggest that some Swift Creek vessels were manufactured for special or ritual purposes while others were intended for domestic use. Finally, her observations pertaining to distribution of designs at different sites may represent such cultural processes as diffusion of ideas, trade, or movement of people.

Another individual noted for his study of Swift Creek designs is Frankie Snow. An avocational archaeologist, Snow has studied and reconstructed Swift Creek designs from the Ocmulgee Big Bend region of south-central Georgia for more than twenty years. His published research (Snow 1975, 1977) has shown that pottery made with the same paddle occurs on different sites in the region. Some of the sites are found on the floodplain and others on oak-hickory sand ridges, suggesting a seasonal pattern of site utilization. In addition, designs identical to those found at Kolomoki and Fairchild's Landing (more than 160 kilometers distant) have been recognized by Snow.

More recently, Jim Stoltman (Chapter 9 herein) has been conducting microscopic analysis of the paste of selected Swift Creek sherds in an attempt to determine whether sherds with identical paddle characteristics (as determined by Frankie Snow) but found at different sites represent movement of the pottery or of the paddle used to create the stamped design. Implications of this research include strengthening hypotheses concerning seasonal movement of people and trade as possible explanations for the distribution of Swift Creek ceramics. Stoltman and Snow's paper (Chapter 9 herein) presented at the 1993 Lamar Institute Conference on Swift Creek reminded me of a research project that was conducted more than twenty years ago involving neutron activation analysis of ceramics from Mandeville and the Swift Creek site.

The research project, as it was conceived in 1975, was an attempt to show that the reliability of neutron activation test results could be increased by the careful screening of the archaeological samples prior to the actual neutron activation process. Having recently completed both my dissertation on the Mandeville site (B. A. Smith 1975) and the analysis of the Swift Creek site ceramics (Kelly and Smith 1975), I attempted to select artifacts that should be local to each site along with others (from Mandeville) that probably were not local to that site. Other artifacts were also included in the sample, as will be described later. This hypothesis, that the careful screening of archaeological samples should increase the probability that the trace element patterns of artifacts manufactured from a common clay source and artifacts manufactured in different regions would be so identified by the neutron activation method, was not conclusively demonstrated. With that rather disappointing result the project data were put away, even forgotten, until now. The following are some edited excerpts from a paper that described this research project (Smith, Noakes, and Spaulding 1976).

Neutron activation analysis of ceramic artifacts is based on the theory that impurities in the form of trace elements occur in clays and that the percentage composition of these various trace elements in pottery will mirror that of the source clays. These trace elements frequently occur in small quantity, such as parts per million. Neutron activation is an analytical process with the necessary sensitivity to accurately detect the presence of such elements.

The Sample

Seventy-five items (sherds and figurines) were included in the neutron activation analysis (Table 8-1). Of these, forty-seven were from Mandeville (9CY1), twenty were from the Swift Creek site (9BI3), six were from the Block-Sterns site (8LE148), and two were miscellaneous sherds (one from northern Georgia and one from the Georgia coast).

Mandeville was a multicomponent site, the major occupation of which was by a Middle Woodland Hopewell-related group that manufactured Early Swift Creek and associated ceramics. Mound A was a flat-topped occupational mound measuring approximately $70 \times 50 \times 4$ meters. The uppermost 1.2 meters was a Mississippian cap added to the mound several hundred years after the Middle Woodland occupation. The Middle Woodland portion, from which most of the samples used in this study were taken, was composed of a series of four midden layers separated by three fill layers. Mound B was a conical burial mound containing such diagnostic Hopewellian items as copper-covered earspools and panpipes, a clay human figurine, and clay platform pipes. Mound B was contemporary with the Middle Woodland portion of Mound A (B. A. Smith 1975).

Forty-seven of the seventy-five artifacts used in this project were from the Mandeville site. Nineteen of the samples were taken from Feature 28, a brown sand layer associated with the first mound-building activity (Layer IA) in Mound A. Thirteen samples came from Feature 29 in Layer IV, the last of the Middle Woodland midden layers in Mound A. Eight samples were figurine fragments from various proveniences, including Mounds A and B

Table 8-1. Artifacts Used for Neutron Activation Analysis

Sample	Site	Provenience	Surface Finish
1	9BI3	Layer 4	Indeterminate
2	9BI3	Layer 4	Swift Creek Complicated Stamped
3	9BI3	Layer 4	Swift Creek Complicated Stamped
4	9BI3	Layer 4	Plain
5	9BI3	Layer 4	Swift Creek Complicated Stamped
6	9BI3	Layer 4	Plain
7	9BI3	Layer 4	Swift Creek Complicated Stamped
8	9BI3	Layer 4	Plain
9	9BI3	Layer 4	Plain
10	9BI3	Layer 4	Swift Creek Complicated Stamped
11	9BI3	Layer 4	Plain
12	9BI3	Layer 4	Swift Creek Complicated Stamped
13	9BI3	Layer 4	Fiber-tempered plain
14	9BI3	Layer 4	Plain
15	9BI3	Layer 4	Plain
16	9BI3	Layer 4	Plain
17	9BI3	Layer 4	Plain
18	9BI3	Layer 4	Swift Creek Complicated Stamped
19	9BI3	Layer 4	Plain
20	9BI3	Layer 4	Swift Creek Complicated Stamped
21	9CY1	Mound A, F28	Plain
22	9CY1	Mound A, F28	West Florida Cordmarked
23	9CY1	Mound A, F28	Crooked River Complicated Stamped
24	9CY1	Mound A, F28	Plain
25	9CY1	Mound A, F28	Plain, tetrapod
26	9CY1	Mound A, F28	Gulf Check Stamped
27	9CY1	Mound A, F28	Simple stamped
28	9CY1	Mound A, F28	Swift Creek Complicated Stamped
29	9CY1	Mound A, F28	Polished plain
30	9CY1	Mound A, F28	Plain, T-rim
31	9CY1	Mound A, F28	St. Andrews Complicated Stamped
32	9CY1	Mound A, F28	Simple stamped
33	9CY1	Mound A, F28	Swift Creek Complicated Stamped
34	9CY1	Mound A, F28	Indeterminate
35	9CY1	Mound A, F28	Plain
36	9CY1	Mound A, F28	Plain
37	9CY1	Mound A, F28	Simple stamped
38	9CY1	Mound A, F28	Gulf Check Stamped
39	9CY1	Mound A, F28	Crooked River Complicated Stamped
40	9CY1	Mound A, 40-50L0	Cord-marked rim
41	9CY1	Layer I, 0-6"	Cord-marked middle

continued on next page

Table 8-1, continued

42	9CY1	Layer I, 0-6"	Cord-marked base
43	9CY1	Mound A, Trench 4	Red filmed
44	9CY1	Mound A, F29	Swift Creek Complicated Stamped
45	9CY1	Mound A, F29	Swift Creek Complicated Stamped
46	9CY1	Mound A, F29	Swift Creek Complicated Stamped
47	9CY1	Mound A, F29	Crooked River Complicated Stamped
48	9CY1	Mound A, F29	Plain
49	9CY1	Mound A, F29	Swift Creek Complicated Stamped
50	9CY1	Mound A, F29	Rectilinear Complicated Stamped
51	9CY1	Mound A, F29	Swift Creek Complicated Stamped
52	9CY1	Mound A, F29	Plain
53	9CY1	Mound A, F29	Swift Creek Complicated Stamped
54	9CY1	Mound A, F29	Swift Creek Complicated Stamped
55	9CY1	Mound A, F29	Swift Creek Complicated Stamped
56	9CY1	Mound A, F29	Swift Creek Complicated Stamped
57	Ga. Coast		Deptford Linear Check Stamped
58	9CK62		Cartersville Check Stamped
59	9CY1	Unknown	Simple stamped
60	9CY1	Unknown	Simple stamped/brushed
61	9CY1	Unknown	Simple stamped
62	8LE148	Mound	Plain, scalloped rim
63	8LE148		Plain
64	8LE148		Plain
65	8LE148		Gulf Check Stamped
66	8LE148		Swift Creek Complicated Stamped
67	8LE148		Figurine
68	9CY1	Mound A, Layer II	Figurine, head
69	9CY1	Spring	Figurine, turban
70	9CY1	Village	Figurine, female
71	9CY1	Mound B, F10	Figurine, female
72	9CY1	Mound A, 30L0, 96-102"	Figurine, leg
73	9CY1	Mound A, Layer IA	Figurine, Fragment 8610
74	9CY1	Mound A, Layer IA	Figurine, female fragment
75	9CY1	Mound A, Layer IA	Figurine, foot

and the village area between the two mounds. The remaining seven samples were taken from various portions of Mound A.

The Swift Creek site was a mound and village site in central Georgia. The mound was structurally similar to Mound A at Mandeville in that it was apparently constructed of midden layers separated by fill layers. The midden layers were not as thick as those at Mandeville, however, and the Swift Creek mound was apparently circular, not rectangular. The site is the type site for Swift Creek Complicated Stamped ceramics and Early to Late Swift Creek is represented in a stratigraphic sequence in the mound. All twenty samples from this site were taken from Midden Layer 4 (counting from the bottom from a total of six occupation levels) (Kelly and Smith 1975). It was, and still is, my belief, based on subjective knowledge of the ceramics from both sites, that the Mandeville site was occupied somewhat earlier than the Swift Creek site and that contact between the two was not likely to have occurred; thus, the neutron activation analysis should have revealed some distinctive differences between the two pottery samples.

Several samples came from the Block-Sterns site near Tallahassee, Florida (see Chapter 13 herein). They were included in this study because artifacts recovered during the 1973 excavations of the site (see Chapter 13 herein) suggested that it was probably contemporary with the Middle Woodland component at Mandeville.

Eight of the Mandeville artifacts and one of the Block-Sterns artifacts were figurines. Sample 71 was a figurine that was recovered from a feature in the burial mound at Mandeville. It bears a striking resemblance to Hope-wellian figurines from the Knight mound in Illinois. A charcoal sample from the feature in which the artifact was found was radiocarbon dated at A.D. 250. Other Mandeville figurine fragments were recovered from Mound A and the village area. The Block-Sterns figurine is similar in appearance to Sample 68 and it was this similarity that led to the inclusion of the Block-Sterns artifacts in the study.

Samples 40, 41, and 42 were taken from different portions of a single cord-marked vessel from Mandeville.

Sample Preparation

The samples were prepared as follows: a small piece was cut from each potsherd with a diamond cutting saw. All exterior surfaces were removed and the pieces were rubbed against a Carborundum stone to remove possible brass particles picked up from the saw. They were then leached at least twenty-four hours in distilled water to remove soluble salts and then allowed to air dry. The pieces were broken so that all were of uniform size, weighing approximately 200 milligrams each, and individually wrapped in aluminum foil.

The figurines were handled somewhat differently. A tungsten-carbide drill was used to collect approximately 200 milligrams of powdered clay. The surface material was discarded and the powdered clay was sealed in individual plastic vials, which were also wrapped in aluminum foil.

Seven standard rock samples (USGA) were also sealed in plastic vials and wrapped in aluminum foil.

Irradiation and Counting

The samples and the standards were irradiated at the Georgia Institute of Technology Research Reactor for seven hours at a flux of 5×10^{13} neutrons per square centimeter per second. After seven days of decay, they were transported back to the Geochronology Lab (now the Center for Applied Isotope Studies) at the University of Georgia where targeted elements were counted for 100 seconds using a 9-percent lithium-drifted germanium (Ge-Li) detector and a 4096 computer-based multichannel analyzer.

Results and Discussion

Eight trace elements were identified for analysis: scandium, chromium, iron, cobalt, lanthanum, cerium, samarium, and ytterbium. The elements were plotted on log-graph paper, creating scattergrams showing the proportion of these elements in each artifact. Figures 8-1 through 8-3 show these scattergrams. The proportions are given in parts per million for all elements except iron, which is given as a percentage.

The first of these scattergrams is of scandium (Figure 8-1). The top group represents the Swift Creek sample, the middle group is the Mandeville sample, and the bottom group is a mixed sample, including the Block-Sterns sherds, the miscellaneous sherds, and all of the figurines. The same groupings are shown on all of the element graphs (Figures 8-1, 8-2, and 8-3).

Within each of these three groups, the elements tend to cluster. It should be expected that the middle and bottom groups show similar clustering since several of the specimens in the bottom group are Mandeville figurines. Some

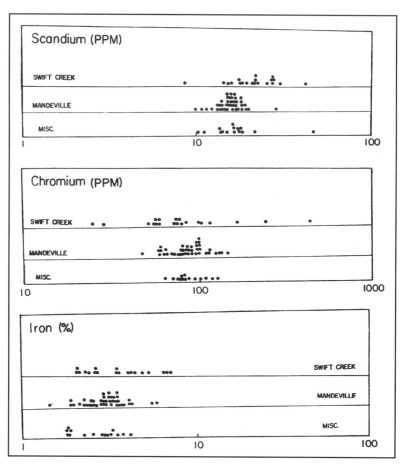

Figure 8-1. Scatterplot of scandium, chromium, and iron in neutron activation analysis of Swift Creek sherds.

differences do show up between the Swift Creek and Mandeville sites, but they are not as distinctive as had been anticipated. It seems likely that these two samples are indicating the homogeneity of Coastal Plain clays, at least within the state of Georgia. The one northern Georgia sherd (Sample 58) is isolated on a couple of the scattergrams (scandium and samarium), suggesting that there may be more distinctive differences between Piedmont and Coastal Plain clays than there are for clays from within the Coastal Plain.

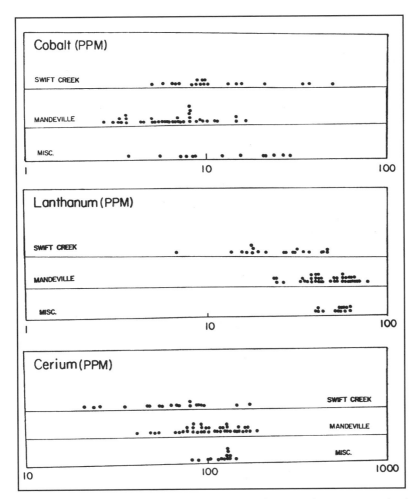

Figure 8-2. Scatterplot of cobalt, lanthanum, and cerium in neutron activation analysis of Swift Creek sherds.

The hypothesis with which this study was begun, that the careful screening of archaeological samples should increase the probability that the trace element patterns of artifacts manufactured from a common clay source and artifacts manufactured in different regions would be so identified by the neutron activation method, was not conclusively demonstrated; however, neither was it necessarily invalidated. It is possible that the nature of the source clays

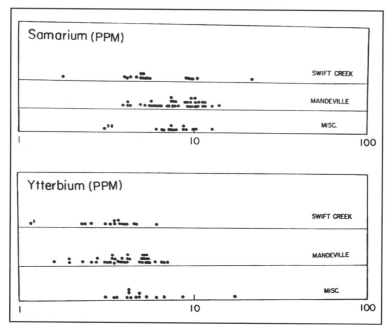

Figure 8-3. Scatterplot of samarium and ytterbium in neutron activation analysis of Swift Creek sherds.

(Coastal Plain) for the sites used in this study obscured the trace element pattern distinctions.

This, then, was the status of the project in 1976. Returning to the data in 1993, I asked Carol Pierannunzi (professor of political science at Kennesaw State College) to conduct various statistical analyses, this time to see whether a hypothesis of trade to account for the distribution of at least some Swift Creek ceramics could be supported. For purposes of this study, only four of the original eight trace elements—scandium, chromium, iron, and cobalt—were included.

I first divided the seventy-five samples into seven groups as follows: (1) Swift Creek (9BI3); (2) Mandeville (9CY1), Feature 28; (3) Block-Sterns (8LE148); (4) 9CK62; (5) miscellaneous; (6) Mandeville (9CY1), Feature 29; and (7) Mandeville (9CY1) figurines. Groups 4 and 5 were later combined since they represented so few artifacts (Samples 57 through 61).

I began by briefly reconsidering the original question: could significant differences be identified among the sites? The statistical analysis of the four trace elements yielded basically the same conclusion as had been reached originally: there is no significant difference among the levels of minerals; thus, what is found at one site is not significantly different from what is found at other sites. Next, I examined means and standard deviations of the elements for each of the above-listed groups individually and found very little of note. Sample 5 from the Swift Creek site was shown to be distinctive in terms of scandium and Sample 29 from Feature 28 at Mandeville was found to be distinctive in terms of iron.

Cluster analysis provided some of the more interesting suggestions about the samples. Cluster analysis compares each artifact with all others in terms of the proportions of the four trace elements and groups the artifacts accordingly. Five clusters were generated (Table 8-2). Clusters 1, 2, and 3 contain samples from both Swift Creek and Mandeville and Clusters 1 and 3 contain samples from Swift Creek, Mandeville, and Block-Sterns. This would seem to support the conclusion reached earlier concerning homogeneity of Coastal Plain clays.

Cluster 4 consisted of only one case, Sample 5, a Swift Creek Complicated Stamped sherd from the Swift Creek site. This is the same artifact that was found to be unique in terms of scandium in the examination of means and standard deviations of the elements. Looking back over the scattergrams, Sample 5 also separates out for ytterbium and lanthanum. It seems likely, therefore, that this particular sherd represents a vessel imported into the Swift Creek site.

Cluster 5 included eight specimens from Mandeville and one from Block-Sterns.

Of interest was the grouping of the figurines (Figures 8-4 and 8-5). Of the eight Mandeville figurines, five appeared in Group 1 and three in Group 2. The Block-Sterns figurine appeared in Group 3. One of the three figurines in Group 2 (Sample 71) was the female figurine from the burial mound at Mandeville. As previously described, this figurine is very similar to Hopewellian figurines illustrated from the Knight mound in Illinois; thus, a nonlocal origin for this artifact would not be unexpected.

The groupings of Samples 40, 41, and 42 were interesting also. These three samples were taken from three sections of a partially restored cordmarked vessel. Sample 40 was taken from the rim, 41 from the mid-portion

Table 8-2. Groups Generated by Cluster Analysis

Group	Sample	Site	Decoration
1	1	9BI3	Indeterminate
1	7	9BI3	Swift Creek Complicated Stamped
1	10	9BI3	Swift Creek Complicated Stamped
1	12	9BI3	Swift Creek Complicated Stamped
1	14	9BI3	Plain
1	15	9BI3	Plain
1	17	9BI3	Plain
1	18	9BI3	Swift Creek Complicated Stamped
1	21	9CY1	Plain
1	23	9CY1	Crooked River Complicated Stamped
1	24	9CY1	Plain
1	25	9CY1	Plain, tetrapod
1	33	9CY1	Swift Creek Complicated Stamped
1	49	9CY1	Swift Creek Complicated Stamped
1	50	9CY1	Rectilinear Complicated Stamped
1	55	9CY1	Swift Creek Complicated Stamped
1	58	9CK62	Cartersville Check Stamped
1	60	9CY1	Simple stamped/brushed
1	62	8LE148	Plain, scalloped rim
1	63	8LE148	Plain
1	65	8LE148	Gulf Check Stamped
1	68·	9CY1	Figurine, head
1	69	9CY1	Figurine, turban
1	72	9CY1	Figurine, leg
1	74	9CY1	Figurine, female fragment
1	75	9CY1	Figurine, foot
2	2	9BI3	Swift Creek Complicated Stamped
2	3	9BI3	Swift Creek Complicated Stamped
2	6	9BI3	Plain
2	9	9BI3	Plain
2	11	9BI3	Plain
2	13	9BI3	Fiber-tempered plain
2	20	9BI3	Swift Creek Complicated Stamped
2	31	9CY1	St. Andrews Complicated Stamped
2	32	9CY1	Simple stamped
2	34	9CY1	Indeterminate
2	35	9CY1	Plain
2	37	9CY1	Simple stamped
2	38	9CY1	Gulf Check Stamped
2	42	9CY1	Cord-marked base
2	53	9CY1	Swift Creek Complicated Stamped

continued on next page

Table 8-2, continued

2	70	9CY1	Figurine, female
2	71	9CY1	Figurine, female
2	73	9CY1	Figurine, Fragment 8610
3	4	9BI3	Plain
3	8	9BI3	Plain
3	16	9BI3	Plain
3	19	9BI3	Plain
3	22	9CY1	West Florida Cordmarked
3	26	9CY1	Gulf Check Stamped
3	27	9CY1	Simple stamped
3	28	9CY1	Swift Creek Complicated Stamped
3	39	9CY1	Crooked River Complicated Stamped
3	40	9CY1	Cord-marked rim
3	41	9CY1	Cord-marked middle
3	43	9CY1	Red filmed
3	46	9CY1	Swift Creek Complicated Stamped
3	47	9CY1	Crooked River Complicated Stamped
3	48	9CY1	Plain
3	51	9CY1	Swift Creek Complicated Stamped
3	52	9CY1	Plain
3	56	9CY1	Swift Creek Complicated Stamped
3	57	Ga. Coast	Deptford Linear Check Stamped
3	64	8LE148	Plain
3	67	8LE148	Figurine
4	5	9BI3	Swift Creek Complicated Stamped
5	29	9CY1	Polished plain
5	30	9CY1	Plain, T-rim
5	36	9CY1	Plain
5	44	9CY1	Swift Creek Complicated Stamped
5	45	9CY1	Swift Creek Complicated Stamped
5	54	9CY1	Swift Creek Complicated Stamped
5	59	9CY1	Simple stamped
5	61	9CY1	Simple stamped
5	66	8LE148	Swift Creek Complicated Stamped

of the vessel, and 42 from the base of the vessel. Samples 40 and 41 appeared in Group 3 and Sample 42 appeared in Group 2 in the cluster analysis. As can be seen in Figure 8-6, there are surface color differences that suggest differences in firing temperature. This suggests that differences in firing temperature might affect the trace element distribution. Alternatively, the base

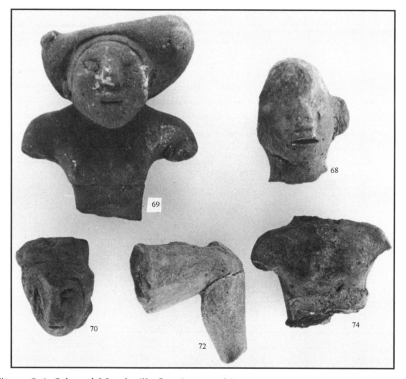

Figure 8-4. Selected Mandeville figurines used in neutron activation analysis.

would have been in closest proximity to fire if the vessel was used in cooking, and this heat, again, might have affected the trace element distribution. If either of these explanations is valid, a real problem with trace element analysis would be indicated.

Four sherds had been included in the original study because they were believed to definitely be nonlocal to either Mandeville or Swift Creek. Sample 29 was a polished plain sherd and Sample 43 was red filmed. Both of these sherds, found at Mandeville, were probably trade items from the Santa Rosa–Swift Creek complex on the Florida Gulf Coast; however, only the polished plain sherd stood out in any way. It was shown to be unique in terms of iron in the examination of means and standard deviations of the elements. Sample 57 was a Deptford Linear Check Stamped sherd from the Georgia coast and Sample 58 was a Cartersville Check Stamped sherd from site 9CK62 in northwestern Georgia. As has already been described, this artifact is isolated

Figure 8-5. Figurine from Mound B, Mandeville, used in neutron activation analysis.

on the scattergrams for scandium and samarium. Otherwise, neither of these two sherds appeared to be especially distinctive.

Conclusion

The various statistical analyses of the data from the neutron activation analysis of selected ceramic artifacts from the Mandeville and Swift Creek sites offer limited support to a hypothesis of trade as one of the cultural processes involved in the distribution of Swift Creek ceramics. At least one sherd (Sample 5) from Swift Creek and one (Sample 29) from Mandeville

Figure 8-6. Cord-marked vessel from Mandeville used in neutron activation analysis.

may have been trade items. Also, the three Mandeville figurines that clustered in Group 2, including the complete specimen (Sample 71) found in the burial mound, may have been nonlocal artifacts.

One factor that may limit the results in the case of this particular set of data is that no clay samples from the vicinity of the two main sites were included in the study. Any future project involving neutron activation analysis of ceramics to test hypotheses about trade should certainly include local clay samples. At the very least, inclusion of such samples for Coastal Plain Swift Creek sites should resolve the question about the overall homogeneity of Coastal Plain soils with which the original research project ended. In addition, the questionable result of the cluster analysis involving the three samples from a single cord-marked vessel (Samples 40, 41, and 42) limits any conclusions based on this study.

Despite these limitations, it is hoped that this study has demonstrated that neutron activation analysis does have the potential to yield valuable insight into the cultural processes at work as archaeologists attempt to unravel the prehistoric past.

Acknowledgments

This chapter was possible only because of the assistance of several people: Carol Pierannunzi (professor of political science at Kennesaw State College) and Robin Acree (computer lab assistant at Kennesaw State College), both of whom assisted with the statistical analyses; Donald F. Smith, who prepared the scattergrams used in the original paper; John E. Noakes (director, Center for Applied Isotope Studies, University of Georgia), who sponsored the original study; and James D. Spaulding (Center for Applied Isotope Studies), who provided technical help with the original project.

Cultural Interaction within Swift Creek Society
People, Pots, and Paddles

James B. Stoltman and Frankie Snow

Swift Creek Complicated Stamped ceramics are special (Anonymous 1939). Not only are the designs that were impressed into their surfaces from elaborately carved wooden paddles aesthetically pleasing to almost anyone's eyes, but the designs are unusually varied and complex as well (see Figure 9-1). While the former feature allows one to enjoy studying them today, it is the latter characteristic that renders them a potentially rich reservoir of information about the social behavior of their makers (Broyles 1968).

For more than twenty-five years, Frankie Snow (Snow 1975, 1993; Snow and Stephenson 1993) has been systematically analyzing the design repertoire of Swift Creek potters in south-central Georgia. His research has identified numerous designs that are shared between Swift Creek sites, some as far apart as 190 kilometers. In addition to design sharing, however, his meticulous observations and measurements of paddle impressions have led to the identification of numerous instances of two or more sites possessing pottery vessels impressed with the same paddle.

It was against this background a few years ago that our conversations led to the idea of using petrographic analysis of complicated stamped ceramics as an independent line of evidence to evaluate whether it was paddles or pots that were being circulated among the Swift Creek peoples of central Georgia. Accordingly, Snow selected a series of sherds from vessels that he had analyzed and whose contexts and/or designs were known. These sherds,

Figure 9-1. Major carved paddle-stamped designs from sherds used in petrographic analysis.

presently totaling sixty-nine from eleven sites (Figure 9-2), were forwarded to Stoltman for thin sectioning. Within this sample were twenty-two vessels that had been identified by Snow as possessing one of the distinctive designs whose occurrence had been documented at two or more sites (Figure 9-1). The remaining forty-seven vessels, all also of the type Swift Creek Complicated Stamped, were included in the petrographic analysis to provide a basis for identifying the physical characteristics, and their ranges of variation, of the locally produced ceramics from each site. As can be seen from Table 9-1, the number of vessels thin sectioned from each site is uneven. In the cases of only two sites, Hartford and Milamo, are the samples large enough to

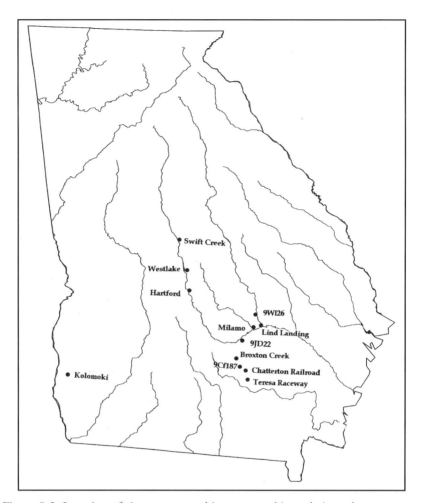

Figure 9-2. Location of sites represented in petrographic analysis study.

offer some hope of representativeness. Thus, it is these sites that will receive the greatest emphasis in the discussion to follow.

In evaluating the results of this study it is important to appreciate that the design and petrographic analyses were conducted completely independently of one another. All sherds were initially selected by Snow and the motifs identified before the sherds were forwarded to Stoltman. On receipt of the sherds, Stoltman assigned them thin-section numbers and conducted

Table 9-1. Numbers of Vessels per Site Analyzed Petrographically along with Temper Class Frequencies

		I--------------------Temper--------------------I					
Site	**N**	**Sand**	**Grit 1**	**Grit 2**	**Grit 3**	**Grit 4**	**Grit 5**
Westlake	5	2	1	1		1	
Hartford	19	8	3	3	1	4	
Milamo	15	14		1			
9WL26	1		1				
Lind Landing	6	6					
9JD22	1						1
Chatterton Railroad	2	2					
9CF187	1	1					
Teresa Raceway	6	5				1	
Broxton Creek	7	6				1	
Kolomoki	6	6					
Totals	69	50	5	5	1	7	1

all subsequent analyses on the basis of those numbers only, which ensured that the motif and, in most cases, even the site remained unknown until all the petrographic data were finally tabulated.

Our basic goal in this study was to employ the physical characterization of the sherds provided by the petrographic analyses to evaluate the between-site distribution of seven different Swift Creek paddle-stamped designs by ascertaining, if possible, whether it was the pots or the paddles that had circulated. If vessels were manufactured at one site and redistributed to other sites in finished form, it is our expectation that such vessels will constitute a homogeneous group that will physically resemble locally produced vessels at the production center while at the same time being physically distinct from the locally produced vessels at the recipient sites. On the ternary graphs used in this study to provide a visual representation of the data this expectation will be manifest by clustering of the data from vessels that possess the same design within the range of variation of only one of the sites, the presumed production center. By contrast, if paddles moved from site to site, vessels with identical designs at two or more sites will not constitute a physically homogeneous group or cluster but will resemble the locally produced ceramics at the respective sites at which they were found. For ease of reference, we shall refer to these as clustered versus dispersed distributions, respectively, when discussing the ternary plots below.

To operationalize these expectations it is first necessary to define the essential physical properties that characterize the local ceramic products of each of the sites included in the analysis. The best way to do this is to have samples of local clay-rich sediments from each site for use as standards against which to compare the observed paste properties of the vessels themselves. Three lumps of what are presumed to be potters' clay recovered at the Milamo site and alluvium collected from the nearby Ocmulgee River valley at Hartford are the only local soil samples presently available for this study. An alternative approach to defining the physical properties of local ceramics is to analyze petrographically a representative sample of demonstrably local sherds from each site for comparison with the presumed trade vessels. This approach has important limitations—such as uncertainty over what constitutes a representative sample, how to be certain that only local vessels are included in each site's sample, and how to interpret overlapping ranges of variation—but at least it provides an explicit matrix of data against which competing hypotheses can be evaluated, and thus it provides a valuable complement to whatever local soils data are available.

Thin sections from the sixty-nine Swift Creek Complicated Stamped vessels were analyzed using procedures described by Stoltman (1989, 1991), with one modification. Because the majority of the vessels (fifty of sixty-nine) were tempered with sand (Figures 9-3 and 9-4), that is, preponderantly monocrystalline grains of quartz with minor amounts of feldspars and mica also present, it was impossible to distinguish human additives (temper) objectively from natural inclusions (sand). Therefore, instead of recording separate paste and body indices for each vessel, a single combined Bulk Composition index was used, which could then be employed for both sand-tempered and grit-tempered vessels. This quantitative index was recorded on ternary graphs with the following values at the poles: (1) Matrix = percent clay, (2) Silt = percent mineral grains of silt size, that is, of less than 0.0625 millimeters in all dimensions, and (3) Sand and Gravel = percent mineral grains 0.0625 millimeters or larger in at least one dimension. For each sand/gravel grain counted the mineral species was determined and the size was recorded

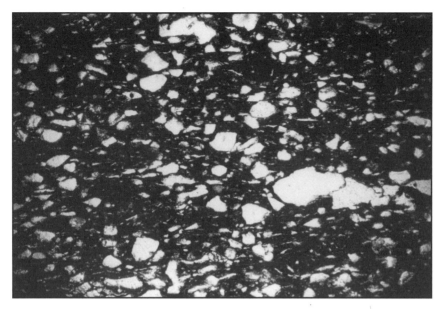

Figure 9-3. Photomicrograph of finely sand-tempered Vessel 9-69 from Milamo viewed in plane-polarized light at 10 times magnification. Long dimension of the largest mineral grain is 0.575 millimeters. Temper is composed mostly of fine, monocrystalline grains of quartz. The size index of this vessel is 1.03.

in terms of the following ordinal scale values: 1 = fine sand (0.0625 to 0.249 millimeters); 2 = medium sand (0.25 to 0.499 millimeters); 3 = coarse sand (0.50 to 0.99 millimeters); 4 = very coarse sand (1.0 to 1.99 millimeters); and 5 = gravel (> 2.0 millimeters).

On the basis of this ordinal scale, a bulk sand/gravel size index was determined for each vessel. This index was calculated by multiplying the number of grains per class by the weighted value of each class, summing these totals, and then dividing by the total number of grains counted per vessel. The value of this index for each vessel ranges between 1 and 5.

The Hartford Site

We begin discussion of the results of the petrographic analyses with the Hartford site (9PU1). As reported by Snow (1993) and Snow and Stephenson (1993), Hartford was a substantial Early to Middle Swift Creek

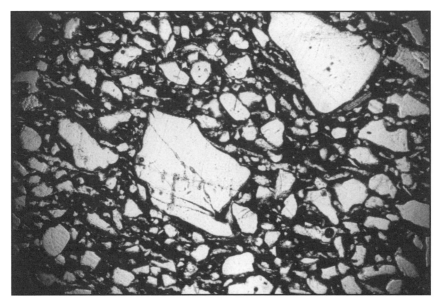

Figure 9-4. Photomicrograph of Vessel 9-70 from Kolomoki viewed in plane-polar-ized light at 10 times magnification. Long dimension of the longest grain measures 0.925 millimeters. Temper is coarse sand, composed mostly of monocrystalline grains of quartz. The size index for this vessel is 1.59.

community located along the Ocmulgee River in Pulaski County less than 80 kilometers downstream from Macon (Figure 9-2). Two mounds were for-merly present at the site, along with evidence for at least two episodes of Swift Creek occupation, the earlier referred to as the submound midden and the later as the village. As evidenced by the high percentage of shared designs with other Swift Creek sites—so far Snow (Snow and Stephenson 1993:3) has recorded twenty-one designs from the submound midden at thirteen other sites and sixteen designs from the Hartford village at twenty-one other sites—it is evident that the occupants of the Hartford site were intensively interacting with their Swift Creek neighbors throughout the site's duration.

Nineteen vessels from the Hartford site have thus far been subjected to petrographic analysis; eleven of these vessels are grit tempered and eight are sand tempered. The results of the petrographic analyses of these vessels and the local clay are summarized in Table 9-2 and presented graphically in Fig-ure 9-5.

Table 9-2. Bulk Composition and Size Indices for Sand-and-Gravel Inclusions for the Nineteen Vessels from Hartford (Means and Standard Deviations Recorded Separately for Sand- and Grit-Tempered Vessels)

Vessel	Matrix %	Silt %	Sa./Gr. %	Size Index	Temper
9-61	63	3	34	2.10	Grit 1
9-62	57	4	39	1.97	Grit 3
9-63	58	3	39	2.00	Grit 2
9-64	67	5	28	2.63	Grit 2
9-65	53	4	43	2.29	Grit 4
9-67	63	3	34	2.63	Grit 2
9-68	56	7	37	1.97	Grit 1
9-73	62	4	34	2.09	Grit 1
9-75	53	3	44	2.31	Grit 4
9-114	69	3	28	2.06	Grit 4
9-138	62	2	36	2.19	Grit 4
Means (11)	60.3	3.7	36.0	2.20	
S. D.	5.3	1.4	5.2	0.24	
9-66	68	2	30	1.46	Sand
9-81	82	5	13	1.32	Sand
9-137	69	5	26	2.15	Sand
9-143	72	4	24	1.56	Sand
9-144	77	4	19	1.49	Sand
9-146	81	4	15	1.78	Sand
9-147	68	1	31	1.75	Sand
9-148	77	3	20	1.79	Sand
Means (8)	74.25	3.5	22.25	1.66	
S. D.	5.8	1.4	6.6	0.26	
Local clay	64	3	33	2.04	

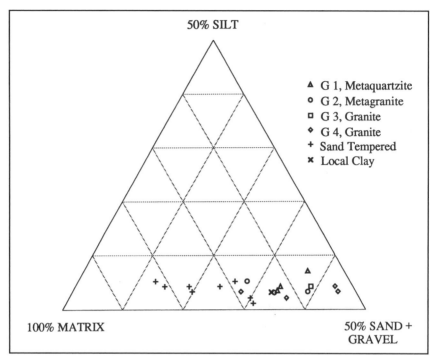

Figure 9-5. Ternary graph showing bulk composition of nineteen Hartford vessels by temper class. *G*, Grit.

On the basis of the data presented in Table 9-2 and Figure 9-5, a number of observations concerning ceramics from the Hartford site may be offered. Interestingly, two different temper types occur, grit (represented by four subtypes) and sand. Both temper types are so well represented at the site that the local production of both seems likely. Confirmation of this inference is lacking, however, for the one local clay sample analyzed resembles none of the vessels so far analyzed from the site (it lacks grit altogether and is distinctly sandier than any of the sand-tempered vessels; see Figure 9-5).

It is possible that grit temper was preferentially used during the early (submound midden) occupation, because eight of the eleven grit-tempered vessels in the thin-section sample derive from that component. Expressed another way, 67 percent of the vessels analyzed from the submound midden (eight of twelve) are grit tempered versus 43 percent (three of seven) from the village. Until a larger sample of local vessels has been analyzed, this suggested temporal trend should be regarded as a working hypothesis in need of further confirmation.

What is especially noteworthy about the Hartford sample—remember that the sole criterion for selecting these vessels was the nature of their stamped designs—is that the majority (eleven of nineteen) was grit tempered. The grit-tempered sample from Hartford exceeds the total number of grit-tempered vessels from the remaining ten sites combined: only eight of forty-seven vessels from the latter sites have grit temper. Moreover, with the exception of Westlake (where three of five vessels have grit temper), no site has more than one grit-tempered vessel. Such a distribution pattern suggests geographically limited production and, in light of the close proximity of the Hartford and Westlake sites both to one another and to the Piedmont (Figure 9-2), the ultimate source of the metamorphic, crystalline rocks used as grit temper.

Four grit temper subtypes were recognized in the Hartford sample. Grit 1, observed in three vessels, is a metaquartzite. It is represented primarily by angular grains of polycrystalline quartz that is deformed, has undulose extinction, and shows other such signs of metamorphic alteration (Figure 9-6). By contrast, Grit 2, observed in three vessels, is a rock of granitic composition that has undergone considerable alteration (Figure 9-7). Unlike mineral inclusions in Grit 1 vessels, among which feldspars are observed in fewer than 12 percent of the grains counted, more than 50 percent of the mineral grains counted in Grit 2 vessels contain altered feldspars. Grit 3 was observed in only one vessel. Its primary constituent is polycrystalline quartz that shows distinctive fracturing, but a few polymineralic grains containing combinations of quartz, feldspar, and amphibole are also present. Notably, however, the feldspars do not display the extensive alteration of Grit 2. A fourth grit type (Grit 4) was observed in four vessels. It is granitic in composition, containing polycrystalline quartz (with sutured boundaries and undulose extinction) along with "fissured" feldspars and green amphibole. At the present it is unknown whether the metamorphic rocks observed in the Hartford vessels were obtained directly from bedrock sources (which would have involved either exchange with peoples resident on the Piedmont or procurement trips to the Piedmont by Hartford residents) or were collected locally in outwash

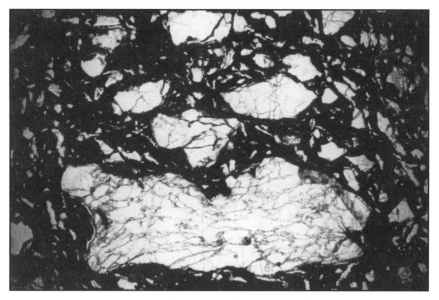

Figure 9-6. Photomicrograph of Vessel 9-61 from the Hartford site viewed in plane-polarized light at 10 times magnification. Temper is metaquartzite, or Grit 1. Largest grain measures 2.5 millimeters; it is composed of multiple grains of deformed quartz. Size index for the mineral inclusions of this vessel is 2.10.

deposits. If the alluvial clay sample that we collected from the nearby Ocmulgee Valley is at all representative of local resources, the latter alternative must be considered improbable, because the sand/gravel fraction of this sample (33 percent by volume; Table 9-2 and Figure 9-5) included none of the metamorphic rock types observed in the grit-tempered vessels.

Two additional features of the vessels from the Hartford site merit emphasis. First, for the grit-tempered vessels, the amount of mineral inclusions in the sand/gravel size range normally exceeds 30 percent by volume (the mean for the eleven grit-tempered vessels is 36.0 ± 5.2 percent; Table 9-2), whereas the comparable value for the eight sand-tempered vessels is less than 25 percent (mean = 22.25 ± 6.6 percent; Table 9-2). Second, the mean size index of sand and larger inclusions is much higher for the eleven grit-tempered vessels (mean = 2.20 ± 0.24 percent) in contrast to that of the eight sand-tempered vessels (1.66 ± 0.26 percent; Table 9-2). Of course, the larger size of grit as opposed to sand temper may be a mechanical correlate of

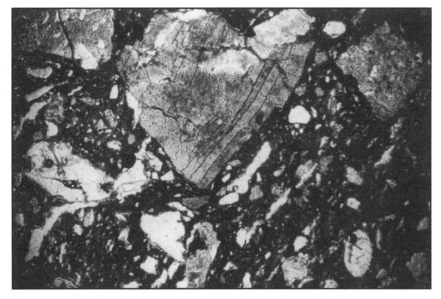

Figure 9-7. Photomicrograph of Vessel 9-64 from the Hartford site viewed in plane-polarized light at 10 times magnification. Temper is metagranite, or Grit 2. Largest grain has a maximum dimension of 1.625 millimeters. It is composed of quartz (clear areas of grain) and heavily altered feldspar (dark area of grain). The size index for this vessel is 2.63.

crushing hard rocks for temper as opposed to selecting finer, natural sands. Nevertheless, the size differential between grit and sand tempers is potentially significant, for it may reflect not simply resource availability but also functional considerations on the part of the potters.

Combining the foregoing petrographic observations with the design analyses of Snow, we are now in a position to consider the issue of whether paddles or pots were being circulated between Hartford and other Swift Creek sites. The strongest case for the local production and subsequent intersite exchange of ceramic vessels occurs when identical designs and identical pastes are observed among ceramic vessels from two or more sites. This appears to be the case for the four vessels that have the box-center motif (Figure 9-1) selected by Snow for thin-section analysis (see also Snow 1993:figure 3, *lower right*). These four vessels come from four separate sites: (1) the Westlake site in Twiggs County about 30 kilometers upstream from

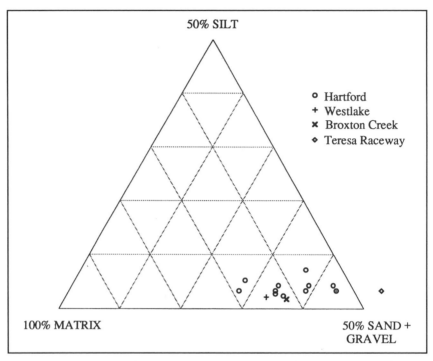

Figure 9-8. Ternary graph showing bulk composition of the eleven grit-tempered vessels from Hartford versus vessels with the box-center design from the Broxton Creek, Teresa Raceway, and Westlake sites. *Dotted circle* denotes the Hartford vessel with the box-center design.

Hartford on the Ocmulgee, (2) the Broxton Creek (9CF3) and (3) Teresa Raceway (9CF100) sites, both in the Satilla drainage in Coffee County, and (4) the Hartford village (Figure 9-2). All four of these vessels are grit tempered, with the Westlake vessel (9-76) possessing Grit 1, or the metaquartzite, while the vessels from Hartford (9-75), Broxton Creek (9-77), and Teresa Raceway (9-78) are all characterized by Grit 4.

As can be seen from Figure 9-8, the three vessels in this group not found at Hartford all follow the quantitative pattern of amount of mineral inclusions of sand size and larger observed for the grit-tempered vessels at Hartford, that is, more than 30 percent. The Teresa Raceway vessel, with its high sand and gravel amount (51 percent), is unusual, but the magnitude of the differences between it and the remainder of the vessels in this category do not seem great enough to warrant its exclusion. In addition, the sand/gravel size indices for the three non-Hartford vessels (2.22, 2.23, and 2.25) are well within the observed range of variation for the Hartford sample (1.97 to 2.63). With all of these factors considered, then, it is here suggested that all four vessels with the box-center motif most probably derive from a common source. Because of the nature of the metamorphic rocks used as temper in these vessels, that common source must be on or near the Piedmont. Since five of six vessels from Teresa Raceway and six of seven from Broxton Creek are sand tempered (Table 9-1), the two grit-tempered vessels from these sites are presumed to be imports. That the only grit-tempered vessels at these sites are also characterized by the box-center design accentuates all the more the apparent nonlocal origin of these vessels. For the moment, at least, the Hartford site would appear to be the leading candidate for the production center of some of the vessels with the box-center design.

For the purposes of this analysis, Snow identified a second design match between Hartford and another site. This match involves the horseshoe motif, represented by Vessels 9-61 and 9-73 from the submound midden at Hartford (both tempered with metaquartzite, or Grit 1) and Vessel 9-74 from 9WL26, a small extractive site on the Oconee River near its confluence with the Ocmulgee. The vessel from 9WL26 is also tempered with metaquartzite (Grit 1) but is somewhat different from the Hartford Grit 1–tempered vessels in that it has a lower percentage of sand and gravel—24 percent. This is outside the range of variation observed for the Hartford site (34 to 37 percent), but we are inclined to attribute this to sampling error, considering the small sample presently analyzed. Again, we feel it is highly significant that vessels from two sites that were originally selected for petrographic analysis on purely stylistic grounds have proved to possess identical tempers.

The Milamo Site

The second-largest sample (fifteen) of thin-sectioned vessels from a single site analyzed in this study came from the Milamo site (9WL1). In addition, three lumps of unshaped clay recovered at the site by Snow and presumed to be by-products of vessel manufacture were included in the thin-section analysis. These samples should provide a firm basis for characterizing local clay resources available to Milamo potters. This site is located about 120 river

Table 9-3. Bulk Composition, Size Indices for Sand-and-Gravel Inclusions, and Designs for the Fifteen Vessels plus Three Clay Samples from Milamo

Vessel	Matrix %	Silt %	Sa./Gr. %	Size Index	Design
9-69	77	3	20	1.03	Turtle
9-79	73	5	22	1.11	Eye?
9-82	74	5	21	1.31	Turtle
9-83	74	4	22	1.47	Turtle
9-86	78	4	18	2.05	Eagle
9-91	65	2	33	1.80	Mosquito
9-92	70	7	23	1.33	Tongue
9-93	78	6	16	1.27	Tongue
9-94	68	8	24	1.40	Bird in flight
9-95	76	5	19	1.46	Dunce-cap man
9-96	73	6	21	1.12	UGA
9-97	71	8	21	1.11	?
9-98	64	4	32	1.20	?
9-99	72	7	21	1.18	?
Means (14)	72.3	5.3	22.4	1.35	
S.D.	4.4	1.8	4.8	0.28	
9-71*	64	5	31	2.30	Plate Ten UR
Clay 1; 9-149	60	6	34	1.68	
Clay 2; 9-150	77	3	20	1.78	
Clay 3; 9-151	90	5	5	1.60	

*Vessel 9-71 grit tempered; all others sand tempered.

kilometers downstream from the Hartford site on the lower Ocmulgee in the southeastern corner of Wheeler County (Figure 9-2). Unlike those from the Hartford site, the vast majority of the vessels analyzed from Milamo—fourteen of fifteen—are sand tempered (Figure 9-3). The basic data gathered through the petrographic analysis of the fifteen vessels and three clay samples from Milamo are presented in Table 9-3 and in Figure 9-9.

The task of characterizing the physical properties of the locally made ceramics at Milamo was facilitated by the recovery from the site of lumps of clay that are presumed to be remnants of pottery manufacture. Thin sections of three of these clay lumps revealed them to be remarkably variable in their sand/gravel content, which ranged between 5 percent and 34 percent (Table

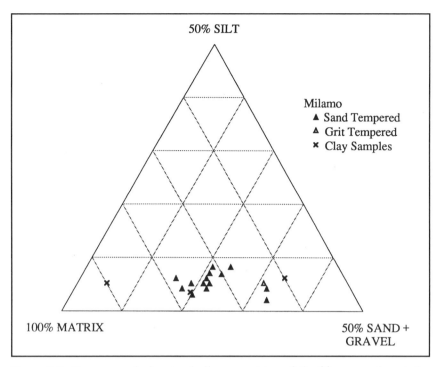

Figure 9-9. Ternary graph showing bulk composition of the fifteen vessels and clay samples from Milamo.

9-3; Figure 9-9). The sand/gravel size indices for the clay lumps are well within the range of variation recorded for the fourteen sand-tempered vessels from the site. As can be seen from Figure 9-9, twelve of the sand-tempered vessels in the Milamo sample have paste properties that conform closely to that of one of these clay samples (Clay 2 in Table 9-3), while two of the sand-tempered vessels more closely resemble Clay 1 (Table 9-3). One clay sample, the one with only 5 percent sand/gravel (Clay 3), is unlike any of the vessels in the current sample.

An important lesson from these data would seem to be that locally made ceramics from a site need not necessarily have uniform physical properties. Exactly what this variability means in terms of human behavior, however, is uncertain. Some alternatives might be that (1) multiple local clays were used by the local potters, (2) differential amounts of sand/gravel were added to a local clay because of functional or personal considerations on the part of

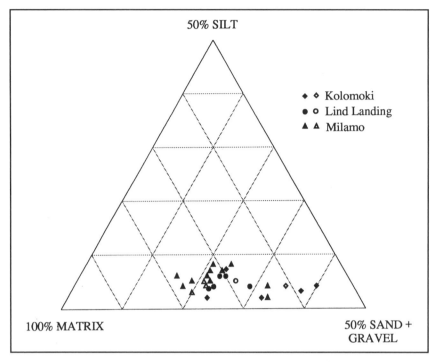

Figure 9-10. Ternary graph showing bulk composition of sand-tempered vessels from Milamo ($N = 14$), Lind Landing ($N = 6$), and Kolomoki ($N = 6$). *Open symbols* denote vessels with the turtle design.

the potters, or (3) multiple episodes of occupation had occurred, each with its own pattern of clay exploitation/preparation. For the present, it seems reasonable to view Clay 2 and the twelve similar sand-tempered vessels as best characterizing the local products of Milamo artisans. The other two sand-tempered vessels could also be of local origin (made of Clay 1?), although their outlier status on the ternary graphs (see especially Figures 9-9 and 9-10) raises the possibility that they could be of nonlocal derivation (from Kolomoki?).

Against this background, let us now turn to the evidence for shared designs between Milamo and other Swift Creek sites. Within the current sample, Snow has identified five instances of design sharing between Milamo and at least one other site. We shall discuss each of these instances in turn below.

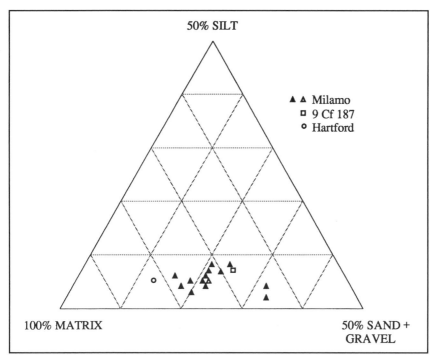

Figure 9-11. Ternary graph showing bulk composition of Milamo vessels versus vessels with the eye(?) design from Hartford and 9CF187. *Open triangle* denotes the Milamo vessel with the eye(?) design.

The first case of design sharing between Milamo and other sites involves the eye(?) design, which appears on Vessel 9-80 from 9CF187 (unfortunately the sole vessel thin sectioned from that site), on Vessel 9-81 from the Hartford village, and on Vessel 9-79 from Milamo. All three of these vessels are sand tempered and have reasonably fine sand/gravel size indices: 1.18, 1.32, and 1.11, respectively. As can be seen from Figure 9-11, these three vessels do not form a discrete cluster but rather are dispersed across the ternary diagram in a way that suggests independent production rather than a common derivation (see also Figure 9-5). It seems more likely that paddles rather than pots moved between sites in this case.

The second set of design shares involving the Milamo site is represented by the turtle design, which appears on three separate vessels at Milamo (9-69, 9-82, and 9-83) and on Vessels 9-70 at Kolomoki and 9-84 at Lind Land-

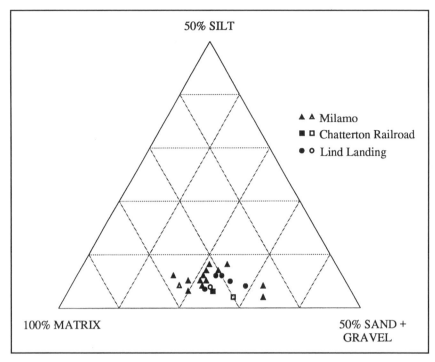

Figure 9-12. Ternary graph showing bulk composition of sand-tempered vessels from Milamo (*N* = 14), Lind Landing (*N* = 6), and Chatterton Railroad (*N* = 2). *Open symbols* denote vessels with the eagle design.

ing (9WL7), which is located just 8 kilometers east of Milamo. The basic petrographic data pertaining to these vessels, all of which are sand tempered, are plotted on Figure 9-10. As can be seen from this figure, the vessels with the turtle design all fall within or near the grid lines of other vessels from their respective sites rather than forming a common cluster. Such a dispersed pattern is consistent with the view that each of the vessels with the turtle design in this sample was manufactured at the respective site of discovery. In this case it appears that paddle rather than vessel exchange connected the Milamo site to Lind Landing and Kolomoki.

The third set of design shares linking Milamo with its neighbors involves the eagle design, which appears on three vessels: Vessel 9-88 from Chatterton Railroad (9CF80), Vessel 9-85 from Lind Landing, and Vessel 9-86 from

Milamo. These three vessels, too, are all sand tempered. As can be seen from Figure 9-12, the bulk compositions of these vessels fail to form a common cluster as one would expect if they were derived from a single production center. Instead, each of the eagle vessels has a bulk composition that closely resembles that of other vessels from its respective site. Because the ranges of variation in bulk composition overlap among the three sites, and the Chatterton Railroad sample is inadequate (only two vessels, versus fourteen for Milamo and six for Lind Landing), inferences based on these data must necessarily be tentative. Nonetheless, the most parsimonious explanation of the observed pattern expressed in Figure 9-12 is that paddles rather than pots circulated among these sites in this particular case.

The fourth design share between Milamo and neighboring sites within the present data set involves the mosquito design, which appears on three vessels from as many sites: Vessel 9-89 from 9JD22, Vessel 9-90 from Lind Landing, and Vessel 9-91 from Milamo. Two of these vessels are sand tempered, but the vessel from 9JD22 has a unique, coarsely crystalline granite temper (Grit 5) that sets it apart from all other vessels in the current sample. Further accentuating the paste differences among these vessels is the fact that the Milamo vessel is one of the two atypical vessels from the site that have a Kolomoki-like composition (compare Figures 9-10 and 9-13). The compositional data, as summarized in Figure 9-13, suggest that two or more centers of production were involved in the manufacture of these vessels. In this case it appears likely that paddles rather than pots were moving from site to site.

The fifth and final design share observed between Milamo and another site involves the Plate Ten UR design (not shown in Figure 9-1), which has been recorded on two vessels in the current sample, Vessel 9-72 from Kolomoki and Vessel 9-71 from Milamo. It is notable that this design has also been observed on pictures of sherds from the Swift Creek site (see Kelly 1938:plate 11a, *middle row, right;* Kelly and Smith 1975:plate 10, *upper right*), but since these sherds have not yet been studied by Snow, it is uncertain whether a precise paddle match exists with Vessels 9-71 and 9-72. What is especially distinctive about this design share is that it involves the sole grit-tempered vessel among the fifteen thin-sectioned vessels from Milamo. This vessel, with its Grit 2 (metagranite) temper, is distinctly different from the

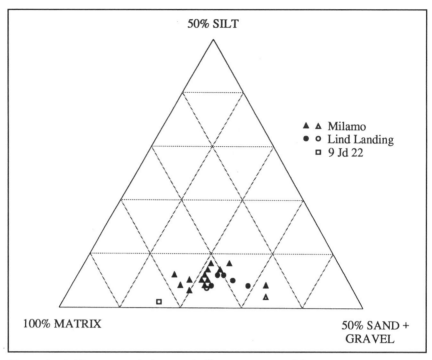

Figure 9-13. Ternary graph showing bulk composition of fourteen vessels from Mi-lamo, six vessels from Lind Landing, and one vessel from 9JD22. All except the 9JD22 vessel (which is grit tempered) are sand tempered. *Open symbols* denote vessels that share the mosquito design.

six sand-tempered vessels (including Vessel 9-72) from Kolomoki. Instead, it falls fully within the observed range of variation of the three Grit 2 vessels from Hartford (compare Figures 9-9 and 9-5), consistent with the view that it is an intrusive vessel, most probably derived from the Hartford vicinity, if not from Hartford itself. On the other hand, Vessel 9-72 has a bulk composition—66 percent Matrix/3 percent Silt/32 percent Sand/Gravel—that is virtually identical to the mean for the six sand-tempered vessels from Kolomoki—64.5 percent Matrix/3.7 percent Silt/31.8 percent Sand/Gravel—suggesting that it was locally produced. It thus seems likely that the two Plate Ten UR vessels were produced at different sites; that is, paddles rather than pots must have circulated in this case.

Summary and Conclusions

The goal of this study was to employ a form of materials analysis of ceramics, that is, petrography, to complement Snow's stylistic analyses of carved paddle impressions that have led to the recognition of identical designs at multiple Swift Creek sites in south-central Georgia. In particular the objective of the materials analysis was to ascertain, if possible, whether it was paddles or pots that were being circulated among Swift Creek communities. The basic expectations guiding this analysis were (1) if paddles were being circulated, the paste properties of the vessels sharing specific designs will differ from site to site (i.e., display a dispersed distribution on the ternary graphs) and, conversely, (2) if pottery vessels were being circulated, pots from different sites with the same design will also have similar pastes (i.e., display a clustered distribution on the ternary graphs). The results of this analysis must be regarded as tentative because of the small samples so far analyzed, but there are, nonetheless, a number of tantalizing patterns in the data whose implications merit serious consideration.

One surprising finding was the recognition of metamorphic rock temper in vessels from seven sites, all of which are located on the Coastal Plain well removed from the Piedmont where such rocks must have originated. At the present it is impossible to ascertain how these rocks were obtained for use as temper. There are at least three possibilities to be considered: (1) finished *vessels,* not temper, were procured by the Coastal Plain residents from Piedmont production centers, (2) the metamorphic *rocks* for use as temper were procured by Coastal Plain residents either by trade or by travel to the Piedmont, or (3) local sources on the Coastal Plain, presumably in alluvium, were exploited. While a single alluvial clay sample can hardly be considered adequate, the absence of metamorphic rock fragments from the local Hartford clay that was sampled is inconsistent with the third alternative above.

Related to this is a second interesting discovery, namely, that these grit-tempered ceramics are concentrated primarily at two sites, Hartford and Westlake, the two sites located nearest the Piedmont. While these two sites produced fourteen of the nineteen grit-tempered vessels in the current sample, the remaining five grit-tempered vessels are distributed among nine sites, with none of the latter having more than a single grit-tempered vessel. Assuming that the current sample is not seriously biased, these data suggest a highly localized production of grit-tempered Swift Creek ceramics in the middle Ocmulgee Valley.

The third, and most important, outcome of this study is the generation of strong, suggestive evidence that both paddles and pots circulated among Swift Creek communities of the Georgia Coastal Plain. Of the seven carved paddle designs used in this study whose occurrence Snow has documented at two or more Swift Creek sites, two, the box-center and horseshoe designs, appear to be represented at multiple sites because of vessel exchange, while four, the eye, turtle, eagle, and mosquito designs, apparently appear at multiple sites because of paddle exchange. The seventh design, Plate Ten UR, appears at Milamo on a grit-tempered vessel that must have been imported, while the identical design on a sand-tempered vessel from Kolomoki suggests its local derivation there. Because a Coastal Plain site like Kolomoki almost certainly could not be the source for the Milamo vessel, a third site must be involved, suggesting that both paddle and vessel exchange must have occurred in this case.

In conclusion it is relevant to address the issue of what the inferred occurrence of paddle and vessel exchange meant within the context of Swift Creek society. The simplest, hence the most likely, explanation for the intersite circulation of paddles involves the physical movement of potters. The movement of a newly married potter from one community to another and seasonal movements of whole social groups or communities are two common processes that could have fostered intercommunity paddle movement. These possibilities seem especially likely considering that many Swift Creek sites "appear as small campsites used intermittently from year to year" (Snow 1977:22) and that spousal exchange between communities is a virtually universal practice in tribal-level societies such as Swift Creek appears to have been. This alternative can be referred to as the social model because it was primarily people, rather than pots, who were the main links between interacting communities.

On the other hand the intercommunity circulation of pottery vessels is more likely to have been associated with either gift giving or ritual feasting or, possibly, even the redistribution of local surpluses within the framework of some kind of exchange network. In this case it seems more likely that the pots circulated independently of seasonal or permanent residential shifts by the potters. This latter alternative, or set of alternatives, can be referred to as the economic model in that it was primarily the circulation of goods (i.e., pots and, no doubt, their contents) that served to define, establish, and maintain intercommunity interaction.

In sum this study suggests that paddles circulated among Swift Creek communities, most likely as correlates of social mechanisms like marriage and residential mobility, but that in some instances, especially involving the near-Piedmont sites of Hartford and Westlake, pottery vessels also circulated among Swift Creek communities. This latter discovery suggests that economic and possibly political, not purely social, motives must be given serious consideration in our efforts to understand the processes underlying the production and distribution of pottery in Swift Creek society.

Swift Creek Phase Design Assemblages from Two Sites on the Georgia Coast

Rebecca Saunders

Perhaps because I received my first training in archaeological analysis techniques in the mid-1970s, when social archaeology and particularly the works of Hill (1968), Longacre (1964), Hardin (1977), Washburn (1978), and others were in vogue, I have long been fascinated with the potential of design analysis to illuminate social relationships in the past. These early "social archaeologists" relied on the idea of varying degrees of interaction to explain stylistic similarities within or between assemblages. In this diffusionist interaction approach, style was conceived of as a residual category—adaptively neutral, involving little decision making on the part of the potter, and consequently socially passive. Style was transmitted directly from mother to daughter; errors in transmission or in copying were responsible for the drift in style through time. The attributes of a style were distributed clinally from the center of a tradition outward, slowly and regularly dissipating until they merged with the edges of another tradition.

In the late 1970s, Wobst (1977) applied information theory to the study of design. In this approach, style is not a by-product of boundaries. Instead, because of conscious selection of design attributes that symbolize political affiliation, status, wealth, and/or religious beliefs, style plays an active role in the establishment and maintenance of territorial boundaries and promotes social integration within those boundaries (see Saunders 1986a:30–44 for a more comprehensive discussion of the theories of style). Therefore, expectations of design distribution differ from those of the interaction approach. Instead of clinal distribution and a merging with styles of other social groups, in which system style is used as information, the boundaries of the distribution of meaningful symbols are expected to be sharply defined. This has been best illustrated by Hodder (1977, 1979, 1982a), whose ethnographic research in Kenya demonstrated that items of material culture were more diverse between competing groups than between ethnic groups that were not competing for resources. In addition, within the acephalous groups that he studied, Hodder (1979) noted that stylistic attributes were homogenized as a result of strong pressures to conform. From these data, Hodder (1982a:56) argued that material culture not only reflects or symbolizes ethnic groups, but also "actively forms ethnic differences and makes them acceptable."

In Wobst's formulation, only certain elements of a design contain information, and other elements might indeed be neutral (Wobst 1977:321). Thus, the information approach was not intended to supplant interaction as an explanation for all aspects of design variability. Rather, and as subsequent researchers have emphasized (Carr 1985; Graves 1981; Plog 1983), a synthesis of the two theories reveals the multidimensional nature of style. In the synthetic approach, variation in style can result from several different factors including individual variation, interaction, and interaction intensities and the necessity to convey information about cosmology, religion, and/or political or other social affiliations. There is, then, a design hierarchy (Redman 1978), different levels of which (e.g., the design element, the motif, the design structure) may respond differently to varying stimuli (Friedrich 1970; Hardin 1977, 1984).

It remained for the contextual approach of the post-processual school, and especially the earlier work of Hodder (e.g., Hodder 1977, 1979, 1982b), to operationalize the concepts of the information approach. Hodder stipulated rules of inference that can be used to test hypotheses concerning the function (or, more controversially, the meaning[1]) of stylistic elements within a particular cultural assemblage. More recently, David et al. (1988) have used this method to argue that cosmological symbols can be identified on the basis of their redundancy in various media and contexts in a particular culture (see also Saunders 1992a, 1992b for a southeastern example).

Information Theory and Swift Creek Phase Pottery

The idea that the repetition of a small number of motifs in a single medium or in various media is likely to convey information (cosmological or otherwise) seems particularly relevant for the study of Swift Creek phase designs (see Chapter 6 herein). In Swift Creek designs, a relatively small repertoire of design elements was used in a virtually limitless number of design motifs.

A variety of researchers have suggested that Swift Creek phase designs conveyed information. Kellar, Kelly, and McMichael (1962), for instance, suggested that particular designs belonged to certain families. Broyles (1968:51), who began a design analysis of Late Swift Creek phase pottery excavated at Kolomoki, may have given some support to this idea when she observed that "in the vast majority of cases . . . one design seems to be restricted to one area, even when more than one paddle was carved with the same design." On the basis of his work tracing vessel trade routes through paddle flaws, Snow (1975) reported his belief that regional production centers or specific villages were represented by particular design elements. Shannon (1979) extended the concept to a still higher level of social integration, speculating that certain designs symboled political affiliation within a priest state. These are not necessarily conflicting hypotheses; they could relate to distinct functions of different levels of the design hierarchy in different social contexts.

In my own work at the Late Swift Creek component of the Kings Bay site (9CM171a) (Figure 10-1) in southeastern Georgia (Saunders 1986a, 1986b), I tested whether individual variation might be visible in the complicated stamped designs on the pottery in the contemporaneous, discrete household middens at the site.[2] Both technological attributes (vessel wall thickness, rim fold depth, rim diameter, paste composition, interior and exterior color and surface finish, vessel form, lip form, lip finish, regularity of rim fold base) and stylistic attributes (presence or absence of stamping, zoned stamping, presence or absence of exterior smoothing, depth of smoothing, degree of overstamping, land and groove width, groove depth, character of lands and grooves, elements present, design group) were recorded for sherds from seven middens. When the attributes were clustered (with technological and stylistic attributes clustered separately), both resulting diagrams ap-

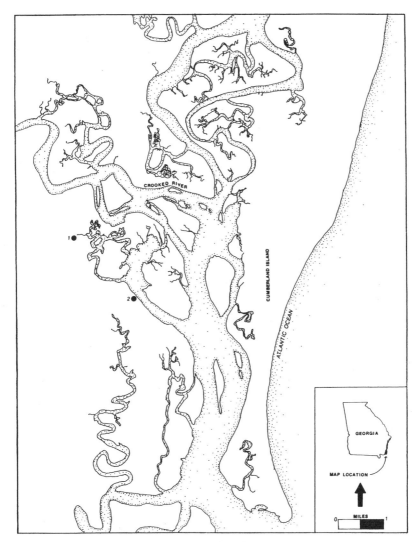

Figure 10-1. Location of (*1*) Mallard Creek and (*2*) Kings Bay sites.

peared to indicate two "analytical individuals" at the site.[3] Certain design groups were restricted to the spatially discrete "individuals." I speculated that the designs might represent some degree of lineal affiliation.[4]

More recently, I completed a study of the cosmological concepts embedded in the four-field design common to many of the Lamar-related designs

(Saunders 1992a, 1992b). Returning to contemplate Swift Creek designs after that study, I am more convinced than ever that southeastern Indian pottery designs were composed of symbols that had specific meanings to the populations. Some of these symbols represent religious or cosmological beliefs that have both deep roots and widespread adherence in the prehistoric Southeast (Hudson 1984:4; Snow, Chapter 6 herein). This seems particularly plausible for the most durable symbols, for instance the scroll, that more or less originated (at least on the medium of pottery) in the Swift Creek phase and continued to be emphasized in stamping and incising up to and even after contact.[5]

An additional piece of evidence may be found in what Willey (1949:431) and Sears (1952:103) perceived as the reductionist character of Late Swift Creek designs: "Total stamps are simpler than in the preceding period, since one motif is either obviously the central one, in some collections, or is repeated two or more times in other collections. . . . Fewer lands and grooves are employed in the delineation of each motif than was the case in early Swift Creek stamping, and fill elements are fewer and simpler" (Sears 1952:103). The relative simplicity of Late Swift Creek design motifs can be seen by comparing Snow's (this volume) Early and Middle Swift Creek motifs with the Late Swift Creek designs from Kings Bay in Figures 10-2 through 10-10. While some might regard this as the devolution inherent in the trajectory of a style, the trend toward simplification conforms to one of Wobst's stipulations for style as information exchange—that the symbol be legible and unambiguous.

Nevertheless, the problem of interpreting symbols is complex, first because each is unique to its social context and second because symbols can be active on so many levels and meaning can change in space and time (Hodder 1982a:14).

An Application to Late Swift Creek Pottery on the Georgia Coast

As originally conceived, this chapter was to report on the attempt to trace Swift Creek phase designs or design elements through time to isolate short-lived from longer-lived symbols. For instance, did the scroll/spiral become the most common element in Late Swift Creek assemblages first in a particular area (perhaps the Kolomoki area?). Could that area then be seen

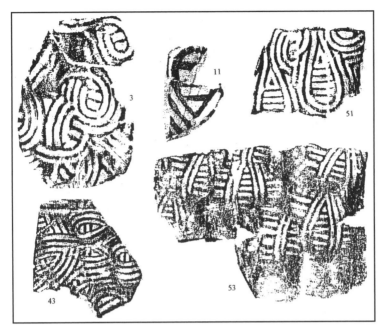

Figure 10-2. Swift Creek designs at the Kings Bay site: DG1.

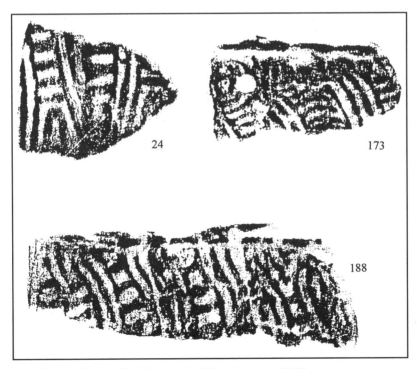

Figure 10-3. Swift Creek designs at the Kings Bay site: DG2.

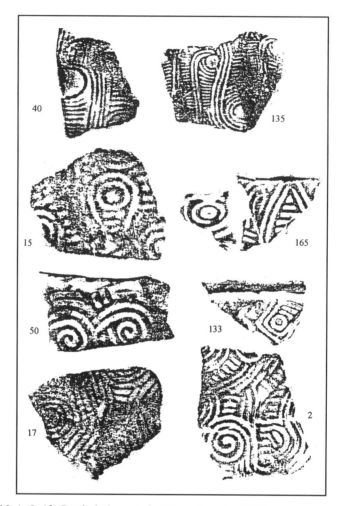

Figure 10-4. Swift Creek designs at the Kings Bay site: DG3.

as the major political player responsible for the subsequent dominance of the scroll in design motifs of the Mississippian period?

However, I became convinced that unfortunately adequate published data were not available. What will be necessary for a study of that sort is adequate reportage of design element and motif inventories from a variety of sites and a number of different contexts.[6] The intrasite and intersite distribution of the assemblages will have to be analyzed in terms of the design

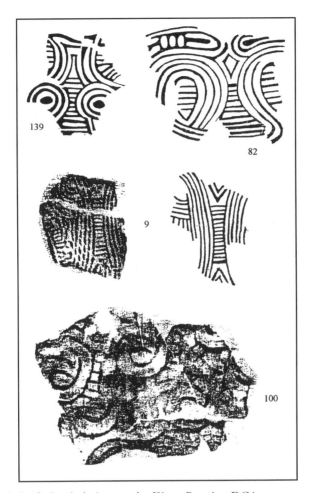

Figure 10-5. Swift Creek designs at the Kings Bay site: DG4.

hierarchy, in other words, the elements present, what elements appear or do not appear in combination, and how elements are combined (design structure and symmetry), if archaeologists are to understand what part of the social hierarchy the symbols represent.

In the following small study, I use the concept of design hierarchy to try to ferret out the relationship between two sites in southeastern Georgia, the Kings Bay site (9CM171a) and the Mallard Creek site (9CM185; Figure 10-1). The two sites provide an interesting contrast in settlement pattern.

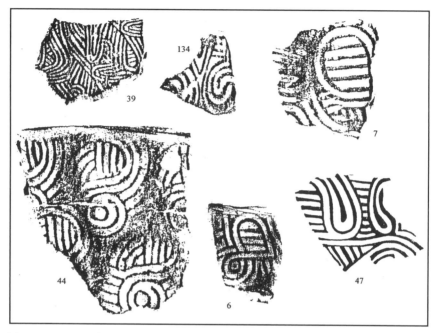

Figure 10-6. Swift Creek designs at the Kings Bay site: DG5.

The Swift Creek portion of the Kings Bay site was located on a relatively exposed, high bluff overlooking Kings Bay. The site consisted of a series of individual shell middens arranged in the arc-like pattern typical of Swift Creek phase sites on the Gulf Coast (see Bense, Chapter 14 herein). Fresh water may have been provided by the artesian spring now present at the site; otherwise the only immediate source of fresh water would have been a natural slough that borders the northwestern side of the site. Zooarchaeological studies of vertebrate and invertebrate fauna at the site suggested either intermittent use throughout the year or year-round occupation (Quitmyer 1985:89). However, the size of the middens, and of the site itself, indicated that site residency was relatively brief.

The Mallard Creek site occupies a more sheltered location 1.5 linear kilometers north of 9CM171. The site is on the western bank of Sandy Run, a small freshwater creek that drains into salt marsh and then into Marianna Creek. Site structure at the Mallard Creek site is decidedly different from

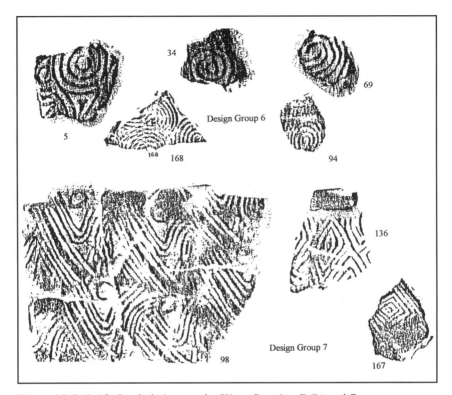

Figure 10-7. Swift Creek designs at the Kings Bay site: DG6 and 7.

that at the Kings Bay site. Shell and bone were discarded in a central location at the site, instead of on a horseshoe-shaped or arc-like midden. Lithics and pottery were found predominantly outside the refuse area, suggesting "that domestic activities took place on the periphery of a centralized refuse disposal area" (Smith et al. 1985:140). Results of a growth ring study of the *Mercenaria mercenaria* clam shells from Mallard Creek ($n = 6$, the total encountered in the test excavations) indicated exploitation almost exclusively in the spring, a pattern distinctly different from that identified for the Kings Bay site (Irv Quitmyer, pers. comm. 1994; Saunders 1994). These are the only seasonal data available from the site at present, and these should be bolstered with other invertebrate and vertebrate faunal analyses. At present, site settlement pattern and the regrettably small *Mercenaria* study suggest that

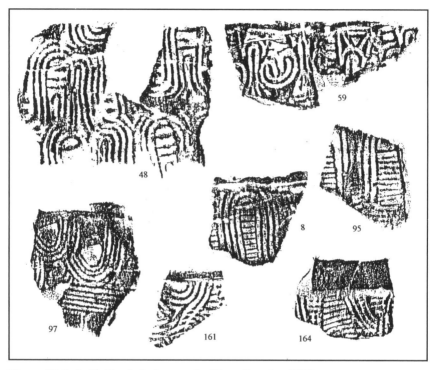

Figure 10-8. Swift Creek designs at the Kings Bay site: DG8.

the Mallard Creek site was a seasonal encampment. As at the Kings Bay site, the size and depth of the Mallard Creek site do not indicate long-term occupancy.

Ever since the excavation of the Mallard Creek site, I have wondered whether the same population inhabited both the Kings Bay site and Mallard Creek as part of a seasonal subsistence round. The same resources are actually available to both sites within a relatively small area; however, the Mallard Creek site is in a more protected location. No radiocarbon dates are available from Mallard Creek, but paddle matching between the sites (to be discussed more fully below) indicates that occupation at the two sites was contemporaneous.

I thought one way to determine the relationship between the sites would be to compare the design assemblages. Initially I postulated that if there was a great deal of paddle matching between the two sites, the same people prob-

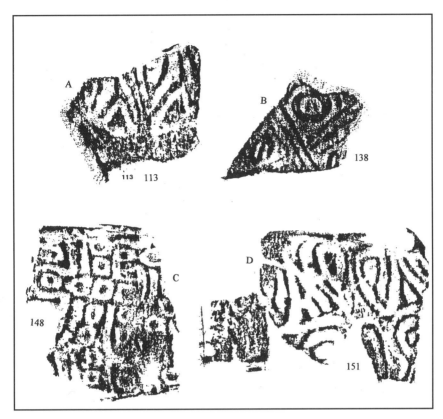

Figure 10-9. Swift Creek designs at the Kings Bay site: DG10.

ably occupied both locations. On the other hand, a limited number of matches would indicate interaction between the sites.[7] If the latter result were obtained, other avenues of research could be explored. How similar were the design assemblages? Did they contain the same elements? The same design groups? Using the hierarchical concept of design described above, one might speculate that elements and/or design groups common to both sites represent one level of social structure, perhaps political affiliation, while those restricted to specific sites or locations within sites represent a lower-level relationship, perhaps lineage. Very common elements or designs that appear throughout Swift Creek phase assemblages may represent cosmological concepts. While the specific information (e.g., political relationship versus cosmology, lineage versus clan) may not be recoverable, archaeologists can at-

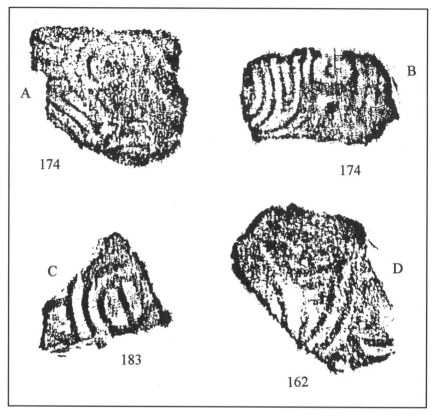

Figure 10-10. Swift Creek designs at the Kings Bay site: DG11.

tempt to understand the hierarchical relationship between the symbols by exploring their spatial distribution.

For the Kings Bay sherd assemblage, I sorted 127 designs (culled from 1,270 sherds) into ten design groups (Figures 10-2 through 10-10; a complete design inventory for the Kings Bay site is presented in Saunders 1986a). These design groups were higher on the hierarchical scale than design elements, but below motifs, as in most cases the entire design could not be reconstructed. Because of the fragmentary nature of the designs, groups were conceived to emphasize design configuration, defined as the combination of elements, rather than the more holistic structural aspects of complete motifs. This distinction should become clearer as the criteria for membership in the different design groups are enumerated below.

The design group descriptions should make it apparent that there is some coherency to the design assemblage at Kings Bay. For instance, Design Groups (DG) 1, 2, 6, 7, and 8 each emphasize a single element: teardrops, ladders, circles, diamonds, and lobes, respectively. Two groups (DG3 and 4) involve teardrops, ladders, and circles and/or spirals in two different configurations. DG5 contains complex designs made up of the foregoing, as well as barred eccentrics. DG10, however, is completely different. In this group, design elements are different and the relationship of land to groove width is very different. DG11 is intermediate between the primitive cast of DG10 and the more sophisticated designs of other groups. (More information, in particular a discussion of design symmetry for these groups, is available in Saunders 1986a.)

Design Group 1. DG1 contains complete designs with only one major element, the teardrop (Figure 10-2). Interior elaborations and external fill areas vary, but the teardrop is the focus of the design. One variant of this theme was allowed. Two designs had teardrops that had been "stretched" (e.g., Figure 10-2, Design 3). Because the similarity coefficient used would not have recognized any similarity between the stretched teardrop and the teardrop if they had been assigned to different design groups, the two stretched elements are included within DG1.

Design Group 2. DG2 also contains designs with only one major element, in this case the ladder (Figure 10-3). Interior elaboration of this element is limited to the insertion of a diamond at either end where the ladder begins to broaden.

Design Group 3. DG3 is more complex than the preceding groups. The central figure is a combination of a vertical element—either the ladder, the lobe, or the more linear, barred portion of the teardrop—and a spherical element, most commonly a circle but occasionally a spiral. This is a good example of what Clarke (1968) and others (e.g., Redman 1977) have called "substitutability" in the decision-making processes of design execution. That is, the vertical elements all serve the same function in the design; conscious choice is involved in the selection of one option over another.

To be admitted to DG3 the elements had to be combined vertically. This vertical combination of the two classes of elements can be appreciated when members of this group are compared with those in DG4, which contains the same elements combined horizontally.

Design Group 4. DG4 contains most of the same elements as DG3: a vertical element, almost always a ladder, combined with either a circle, scroll, or teardrop. In this group, however, the linear element is flanked by the spherical ones. In addition, while in DG3 the teardrop could be substituted for the linear elements, in DG4 it is substituted for a circle.

Design Group 5. DG5 contains the barred eccentrics and the complex (having more than two elements) designs recovered. These two subgroups are nearly, but not exactly, symmetrical. That is, all the complex designs include barred eccentrics, but not all designs containing barred eccentrics are complex.

Design Group 6. DG6 is composed of designs with an emphasis on spherical elements—circles and spirals. The group has only six members; three have circles or spirals only and three combine circles with triangle elaborations.

Design Group 7. DG7 contains those designs with diamonds as the major element. The group has only five members, and all triangles are filled in some manner.

Design Group 8. DG8 includes those designs composed with lobes as the principal element.

Design Group 9. DG9 is used for designs that are too fragmentary to be assigned to a design group.

Design Group 10. DG10 designs, as noted above, are comparatively simplistic, with a high ratio of groove to land width. This is the distinguishing factor in assignment to this category; a number of different elements, either shared with other groups or unique to this group, are executed in this manner.

Design Group 11. DG11 is also unusual with respect to the rest of the collection. The designs in this group consist of a "stretched" teardrop in combination with a circle. The circle is within the bend of the teardrop. Designs in this group also have relatively thin lands and wide grooves.

In terms of the assemblage as a whole, DG3 was the most prevalent at 30 percent of the assemblage; DG5 and DG4, at 14.8 percent and 14.1 percent, respectively, were the next most common designs (Table 10-1). The relative frequency of each design group dictated the frequency of elements. Of the 275 elements in the assemblage, teardrops constituted 22.5 percent, circles 24.5 percent, ladders 15.6 percent, barred eccentrics 8.0 percent, and

Table 10-1. Design Group Frequencies at the Mallard Creek and Kings Bay Sites

Design Group	Mallard Creek Frequency	Mallard Creek Percent	Kings Bay Frequency	Kings Bay Percent
DG1	4	9.09	13	10.2
DG2	1	2.27	7	5.5
DG3	10	22.73	38	29.7
DG4	5	11.36	18	14.1
DG5	6	13.64	19	14.8
DG6	5	11.36	8	6.3
DG7	3	6.82	5	3.9
DG8	2	4.55	10	7.8
DG9	8		29	
DG10	6	13.64	5	3.9
DG11	2	4.55	5	3.9
DG new	1			
Total	53	100.01	128	100.1

triangles 7.6 percent. Spirals, scrolls, and diamonds were relatively rare in the assemblage (Table 10-2).

Two design groups, or, more specifically, certain design options within the groups, were correlated with either the northern or the southern half of the site. Within DG3, the options of lobes and circles or tears and circles were distributed evenly across the site as indicated by low chi-square cell values. However, the other options, tears and spirals, circles/spirals and ladders, and a residual category, were associated with one side of the site or the other (Table 10-3). Similarly, all options within DG4 were evenly distributed across the site except when the curvilinear element was a scroll. Those designs

Table 10-2. Element Frequencies at the Mallard Creek and Kings Bay Sites

Element	Mallard Creek Frequency	Mallard Creek Percent	Kings Bay Frequency	Kings Bay Percent
Teardrop	7	11.86	62	22.5
Lobe	7	11.86	25	9.1
Circle	21	35.59	67	24.5
Spiral	4	6.78	9	3.3
Scroll	1	1.69	12	4.4
Triangle	2	3.39	21	7.6
Ladder	12	20.34	43	15.6
Eccentric	3	5.08	22	8.0
Diamond	2	3.39	14	5.1
Total	59	99.98	275	100.10

were very highly correlated with the southern half of the site. DG6 (circles and spirals) and, to a lesser extent, DG7 (diamonds) were correlated with the northern half of the site.

Other design groups appeared in more or less expectable frequencies across the site. In particular, lobes (DG8), teardrops (DG1), and complex designs (DG5) appeared across the site in even distributions. I have suggested (Saunders 1986a:206–7) that the designs restricted in space symbolize lineages, clans, or moieties while the designs distributed site-wide might be symbolic of the settlement or a larger polity.

I did not have the opportunity to study the Mallard Creek pottery assemblage in the detail that the Kings Bay materials were studied. Indeed, the settlement pattern at the site, specifically the central disposal area, negates the ability to analyze the spatial distribution of a major portion of the design assemblage.[8] However, I did roll all the complicated stamped designs.[9] Fifty-

Table 10- 3. Chi Square Test (with Yates Correction for Small Cell Size) of Design Group Distribution, Northern versus Southern Half of the Kings Bay Site

	South	Chi Square	North	Chi Square	Total	Description
DG1	8	0	4	0	12	Teardrops
DG2	3	.2	0	.4	3	Ladders
DG3a	3	.2	0	.4	3	Tears and spirals
DG3b	6	.1	2	.1	8	Tears and circles
DG3c	7	.5	1	.8	8	Ladders and circles/spirals
DG3d	4	0	4	.1	8	Lobes and circles
DG3e	0	2.1	5	3.4	5	Circular element UID
DG4a	6	0	4	0	10	Ladders and circles
DG4b	6	.9	0	1.4	6	Ladders and scrolls
DG5a	5	.2	1	.3	6	Barred eccentrics
DG5b	7	0	5	0	12	Complex designs
DG6	2	.7	5	1.2	7	Circles, circles and triangles, spirals
DG7	1	.4	3	.6	4	Diamonds
DG8	5	0	3	.1	8	Lobes
DG9*	8		13		21	UID design
DG10	1	.4	3	.6	4	Simplistic designs with large grooves
DG11	1	.1	1	.1	2	Stretched teardrop
Total	73		54		127	

Note: Ninety-one percent cell E < 5, X^2 = 15.358, p < 0.500. *UID*, Unidentified.
*Missing data.

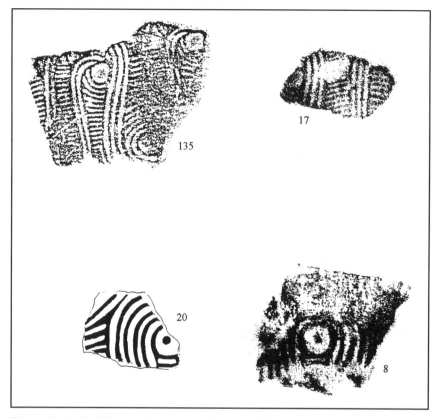

Figure 10-11. Paddle matches between Designs 135 and 17 and Designs 20 and 8. *Left*, Kings Bay sherds; *right*, Mallard Creek sherds.

three separate designs were isolated from an assemblage of 403 complicated stamped sherds. Comparison of the designs with those from Kings Bay indicated two positive paddle matches and five possible matches (Figures 10-11, 10-12, and 10-13; discussed more fully below). Two additional designs were different from all Kings Bay examples but similar enough in overall character to suggest the same paddle carver (one because it is particularly well done and the other because it is particularly poor; Figure 10-14). These data suggest, at the very least, communication between the occupants of the two sites.

All of the design groups present at the Kings Bay site were also present at Mallard Creek. Indeed, the percentage frequencies of the major design

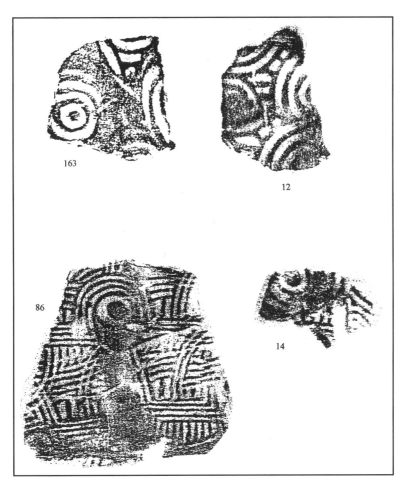

Figure 10-12. Tentative paddle matches between Designs 163 and 12 and Designs 86 and 14. *Left,* Kings Bay sherds; *right,* Mallard Creek sherds.

groups at each site, while not identical, show a similar ranking of the groups (Table 10-1). At Mallard Creek, as at Kings Bay, DG3 predominates, followed by DG5 then DG4 (tied at Mallard Creek with DG6). The major deviation between the two assemblages is in the number of DG10 designs. These comprise only 3.9 percent of the Kings Bay assemblage but are tied at second in order of frequency at Mallard Creek. I almost made a new design category for a few of these designs, especially Design 44 and Design 49 (Fig-

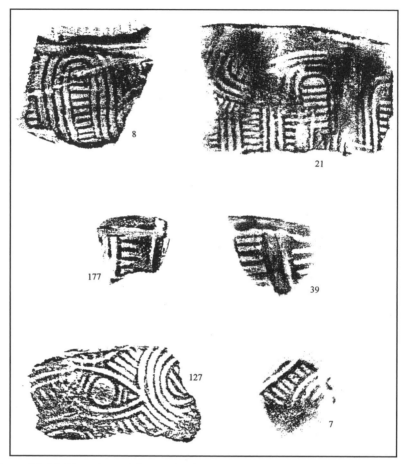

Figure 10-13. Tentative paddle matches between Designs 8 and 21, Designs 177 and 39, and Designs 127 and 7. *Left,* Kings Bay sherds; *right,* Mallard Creek sherds.

ure 10-15), because they are so rectilinear, but I ultimately decided they share too many attributes with the DG10 members at Kings Bay.

One relatively complete design (Design 19, Figure 10-15) could not be assigned to a group. The clear four-field nature of the design, the dotted rectangles, and the unidentified curvilinear element at the lower left confounded designation in the preexisting groups.

A comparison of the frequency of the major design elements (Table 10-

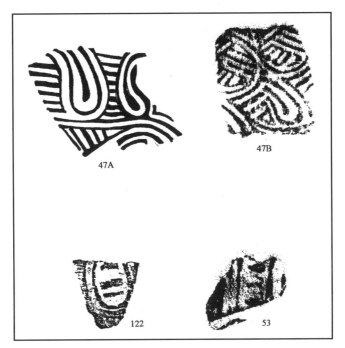

Figure 10-14. Possible same paddle carver for Designs 47A and 47B and Designs 122 and 53. *Left*, Kings Bay sherds; *right*, Mallard Creek sherds.

2) shows slightly less correspondence between the sites, though they are still similar. If rectilinear elements in the aforementioned Mallard Creek DG10 had been included in the table, there would be more divergence. However, rectilinear elements were so rare in the Kings Bay assemblage that they were coded as "other."

As for the specific paddles shared between the two sites, the two positive matches were Kings Bay Design 20 with Mallard Creek Design 8 and Kings Bay Design 135 with Mallard Creek Design 17 (Figure 10-11). Both have DG3 structures. The design in the first set is a fairly typical example of DG3. Kings Bay Design 20 is one of the DG3 options, circles and ladders, found to be restricted to the southern portion of the Kings Bay site. The designs in the second set, with fine lands and grooves and on sherds with uncharacteristically sandy paste, may have come from similar vessels that may have

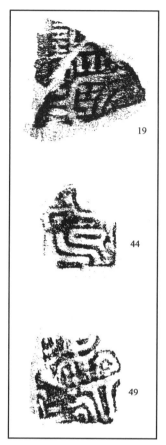

Figure 10-15. Mallard Creek site designs: new design group (Design 19) and DG10 (Designs 44 and 49).

been transported from site to site. In fact, it was the recognition of this possible match during fieldwork at Mallard Creek that stimulated this project. Designs similar in element use (lobes and circles) and structure to Kings Bay Design 135 were found throughout the Kings Bay site.

Other, more tentative, matches are shown in Figure 10-12. Two more DG3 designs are represented, and these are composed of teardrops and circles, a design option not spatially restricted at Kings Bay. The remainder of the possible matches include one member each of DG2, 5, and 8, none of which was restricted in space at Kings Bay. Design matches between the

Kings Bay and Mallard Creek sites, then, constitute something between 4 percent and 12 percent of the designs at Mallard Creek.

Conclusions

How should these data be interpreted? Did distinct populations occupy the two sites or does the correspondence in the frequency of design groups indicate a single population? Here is where the lack of comparative data from other sites on the Georgia coast, and contemporaneous sites outside of what might be considered an isolated style pool (related to either interaction or information), is critical. Despite the small number of paddle matches, on the basis of the similarity in design structure and element use, I am now inclined to think that the same population occupied the two sites. The similarity in carving and style in the DG5 and DG10 cases is particularly persuasive. I did, however, hope to see more paddle matching between the sites before favoring this conclusion. I would also have liked to see more evidence of the designs that were restricted in space at Kings Bay. Another compelling piece of evidence for this conclusion would be stronger evidence for differing site functions to explain why the same population occupied the two sites. However, the difference in intrasite settlement structure between the sites is at least some indirect evidence for different site functions.

In terms of the similarity in the percentage frequencies of design elements and design groups between the two sites, it might be noted that, except for the simple figure-8 designs (and other related teardrops, Figures 10-4, 10-5, 10-6, possibly Figures 10-7 and 10-15, Design 44), a circle (Figure 10-8, Design 97), and a lobe (Figure 10-15, Design 19; note that all of these are unrestricted designs at Kings Bay), none of the designs pictured by Snow (1975:42–55) from sites in south-central Georgia could be incorporated into the design groups found at the Georgia coast sites (17.5 percent of the designs fit a Kings Bay design group).[10] This does not confirm either the social relationship posited between the sites or even the underlying tenet—that the design groups conveyed information. The south-central sites could simply be out of the design interaction zone. It will be necessary to delineate the spatial distribution, and especially the characteristics of the boundaries, of many different design assemblages before any definitive conclusions can be made.

Notes

1. For those archaeologists uncomfortable with the subject of meaning, the papers of Patrick (1985), Kosso (1991), and, to a lesser extent, Emerson (1989) assure us of the compatibility of the level of inference between processual and post-processual archaeology.

2. Individual variation refers to the fact (long employed by art historians) that "individuals are always somewhat different from one another in their motor habits or motor performances; the artifacts they make or use will exhibit slight stylistic differences in execution or use-wear. We can use these differences to identify the works of different individuals" (Hill and Gunn 1977:2). In this study, individual paddle carvers and/or pot stampers should be identifiable in the mix of stylistic attributes recorded.

3. The concept of the analytical individual refers to the fact that at many levels of stylistic analysis, it is difficult to conclude that the smallest identifiable cluster of attributes may in fact have been produced by one individual. An analytical individual may be a single craftsperson or any combination of closely interacting individuals (e.g., sisters or a mother and daughter; see Redman 1977).

4. I have remained quite suspicious of these data. Site structure, paddle matching, and radiocarbon dating did indicate that all middens (and hypothetical adjacent houses) were occupied at the same time. However, the creation of design groups and assignment of more or less ambiguous designs to groups may not be replicable.

5. There is some ethnohistoric basis for the idea that religious symbols were present in southeastern Indian designs. Speck noted:

As regards the artistic expression of this tribe [the Catawba], it seems that, in general, special conventional decorations symbolizing concrete objects are confined to a few articles of clothing such as neckbands, sashes, hair ornaments, leggings, and carry-pouches. The whole field is permeated with a strong religious significance. Decorations of a like sort with a still more emphatic religious meaning are found on pottery, though rarely, as well as on other objects. (Speck 1909:54)

Speck did not elaborate and I have been unable to find any other ethnohistoric references to the meaning of designs on southeastern Indian pottery. There has been some work by archaeologists on the meaning of Mississippian period pottery designs (e.g., Emerson 1989; Griffith 1981; Hall 1973), but they have been more concerned with representational meaning rather than social meaning.

6. Few such complete inventories exist. These include Caldwell's (1978) descriptions from Fairchild's Landing and Hare's Landing; Sears's (1956) sketches from Kolomoki; my own inventory (Saunders 1986a) and that in Smith et al. (1985) from the Mallard Creek site; and also that on the Kings Bay Naval Submarine Support Base in southeastern Georgia (Smith et al. 1985). Snow's (1975) work and Chapter 6 in this volume are also valuable in this regard.

7. Plog (1983) criticized early analyses of design distribution for failing to establish the appropriate controls for the determination of the causes of design variation. Among other necessary controls, he stipulated that site function must be similar, because activities at functionally different sites could affect the assemblage of vessel forms, and different forms might require different decorative treatments. This is certainly true for pottery traditions. However, utilitarian jars were the overwhelming majority of vessel forms at both the Kings Bay and Mallard Creek sites, and there is no reason to suspect that site function affected the design in this case.

8. Another problem with comparability between the assemblages is that the excavation strategies used at the two sites were quite different. The Kings Bay site was taken into Phase III excavation while Mallard Creek has had only Phase II testing.

9. I used a variation of Shannon's (1979) lithographic technique to record the designs on the pottery. I covered the sherds in thin plastic wrap and set them on a pedestal of plasticine. A layer of institutional-grade toilet paper was then placed over the sherd. A semi-soft lithographer's brayer covered with water-based printer's ink was then rolled over the paper; lands of the design were reproduced on the paper. This technique allows one to make a permanent record of the design on the sherd on paper thin enough to be used as a transparency. With use of a light table, the designs or design fragments on different sherds can be overlain and directly compared (Saunders 1986a).

10. Trying to put the supposedly contemporaneous (Caldwell 1978:97;

I think the site might be 200 to 300 years earlier) and much larger Fairchild's Landing design assemblage into the Kings Bay design group format was more frustrating. DG1 was present in large numbers (27 percent), second was DG6 (8 percent), and DG3 and 4 were hesitantly assigned (6 percent and 3 percent, respectively). A full 41 percent of the reconstructed designs could not be assigned to a Kings Bay group.

Kolomoki and the Development of Sociopolitical Organization on the Gulf Coastal Plain

Karl T. Steinen

The Woodland in the Southeast was a period when societies were experimenting with the kinds of economies and social systems that provided the foundation for the establishment of Mississippian period chiefdoms. This experimentation took on different forms across the Southeast with the various manifestations of Swift Creek culture being perhaps both the most spectacular and most perplexing. Much of this problem can be attributed to our on-again and off-again interest in the Kolomoki site in southwestern Georgia. Kolomoki is a large multimound site (Figure 11-1) that was occupied during the Late Swift Creek and Weeden Island I periods and that has many of the characteristics of a Mississippian civic center—large truncated mound, crescent-shaped village area, and elaborate burial mounds—but lacks other features such as village burials, fortifications, strong indications of a stratified society, and the elaborate status markers known from sites such as Moundville, Lake Jackson, and Etowah.

The excavations of the Kolomoki site were conducted more than forty years ago by William H. Sears (Sears 1951a, 1951b, 1953, 1956, 1968). He argued that Kolomoki was a post–Swift Creek cultural phenomenon even though generally accepted interpretations of the ceramics and radiocarbon dates supported a Late Swift Creek affiliation (Table 11-1). Sears felt that the nature of the ceramics in both midden and mound contexts supported a late temporal placement. In an extensive reconsideration of Kolomoki Sears later

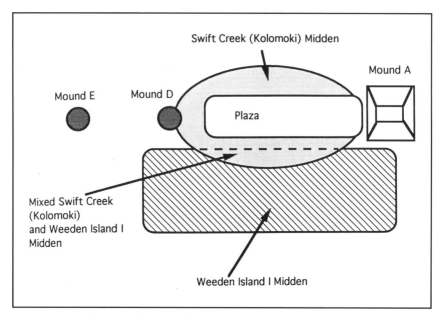

Figure 11-1. Schematic diagram of the Kolomoki site.

emphasized that there are three identifiable periods represented in the village midden (Sears 1992). The first is the Late Swift Creek (Kolomoki) assemblage, the second is a Weeden Island I complex that is a mixed Weeden Island and complicated stamped assemblage, and the third is also Weeden Island I but is a mixed Weeden Island and plain pottery assemblage. The Swift Creek (i.e., Kolomoki) site plan at Kolomoki is a crescent-shaped midden with the open end facing Mound A, and the Weeden Island site plan is an apparent continuous midden on the southern side of the site that extends outside the boundaries of the current park (Sears 1992) (Figure 11-1). The two burial mounds that were excavated, Mounds E and D, date respectively to the Late Swift Creek period or about A.D. 250–300 and to the first of the Weeden Island I assemblages or approximately A.D. 350–600 (Sears 1992:figure 1). A third mound, located outside of the boundaries of the park, which has not been excavated, may date to the final Weeden Island I occupation of the site.

Models of sociopolitical organization for the Kolomoki site and related cultures have varied greatly. Sears (1968) developed a model that argues that Kolomoki was the center for an extremely large Priest State (chiefdom) that

Table 11-1. Radiocarbon Dates from Mandeville and Kolomoki

Site	Provenience	Date B.P.	Date	Lab #	Period	Reference	Good Date?
9CY1	Below Mound A	1960 ± 150*	10 B.C.	M-1042	Late Deptford	1	Yes
9CY1	Below Mound A	1030 ± 150*	A.D. 920	M-1043	Late Deptford	1	Too recent
9CY1	Mound A tertiary midden	1420 ± 150*	A.D. 530	M-1044	Early S.C.	1	Too recent
9ER1	Mound D	1920 ± 300	A.D. 30	M-49	Early W.I.	2	Too old
9ER1	Mound E	2120 ± 300	170 B.C.	M-50	Late S.C.†	2	Too old
9ER1	Midden south of Mound A	1545 ± 225	A.D. 405	I-11482	Late S.C. /W.I. mix	3	Yes
9ER1	Midden south of Mound A	1565 ± 75	A.D. 385	I-11482C	Late S.C. /W.I. mix	3	Yes
9ER1	Midden south of Mound A	2075 ± 85	125 B.C.	I-11481	Late S.C. /W.I. mix	3	Too old

Notes: S.C. Swift Creek; *W.I.,* Weeden Island. References: *1,* Kellar, Kelly, McMichael 1962; *2,* Crane 1956; *3,* Milanich et al. 1984.
*When originally reported 1961 was used instead of 1950 to calculate the A.D./B.C. date.
†Referred to as *Late Swift Creek (Kolomoki)* in the text.

occupied the area from the Kolomoki site in the north, southward to the Gulf Coast, to as far west as Mobile Bay, and to as far east as the Big Bend area of Florida. He argued that there was a single political/religious leadership of the society that exercised control over the entire population and that Kolomoki and the Kolomoki state were the temporal and cultural equivalent of Mississippian chiefdoms. This model is overly ambitious in nature. The projected size for a Kolomoki Priest State (chiefdom) is simply too large to have been successfully administered from a single civic center, especially one located on its northern periphery. Recent analyses of Mississippian chiefdoms indicate that they were much smaller in area, generally only about 23 to 75 kilometers from one end to another (Hally 1993; Scarry and Payne 1986:83; Smith and Kowalewski 1980:6), than Sears's proposed Kolomoki Priest State. Given the level of organization attributed to Mississippian chiefdoms one can say that if there was a Priest State, it was much smaller in size than originally thought.

Few archaeologists were convinced by Sears's interpretations of the Kolomoki chronology or its position in the development of southeastern culture (Griffin 1984:136; Williams 1958). Recent work by Milanich and his colleagues in central Florida and at the McKeithen site in north-central Florida, by Percy and Brose in the Apalachicola Valley, and by me in southern Georgia has developed new data and interpretative models that provide a foundation for the reinterpretation of the Kolomoki site (Brose 1984; Brose and Percy 1974; Hemmings 1974; Milanich 1974; Milanich et al. 1984; Percy 1976; Percy and Brose 1974).

On the basis of a regional survey and excavations at the McKeithen site, a Weeden Island I civic center, Milanich et al. (1984) developed a model to explain the development and decline of sociopolitical organization during the Middle Woodland period. The model argues that these societies consisted of a series of relatively small villages that centered on single burial mounds or, in a few instances, small civic centers. These mounds/civic centers represented the burials and residences of Big Men who were the dominant sociopolitical leaders for each village cluster. These societies, organized on a lineage structure, did not participate in a chiefdom level of political organization as Sears thought but were essentially egalitarian in nature with some of them, such as McKeithen and to a greater extent Kolomoki, representing the culmination of this evolutionary development. Milanich and his colleagues argue that this kind of development eventually failed and did not lead directly to Mississippian societies.

Both Sears's Priest State and the McKeithen Elite Lineage model are based on the assumption that there was a supporting population, found in outlying villages and farmsteads, for the civic centers. Known site distributions along the Chattahoochee and Apalachicola rivers in the area from Stewart County, Georgia, in the north to Gadsden County, Florida, in the south indicate that there are numerous sites present that contain materials attributable to the Late Swift Creek and Weeden Island I periods (Belovich et al. 1983; DeJarnette 1975; Huscher 1959a, 1959b; Kelly 1950, 1960; Kelly et al. 1962; Knight and Mistovich 1984; Steinen 1977:79–81; White et al. 1981). Survey of the area between the Chattahoochee River and Spring Creek around Kolomoki (Steinen 1976b) indicates that there are few if any sites attributable to the Late Swift Creek and Weeden Island I periods present in the interior areas. Recent excavations in Randolph County, Georgia, only a few kilometers to the north of Kolomoki, demonstrate that there were Swift Creek sites in the area away from the Chattahoochee although they may not have been village sites (Espenshade 1992). Thus, there appears to be a discontinuity in site distribution in the Early County area. The largest and most impressive Late Swift Creek/Weeden Island I site seems to sit in isolation in the interior while village sites of the same period are found along the Chattahoochee River.

Environment

Kolomoki is located in an ecotone near the junction of the Dougherty Plain and the Red Hills geological zones. The Dougherty Plain is an area with chocolate-colored sandy loam soils, numerous sinkholes, dense hardwood forests, swampy hammocks, and mesic hammocks (Hubbell et al. 1956:9). The Red Hills are characterized by dark red soils, steep slopes, moist ravines, and forests of the Piedmont aspect. The bottomland of the Chattahoochee is broad and flat and as wide as 2 kilometers in some areas. The transition to the interfluvial zone is steep and abrupt. Numerous tributary streams, usually with narrow bottomlands, cut through the bluff and add to the rugged nature of the terrain (Steinen 1976b:69). The natural forest cover has generally been replaced by extensive pine plantations and agricultural fields on both the river bottoms and interfluvial uplands.

Ceremonial Sites in Southwestern Georgia

Kolomoki is only one of several ceremonial sites known in southwestern Georgia. By far the majority of these sites are conical burial mounds and only a relative few can be classified as civic centers (Brose and Percy 1974; Huscher 1959a, 1959b; Kelly 1960; Kelly et al. 1962; Moore 1903, 1907, 1918; Sears

1973, 1977; Steinen 1976a, 1976b, 1977, 1989). Research in southwestern Georgia has provided information concerning two civic centers, Mandeville and Cemochechobee, that predate and postdate Kolomoki. Both of these sites are only a few kilometers to the north and west of the Kolomoki site, on the eastern bank of the Chattahoochee River. Interestingly, and I think importantly, all three sites are located within the Red Hills physiographic region.

Mandeville, located in Clay County, Georgia, is a ceremonial site that dates to the Late Deptford and Early Swift Creek periods. The most prominent feature of the site is Mound A, also known as the Standley mound. This truncated earthen structure is approximately 70×50 meters at its base and more than 4 meters high (Kellar, Kelly, and McMichael 1962; McMichael and Kellar 1960:1). The final cap on Mound A is Mississippian but the interior layers all date to the Deptford and Early Swift Creek periods (Kellar, Kelly, and McMichael 1962; McMichael and Kellar 1960). Mound B, also known as the Griffith mound, is a burial structure. Associated ceramics, especially tetrapods, vessels with check stamping, and vessels with complicated stamping with notched rims, indicate that this structure dates to the Late Deptford and Early Swift Creek periods (McMichael and Kellar 1960:68–69) and fits Sears's descriptions for the Hopewell-related Yent-Greenpoint ceremonial development on the Gulf coast of Florida (Sears 1962). Although a total of twenty-three 10×10-foot squares were excavated and 10,131 sherds, most of which were from the final Mississippian occupation, were recovered from a midden that was more than 1 meter thick, no subsurface features were recorded (Kellar, Kelly, and McMichael 1962:348). The materials recovered from the village area were predominantly from the Mississippian occupation, but the Woodland sherds were mostly check stamped and complicated stamped (Betty Smith, pers. comm.).

At Mandeville there are two significant structures—a burial mound and a truncated mound—that date to the Deptford/Swift Creek transition during the Woodland period. Radiocarbon dates for Mound A range from 1960 ± 150 B.P. (10 B.C.) to 1420 ± 150 B.P. (A.D. 530) (Table 11-1). By including the standard deviations in the interpretation of these dates one can easily assign the site to a pre–A.D. 300 setting. The mounds, their inclusions, and dates demonstrate that a form of centralized ceremonialism had developed and then disappeared in the Chattahoochee Basin prior to the rise of

Kolomoki during the Late Swift Creek period. The social organization and patterns of adaptation, as shown from our incomplete understanding of settlement patterns in the Lower Chattahoochee, appear to have involved a village-based egalitarian system with only the suggestions of a developing social differentiation associated with a socioreligious authority that was centered on Mandeville. This type of organization closely resembles what Sears (1968:137–40) has called a Village Community system.

There are no identified Weeden Island II (Wakulla) ceremonial centers in the Lower Chattahoochee region or in any other area. Numerous middens and burial mounds date to this period but there are no sites that have village areas, burial mounds, and truncated mounds similar to Mandeville and Kolomoki. The first post-Kolomoki ceremonial center in the Lower Chattahoochee is the Cemochechobee site, a fully Mississippian Rood phase civic center located near Fort Gaines, Georgia, that dates from A.D. 900 to A.D. 1400. A detailed discussion of this site and its role in southeastern prehistory has been presented elsewhere and needs not be repeated here (Schnell, Knight, and Schnell 1981).

There is little overlap between the ceramic complexes at these three sites and no temporal overlap. Mandeville is a transitional Deptford to Early Swift Creek site, Kolomoki is a transitional Late Swift Creek to Early Weeden Island site, and Cemochechobee is a fully Mississippian site. The development of ceramic complexes in the lower Chattahoochee, however, has been well demonstrated and indicates that Mandeville, Kolomoki, and Cemochechobee, while they did not directly develop one from the other, certainly represent a temporally interrupted development.

We are presented with a problem by these patterns. Beginning with Mandeville in the transitional Late Deptford/Early Swift Creek period and continuing with Kolomoki in the Late Swift Creek/Weeden Island I transition there is an evolution to what appears to be a form of pre-Mississippian social organization. The richness of the Kolomoki Mound D and E burials, the size of the site, the crescent-shaped midden surrounding a plaza during the Late Swift Creek occupation, and the presence of the large truncated Mound A (which appears to date to the Kolomoki [Swift Creek] occupation and is definitely not related to the very small Mississippian occupation of the site) all point toward a society that had a significant amount of social differentiation. Sears (1968) argued for this but more recent interpretations (see

Milanich et al. 1984; Steinen 1989) suggest that the kinds of status markers associated with Mississippian chiefdoms are simply absent from Kolomoki and other Swift Creek and Weeden Island civic centers. Even if Kolomoki was not the center of a Mississippian-like chiefdom it was an important site for a social system that was more complex than earlier village-based communities; however, it was not as complex or as strongly structured as the system recognized for Mississippian societies.

Settlement Patterns, Economics, and Political Organization: A Model for the Rise and Fall of Kolomoki

Models of prehistoric political organization generally are based on our ability to recognize the parallel between growing social differentiation (development from an egalitarian society toward stratification) and increasing complexity and regularity in settlement hierarchies, community patterns, artifact distributions, burial loci, and burial furniture (Larson 1960; Peebles 1971; Peebles and Kus 1977; Sears 1968). The more complex levels of social organization have more complex archaeological manifestations. The relatively simple collections and patterns associated with Archaic period sites are easily contrasted with the elaborate status markers, numerous large mounds, and civic centers of Mississippian chiefdoms. Somewhere between these two extremes lies Kolomoki.

The evolution of political systems in the lower Chattahoochee Basin was a pattern of increased centralization and complexity of sociopolitical organization followed by a period of decentralization during the Weeden Island I and II periods and then a reemergence of complex systems during the Mississippian period. It was not, as Sears (1968) hinted, a linear development toward a Mississippian way of life. If this is so, what were the interlocking social and economic dynamics that underlay this sinuous or nonlinear trajectory (Figure 11-2)? Because of the paucity of organized work that has been conducted in the Lower Chattahoochee during the past thirty years a clear answer to this question cannot be given. There are, however, enough data to generate models that can be tested in the future.

My reconnaissance survey of the area around Kolomoki (Steinen 1976b) and an analysis of surveys in the Chattahoochee Basin suggest that Kolomoki may have developed in a pattern that was significantly different from those

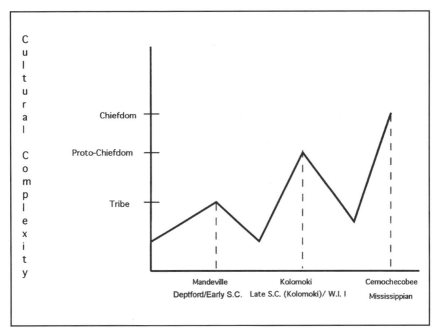

Figure 11-2. Sinuous or nonlinear trajectory of cultural development in the area around the Kolomoki site. *S.C.*, Swift Creek; *W.I.*, Weeden Island.

previously proposed (Milanich et al. 1984; Sears 1968). Our understanding of site distributions in southwestern Georgia is generally limited to the Chattahoochee River. Clarence B. Moore's famous surveys never went inland (Moore 1903, 1907, 1918). River basin projects of the 1950s, principally those conducted by Hurt, Kurjack (DeJarnette 1975), Huscher (1959a, 1959b), and Caldwell (1978), stayed along the river. More recently the Corps of Engineers–sponsored surveys of the Chattahoochee River from the Florida/Georgia border to the Fall Line have provided information concerning shifts in settlement patterns during the Weeden Island I and II periods (Belovich et al. 1983; Knight and Mistovich 1984; Mistovich and Knight 1986; White et al. 1981). The only inland surveys have been associated with cultural resource management projects and my own reconnaissance-level survey of Early County in 1975 (Steinen 1976b). None of this work has contributed greatly to an understanding of the macro-settlement pattern for Kolomoki and it is certainly not sufficient to either support or refute Milanich and his coauthors' statements about the rise and fall of the Kolomoki polity, Sears's proposal for a complex chiefdom level of political organization, or any other interpretation for this site.

Both the Priest State and Elite Lineage models assume that there was a supporting population, found in outlying villages and farmsteads, for the Swift Creek and Weeden Island period ceremonial sites (both the evolving civic centers such as McKeithen and Kolomoki and the individual burial mounds). In north-central Florida such a supporting population was identified through regional survey (Milanich et al. 1984; Siegler-Lavelle 1980). My survey in Early County, however, did not disclose the presence of sites that date to the Swift Creek and Weeden Island periods in either the interior Dougherty Plain or interior Red Hills environments. These kinds of sites are found in abundance along the Chattahoochee River and farther to the south in the area north of Tallahassee (Huscher 1959a, 1959b; Mistovich and Knight 1986; Scarry 1990; White et al. 1981). If this pattern is not a product of sampling error, how can it be incorporated into a model that explains how and why Kolomoki developed into a large civic center and then declined with the advent of Weeden Island society?

Drawing from models generated from surveys farther to the south in the Dougherty Plain (Brose 1984; Scarry 1990; Scarry and Payne 1986; White et al. 1981), I suggest that Kolomoki was first occupied because of the advantages presented by its location on the Dougherty Plain/Red Hills ecotone. Kolomoki Creek, numerous springheads, and the tributary creeks of the Chattahoochee found in the Red Hills, as well as the sinkhole ponds and swampy floodplains found in the Dougherty Plain, provided a rich and varied environment that could be easily and effectively exploited by Woodland economic systems. Research in other areas of Georgia and Florida (Kohler 1991; Milanich 1971; Percy 1976; Percy and Brose 1974) indicates that during the Late Swift Creek and Weeden Island I periods a diffuse economic system that included hunting, fishing, gathering, and farming was practiced (Cleland 1976). By locating on the ecotone between two diverse and varied environments, the occupants of Kolomoki could exploit a wide range of resources. This pattern, which is continued in the following Mississippian period (see Larson 1960; B. D. Smith 1975, 1978; Ward 1965), allowed for the development of a substantial population without the reliance on floodplain agriculture that was crucial for the development of Mississippian society and economics (B. D. Smith 1975; B. D. Smith, ed. 1978:483).

The pre-Woodland settlement pattern in the area around Kolomoki closely reflects a system that would rely solely on exploitation of the resources of the creeks, sinkholes, springheads, and interfluvial environments. My survey and an inspection of private collections indicate that small Middle and Late Archaic period sites are abundant in the uplands adjacent to the creeks and sinkholes of the area (Steinen 1976b). This distribution of lithic sites, with no apparent nucleation, is indicative of an economic system that did not support a settled lifeway or the development of a complex society.

A significant factor that may have led to the shift in settlement distribution and the development of complex ceremonialism during the Woodland period would have been the developing importance of maize agriculture, which was an element of Woodland period economies (Kohler 1991:100–107; Percy 1976:table 1; Percy and Brose 1974:11; Scarry 1990:233; Wood 1981; Wood et al. 1986; Wood and Ledbetter 1988).

Although the overall evidence for the existence of maize in the Southeast prior to the Late Woodland period is scanty, it is sufficient to suggest that it was an element of the overall socioeconomic system. Many archaeologists are quite ambivalent even to the suggestion that maize was present during the Early and Middle Woodland periods at all. In a discussion of the evidence for the presence of maize in the Southeast Fearn and Liu (1995) document the presence of maize pollen as early as 3500 B.P. (50 B.C.). At the Fort Center site in Glades County, Florida, maize pollen was recovered from sealed cultural contexts including human coprolites dating to as early as 2500 B.P. (Sears 1982). Fearn and Liu indicate that isotopic analysis of human bone in both Mesoamerica and the Southeast indicates that a significant reliance on corn did not occur for at least 1,000 years after it is first visible in the microfossil or macrofossil record.

The main question, I believe, is not whether maize was present during the Early and Middle Woodland but what role it had in a diverse system of hunting, fishing, gathering, and cultivation. Sears (1971) has suggested that the growing of maize was an integral aspect of the developing Hopewellian ceremonialism. He feels that they were a complex, the one element dependent on the other, that was adopted as a package. Scarry and others (Hall 1980:430;

Johannessen 1993:75–76; C. M. Scarry 1993:87–88) have suggested that since most of the early corn has been recovered from ceremonial/civic deposits, it may have been a ceremonial food associated with an emerging elite element in the society.

One significant problem with the idea that agriculture was part of the Kolomoki economy is that the site is not located near any large contiguous areas of rich arable land. Most archaeologists generally assume that farming settlements will be located adjacent to their agricultural plots, and for years they have looked at this relationship as an indirect indicator of agriculture (see Bruce Smith, ed. 1978). While this pattern of proximity is an important element in the location of Mississippian sites, especially civic centers (Larson 1970; Ward 1965), other dynamics may have functioned within less centralized socioeconomic systems that allowed for the efficient exploitation of scattered plots of arable land by peoples living in nucleated settlements. A model for such a system comes from Moala Island, Fiji. There, the traditional social system was based on extended family households that subsisted by growing root crops such as taro, yams, sweet potatoes, and sweet manioc using slash-and-burn techniques. Until the 1950s Moala Islanders exploited plots of land adjacent to their villages as well as some that were more than 15 kilometers walking distance away (Sahlens 1957:450). Because of the distances involved and the rough terrain of the island the noncontiguous plots were most effectively worked when the producers remained near them overnight. A few members of the extended family would travel to the distant plot, work it for a few days, and then return to the permanent village. A similar pattern was followed during the harvest.

This kind of economic system would be well suited to the interior of the Red Hills and the Dougherty Plain ecosystems where there is a plentiful supply of water, game, and fish but where the rich land needed to support corn agriculture is found in small plots that are widely scattered along the narrow floodplains of the Red Hills creeks and around the sinkhole ponds of the Dougherty Plain. In a Moalan-like system of absentee agriculture these scattered plots, in conjunction with a diverse system of hunting, fishing, and gathering, could be effectively used to support a fairly extensive population centered at Kolomoki. The archaeological manifestation of this kind of economy would be the nucleated community at Kolomoki in addition to a series of artifact scatters adjacent to the small plots of land (Figure 11-3).

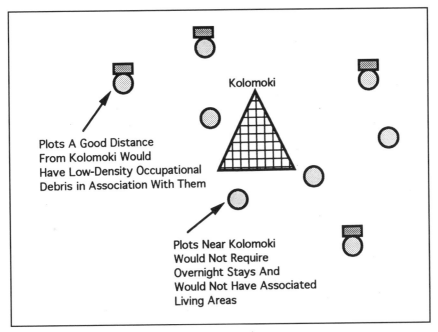

Figure 11-3. Schematic diagram of proposed Moalan (Fijian)-like agricultural system for the Kolomoki area.

These distant sites would be similar to the Sonny Lee site in Thomas County, Georgia (Steinen and Crawford 1990), and 9RH18 near Cuthbert, Georgia (Espenshade 1992:75). In both instances the conclusion was that each site represented long-term low-intensity use, but archaeologists have failed to recognize that this activity might have been related to farming activities.

Direct evidence in support of the presence of corn farming at and around Kolomoki is lacking at this time. However, there is sufficient evidence, cited above, that indicates that maize was cultivated during the Early and Middle Woodland periods in other areas of the Southeast. Perhaps one of the problems with our search for evidence of maize farming has been a reliance on the recovery of macrofossils (Yarnell and Black 1985) and a general avoidance of the search for pollen. The recovery techniques used at Kolomoki were not designed to recover floral remains (Sears 1956) and other sites that have been excavated in the lower Chattahoochee have had poor floral preservation (Knight and Mistovich 1984; Mistovich and Knight 1986). Because maize microfossils or macrofossils have not been identified at this time does not mean that we should assume that maize was absent at Kolomoki or surrounding sites. We should, however, develop testable models, such as the one presented here, concerning its presence or absence at these sites and the role that it had (or did not have) in the overall social and economic systems.

The dispersed Woodland economy of Kolomoki would have limited both the size of the population that could develop and the complexity of the social organization. Mississippian culture seems to have been reliant on the productivity of river bottom agriculture and varieties of corn that did not exist during the Woodland period (see Galinat and Gunnerson 1963; Mangelsdorf 1974:162–63; C. M. Scarry 1993; B. D. Smith, ed. 1978:483, 489). The resources of the floodplain environments provided certain adaptational advantages to Mississippian populations and attracted Woodland period peoples as well. The location of Deptford, Swift Creek, and Weeden Island middens and ceremonial structures along the rivers, and in apparently the same environmental setting as Mississippian sites, suggests that Woodland peoples were attracted to the same rich renewable soils of the river bottoms and the varied seasonal resources of the hardwood forests as were Mississippian populations. These are, however, the very kinds of resources that were not available at Kolomoki.

As the population of Kolomoki increased during the Late Swift Creek period the social organization responded in an expected manner. Indicators of social differentiation increased and were manifested in Mound E with its elaborate effigy ceramics and in the formal crescent-shaped village area and plaza. Details of this development, however, have not been delineated at this time. Sears's extensive testing in the village midden and his analysis were not designed to uncover these kinds of dynamics. Because the notes and catalog for these excavations were misplaced some unknown time after the completion of the analysis and the preparation of the reports, without new excavations in the village area archaeologists may never understand the dynamics of growth of the Late Swift Creek occupation of the site.

If Sears's test-pit data are correct and the Weeden Island I occupation of Kolomoki was concentrated to the south of a line from Mound A to Mounds D and E and was not structured in a formal manner as is generally found in civic centers, this would signal a decline in the centralization of sociopolitical authority at the Kolomoki site. In this moving away from the formally structured village plan toward one that was not oriented around a central plaza in front of the large mound, one would see the long-term decline toward a type of social organization that could be successfully supported by a diffuse hunting, fishing, gathering, and farming economy that is similar to those determined for other Weeden Island societies that are found on the eastern Gulf Coastal Plain (Brose 1984; Milanich 1974; Percy 1976; Percy and Brose 1974). Mound D is associated with this period of occupation and an unexcavated conical mound located to the south of the boundaries of the Kolomoki Mounds Historic Site may relate to the third and final assemblage of the site (Sears 1992; Steinen 1976a). As with the microchronology of the Late Swift Creek occupation little is known of the internal dynamics of the Weeden Island period occupation of Kolomoki.

Concluding Comments

It is time to return to Kolomoki. Models of social organization and our understanding of settlement patterns and chronologies for southern Georgia have been refined, and significant new models of Woodland period society have been generated in recent years since the work at Kolomoki was completed nearly half a century ago. Yet, no direct attempts have been made to conduct organized work in the area surrounding one of the largest and most enigmatic sites of this period. Did Kolomoki sit in isolated splendor for hundreds of years or was there a general shift in settlement away from the Chattahoochee River as Schnell has suggested (Schnell in Knight and Mistovich 1984)? Speculation and theory building will do little to answer the questions that remain about Kolomoki and the development of complex societies during the Woodland period. New excavations in the Kolomoki midden are needed to develop a microchronology for the site and to define possible elite ceramics and residential areas as Kohler did at the McKeithen site (Kohler 1978; Milanich et al. 1984). Excavation methods need to be implemented to develop a more detailed understanding of changes in subsistence patterns, large areas of the midden need to be opened to trace residence patterns, and a detailed survey of the Dougherty Plain and the Red Hills environments needs to be conducted to determine patterns of cultural development in the area away from Kolomoki. Until this is done archaeologists will continue to develop competing models that are not testable from the existing and quite incomplete database.

Acknowledgments

Many of the ideas in this chapter were inspired by conversations with W. H. Sears, J. T. Milanich, T. A. Kohler, E. Bilko, and L. H. Larson. Naturally, they are not to blame for any errors in interpretation that I have presented.

Swift Creek Traits in Northeastern Florida
Ceramics, Mounds, and Middens

Keith H. Ashley

This chapter reviews the occurrence of Swift Creek manifestations as revealed in northeastern Florida. After a brief discussion on local Woodland chronologies, past research and new ideas concerning nontechnological aspects of Middle Woodland ceramics are considered to suggest Early and Late Swift Creek pottery types and possible cultural manifestations. This is followed by a presentation of data gathered from known burial mounds and midden deposits that have yielded Swift Creek wares. The study encompasses sites along the northern or lower St. Johns River in present-day Duval County, Florida (Figure 12-1). This region, extending from Julington Creek to the river's mouth at Mayport, corresponds roughly to the known distribution of Swift Creek ceramics in northeastern Florida. Much of our current data on local Middle Woodland occupations, however, is derived from sites confined to the tidewater zone between downtown Jacksonville and the Atlantic Ocean. Figure 12-2 shows the lower St. Johns River area within the context of the southeastern United States, along with other regions referenced in this chapter.

Before continuing, two points need to be made explicit regarding local Middle Woodland manifestations as perceived in the region. First, in the context of the study area, the term *Swift Creek* is used loosely to indicate Swift Creek pottery-making peoples but does not carry with it specific ethnic or geographic connotations. Second, those St. Johns River mounds yielding Swift Creek pottery will be identified as Swift Creek related, acknowledging

Keith H. Ashley

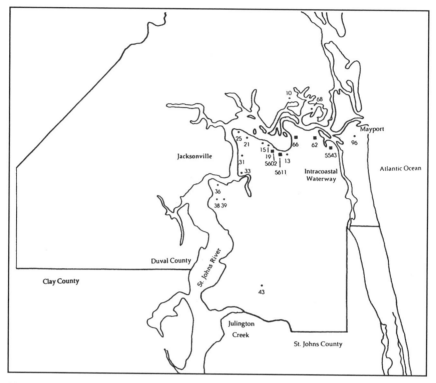

Figure 12-1. Swift Creek mound and midden sites, Duval County, Florida.

ceramic relationships between local Middle Woodland mound builders and Swift Creek peoples to the west and north. Complementary overviews of past research concerning local Swift Creek manifestations and problems in their interpretation are discussed by Ashley (1992) and Russo (1992).

Local Woodland Ceramic Chronology

Archaeologists have routinely affiliated post-Archaic groups in northeastern Florida with the St. Johns tradition, a widespread archaeological manifestation dating from about 500 B.C. until shortly after Spanish settlement of Florida in A.D. 1565 (Goggin 1952; Milanich 1994). The Woodland era within this chronology, circa 500 B.C. to A.D. 750, is referred to as St. Johns I and is characterized by sand burial tumuli, extensive freshwater- and marine-

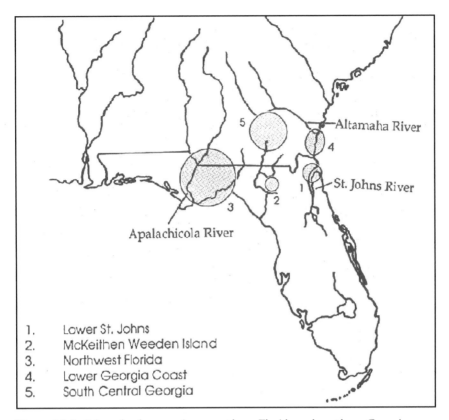

Figure 12-2. Selected culture regions, northern Florida and southern Georgia.

shell middens and mounds, and a prevailing distinctive plain chalky pottery. Recently, Russo (1992; Russo et al. 1993) has reconsidered the archaeological history of the lower St. Johns River valley and southeastern coastal Georgia, suggesting that the regions should be combined and called the St. Marys. The primary premise behind this regional construct is that most sites within the St. Marys area, although containing St. Johns cultural traits, differ from regions to the south, north, and west in terms of pottery assemblages and settlement types (Russo 1992:107).

The first Woodland period occupations of the St. Marys mouth region occurred around 500 B.C. and are represented by Deptford pottery assemblages containing plain, check-stamped, and simple stamped types (Russo

Table 12-1. Radiocarbon Dates from Northeastern Florida Swift Creek Sites

SITE	C14 Date B.P.	C14 Adjusted Date	C13 Adjusted Date B.P.	C13 Adjusted Date
8DU96	1865 ± 95	A.D. 85 ± 95		
8DU68	2640 ± 90	690 ± 90 B.C.		
8DU68	990 ± 60	A.D. 960 ± 60	1360 ± 60	A.D. 590 ± 60
8DU68	1250 ± 70	A.D. 700 ± 70	1610 ± 70	A.D. 340 ± 70

1992:115; Sears 1957:28; Vernon 1984:108). Some time after A.D. 1, there appears to have been a florescence of several decorated minority types (e.g., check stamped, complicated stamped), although undecorated sand-tempered wares, which often tend to be overlooked, dominated local pottery assemblages (Russo 1992:115; Sears 1957:29). Diagnostic decorative pottery types recovered from local Woodland midden contexts include Deptford, St. Johns, Swift Creek, and Weeden Island. In the past, most post-Archaic wares except the chalky St. Johns series were presumed to be of foreign origin (Goggin 1952:47; Milanich and Fairbanks 1980:161). However, site components containing almost exclusively Deptford (e.g., Greenfield site 5, 8DU5541) and Swift Creek (e.g., Greenfield site 7, 8DU5543) series ceramics have been recently identified, suggesting local production (Florida Archaeological Services 1995). Ironically, no pure St. Johns I sites, as defined by the predominance of St. Johns plain wares, have yet been reported locally (Goggin 1952:47; Russo 1992:115).

The lack of unequivocal stratigraphic ceramic information combined with the ubiquitous occurrence of plain wares and the paucity of absolute dates from secure contexts precludes the development of concisely defined and well-dated local Woodland phase designations at this time. In fact, radiocarbon dates have been reported for only two Swift Creek–related sites in northeastern Florida (Table 12-1). Moreover, the date from the Mayport mound (8DU96) and the first date from the Dent mound (8DU68) seem too early for mound interment on the basis of recovered artifacts. As work in the region continues, a clearer, more chronologically refined local Wood-

Table 12-2. Chronologies of Northeastern Florida and Southeastern Georgia

	St. Marys[1]	Lower St. Johns[2]	Lower St. Johns[3]	St. Johns[4]	Kings Bay[5]
800-	Colorinda Creek Swift St. Johns? (Colorinda, Creek, Swift, St. Johns?)	Colorinda			
700-			Sand Tempered Plain	St. Johns 1b	
600-		Weeden Island			
500-		– – –			Swift Creek
400-					
300-		Sand Tempered Plain	Limestone (Charcoal) Tempered Plain	St. Johns 1a	
200-					
100-					
0 A.D.-					
100-	Deptford	Deptford	Deptford	St. Johns 1	Deptford
200-					
300-					
400-					
500-					

References: *1*, Russo 1992; *2*, Sears 1957; *3*, Sears 1959; *4*, Milanich and Fairbanks 1980; *5*, Adams 1985.

land ceramic sequence should emerge. Table 12-2 outlines some of the previously presented ceramic chronologies for the Woodland period in northeastern Florida and/or southeastern Georgia.

Swift Creek Ceramics

John Goggin (1952) was the first researcher to discuss, with heavy reliance on Moore's (1894, 1895, 1896) burial mound data, the distribution of Swift Creek Complicated Stamped ceramics in northeastern Florida. Sketches of various sherds and vessels recovered by Moore clearly indicate Swift Creek design patterns and vessel forms. Goggin (1952:49–50, 70, 106) observed that both notched-rim (early) and folded-rim (late) Swift Creek wares were found at sites on the St. Johns River and emphasized that their association was seemingly restricted to burial mounds along the river's lower course. Subsequent to Goggin's study, Sears (1957, 1959) was the first archaeologist working in the study area to recover Swift Creek sherds through stratigraphic excavation.

Excavating at several shell middens and one mound site on the river's southern bank, Sears uncovered a small collection of Swift Creek II, St. Andrews, Crooked River, and "limestone-tempered" plain and complicated stamped sherds (Sears 1957, 1959). In addition, Sears reported a plain, "hole-tempered" pottery that has been interpreted by Ashley (1992:131) to be synonymous with the limestone-tempered ware. After closer scrutiny, however, it appears that Sears did differentiate between hole- and limestone-tempered ceramics, although specific physical differences between the two were never discussed. Sherds of the former are all undecorated and resemble Pasco pottery of the Florida Gulf Coast, whereas the latter include a complicated stamped variant that mimics Early Swift Creek pottery in terms of surface finish and rim treatment (Sears 1959:3, 12).

As reported earlier (Ashley 1992:131), a microscopic examination of suspected limestone-tempered sherds revealed that these wares actually contained small fragments of wood, some of which have been identified as pine (*Pinus* sp.) charcoal. Furthermore, a recent reexamination of several sherds originally recovered by Sears confirmed the presence of carbonized wood fragments (Ruhl in Russo et al. 1993:35–36). The charcoal is undoubtedly a human additive and thus considered a temper (Ann Cordell, pers. comm.). A brief microscopic inspection of a few sherds from the Mayport mound done by me and Donna Ruhl indicated that they are very similar to Sears's limestone-tempered ware. These Mayport specimens were originally typed as hole-tempered by the excavator (Wilson 1965). Thus, it seems reasonable to conclude that Sears's limestone-tempered and Wilson's hole-tempered wares are actually charcoal-tempered wares. The cultural affiliation and temporal placement of Sears's hole-tempered ware, however, remain in question, although affiliations with Pasco pottery are possible.

More recent investigations have uncovered additional Swift Creek ceramics from sites near the river's mouth, but because of small sample sizes few attempts have been made to discriminate early from late varieties (Ashley 1991; Ashley and Johnson 1990; Ashley and Wheat 1991; Johnson 1988;

Lee et al. 1984; Richter 1993; Russo et al. 1993). In the past, distinguishing among Early, Middle, and Late Swift Creek has involved different criteria depending on the researcher and the specific region under study (Brose 1985:159). For this chapter, the designation of Early Swift Creek is used for assemblages in which scalloped or notched rims are most frequent. In contrast, Late Swift Creek refers to assemblages dominated by folded rim forms. Because of the lack of local radiocarbon dates, comparative temporal data from northwestern Florida and the lower Georgia coast are used. The following descriptions are regularities I have observed in local pottery collections containing Swift Creek wares.

Early Swift Creek (A.D. 100–300)

Vessels and sherds conforming to the Early Swift Creek type include sand-tempered and charcoal-tempered varieties. Charcoal inclusions in the latter, all of which appear to be sand-tempered, range from abundant to sparse. At this time, it is unclear whether wood was added unfired and carbonized during ceramic manufacture or was wood charcoal to begin with and "ashed away" during the firing process, leaving holes of various sizes (Ruhl in Russo et al. 1993:35). Some specimens possess an intentionally smoothed surface, which reduced exterior surface pitting. In contrast, others are so pitted that the friable sherds tend to crumble on contact. A ceramic technological analysis of the charcoal-tempered pottery is needed to define its range of variability and to develop objective and replicable criteria by which to identify the ware (e.g., Cordell 1985, 1992, 1993).

Within local mound and midden pottery assemblages, plain sherds consistently outnumber their complicated stamped counterparts (Tables 12-3 and 12-4). With respect to complicated stamped specimens, many lack distinct or complete design patterns, because of factors ranging from small sherd size to severe surface weathering. Discernible design elements include bull's-eyes, concentric circles, ovals, scrolls, and other curvilinear motifs, as well as various triangular and diamond patterns. Design motifs on charcoal-tempered wares seem to be more similar to northwestern Florida coast Swift Creek designs (Shannon 1979) than to those from southeastern Georgia (Frankie Snow, pers. comm.). In fact, Early Swift Creek pottery assemblages have been reported rarely for sites in south-central and coastal Georgia, and none is presently known for the Kings Bay locality (Adams 1985; Saunders 1986a, Chapter 10 herein).

Table 12-3. Reconstructed Mortuary Vessels from the Mayport and Dent Mounds

Type	Mayport Mound[*]	Dent Mound
Sand-tempered plain	9	10
Charcoal-tempered plain	2	9
Charcoal-tempered Swift Creek (Early)	1	4
Swift Creek (Late)	6	2
Swift Creek	0	3
St. Johns Plain	3	2
Dunns Creek Red	2	1
Weeden Island	1	2
Deptford Simple Stamped	1	0
Totals	25	33

*Additional sherds and vessels are part of an unanalyzed collection in Jacksonville.

Rim treatments associated with plain and complicated stamped charcoal-tempered wares include a simple round style and a wide variety of notched, ticked, crenelated, and pie-crust styles. Occasionally interior or exterior clay extrusion along the lip margin resembles a small, poorly formed fold, but few examples are suggestive of intentional folding. This may suggest an evolutionary trend toward rim folding, although no medium or large rim folds have been reported on charcoal-tempered wares to date. Rim forms on charcoal-tempered wares point to a local Early Swift Creek pottery assemblage. However, vessels or basal sherds with podal supports, generally indicative of Early Swift Creek assemblages, have not been reported locally.

Complete vessels have yet to be recovered from midden contexts, but mended sherds from 8DU5543 suggest open bowls and pots. More definitive answers concerning vessel form are derived from pottery collections from the Mayport (8DU96) and Dent (8DU68) mounds, with reconstructed vessels consisting of simple restricted bowls, straight-sided bowls, collared jars with globular bodies, large conoidal pots, and one boat-shaped vessel. Many of

Table 12-4. Sherd Frequencies, Features 10 and 4, 8DU5543[*]

Feature 10	Number	Percent
Sand-tempered plain	31	19.4
Charcoal-tempered plain	47	29.4
Sand/charcoal-tempered plain	9	5.6
Grog/charcoal-tempered plain	10	6.3
Sand-tempered complicated stamped	4	2.5
Charcoal-tempered complicated stamped	188	11.2
Sand/charcoal-tempered complicated stamped	32	20.0
Sand-tempered eroded	5	3.1
Charcoal-tempered eroded	3	1.9
Other	1	0.6
Total	160	100.0
Feature 4	**Number**	**Percent**
Sand-tempered plain	143	43.5
Sand-tempered complicated stamped	90	27.4
Sand-tempered check stamped	13	4.0
Sand-tempered shell edge impressed	9	2.7
St. Johns Plain	6	1.8
Sand-tempered stamped and incised	1	0.3
Sand-tempered eroded stamped	62	18.8
Sand-tempered eroded	5	1.5
Total	329	100.0

*Ceramic analysis based on nontechnological identification.

Figure 12-3. Swift Creek design contact between the Dent mound (Florida) and the Lewis Island site (Georgia). (Copyright © Frankie Snow. Used by permission.)

the Swift Creek wares from the Dent mound are heavily sooted, implying utilitarian or ritual usage prior to interment (Ashley and Richter 1993).

Late Swift Creek (A.D. 300–700)

Evidence that Late Swift Creek ceramics have been recovered locally is as unambiguous as the presence of Early Swift Creek, since folded-rim complicated stamped sherds and vessels are unquestionably illustrated by Moore (1894, 1895, 1896). More recently, late styles have been recovered from sites such as the Dent mound (8DU68), the Mayport mound (8DU96), the McCormick site (8DU66), and Greenfield site 7 (8DU5543), to name a few. Late varieties generally range from sandy to gritty in paste, with charcoal tempering unreported thus far. It is generally implied that grit-tempered complicated stamped wares as well as micaceous paste wares are extralocal trade acquisitions. Whether these ceramics are indeed the result of foreign production or are local copies indistinguishable from imported Swift Creek wares remains to be tested, however.

To this end, Frankie Snow has recently linked a Late Swift Creek motif from the Dent mound with one from the Lewis Island site near the mouth of the Altamaha River, Georgia (Figure 12-3). A direct sherd-to-sherd comparison indicates that the two vessels (both with folded rims) display identi-

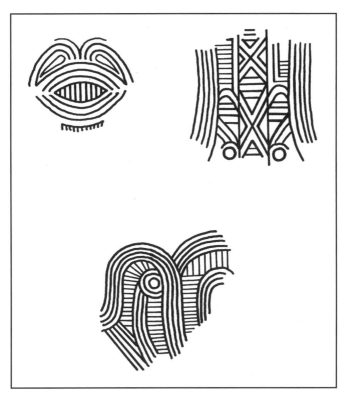

Figure 12-4. Selected Swift Creek designs from the Dent mound. (Copyright © Frankie Snow. Used by permission.)

cal complicated stamped motifs (Frankie Snow, pers. comm.). Furthermore, diagnostic irregularities (i.e., flaw marks) apparent on both sherds strongly suggest that they were stamped with the same paddle. A second design contact has also been uncovered by Snow linking another design from the same Lewis Island site with one from the Mayport mound. Confirmation of these Late Swift Creek design contacts to the north suggests tentatively that the exchange networks involving the movement of Swift Creek people, design concepts, paddles, and/or the wares themselves shifted over time from the northwestern Florida coast during Early Swift Creek times to the Atlantic seaboard of Georgia.

Design elements on Late Swift Creek vessels include snowshoes, scrolls, circles, and various barred elements (Figure 12-4). Information regarding vessel forms comes exclusively from reconstructed mound ceramics. Complicated stamped vessels from mortuary contexts include large conoidal pots and collared jars with globular and elongated bodies. Sooting of the exterior surface of some of these vessels also suggests domestic or ritual use prior to their intentional placement in burial mounds.

Sand Burial Mounds

A review of past mortuary mound studies indicates that at least fourteen burial mounds in the lower St. Johns River valley have yielded Swift Creek Complicated Stamped pottery (Table 12-5). Twelve were excavated during the late nineteenth century by Clarence B. Moore (1894, 1895, 1896), while two were investigated more recently (Ashley and Richter 1993; Wilson 1965). Definitive interpretations of local mound excavations, however, are hampered by the use of biased sampling and recording techniques on the part of past investigators. The problems in interpreting Moore's biased mortuary data have been well chronicled by numerous researchers. Similarly, the Dent mound was excavated twenty years ago by a local amateur group that failed to employ rigorous stratigraphic controls (Ashley and Richter 1993). The field methods used in the partial excavation of the Mayport mound have also met with criticism (Sears 1967). As a consequence of these methodological deficiencies, only broad inferences can be gleaned from these mortuary studies.

Because the only recognized prehistoric complicated stamped ware found in the region is presumed to be Swift Creek, those complicated stamped wares unearthed by Moore are considered to be Swift Creek or a related ware. Moreover, Moore's (1894, 1895, 1896) illustrations of complicated stamped sherds and vessels from the lower St. Johns region are invariably Swift Creek. The only other known complicated stamped ware found in the area is San Marcos, a protohistoric Guale Indian ware not known to occur in local prehistoric burial mound contexts. Outside the lower St. Johns area (e.g., northwestern Florida, lower Georgia coast), however, the assumption that all complicated stamped wares reported by Moore are Swift Creek is more dubious, since other similarly decorated ceramic types also occur in those areas.

According to Goggin's (1952:51) synthesis of Moore's mound data, at least seventeen of the forty-one mounds recorded in Duval County date to

Table 12-5. Swift Creek-Related Mounds on the Lower St. Johns River

SITE	Name	Size (m)	Height (m)	Source
8DU10	Johnson Mound	19.8	2.1	Moore 1895
8DU13	Monroe Mound	19.5	1.0	Moore 1895
8DU15	Low Grant Mound A	11	1.2	Moore 1895
8DU19	Low Grant Mound E	27.7 by 23.8	1.7	Moore 1895
8DU21	Horseshoe Landing Mound A	15.2	1.1	Moore 1895
8DU25	Reddie Point Mound A	24.4	--	Moore 1895
8DU31	Alicia Mound B	26.2	1.0	Moore 1895
8DU33	Arlington Mound	17.4 by 11	0.6	Moore 1896
8DU36	South Jacksonville Mound B	21.9 by 15.2	1.0	Moore 1896
8DU38	Point La Vista Mound A	8.8	0.8	Moore 1896
8DU39	Point La Vista Mound B	15.8	0.6	Moore 1896
8DU43	Beauclerc Mound	--	1.8	Moore 1894
8DU68	Dent Mound	14.0	0.8	Ashley/Richter 1993
8DU96	Mayport Mound	19.8 by 20.4	0.6	Wilson 1965

the Woodland period. Additional mounds near the river's mouth may relate specifically to the Middle Woodland, though others clearly predate or post-date those containing complicated stamped wares. Several Early Woodland burial mounds have yielded Deptford ceramics and Yent ceremonial complex–related artifacts, indicating that exchange networks linking the lower St. Johns with northwestern Florida existed prior to the emergence of Swift Creek–related mortuary mounds (Milanich 1994:261; Sears 1962:15). Two local pyramidal mounds, Shields (8DU12) and Grant (8DU14), also produced several complicated stamped sherds. These monumental sand constructs definitively date to the later Mississippian period, and the few recovered Swift Creek sherds were probably inclusive in the mound fill, which was taken from nearby preexisting middens during construction.

Distribution

To date, the burial mounds in northeastern Florida known to have yielded Swift Creek pottery are restricted almost exclusively to Duval County. The only reported exception is the St. Johns Landing mound (8PU9) located well to the south near Palatka in the central St. Johns River drainage (Goggin 1952:86; Moore 1894:174). As Figure 12-1 indicates, the majority of Swift Creek–related mounds in Duval County are concentrated between Jacksonville and the ocean. Similarly, most habitation sites of the period are shell middens concentrated along the tidewater zone, indicating that the local groups were fisher-hunter-gatherers who took full advantage of the area's abundant tidal marsh and estuarine resources. With populations seemingly congregated along the river's lower course, it would stand to reason that their burial activities would take place nearby. Hypothetically, these mounds may have been used to mark or define territories belonging to specific social entities.

Mortuary Traits

The Swift Creek–related mounds listed in Table 12-5 range in horizontal size from 9 to 30 meters and most were about 1 meter in height at the time they were recorded. Mound shape varies from circular to elliptical, with a few manifesting more amorphous configurations. Although mounds may have occasionally contained thin charcoal lenses, white sand strata, and/or hematite-impregnated sand, mound fill has invariably been described as homogeneous, suggesting little mound complexity. No specialized submound or intramound burial facilities or crypts have been reported for these mounds, although a large subgrade pit containing abundant charcoal but no human remains was found beneath the Monroe mound (Moore 1895). While lenses or amorphous areas of carbonized debris may indicate the remains of burned structures, patterns recognized as such have yet to be reported.

According to the existing literature, fireplaces or fire pits seem to have been a consistently occurring mound feature (Ashley and Richter 1993; Moore 1894:192; Wilson 1965). These typically small, circular areas of charcoal seem to have occurred in association with human burials on a regular basis. Their role in the mortuary ritual is unknown, although the fires may have served for cooking ritual brews or meals. Calcined bone suggestive of intentional cremation was only manifest within a feature beneath the large mound at Beauclerc, 8DU43 (Moore 1894:198). Small collections of paired oyster shells interpreted as food offerings were apparently associated with at least five separate burials at the Dent mound (Ashley and Richter 1993).

A range of variability in burial modes exists and includes extended supine, flexed, bundle, and multiple bundle. Partial burials are also common, particularly of isolated skulls. Incomplete interments may reflect differential bone preservation, postdepositional disturbances, intentional burial modes (i.e., part of the skeleton is symbolic of the entire person), or even recovery biases on the part of excavators. Large accumulations of disarticulated human bones representing multiple individuals are common, whereas single-individual primary burials are less frequent. The depth at which some interments were uncovered at the Dent mound suggests that initiatory burials were placed in premound pits, although archaeological outlines of these pits were not identified (Ashley and Richter 1993).

Demographic data regarding mound burial populations are virtually nonexistent, owing to incomplete burial inventories and the absence of any biocultural analyses during past mound investigations. Tentative age and sex determinations for the Mayport mound mortuary population, however, suggest a possible egalitarian burial population with adults of both genders and few children represented (Wilson 1965:12–13). Because Wilson failed to state his method for sex and age determinations, his demographic data are questionable. Morphological and metric data regarding local Middle Woodland skeletal populations are also wanting.

An inventory of burial goods commonly reported for local Swift Creek–related mounds is presented in Table 12-6. Much of Moore's artifact information, however, consists of nothing more than inconsistent and rarely quantified trait list compilations. Although trait list studies are prone to justifiable criticisms, the frequency with which Moore acknowledges these artifact classes does suggest that a fairly standard suite of mortuary paraphernalia was in use during the Middle Woodland. Moreover, most of the same mortuary accouterments mentioned by Moore were recovered from the Mayport and Dent mounds (Ashley and Richter 1993; Wilson 1965). Raw materials and mortuary goods common to most Swift Creek–related mounds include

Table 12-6. Swift Creek-Related Burial Mounds and Associated Artifacts

	Comp. Stamped Pottery	Shell Bead	Shell, Miscellaneous	Unmodified Pebbles	Pebble Hammerstone	Projectile Points	Flakes	Celts	Tobacco Pipes	Hematite	Sandstone	Mica	Copper
Johnson Mound	X		X	X		X	X	X		X	X	X	X
Monroe Mound	X	X	X	X	X			X			X	X	X
Grant Mound A	X		X	X	X	X	X	X		X	X	X	
Grant Mound E	X	X	X	X	X	X	X	X	X	X	X	X	X
Horseshoe Landing Mound A	X			X		X	X	X					
Reddie Point Mound A	X	X	X	X	X	X		X		X		X	X
Alicia Mound B	X		X	X	X	X	X	X	X	X	X	X	
Arlington Mound	X	X	X	X	X	X	X	X	X	X	X	X	X
South Jacksonville Mound B	X						X						
Point LaVista Mound A	X			X	X	X		X					
Point LaVista Mound B	X		X							X	X	X	
Beauclerc Large Mound	X			X		X	X						
Dent Mound	X	X	X	X		X	X	X		X	X	X	
Mayport Mound	X	X	X	X	X	X	X	X	X	X		X	X

plain and complicated stamped pottery, modified and unmodified marine shell, pebbles, pebble hammers, projectile points, celts, hematite (ocher), sandstone, mica, chert flake concentrations, and to a lesser degree copper.

Archaeological evidence from the Dent and Mayport mounds indicates that mortuary pottery assemblages at these sites consist of plain wares (sand-tempered, charcoal-tempered, and chalky St. Johns), Dunns Creek Red,

Swift Creek and charcoal-tempered complicated stamped wares, and less frequently Weeden Island pottery (see Table 12-3). Both mounds yielded a broken Weeden Island multicompartment bowl. Additional diagnostic artifacts from these mounds include Duval projectile points. The Dent mound also contained Columbia- and Sarasota-like points (Bullen 1975).

Ceramics were intentionally placed in these mounds as whole, partial, and basally perforated vessels. More commonly, however, vessels were apparently broken and scattered across former mound surfaces. Both plain and decorated vessels from the Dent mound displayed extensive exterior sooting, suggesting they were used in association with fire and may have served some domestic or ritual function prior to interment (Ashley and Richter 1993). Burial artifacts were interred in direct association with preserved human remains as well as in small caches in the mound fill seemingly unrelated to human interments. Hypothetically, these artifact deposits may have had a specific or symbolic systemic context. No distinct eastern-side pottery caches, characteristic of later Weeden Island mounds, are reported for local Swift Creek–related mounds.

The areal and vertical arrangement of mound interments combined with the documented presence of temporally distinct ceramics (e.g., Early and Late Swift Creek) in some mounds implies that the local Swift Creek–related mounds were multistage constructs. For the Dent mound, it is speculated that stored human remains, with little or no soft tissue, were periodically interred en masse. Concurrently or at other times, smaller bundles of disarticulated bone, isolated individual and grouped skulls, and/or fleshed corpses were also interred. Burials are suspected to have been placed on former mound surfaces or immediately adjacent to mounded areas and covered with small amounts of earth. Other burials may have been placed in pits dug into the premound surface or into the existing mound itself. In this fashion, the mound would have grown gradually over an unknown period of time, requiring a minimal labor force. These accretionary mounds are akin to what Sears (1958:277) termed the continuous-use type of mound.

Sociopolitical Setting

As described above, gross characteristics of the lower St. Johns River mounds compare favorably to those Swift Creek and mixed Swift Creek–Weeden Island I mounds described for the Florida Gulf Coast by Willey

(1949:369–71, 404–6). Shared mortuary artifacts and similar burial customs presumably grew out of effective trade and communication networks linking the fisher-hunter-gatherers of the lower St. Johns to groups on the Florida Gulf Coast and beyond. Regrettably, a decisive understanding of sociopolitical aspects of the local Middle Woodland culture is hampered by an inadequate and biased regional database.

Comparative ceremonial/mortuary data from northwestern Florida have been synthesized by Sears (1962, 1973). Consequently, Early Swift Creek pottery in sacred contexts has been placed under the rubric of Green Point, whereas sacred Late Swift Creek wares are viewed as part of the Weeden Island I ceremonial complex (Sears 1962, 1973). These ritual components, both of which reportedly postdate Ohio Hopewell, are part of an evolutionary ceremonial continuum (Milanich et al. 1984:21; Sears 1962). Nevertheless, exotic raw materials or finished artifacts suggestive of the widespread Hopewell ceremonial complex occur in mortuary mounds in the southeastern United States after the demise of Midwest Hopewell, circa A.D. 400 (see Brose and Greber 1979). Distinctly Hopewell-like burial customs and mortuary facilities are not reported for any local Swift Creek–related burial mounds.

Beyond the previous methodological problems and biases, however, there does appear to be a distinct regional pattern associated with burial practices exhibited in the local Swift Creek–related mounds. Sequential use of seemingly coeval burial mounds suggests that specific long-standing social entities (e.g., lineages) either lived in close proximity to or periodically returned to a specific burial area to inter their dead. The presence of both primary and secondary burials could easily be construed as representing status differentiation, but such an assumption is unfounded on the basis of the available data. Although some members of the local Middle Woodland societies may have held differential status, there presently is insufficient data to establish whether this was ascribed or achieved. Society on the whole was probably egalitarian, with apparently all members being interred in the mound. At present, little archaeological evidence exists in the area to suggest any hierarchical level of social organization akin to the protochieftainship proposed for McKeithen Weeden Island between A.D. 200 and 600 in northern Florida (Milanich et al. 1984:117–19).

Middens

Non–burial mound sites yielding Swift Creek pottery include shell middens and small ceramic scatters. The former tend to be multicomponent sites demonstrating sparse to dense marine-shell accumulations, whereas the latter are generally nonshell shoreline or nearby sand-ridge deposits (Ashley 1992:131–32). A review of available artifact inventories indicates that complicated stamped wares, variably typed as Swift Creek, Brewton Hill, St. Andrews, Crooked River, and New River, have been recovered from at least twenty-five sites, most of which are on the river's southern side east of downtown Jacksonville. Few reports, however, have attempted to distinguish Early from Late Swift Creek wares. This is usually because few sherds are recovered and those that are often tend to be too small to permit recognition of diagnostic criteria established to differentiate early from late forms. Additional sites have yielded untyped sand-tempered complicated stamped sherds that are presumably Swift Creek or a related ware (Dickinson and Wayne 1987; Rudolph 1980; Rudolph and Gresham 1980; Russo et al. 1993).

To date, little information is available concerning middens presumably associated with local Swift Creek–related mounds. Moore (1894, 1895, 1896) was apparently uninterested in the ubiquitous shell middens near the river's mouth and turned his attention almost exclusively to mortuary mounds. Moreover, no results of subsequent excavations at midden deposits near any of Moore's mounds have been documented. However, shell middens in the general vicinity of the various Grant and Reddie Point mounds have yielded occasional Swift Creek sherds (Ashley and Johnson 1990, 1993; Johnson 1988; Robert Thunen, pers. comm.). Of the two more recently excavated Swift Creek–related mounds, midden information is only available for the Dent mound and is admittedly limited (Ashley and Richter 1993; Russo et al. 1993:116–18, 120).

Two test pits were dug into the midden deposits surrounding the Dent mound by a local amateur group between 1977 and 1984. These tests, which were poorly controlled (30-centimeter levels), yielded predominately Orange, Deptford, and post–A.D. 750 St. Johns and Savannah period ceramics (Ashley and Richter 1993). Plain sand-tempered wares were the predominate post–Late Archaic pottery type; however, it is impossible to correlate these nondescript wares with their associated pottery assemblages. Subsequent shovel testing by the National Park Service unearthed similar pottery types, suggesting Late Archaic and undetermined post-Archaic period occupations in the middens (Russo et al. 1992:116). A more refined ceramic technological analysis on the plain wares from the mound and adjacent middens may lead to a better understanding of the post-Archaic occupations at the Dent mound site.

The documented incidence of Swift Creek pottery at most lower St. Johns River midden sites is typically low, ranging from one to ten sherds. In some instances, however, the infrequent occurrence of these wares could be attributed to either the limited nature of the site's Middle Woodland component or sampling error. Nevertheless, at least four multicomponent sites, 8DU62 (Sears 1957, 1959), 8DU66 (Richter 1993), 8DU5602 (Johnson 1988), and 8DU5611 (Ashley and Wheat 1991), have demonstrated components in which Swift Creek sherds are better represented (i.e., accounting for at least 100 sherds or 15 percent of the midden assemblage). It is unfortunate that because of very limited site testing the structure and extent of each sites' Woodland component is poorly understood. An essentially pure Swift Creek site (8DU5543) has been recently excavated, however, and results provide baseline information on local Swift Creek adaptations (Florida Archaeological Services 1995).

At Greenfield site 7 (8DU5543), the Swift Creek component is represented by an intermittent low-density midden covering an estimated 3 hectares on the southern side of the St. Johns River, within 8 kilometers of the river's mouth (Florida Archaeological Services 1995). Included within the sparse spread of midden debris were several small, localized areas of dense shell interpreted as household middens. Identified shell middens were situated away from the present shoreline, roughly 50 to 200 meters from the tidal marshes. Investigations focused on two adjacent household middens that contained Early Swift Creek pottery and a third that yielded Late Swift Creek pottery.

Excavation of the two closely spaced house middens revealed a thin (10 to 15 centimeter) shell refuse layer densely packed with oyster shell, abundant vertebrate faunal bone, charcoal, and plain and complicated stamped pottery. One shell midden (designated Feature 10), measuring 2 × 7 meters, produced 160 sherds (Table 12-4). Of these, 60 percent were plain, 34 percent were complicated stamped, and 6 percent were eroded. The second midden (contained in Test Units 15 through 22) was slightly larger (6 × 12 meters) and yielded 475 sherds, with 52 percent plain, 28 percent complicated stamped, and 20 percent eroded. No St. Johns wares and only two decorated sherds (both cord marked) other than complicated stamped were recovered from the two shell middens.

A third shell deposit (designated Feature 4) was delineated about 150 meters southeast of the two aforementioned house middens, and it produced sandy-paste plain and complicated stamped wares (Table 12-4). No charcoal-tempered sherds were recovered from this shell midden feature. Additional excavations and controlled mechanical stripping operations near the three middens exposed few features and failed to uncover any structural evidence.

In the absence of available radiocarbon dates, relative dating of the various middens at 8DU5543 is based solely on currently accepted dates for the two distinct Swift Creek assemblages at the site (see Ashley 1992:129). Modified rims from Feature 10 and Test Units 15 through 22 were dominated by various notched varieties, whereas simple rounded rims dominated among the sandy-paste sherds in Feature 4, although a few medium to large folded rims were recovered. This strongly implies sequential midden deposits with the former middens interpreted as Early Swift Creek (circa A.D. 100–300) and the latter as Late Swift Creek (circa A.D. 300–500+).

Nonceramic artifacts from the various midden deposits were limited and include a whelk hammer, a pearl, a sherd hone, two flakes, and several modified animal bone fragments. A trash pit discovered nearby at Greenfield site 6 (8DU5542) yielded charcoal-tempered ceramics and a Duval projectile point. Site 8DU5543 is located only a short distance across the tidal marshes from 8DU62, the only other nonmound site in the region yielding appreciable quantities of charcoal-tempered pottery. At 8DU62, Sears's few scattered midden tests generated meager data concerning site settlement and depositional patterning. It is possible that the Middle Woodland component at 8DU62 maintains a site structure similar to that found at Greenfield site 7, but this remains to be investigated.

The composition of the three sampled middens at 8DU5543 was uniform, with oyster representing the primary shellfish constituent. Small traces of stout tagelus, quahog clam, ribbed mussel, mud nassa, marsh periwinkle, and whelk were observed. Metric analysis of a sample of 100 impressed odostomes, a small gastropod that feeds on oyster, suggests that the oysters from the Late Swift Creek midden were intensively harvested during the later summer and fall months, with a drop in oyster collection during the colder months (DeFrance 1993:7).

Zooarchaeological analysis of faunal samples from both the Early and Late Swift Creek middens indicates an economic emphasis on the exploitation of aquatic fauna, particularly small estuarine fish (deFrance 1993). Mass-capture techniques of fishing that involved fine-mesh nets used in shallow, inshore marine waters can be inferred on the basis of the size and kinds of fish present in the samples, along with the recovery of shrimp remains. Furthermore, the data reveal little evidence for the exploitation of marine fauna that inhabit deep ocean waters. In the analyzed Early Swift Creek feature menhaden, spots, mullet, and hardhead catfish were the dominant vertebrate species, while gaff-topsail catfish, Atlantic croaker, and goby were most common in the Late Swift Creek feature (deFrance 1993). Zooarchaeological data combined with artifactual evidence suggest intensive, but short-term, episodes of site occupation.

Preliminary Model

Explaining the mechanisms responsible for the occurrence of Swift Creek pottery in an area customarily thought to be outside the effective distribution of the Middle Woodland ware is a topic that we must begin to address. While Swift Creek pottery was originally thought to represent only a mortuary ware in lower St. Johns River mounds (Goggin 1952), more recent studies have demonstrated clearly that it was not exclusively a sacred ware. By and large, local Middle Woodland midden assemblages tend to be characterized by large percentages of sand-tempered plain wares; however, decorative styles (i.e., check stamped, complicated stamped) seemingly underwent periods of local florescence. On the basis of the present database, the following tentative hypothesis has been suggested for the appearance of Swift Creek wares in northeastern Florida (Ashley 1992:134).

Long before the emergence of Swift Creek manifestations, exchange networks linking the lower St. Johns with sites on the northern Gulf Coast of Florida were well established. Evidence of such interaction is revealed in local Early Woodland Deptford mounds, from which nonlocal Yent-related artifacts have been recovered (Milanich 1994:262). During the Middle Wood-land period (A.D. 100–300) contact along these communication pathways seems to have resulted in the movement of Early Swift Creek ceramic styles, vessels, and/or possibly less-cumbersome carved paddles by means of people coming overland into the lower St. Johns region. Because no Early Swift Creek sites have been recorded in the extreme north-central part of Florida, a massive transpeninsular migration of Early Swift Creek people from north-western to northeastern Florida seems unlikely. At some point, a charcoal-tempered ware affiliated with Early Swift Creek manifestations (both mounds and middens) emerged in the lower St. Johns area. On the basis of nontech-nological ceramic evidence, this ware may further be a local product as asso-ciated with sites such as 8DU68, 8DU62, and 8DU5543, which presumably date to A.D. 100–300. The production origin of the many sand-tempered Early Swift Creek wares found in the area is much less clear, however.

Late Swift Creek designs in northeastern Florida tend to exhibit a marked similarity to those found in south-central and coastal Georgia. In fact, two separate design contacts have been positively established linking groups on the St. Johns to a site near the mouth of the Altamaha River on the Georgia coast. Thus, as the geographic distribution of Swift Creek pottery broadened over time, local contact with Swift Creek pottery-making people seems to have shifted from northwestern Florida to the lower Georgia coast. Reasons for this conjectured shift in interaction have not been discussed previously, but the emergence in northern Florida of McKeithen Weeden Island around A.D. 200–300 could have been a contributing factor (Milanich et al. 1984).

The rise in the popularity of pottery assemblages dominated by Weeden Island wares (and lacking Late Swift Creek ceramics), as exhibited at the McKeithen site, in northern Florida may have served to curtail the spread of Late Swift Creek ceramics from the Gulf Coast area into northeastern Flor-ida. It is not suggested that transpeninsular communications broke down, but only that the movement of Late Swift Creek wares (or design styles) discontinued or was greatly diminished. In fact, it is very probable that many of the exotic Weeden Island vessels found in local Swift Creek–related mounds have northern Florida pottery origins. As a consequence, local in-teraction with Late Swift Creek peoples possibly shifted to the Georgia coast, an area uninhabited (or sparsely inhabited) by Early Swift Creek peoples. That Late Swift Creek groups residing on the lower Georgia coast (e.g.,

Kings Bay locality) actually migrated into northeastern Florida has been previously suggested (Ashley 1992:134). This contention is supported by the recovery of Late Swift Creek pottery from sites in the St. Johns River estuary and to the north on Black Hammock Island, Big Talbot Island, and Amelia Island. The latter is less than 16 kilometers from the Kings Bay locality. Reported data from the island sites, other than surface-collection compilations, are presently lacking, however.

Conclusions

Traditionally, Swift Creek pottery has been viewed as nonlocal trade wares when recovered at sites on the St. Johns River (Goggin 1952). The reason for this assumption is simple: northeastern Florida is peripheral to the known geographic distribution of Swift Creek pottery. While the manufacturing origin of locally recovered Swift Creek pottery has yet to be investigated at the technological level, the relative abundance of the pottery type at habitation sites such as 8DU66, 8DU5602, 8DU5611, and 8DU5543 strongly suggests local production. This is not to insinuate that all Swift Creek wares are local products, since dual factors (local production and extralocal trade) are probably responsible for the varied-paste Swift Creek wares found in the region. Regardless of the production origin of these wares, Swift Creek pottery was an important part of the Middle Woodland pottery tradition of the lower St. Johns River area.

In-depth research on Swift Creek manifestations in northeastern Florida is just beginning, and thus definitive interpretations regarding these manifestations must be postponed until more and better data are available. The model presented in this chapter is a slightly expanded version of one I presented earlier (Ashley 1992), so its hypothetical nature should be reiterated. Although the model is rather simplistic and contains obvious gaps, it does provide a workable hypothesis that can guide future research.

In conclusion, the present study has raised numerous questions concerning Early and Late Swift Creek manifestations. If charcoal-tempered wares are a local manufacture what was the incentive for their inclusion? Is there a forerunner for this ware outside the lower St. Johns River valley? Why was charcoal tempering seemingly so short-lived? How do local Early and Late Swift Creek designs compare with those from northwestern Florida and coastal Georgia? What Late Swift Creek manifestations are present locally? Did Late Swift Creek groups from the lower Georgia coast actually immigrate into northeastern Florida? It is hoped that some of these questions will be addressed in the near future.

Acknowledgments

I would like to thank Donna Ruhl, Buzz Thunen, and Bob Richter for commenting on an earlier draft of this chapter. Donna Ruhl and Ann Cordell kindly examined several charcoal-tempered sherds from the Dent mound and provided helpful comments on the ware. Thanks to Bob Johnson for allowing use of the Greenfield site 7 data. Frankie Snow was of enormous assistance, providing comparative Swift Creek information from Georgia as well as valuable references. Frankie Snow is also responsible for the design drawings in Figures 12-3 and 12-4, which along with Figure 12-2 were inked by Alan Basinet. I owe a great deal of gratitude to Angela Ashley for her help in the layout of all figures and tables.

1973 and 1994 Excavations at the Block-Sterns Site, Leon County, Florida

B. Calvin Jones, Daniel T. Penton, and Louis D. Tesar

From the primarily ceramic manifestation defined by Arthur R. Kelly in 1938, the concept of Swift Creek has grown to a progressively well-defined archaeological culture through the work of Willey (1949), Sears (1962, 1966), Phelps (1969), and others. Its linkages with other Hopewellian manifestations to the north and with Marksville–Santa Rosa to the west have long been recognized. In northwestern Florida, the developmental sequence is from Deptford, to Swift Creek, thence to Weeden Island.

The northwestern Florida region has been subdivided, with the Apalachicola River drainage serving as the boundary (Phelps 1969). Penton (1970, 1974) provided an excellent summary of Swift Creek in the eastern portion of northwestern Florida, the area in which the Block-Sterns site (8LE148) is located. Bense (1992) has summarized Santa Rosa–Swift Creek in western Florida.

In both areas, roughly 90 percent of the known sites are located in the Coastal Lowlands. For the western area, Bense (1992:2) suggested that during these periods people were concentrated on the coastal strip, while "the interior was essentially vacant and used only for special-purpose, short term activities." In contrast, in the upper Chipola River basin west of the Apalachicola, Jones (Butterfield 1973:1–2) has noted significant inland sites with at least one Mandeville-like mound complex (Waddell's Mill Pond). In the eastern area, Penton (1974:4) observed that "the bulk of the coastal sites are located either on, or immediately inland from, rich estuarine areas," while "all the upland sites are situated upon what is now considered excellent agricultural lands." David Phelps (1969:23) suggested that there is some indication that interior sites have more permanent, clay-floored houses in contrast to coastal sites and that "this may indicate seasonal ranging to different micro-environments within the territory." Penton (n.d.) concluded, "if this is the case, then the more permanent settlements would probably be back inland, especially if agriculture was being practiced to any extent. This may also be the reason coastal sites have revealed little in the way of structural remains."

Penton (1974:4) identified only seven interior sites in his sample of Swift Creek sites in the Tallahassee Hills. These include two mound/midden sites—one of which is the Block-Sterns site—and five village areas with no recorded mounds. Another nonmound village site was added by Tesar (1980:594), and since the time of that report eight others have been added to the list (Tesar 1994:125–28). Jones adds that one or more of the two dozen sites within the Letchworth complex at the southwestern end of Lake Miccossukee, located adjacent to the eastern Leon County line, appear to belong to Swift Creek, on the basis of associated village remains.

The Block-Sterns Site

The Block-Sterns site is located southeast of Tallahassee, Florida, spread along the northern shoreline of Piney Z Lake, an artificially segmented portion of Lake Lafayette (Figure 13-1). The area lies within the southern limits of the Tallahassee Red Hills, near the northern interface with the Gulf Coastal Lowlands. The natural amenities associated with this ecotonal setting attracted both transient and semipermanent residents over a span of some 10,000 years. Physical remains reported from this site represent Paleo-Indian, Archaic, Deptford, Swift Creek, Weeden Island, Fort Walton, and Apalachee occupations. Current data are insufficient to delineate properly the extent of the various occupations on the site.

The Block-Sterns site is by far the largest of the sixteen known Swift Creek sites in Leon County, Florida. It was first recorded in the Florida Master Site File by B. Calvin Jones in 1968, and investigations expanded thereafter to encompass roughly 80 acres. The site contains four known mounds,

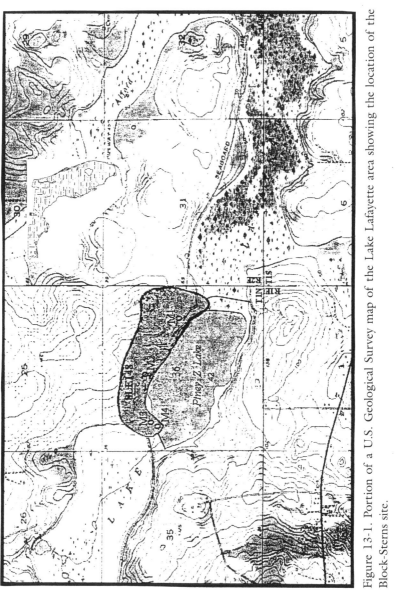

Figure 13-1. Portion of a U.S. Geological Survey map of the Lake Lafayette area showing the location of the Block-Sterns site.

a village area, and activity areas. In 1969 the first two mounds were identified as A and B; however, with the use of letter designations for subareas of the final expanded site area, the mounds were redesignated numerically. Mound 1 (formerly A) dates to late Deptford–Early Swift Creek times, and two other mounds belong to the later Weeden Island time (Mounds 3 and 4). All three of these mounds are known to have mortuary components. The fourth mound (Mound 2, formerly B), presumed from its setting to be of Swift Creek date, remains essentially untested, although in 1979 two 2 × 2-meter test units were placed near the mound crest and on its northern slope during a Florida State University field school project. When Jones and Tesar observed the open units, several red clay floor levels were noted in one unit and the excavation at the other was discontinued when a whitish-colored feature or zone was reached.

Mound 1 Excavations: 1973

During the summer of 1973, preliminary excavations were conducted in Mound 1 of the Block-Sterns site. The excavations were designed to sample and evaluate Mound 1 in anticipation of private development. Before the 1973 research, virtually nothing was known about the functional and chronological nature of this mound.

Prior to the 1973 work, Mound 1 had remained relatively undisturbed except for the incidental impacts associated with agricultural activities. The area immediately north of Mound 1 had been a tung grove, and upslope cultivation had created erosional conditions that resulted in the masking of the external mound configuration. Several modern post molds were located during the course of excavations, and at least one fire lane was noted on the mound slope, but otherwise modern disturbances were minimal.

Six 3 × 3-meter units and three 1 × 1-meter units were excavated during the 1973 season, representing approximately 20 percent of the mound. The primary emphasis of the unit placement was on a north-south axis, which was designed to provide a comprehensive stratigraphic cross section of the apparent mound summit (Figure 13-2). As work progressed on the first unit, it became obvious that Mound 1 was something more than our original assumptions had prepared us for. The encounter of the initial hard clay mound "mantle" was the first surprise.

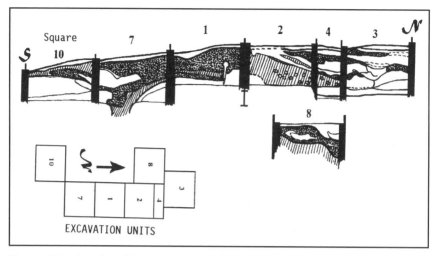

Figure 13-2. Stratigraphic cross section of Block-Sterns Mound 1 excavation units.

As we subsequently learned, the mound consisted of several construction stages, each presumably spanning a certain (undetermined) period of time. This assumption was reinforced by the presence of erosion features on some of the mantle surfaces, as well as by several areas of silt deposition. The easily discernible mantles consisted of relatively uniform, hard-packed clay surfaces. The clay of these mantles was usually red or bright reddish orange.

The intervening layers of fill were usually very mottled dark brown and tan soil, with a less compact consistency than that of the sandwiching mantles. Certain fill areas clearly reflected basket loading.

A substantial number of probable post molds was recorded during excavations, but a definitive projection of their structural function(s) has not been completed. Subjectively, it appears that the most distinctive of the various mantles also contain the most likely evidence of mound structures, including a section of what appears to be a wall trench. Considerable quantities of daub were also observed throughout the mound fill and in the fill of some of the burial pits.

The poorly preserved remains of seventeen individuals were located during the 1973 season. In each instance, the remains were found within pit features, including one located during sectioning of a possible post mold. The acidic soil and weather conditions had reduced the skeletal elements to little more than bone paste and teeth caps. A number of pits containing no discernible skeletal remains were also encountered, some of which appeared similar to the burial pits. Artifactual materials were present in some of these pits.

Seven of the individuals were located within Square 2, four in Square 8, and two each in Squares 1, 3, and 4. David Dickel conducted a brief analysis of the remains in early 1990 and a subsequent more detailed analysis for Native American Grave Protection and Repatriation Act (NAGPRA) compliance reporting. On the basis of field records and fragmentary remains he concluded that there were apparently twelve adults and five children or subadults represented in the collection he examined. He also concluded that the physical condition of these remains rendered them of little further research value.

Although no complete cremations were noted during excavations, there was abundant evidence of fire throughout the mound. Dickel states that "some of this (skeletal) material may have been heat altered, possibly from cremation . . . [Burial 7 and] many of the other fragments are white and chalky and at least partially calcined." Burial 7 exhibited charring and "check" fractures, and Burial 14 contained a charred log or plank fragment.

Burial pits were encountered at various depths in the mound, ranging from 45 to 165 centimeters below the present surface. The pit origins appear to cluster in two depth ranges (45 to 65 centimeters and 140 to 165 centimeters) associated with mound construction stages, although one burial pit was encountered at 80 centimeters and one at 110 centimeters below the present surface.

Mound 1 Artifacts

The artifact assemblage from Mound 1 appears to belong exclusively within an Early Swift Creek context. Distinctive items included a ceramic platform pipe, a multicolored painted female ceramic figurine (Figure 13-3), a slate bar gorget, several ceramic vessels with crenelated rims and tetrapodal bases, a "Brangenberg" vessel fragment, a T-lip rimsherd, Swift Creek Complicated Stamped sherds, expanded-base chert projectile points, and a mica-covered cache of twenty-six chert blades or preforms. Conch shell fragments, bear teeth, and skull fragments were also present.

Burial 14 contained the greatest variety of accompanying items, including five ceramic vessels, two groups of quartz crystal flakes, a ceramic figur-

Figure 13-3. Female figure from Block-Sterns Mound 1, front and back views (photograph courtesy of the Florida Department of State, Division of Historical Resources).

ine, a conch shell (dipper?), a large bear mandible, a quartz pebble hammer stone, and a charred plank or log fragment. This mound base burial, possibly the central feature, was encountered at 148 centimeters below the present surface.

Mound 1 Radiocarbon Dates

Radiocarbon samples were taken from several mound contexts, including the charred log or plank in Burial 14. Two separate samples from the charred log or plank were submitted for dating. David Brose sent the first sample to

Dicarb Radioisotope Laboratory in June 1974. This sample (DCR No. 217) was dated to 2680 ± 120 B.P., or 730 ± 120 B.C. This date was considered to be too early, so a second sample was submitted to Teledyne Isotopes in May 1976. This sample (I-9923) dated 2020 ± 80 B.P., or 70 ± 80 B.C.

Mound 1 Summary

The 1973 excavations at Block-Sterns provided convincing evidence that the ceremonial construction activities of northern Florida Swift Creek peoples were somewhat more sophisticated than had generally been presumed. The Mound 1 research provided irrefutable evidence that both clay-capped mounds with multistage construction and mound summit structures, including possible wattle-and-daub structures, were being built in northern Florida by the time of Christ.

At the outset of excavations, Mound 1 was presumed to have been a "typical" burial mound, and intentional burials were, indeed, encountered within the mound. Some twenty-three years later, we are not entirely satisfied with this interpretation. Penton is becoming comfortable with the idea that the burials may have been dedicatory or commemorative in nature, with much the same ceremonial intent as the blade cache or other artifact deposits.

A review of the field notes and drawings from 1973 showed subtle hints that at least some of the burials were carefully placed on the mound slope in conjunction with either the initiation or termination of a particular mound stage. There are also suggestions that one or more of the mound configurations may be at least partially pyramidal and truncated. The construction axis appears to be approximately 45 degrees off of the current magnetic alignment.

The combined elements of this mound indicate that it is an important and early expression of Early Swift Creek ceremonial life, perhaps bridging the space between Deptford and Swift Creek.

Village Excavations: 1994

Artifacts previously surface collected from the surrounding 30 to 40 acres of the central site area when it was under cultivation range in age from Middle Archaic through early Territorial times. During the past twenty years, the east-central portion of the site, the area around the mound sampled by the Florida State University field school, has yielded hundreds of projectile points, chert and quartz crystal cores and debitage, plain and Swift Creek Complicated Stamped sherds and other ceramic types, a male figurine torso, daub, and the like to surface collectors. In the early 1970s, while excavating at Mound 1, Penton also made a brief surface collection in this portion of the site. Public acquisition of this important archaeological site has long been recommended.

The Bureau of Archaeological Research was notified in March 1994 by the property owner that the east-central portion of the site was to be conveyed to the Leon County School Board for use in the construction of a middle school. It was determined that there was no federal or state funding, licensing, or permitting required for the project. Thus, this locally funded project was not subject to the historic preservation provisions of federal and state laws. However, Byron Block, managing trustee of the estate selling the property, maintained his father's long-standing offer for the Bureau of Archaeological Research to conduct research on the property. Further, in consultation with Calvin Jones and State Archaeologist James Miller, Mr. Block negotiated with the school board to adjust a proposed construction/stormwater retention pond to ensure preservation of the central mound (Mound 2) and a surrounding site buffer area. This action essentially removed concerns that unmarked human burials might be adversely affected by the project.

While 3.5 acres of the most significant portion of the site area included in the sale are to be permanently preserved, design and fiscal constraints precluded preservation of the entire affected sensitive site area. Thus, Mr. Block delayed title transfer for the property to permit the Bureau to conduct archaeological salvage activities and provided limited financial assistance for these efforts. Several informal shovel tests excavated by Jones within the proposed pond area revealed a 40-centimeter-deep plow zone. The property had been under cultivation for nearly a century, with slash pine having been planted in the old fields in 1986.

Work was begun in late March 1994 under the direction of B. Calvin Jones with volunteer labor and a donated bulldozer and operator. At that time it was believed that pond excavation work would begin around the beginning of May. For that reason it was decided to sacrifice the disturbed plow zone to expose pit and structural features to maximize the recovery of in situ cultural data (Figure 13-4). Mechanical stripping was conducted under the

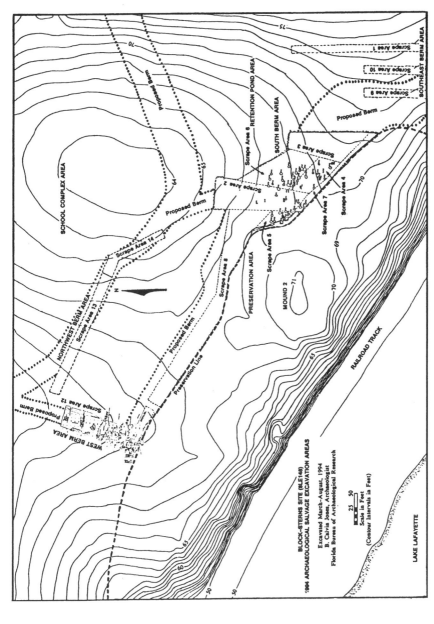

Figure 13-4. Block-Sterns site, 1994 excavation areas.

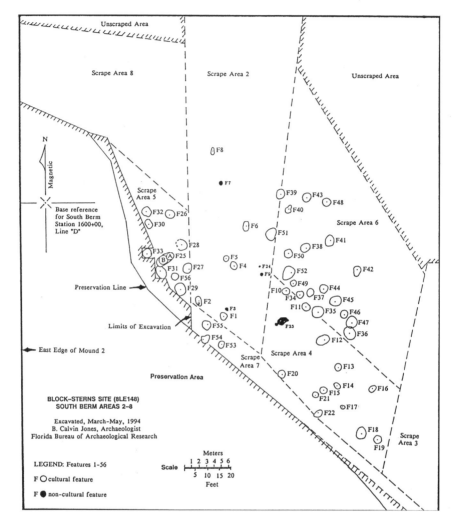

Figure 13-5. Southern berm excavations, Block-Sterns site.

direction of Jones, who limited scrape levels to a thickness of 5 to 10 centimeters.

Fifty-six features were identified within the first (southern berm) scrape areas as well as within a few formally excavated units systematically dug from the ground surface downward (Figure 13-5). Nearly all were pits containing cultural material, a few were determined to be the remains of tree stumps, and none were identified as post molds. Another 125 features were identified in the second (western berm) scrape area, including post molds from two structures as well as pit features (Figure 13-6). The pits in the western area were generally larger than those in the southern berm area.

Contracting delays permitted work to be extended first until June 30 and then until the end of July. At that time title to the property was formally transferred to the school board and formal archaeological salvage activities ended, although we had permission to monitor construction activities to record fortuitous discoveries.

After mechanical scraping, identified features and their surroundings were thin scraped with a flat-bladed shovel to remove mixed soils. The thin-scraped soils were then processed through ¼-inch mesh hardware cloth screens. All identified pit features were excavated with trowels, bamboo picks, and brushes to permit the in situ exposure and recording of cultural remains. All excavated soil was either screened through ¼-inch mesh hardware cloth in the field or transported to the lab for water screening through ¹⁄₁₆-inch mesh window screen. In addition to the preparation of written records, every feature was photographed and sketched. A photographic record was maintained of overall project activities. Project activities were also periodically videotaped.

The weather was cold to very hot and dry during the first half of the project, during which period soil had to be moistened to permit excavation and the units covered to provide workers with limited shade. During the latter half, the weather changed to extremely wet, during which time features under excavation periodically had to be bailed out. Indeed, recording and recovery of exposed material had to be expedited during this latter period because of the threat of inundation, with the result that more soils from the western berm area were fine screened than had occurred in the southern berm area. Selected bone artifacts were treated with diluted (5 percent) Rhoplex (an acrylic preservative) in the field and removed along with their soil columns for final cleaning and preservation in the lab.

While most features could be mapped in a single level, many pits contained sufficient quantities to necessitate the exposure and mapping of two or three levels of material. Bone in single-level pits and in the top level of multiple-level pits was much eroded by the natural soil acidity. However, the process of bone erosion helped neutralize the soil's acidity and thereby pro-

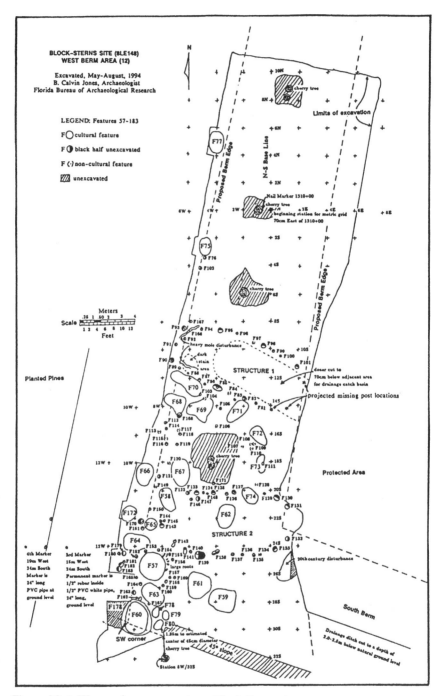

Figure 13-6. Western berm excavations, Block-Sterns site.

tected more deeply buried bone. Features were photographed and mapped by exposed level. Recovered material was washed, rough sorted, and bagged while excavation was ongoing, and this process was completed shortly thereafter.

The four-and-a-half-month fieldwork portion of the project resulted in the recovery of more than 200,000 artifacts and subsistence remains, mostly the latter. The processed collection, representing more than 500 accession numbers, is contained in eighty-nine 1-cubic-foot record archive boxes and eighteen smaller boxes. The material is sorted into the following categories: selected lithics (i.e., projectile points, other worked lithic tools, quartz crystal tools and waste, mica, graphite, galena, ochre, copper ore, and so forth) and general lithics (cores and debitage); selected ceramics (rims, diagnostic decorated sherds, appendages, and unusual plain ware) and unselected ceramics, including ceramic manufacture waste material; general bone (unmodified and common elements) and selected bone (worked elements and teeth); charred plant remains; unsorted fine-screened material (mostly char and very small fish bones, along with grit); radiocarbon samples (seventy-seven bags representing nearly all features with diagnostic artifacts); and unprocessed soil/flotation samples. About fifty of the accessions are the result of fine screening between five and twenty-five or more gallons of soil for each pit feature.

The unforeseen three-month extension of the fieldwork ending date permitted the recovery of more than twice the quantity of cultural remains that would otherwise have been recovered. It also extended the time required to process recovered material and delayed the beginning of formal artifact analysis efforts.

This chapter simply highlights the wealth of cultural data contained in the collection. Artifacts collected during the project range in age from traditional late Paleo-Indian/Early Archaic through early historic times. However, this chapter will focus primarily on those remains collected from in situ contexts, with only minimal discussion of the broader range of site artifacts.

From the cultural synthesis prepared by Milanich (1994:141–54) and others on the Swift Creek and related cultures, we anticipated the recovery of quantities of stone and bone tools, including Columbia, Taylor, and related stemmed projectile points/knives; Swift Creek triangular, bifacial blade knives; expedient scrapers/shavers; bone awls, polished pins, flakers, and bone scrapers; and cut and polished carnivore mandibles and drilled carnivore teeth. Milanich (1994:146) notes that "other stone tools include spoke shaves, hammer stones made from expended cores, flake scrapers, limestone and chert nutting stones (with one to four indentations), and sandstone abraders used to sharpen the bowl awls." Mica and quartz crystal and greenstone celts are frequently reported exotic stone items. Ceramics from these cultures are primarily plain and complicated stamped varieties, with a minority of earlier Deptford and later Weeden Island ceramics evidencing the cultural progression from Deptford to Swift Creek to Weeden Island varieties. Ceramic figurines are also mentioned as relatively frequently occurring in village as well as mound contexts. Subsistence remains include a wide variety of terrestrial animals, primarily deer, a variety of fish and shellfish, and charred hickory nuts and acorns. Horticulture has long been suggested, although evidence is essentially lacking. Evidence of permanent structures has long been sought.

It was within the above context that we began work at the Block-Sterns site. Within time and budget constraints, we designed the project to maximize data collection to determine whether permanent structures were present at the site, whether horticulture was practiced at the site, what role the site played within the broader Hopewellian Interaction Network as well as within the immediate area, and the site's placement within area cultural development.

Village Features

Features 1 through 56 were located in the southeastern portion of the southern berm area of the salvage archaeology project. Five of these were determined to be natural, rather than cultural, features. The fifty-one cultural features were all oval pits, with 75 percent ranging between 0.5 and 1.5 square meters. Pits were dug into culturally sterile red sandy clay soils. Only one pit had a baked clay lining. Forty-seven pits were round to flat bottomed, while three were bell shaped or at least widened near the bottom. Nonfood remains were only occasionally found on pit floors. Artifacts and food remains generally occurred beginning 10 to 15 centimeters above the pit floor and were concentrated in a 15- to 20-centimeter-thick zone. Pit contents were primarily food debris (mostly bone) followed by artifacts.

White-tail deer overwhelmingly dominates the faunal sample, followed by turtle and fish and minor amounts of other animals. Shark, jack, mullet, and stingray are represented among the bones and teeth of recognized coastal fauna. The consistent absence of spinal elements suggests that the coastal fish were brought to the site as fillets, presumably having been smoke dried during seasonal fishing excursions. Nearly all of the deer leg bones have been shattered, presumably to permit extraction of the marrow. Here, too, missing elements suggest butchering elsewhere and transport to the pits for cooking. The missing elements include the cannon bones used in the manufacture of bone points and pins and antler; unmodified antler occurred only in two pits. Floral food remains consist almost exclusively of charred hickory-nut fragments. While fine screening yielded a mass of very small fish bones and scales (primarily from Feature 26), as well as quantities of very small chert and quartz pressure and shatter flakes and mica flecks, no evidence of maize has been identified in the macrofloral sample. Horticulture is among the subsistence activities we hoped to demonstrate from the site data. The site is situated on some of the finest agriculturally suited soils in the region, and several metates and manos were found.

Ceramic and lithic artifacts are dominated by those characteristic of late Deptford, Early Swift Creek, and Late Swift Creek sites, with a very few older ceramics and a fair quantity of Archaic points and blades. The artifacts are those expected in food acquisition and preparation activities, although the pristine quality of many of the projectile points/knives suggests ritual discard. Other artifacts found in the pits represent tool maintenance and manufacture activities, as well as wood, bone, and hide working. Indeed, some of the artifacts are of special-use classes, such as red and yellow ochres, white kaolin, chalk, and graphite pigments; serrated microblades; sheet mica (both cut and uncut); and quartz crystal debitage and expedient tools, as well as pecked, ground, and polished clear quartz crystal objects and turtle carapace cups and bowls. The range of artifacts suggests the conduct of both mundane and ceremonial activities. Indeed, the quantity and quality of pit contents increase in pits closer to the mound.

Some 107 cultural features (pits and post molds) and nineteen noncultural features (root and mole holes) were identified in the western scrape area. The pit features in this area were generally larger (only 57 percent were between 0.5 and 1.5 square meters) and the midden soil deeper and darker than in the southern scrape areas. While Feature 57 had a slight belling or enlargement near its bottom, the rest had flat to rounded bottoms. As in the southern area, cultural material in most of the western-berm pits began 15 centimeters above the pit floor.

All but four of the 107 cultural features were found in the southern half of the bulldozed area, suggesting that such features extend southward and westward from the area of concentration. Interestingly, unlike those in the southern area, the features in the western area do not seem to be clustered toward Mound 2 (eastward). Further, the refuse appears to be the result of domestic rather than ritual activities, although here too red and yellow ochre, graphite, copper ore, and chalk pigments; cut and uncut mica; crystal; and a fragment of a cut-away copper object were found in the area. Worked *Busycon* shell and bone are also of note because of their unexpected variety at the site.

The twenty-two largest pits (eighteen of which are oval) appear to be directly associated with the two Deptford–Swift Creek oval structures. The pit contents consist primarily of food and food-preparation refuse in addition to artifact manufacture and maintenance debitage. Projectile points/knives are larger, more numerous, and include a greater number of possibly reused Early and Middle Archaic points than in the southern area. It is noted, however, that this portion of the Deptford–Swift Creek village area is adjacent to and may overlap the portion of the site area dominated by Middle Archaic remains.

Of the eighty-one identified post molds, twenty-two are associated with Structure 1 while approximately twenty-five are associated with Structure 2. About twenty post holes were found between the two structures, but their purpose is uncertain. At least fifteen post holes surround the second-largest cooking and/or refuse pit (Feature 57). They likely are the remains of a cooking rack or structural cover over the pit.

From the placement of the cooking/refuse pits and structural post molds, we suggest that Structure 2 is the oldest and that pit Features 68 through 71 are contemporary with that structure. Additional evidence that the pits adjacent to the southern wall of Structure 1 predate that structure's usage consists of the clay fill covering these pits, which is part of the same clay layer used to form the floor of Structure 1. In contrast, while pit Feature 62 located within Structure 2 might have been used when the structure existed, pit Features 58, 65, 67, and 74 are so close to the side of Structure 2 (posing a potential fire hazard) that we believe them to be contemporary with Structure 1 or, at least, not contemporary with Structure 2.

Structure 2 measures 9.3 meters long by 4.35 meters wide. Structure 1 appears to have been about the same size. The long axis of Structure 1 is oriented slightly south of east, while Structure 2 is oriented roughly east-west. Both are generally parallel to the edge of the bluff and the nearby lake shoreline in this area of Lake Lafayette. The entryways of both structures appear to have faced eastward toward Mound 2 and generally toward the rising sun. This orientation also served to shield structure occupants from the prevailing northerly and westerly winds in the fall and winter months.

Village Artifacts

While the analysis phase of the project has only just begun, we are able to make a few preliminary observations. First, the expected projectile point/knife lithic tools are abundantly represented. These reflect all stages of maintenance reduction. However, we note that to us an unusual quantity of pristine points—that is, unexhausted, unbroken, relatively sharp points—have been discarded in the pits, particularly in the southern-berm pits nearest to Mound 2. We have hypothesized that their discard reflects a cultural bias against the reuse of points once they have been successfully used.

Whether this is the norm or restricted to activities associated with manhood or new-year ceremonies, for instance, we do not know. While pits in the southern berm area contained an average of two stone points each, western-berm pits contained considerably more whole and broken points: more than twenty-five in the case of Feature 57, for instance. The reuse of older points and the use of a wider variety of points than expected are also noted. Indeed, one point tip appears to be made of obsidian (or a black opalized chert) and an expedient scraper/shaver of grayish-brown tabular chert (similar to that found in Tennessee) also represents the range of exotic stone. While a few exhausted chert cores were used as hammer stones, granular quartz pebble and cobble hammer stones were clearly preferred by site flint knappers.

Faunal food remains are well represented. Deer stand out because of their quantity and size—the bones and antlers generally are much larger than those of contemporary deer in the surrounding area. Fish and turtles are also present. Because of their fragility, Jones removed several examples of turtle carapaces (cups and bowls?) in their soil matrix for lab cleaning and preservation. The presence of coastal species, including shark and jack, suggests seasonal trips to coastal resource locations, while smaller fish and turtle remains suggest exploitation of the adjacent Lake Lafayette. The absence of jack skull and back bones suggests that the samples represented at the site were part of fillets, presumably smoke dried at the coast for transport to the interior. While such items were not identified in the sample, we believe that trips to the coast were also used to obtain salt, *Ilex vomitoria*, and sea turtles, as well as shells, especially *Busycon* shells.

Worked bone was very underrepresented from what we expected. Inspection during the sorting of thousands of faunal remains (some fifteen cubic-foot boxes) yielded fewer than a dozen worked-bone items, including two teeth, one cut jaw, an antler punch or peg, and generally minimally worked bone splinters.

Although we water screened through $\frac{1}{16}$-inch window screen mesh roughly 400 to 500 gallons of soil, we found NO corn, squash, gourd, or other cultigens recognizable by us. We did recover quantities of charred mockernut hickory nut fragments but failed to identify any of the expected acorns or persimmons. The several metates and manos suggest the grinding of seeds—Donna Ruhl (pers. comm.) suggests grass seeds; perhaps microscopic analysis of the grinding surfaces will yield the answer. We have three cubic-foot boxes of sorted charred wood and nuts, another five boxes of small unsorted floral and faunal remains, and two boxes of liter soil samples for those interested in processing their own samples. We also have seventy-seven radiocarbon samples from most of the key features with diagnostic artifacts. We hope to obtain a range of dates to support the artifact seriation sequences evident in the artifact sample.

Tool manufacture and maintenance activities occurred around these pits or at least the results of those activities were discarded in the pits. Chert and quartz debitage and expedient tools, including smooth and grooved abraders, occur with some regularity. The abundance of clear to opaque quartz debitage and the general lack of flaked quartz tools may indicate their use in fire starting. So-called nutting stones are also present. However, because they are made of a soft sandstone, we believe that these specimens functioned as circular abraders or perhaps as fire-starting implements. The more durable anvils made of chert more likely served the function generally attributed to nutting stones.

A large quantity of cut mica debitage and expedient quartz blades and gravers indicates the processing of the raw material at the site. Unfortunately, no discarded finished or partially finished mica specimens have yet been recognized in the sample, although some forms are vaguely suggestive of zoomorphic shapes. A possible bear effigy was found in pit Feature 52 in the southern berm area. There is, however, a repetitive pattern in the forms of the cut mica discards and these excised elements will be used to better understand the form of the cutaway final products. Pecked and ground quartz crystal objects are present as a consequence of manufacture failures. They may have been intended to become beads or pendants when finished, although they might also have served to focus a beam of sunlight much like a magnifying lens. All of the worked quartz objects come from the southern berm area.

Ground stone celts are notable by their absence. Likewise, ceramic figurines are also noted by their absence. However, Penton (1974) reported the occurrence of a figurine torso from the plowed field near the southern berm area. One small fragment of worked copper, part of a cutaway sheet, was recovered during the fine screening of Feature 64 soil samples. The only other evidence of processed copper is restricted to three stained bone fragments.

A wide range of pigments is represented in the sample. These include copper ore (all from the western berm area) for light and dark greens and blues, graphite and galena for grays, charcoal for blacks, chalk for white, hematite for various shades of red, and limonite for yellows. A palette of nonlocal stone retains a red ochre stain. Further, a broken hematite single-hole plummet has a ground surface, indicating its reuse as a source of red ochre pigment.

Finally, a major component of our sample consists of a wide range of ceramics—some twenty-six boxes of general material and another eight boxes of selected samples. The selected samples are those with recognizable decorative motifs, rimsherds, and specimens that represent the temper range from each accession. They also include a considerable quantity of fired and unfired ceramic-manufacture discard material. We have the full range of ceramics spanning late Deptford through Swift Creek into early Weeden Island, as well as a small sample of Fort Walton and Leon-Jefferson ceramics. These include a noticeable amount of cord-impressed, simple stamped, and bold check-stamped sherds, as well as an extreme minority of fiber-tempered and steatite sherds. However, sherds of Franklin Plain and Swift Creek Complicated Stamped, early variety, dominate the sample. Other Swift Creek stamped varieties also occur, including some not previously identified.

We plan to follow the lead of Frankie Snow and others in reconstructing Swift Creek design patterns. So far, none of our identified stamp patterns match those of Snow. A wide variety of rims were located at the site. Along with expected samples are sherds with a cross-in-circle pattern that somewhat resembles the back of some of the Spanish coins found in Florida's waters (Figure 13-7). Rim and body sherds from a St. Andrews Complicated Stamped vessel indicate that it was made and stamped in three stages: base, midsection, and upper third. Note the impression of the curved edge of the paddle (Figure 13-8). We also recovered sherds with an unusual barred-circle stamp pattern that we are tentatively calling Block Stamped in honor of the support of the Block family in our project work at the Block-Sterns site (Figure 13-9).

Summary

The Block-Sterns site appears to be a regional Swift Creek center. We believe that it was occupied year-round, although many of its inhabitants may have been seasonally absent. Further, we believe that the site occupants were those with high status within the local society, with the support population dispersed in clusters elsewhere in the surrounding area. The sources of the obsidian (a point tip), galena, worked copper, copper ore, graphite, red and yellow ochres, hexagonal quartz crystals, clear to milky-colored quartz crystals, igneous stone bar gorget, palettes, celt fragments, and other exotic materials will be of interest. The presence of worked coastal shell indicates a possible trade item. We believe that yaupon (*Ilex vomitoria*) leaves, used to make cassina tea (Black Drink), were also collected during coastal trips for trade with interior people. Certainly mica, quartz crystals, and other exotic materials were brought to the site where they were modified to fin-

Figure 13-7. Sherds with cross-in-circle motif from the Block-Sterns site, Features 67 and 146 (photograph courtesy of the Florida Department of State, Division of Historical Resources).

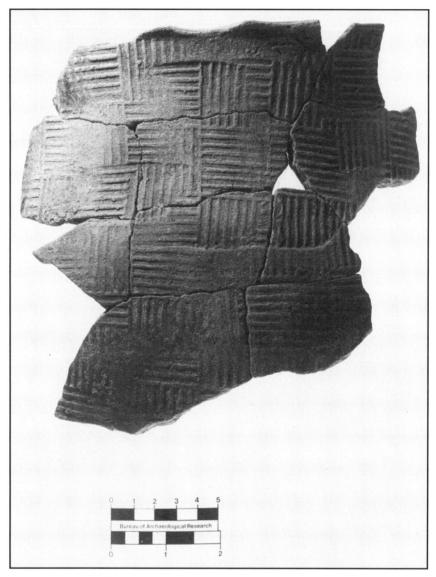

Figure 13-8. St. Andrews Complicated Stamped sherds showing paddle outline from the Block-Sterns site, Feature 8 (photograph courtesy of the Florida Department of State, Division of Historical Resources).

Figure 13-9. Block Stamped sherds from the Block-Sterns site, Feature 61 (photograph courtesy of the Florida Department of State, Division of Historical Resources).

ished products for exchange. Our knowledge of exchange networks and subsistence patterns will also be considerably expanded. The two structures, albeit sequential rather than contemporary, fill an important information gap. We have just begun to mine the wealth of data obtained from our brief project.

Acknowledgment

We wish to acknowledge our debt to avocational (and professional) volunteers and concerned citizens who made this project possible.

Santa Rosa–Swift Creek in Northwestern Florida

Judith A. Bense

Santa Rosa–Swift Creek is a Middle Woodland culture located on the northern Gulf Coast in northwestern Florida. The primary purpose of this chapter is to provide an overview of the available information on Santa Rosa–Swift Creek as of 1994. This overview will include a description of the Santa Rosa–Swift Creek culture area, the general artifact assemblage, chronology, site types, and settlement patterns. Next, within this larger cultural context, I will present preliminary results of investigations at a single-component Santa Rosa–Swift Creek site, Bernath Place, in the Pensacola Bay system as an example of a fairly typical small settlement site of this period.

The Santa Rosa–Swift Creek Culture Area

The Santa Rosa–Swift Creek culture area is located on the northern Gulf Coast in the western panhandle of Florida (Figure 14-1). It stretches 240 kilometers along the coast, from Perdido Bay on the west to St. Andrews Bay on the east and extends into the interior between 50 and 120 kilometers. The interior is characterized by a series of sandy, well-dissected marine terraces and southward-flowing streams organized into four drainage systems that form bays at their confluence with the Gulf, as shown in Figure 14-1. The Pensacola Bay watershed is the largest in the area and is fed by three major rivers. The Choctawhatchee watershed is second in size with only one major river, and the St. Andrews Bay drainage system is the smallest and is fed by only a few third- and fourth-order streams draining the karst–sand

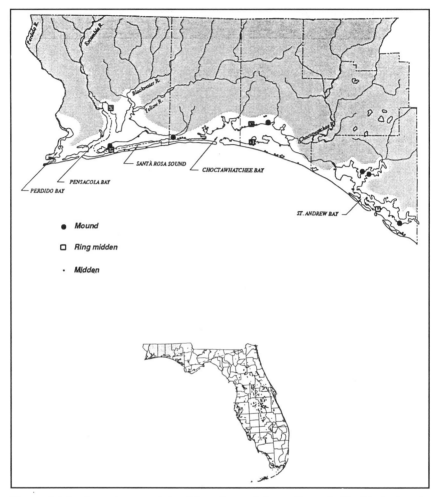

Figure 14-1. Coastal versus inland locations of Santa Rosa–Swift Creek sites in northwestern Florida.

hill region just to the north. This karst region is confined to a relatively small area where limestone containing the Florida aquifer is at the surface and sink-hole lakes dot the landscape along with overflow streams and wetlands.

On the coast, barrier islands and spits protect much of the shoreline and separate the bay systems from the Gulf. Only the Pensacola Bay system has a permanent opening to the Gulf. The other three bay systems have mouths that are alternately closed and open to the Gulf and, consequently, have considerable fluctuations in salinity, relative water level, and marine life. The coastline in the eastern part of the area is not protected by barrier islands, and there are tall dunes up to 25 meters high directly on the coast. Within these dunes, between the mouths of Choctawhatchee and St. Andrews bays, are a series of freshwater lakes that are isolated, rich wetlands within the desert-like environment of dunes and scrub.

The bays have large expanses of sea grass beds and marshes with high populations of fish and shellfish. These protective environments are estuaries for a continual series of migrating fish that come in from the Gulf to spawn. In addition, there are large permanent populations of fish such as mullet and catfish. The specific species composing the marine communities vary within the bay systems primarily with salinity and depth.

The forests in this area are dominated by southern pine, representing a fire climax community. In areas protected from fire, the vegetation reaches the successional climax of an oak-hickory-magnolia forest. Along the bay and sound coasts, hammocks of these mature forests occur frequently on slightly higher and well-drained areas protected from fire by adjacent wetlands. These hammocks have been the primary locations selected for settlement by human populations for the past 3,000 years.

Material Culture

At present, there are few published artifact counts from Santa Rosa–Swift Creek middens. Table 14-1 presents the ceramic counts from five coastal Santa Rosa–Swift Creek shell middens, four in the Pensacola Bay system and one on Santa Rosa Sound. For the two sites with more than 550 sherds, greater than 75 percent are plain and the Santa Rosa and Swift Creek series sherds together make up less than 15 percent. The temper of most pottery is micaceous sand, but the Santa Rosa series vessels often have clay temper, which might indicate that they were from the Marksville culture area, but this has not been confirmed. Rims of plain and complicated stamped vessels are usually notched or crenelated in pie-crust fashion or they are wavy or undulating. Santa Rosa series pottery rims are usually smooth and even. Swift Creek series and plain containers are usually large open bowls that appear to be utilitarian cooking vessels and often have signs, especially sooting,

Table 14-1. Ceramics Recovered from Selected Santa Rosa-Swift Creek Shell Middens

	Pensacola Bay					Santa Rosa Sound	Choctawhatchee Bay	
Ceramic Series	8SR8	8SR986	8SR684	8SR70	Avg. %	8OK1	8WL58	8WL36
Early Swift Creek	8.1	1.0	7.4	5.3	5.5	10.7		
Santa Rosa	6.2	10.0	0.0	59.7	18.8	6.9	6.0*	6.0*
Plain	74.6	89.0	28.4	19.7	52.9	81.8		
(Franklin)	(2.0)	(2.0)	0.0	0.0	0.0	(2.4)		
Other	11.1	1.0	63.9	15.8	22.9	0.5		
Total Sherds	2209	756	529	76	3570	2579	?	?

Summary
Santa Rosa series   6.0 - 59.2 percent
Early Swift Creek series   1.0 - 18.9 percent
Plain   19.7 - 89.0 percent
  (Franklin Plain)   2.0 - 2.4 percent

*Average of percentages given for different units at the site; counts and totals not available.

of having been used directly on an open fire. Santa Rosa series containers are usually small bowls or beakers that do not show signs of having been used for cooking. These same correlations between vessel types and decorations have been previously documented in a Deptford component in the Pensacola Bay system at the Hawkshaw site (Bense 1985).

Other ceramic artifacts from Santa Rosa–Swift Creek sites in northwestern Florida include solid clay female figurines. One ceramic paddle stamp has also been found in the Choctawhatchee Bay system that has a complicated pattern on one side and a check pattern on the reverse side (Phelps 1969).

The typical chipped-stone point in Santa Rosa–Swift Creek assemblages is small with a triangular blade and expanding stem made by corner or side notching. Phelps (1969) refers to these points as Swift Creek points and they are similar to the Columbia type (Bullen 1975). The points are usually made out of Tallahatta quartzite, which occurs just north of the state line in south-

Table 14-2. Typical Santa Rosa-Swift Creek Archaeological Assemblage in Northwestern Florida

<u>Ceramics</u>
    Swift Creek series
        Swift Creek Complicated Stamped, Early variety
        St. Andrews Complicated Stamped
        Crooked River Complicated Stamped
        New River Complicated Stamped
        Horseshoe Bayou Complicated Stamped
        West Florida Cord Marked
    Santa Rosa series
        Alligator Bayou Stamped
        Basin Bayou Incised
        Santa Rosa Stamped
        Santa Rosa Punctated
        Porter Zone Incised
    Plain
        Micaceous sand
        Clay tempered (Baytown-like)
    Vessel features
        Podal supports (usually small)
        Pie-crust rim treatment
        Undulating rims
    Vessel shapes
        Large and small bowls
        Figurines (small, female, solid clay)
    Paddles for stamping decoration

<u>Lithics</u>
    Triangular blade, stemmed or side-notched stone points
        Split quartz pebbles
        Cut mica pieces

<u>Bone</u>
    Bipointed points
    Awls
    Drilled carnivore canine teeth
    Perforated animal vertebrae

central Alabama. Other documented lithics include pieces of the local ferruginous sandstone and small split quartzite pebbles.

Bone artifacts include bipointed points, some with transverse lines, which likely were used as fishing gouges or parts of composite fishing harpoons or spears. The few other bone artifacts include drilled animal teeth and vertebrae.

In Table 14-2, I have proposed a general archaeological assemblage for

Santa Rosa–Swift Creek middens. Although the artifact frequencies are not well documented yet, this assemblage is at least a beginning in establishing the basic material culture of Santa Rosa–Swift Creek in northwestern Florida.

Four Santa Rosa–Swift Creek burial mounds were excavated by Clarence B. Moore at the turn of the twentieth century. The materials recovered from these mounds were used as part of William Sears's definition of the Green Point Hopewellian burial complex (Sears 1962). Burial mounds in the Santa Rosa–Swift Creek culture area, however, have contained only ceramic vessels of Early Swift Creek Complicated Stamped, Basin Bayou Incised, Alligator Bayou Stamped, and plain. In fact, of all the traits noted for the Yent or Green Point burial complexes defined by Sears, only pottery vessels have been recovered from Santa Rosa–Swift Creek mounds. Thus far, no exotic items such as copper panpipes or copper-covered earspools, such as illustrated in Sears's definitive work in 1962, have been found in Santa Rosa–Swift Creek mounds.

Chronology

Ten radiocarbon dates have been obtained from four Santa Rosa–Swift Creek sites (Table 14-3)—two in Choctawhatchee Bay (Thomas and Campbell 1990, 1992) and two in Pensacola Bay (Phelps 1969). No dates have yet been obtained from sites in the St. Andrews Bay system. The dates indicate that while this cultural period lasted about three centuries in both areas, it may have begun up to 150 years earlier in Choctawhatchee (A.D. 150–450) than in Pensacola (A.D. 350–670). A similar time differential has been documented for the preceding late Deptford culture in these bay systems, as shown in Table 14-4. The late Deptford Okaloosa phase in Choctawhatchee Bay has been dated at three sites to between 50 B.C. and A.D. 150, while in Pensacola the culturally similar Hawkshaw phase has been dated at one site to between A.D. 1 and A.D. 260 (Bense 1985).

From these first few dates, it appears that the Deptford and Santa Rosa–Swift Creek phases in the Pensacola Bay system were later than similar manifestations to the east. This possibly could be a result of diffusion lag, considering that the Pensacola area was the farthest west that either Deptford or Swift Creek pottery styles were made and used on a regular basis. The early

Table 14-3. Santa Rosa-Swift Creek Radiocarbon Dates in Northwestern Florida

Bay System	Site	Name	C14 Date
Choctawhatchee	8WL36	Horseshoe Bayou	A.D. 150 $\pm$ 60
Choctawhatchee	8WL36	Horseshoe Bayou	A.D. 200 $\pm$ 60
Choctawhatchee	8WL176		A.D. 330 $\pm$ 70
Choctawhatchee	8WL36	Horseshoe Bayou	A.D. 450 $\pm$ 60
Pensacola	8SR986	Bernath	A.D. 350 $\pm$ 50
Pensacola	8SR986	Bernath	A.D. 430 $\pm$ 50
Pensacola	8SR8	Third Gulf Breeze	A.D. 465 $\pm$ 75
Pensacola	8SR8	Third Gulf Breeze	A.D. 600 $\pm$ 75
Pensacola	8SR986	Bernath	A.D. 590 $\pm$ 50
Pensacola	8SR986	Bernath	A.D. 670 $\pm$ 50

appearance of the Santa Rosa ceramic series, dated 1 B.C. at the Hawkshaw site, in the Pensacola area may be because of its proximity to the Marksville culture area along the coast where these pottery types originated and persisted throughout the Woodland stage. Also, remember that only one Deptford and two Santa Rosa–Swift Creek sites have been dated in the Pensacola Bay system, and they may not be representative of either cultural period.

Subsistence

There have been only preliminary summaries of the fauna from a few Santa Rosa–Swift Creek shell middens (Phelps 1969; Quitmyer 1994; Thomas and Campbell 1990, 1992). From these analyses, it appears that the bulk of the shell middens is made up of either oyster (*Crassostrea virginica*) or marsh clam (*Rangia cuneata*), which differ in salt tolerances. In areas with

Table 14-4. Deptford Radiocarbon Dates in Northwestern Florida

Bay System	Site	Name	C14 Date
Choctawhatchee	8OK183	Pirate's Bay	50 B.C. ± 55
Choctawhatchee	8WL36	Horseshoe Bayou	30 B.C. ± 70
Choctawhatchee	8WL36	Horseshoe Bayou	20 B.C. ± 60
Choctawhatchee	8WL36	Horseshoe Bayou	A.D. 60 ± 70
Choctawhatchee	8OK153		A.D. 110 ± 90
Choctawhatchee	8OK183	Pirate's Bay	A.D. 120 ± 50
Choctawhatchee	8OK183	Pirate's Bay	A.D. 120 ± 50
Choctawhatchee	8OK153		A.D. 130 ± 70
Choctawhatchee	8OK183	Pirate's Bay	A.D. 140 ± 50
Pensacola	8ES1287	Hawkshaw	1 B.C. ± 50
Pensacola	8ES1287	Hawkshaw	1 B.C. ± 60
Pensacola	8ES1287	Hawkshaw	A.D. 160 ± 60
Pensacola	8ES1287	Hawkshaw	A.D. 180 ± 70
Pensacola	8ES1287	Hawkshaw	A.D. 200 ± 70
Pensacola	8ES1287	Hawkshaw	A.D. 220 ± 60
Pensacola	8ES1287	Hawkshaw	A.D. 260 ± 60
Pensacola	8ES1287	Hawkshaw	A.D. 260 + 60

low salinity, marsh clams dominate the shell middens, and in areas that are more saline, oysters dominate. Other shellfish also were regularly exploited such as the quahog (*Mercenaria*), lightning whelk (*Busycon*), coquina (*Donax*), scallop (*Pecten*), and various conchs and whelks.

While shellfish dominate the bulk of the shell middens, fish appears to have been the primary food source. At the Horseshoe Bayou ring midden on Choctawhatchee Bay, twenty-six species of fish were identified, including blue runner, Crevalle jacks, sheephead, catfish, Atlantic croaker, flounder, red

and black drum, speckled trout, and sea bass. Ten mammal species, dominated by deer, were also identified. Eight reptile species, seven bird species,
and one crustacean species were identified. These faunal remains indicate that
this site was occupied for most, if not all, of the year. The presence of sea
bass and coquina indicates that the occupants ventured to the nearby Gulf
of Mexico for food, but most marine food was procured from the bays. Unfortunately, no botanical studies have been reported for any of the ninety-
nine Santa Rosa–Swift Creek sites.

Site Types and Distribution

On the basis of a review of the literature and the Florida Master Site
File, ninety-nine Santa Rosa–Swift Creek sites have been recorded in the
Santa Rosa–Swift Creek culture area. As is true for most areas, northwestern
Florida has not been systematically surveyed and there are many gaps in sur-
vey coverage and intensity, but these ninety-nine sites make up the present
population of known Santa Rosa–Swift Creek site locations.

The first concern in any site distribution analysis is the credibility of
cultural affiliation. In this area, archaeologists benefit from the fact that the
regional ceramic chronology was developed by Willey in 1949, and it has
stood the test of time. His Smithsonian publication, which defined the culture periods and diagnostic ceramic types, was widely distributed and often
reprinted. Consequently, the diagnostic ceramic types for Santa Rosa–Swift
Creek, shown in Table 14-5, have been well known by regional archaeologists
for more than forty years. In addition, Willey (1949) and Sears (1962) inte-
grated the extensive work of Clarence B. Moore (1902a, 1902b) in northwestern Florida burial mounds at the turn of the twentieth century into
the cultural chronology. Also, many of these ninety-nine Santa Rosa–Swift
Creek sites have been revisited during the past ten years in cultural resource
management projects. In sum, my own spot checking indicates that the affiliation of these ninety-nine sites to the Santa Rosa–Swift Creek period appears
to be reliable.

There are several patterns in the locations of the ninety-nine Santa
Rosa–Swift Creek sites. The first pattern is the concentration of sites on the
coastal strip, shown in Table 14-6 and Figure 14-1. Eighty-seven percent of
the sites are on or near the coast and only twelve small sites are in the interior.

Table 14-5. Santa Rosa-Swift Creek Diagnostic Ceramic Series in Northwestern Florida

Ceramic Series	Type
Swift Creek	Swift Creek Complicated Stamped, Early variety
Swift Creek	St. Andrews Complicated Stamped
Swift Creek	Crooked River Complicated Stamped
Swift Creek	New River Complicated Stamped
Swift Creek	West Florida Cord Marked
Santa Rosa	Alligator Bayou Stamped
Santa Rosa	Basin Bayou Incised
Santa Rosa	Santa Rosa Stamped
Santa Rosa	Santa Rosa Punctated
Santa Rosa	Porter Zone Incised

Table 14-6. Santa Rosa-Swift Creek Site Locations in Northwestern Florida

Bay System	Coastal				Interior		Totals
	Bay	Sound	Gulf	Total	Main River	Total	
Pensacola	11	10	0	21	6	10	31
Choctawhatchee	36	0	6	42	2	2	44
St. Andrew	24	0	0	24	0	0	24
Totals	71	10	6	87	8	12	99

The pattern of site concentration on the coastal strip has been suspected for decades, but there has also been the concern that this concentration may have been the result of survey concentration along the coast rather than an actual site distribution pattern. However, in the past ten years there have been several surveys in the interior of the Santa Rosa–Swift Creek area (Bense 1983; Jenkins and Mann 1985; Thomas and Campbell 1992), in the Pensacola and

Table 14-7. Santa Rosa-Swift Creek Site Types in Northwestern Florida

Site Classes
    A. Multiple mound centers (none in Santa Rosa-Swift Creek culture area)
    B. Middens with associated mound
    C. Middens without mounds

Site Shape
    1. Circular and horseshoe-shaped shell midden rings
    2. Linear middens
    3. Small midden dumps
    4. Mounds

Choctawhatchee upland drainages, and very few Early or Middle Woodland sites have been located. These results indicate that the Santa Rosa–Swift Creek population did prefer the coastal strip for settlement, and the interior appears to have been used only for special-purpose, short-term activities.

The second pattern observed in Santa Rosa–Swift Creek sites is variation in their shape (Table 14-7). There are three types of midden shapes: ring middens, linear middens, and small midden dumps. Small midden dumps are usually less than a hectare in size and circular or amorphous in shape. Linear middens are of varying lengths, have a single ridge between 1 and 2 meters high and 30 to 50 meters wide at the base, and are parallel to the adjacent shoreline. Ring middens are large (about 100 meters in diameter), often have well-formed ridges a meter or more high, and have clean central plazas. Five Santa Rosa–Swift Creek ring middens have been identified in northwestern Florida (Figure 14-1). Two ring middens are circular: Baker's Landing (8BY26), on the southern shore of East Bay in the St. Andrews Bay system, and the Old Homestead site (8WL58), on the northern shore of Choctawhatchee Bay. Three ring middens are U shaped: the Horseshoe Bayou site (8WL36), on the southern shore of Choctawhatchee Bay; the Third Gulf Breeze site (8SR8), on Santa Rosa Sound near Pensacola; and the Bernath site (8SR986) at the head of Escambia Bay. Investigations have been conducted at all three of the U-shaped ring middens. Testing at the Third Gulf Breeze ring midden, shown in Figure 14-2, revealed that the ring was well formed, about a meter high, and 95 meters in diameter (Doran and Piateck

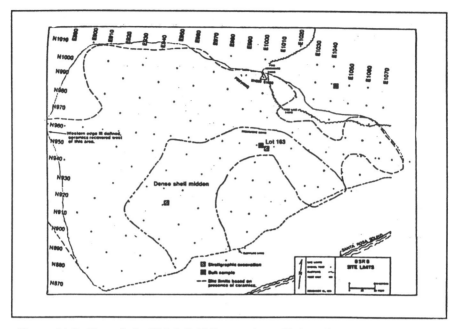

Figure 14-2. Map of the Third Gulf Breeze site, a U-shaped ring midden (Doran and Piateck 1985).

1985; Houston and Stoutamire 1982; Willey 1949). Testing at this site by several investigators has documented that while the site has several cultural components, the shell midden ring was built and used only during the Santa Rosa–Swift Creek period. The area within the horseshoe of shell midden is sterile. Interestingly, shell midden extends outside the shell ring to the north to a thickness of 50 to 75 centimeters. This midden area is flat and contains abundant cultural material. The midden eventually thins out between about 50 and 80 meters north of the ring.

The Horseshoe Bayou site on the southern shore of Choctawhatchee Bay, shown in Figure 14-3, has been extensively excavated (Thomas and Campbell 1990, 1992). The shell midden from the Santa Rosa–Swift Creek period was confined to the ring and a few elevated spots inside the ring. The area inside the ring is characterized as swept clean. This shell midden was composed of discrete lenses of shells, and it had more than 330 features including trash pits, shell concentrations, fire hearths, and almost 200 post

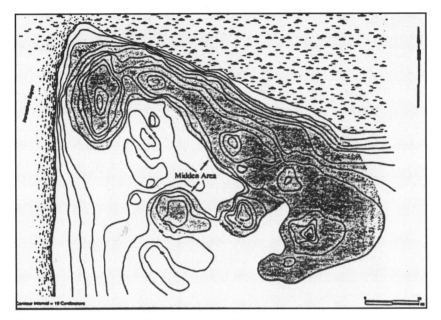

Figure 14-3. Map of the Horseshoe Bayou site, a U-shaped ring midden.

molds. The reports stated that the overwhelming majority of the features were affiliated with the Santa Rosa–Swift Creek culture.

There are six Santa Rosa–Swift Creek burial mounds in northwestern Florida, shown in Figure 14-1. Available information from four of the mounds indicates that they are oval or circular, between 20 and 30 meters wide at the base, and between 1 and 2 meters high. Most mounds appear to have been constructed in a single event. The Manly mound in the Gulf Breeze cluster has a ramp on the western side leading to the summit. Two mounds had a basal layer of oyster shells, and one of these (Baker's Landing in St. Andrews Bay) had nine burials under the basal oyster shell layer. Cremations and multiple skull burials were probably present in the Anderson's Bayou mound in St. Andrews Bay, excavated by Clarence B. Moore (1902a, 1902b). One mound in the St. Andrews Bay system, Alligator Bayou, had sixty-six vessels in an eastern-side cache.

The affiliation of four burial mounds with the Santa Rosa–Swift Creek culture is through the material excavated from them by Moore at the turn of the twentieth century, which was reexamined by Sears in the 1950s. The presence of Santa Rosa and Early Swift Creek pottery vessels in these four mounds as reported in Moore's publications (1902a, 1902b) and by Sears (1962) is the basis for their cultural assignment to the Santa Rosa–Swift Creek period. One mound, the Manly mound near Pensacola, has not been investigated, and it is provisionally assigned to this culture period on the basis of a surface collection on and around the mound and its close proximity to two single-component Santa Rosa–Swift Creek sites. The sixth mound (and possibly a seventh), at Wynnhaven, has been destroyed for more than 100 years. It is provisionally assigned to this period because of its close proximity to a very large single-component Santa Rosa–Swift Creek linear shell midden. Of these six Santa Rosa–Swift Creek burial mounds, four have been destroyed, one is partially preserved, and one is virtually undisturbed.

The third pattern observed in Santa Rosa–Swift Creek sites is that there are two classes of sites. Phelps (1969) and Penton (1974) defined three site classes for the Santa Rosa–Swift Creek period two decades ago: multimound centers, middens with mounds, and middens without mounds. As indicated in Table 14-7, there are no multimound centers in northwestern Florida, and the nearest such centers are the Mandeville site on the Chattahoochee River near Dothan, Alabama, and the Waddell's Mill Pond site near Marianna, Florida, both of which are in the Apalachicola River drainage. In the Santa Rosa–Swift Creek culture area, there are four middens with associated mounds (Class B sites) and scores of middens without mounds (Class C sites).

On closer examination of site locations, there appears to be the possibility of a pattern of site clustering in the Santa Rosa–Swift Creek culture area. Eight site clusters have been tentatively identified there (Figure 14-4). There may also be a ninth cluster at the head of East Bay in the Pensacola Bay system. The site clusters consist of one large midden and several nearby smaller middens. Four clusters of sites have a Class B site (midden with a mound) as the largest settlement. The four other site clusters have a Class C site (midden without a mound) as the largest settlement. Two clusters, Strange Bayou and Gulf Breeze, have ring middens with associated burial mounds. Similarly, the Hammock Point and Fourmile Point clusters have a ring midden without an associated mound as the largest site. Curiously, there are two mounds in the St. Andrews Bay system on North Bay, Alligator Bayou and Anderson's Bayou, that do not have any recorded middens nearby.

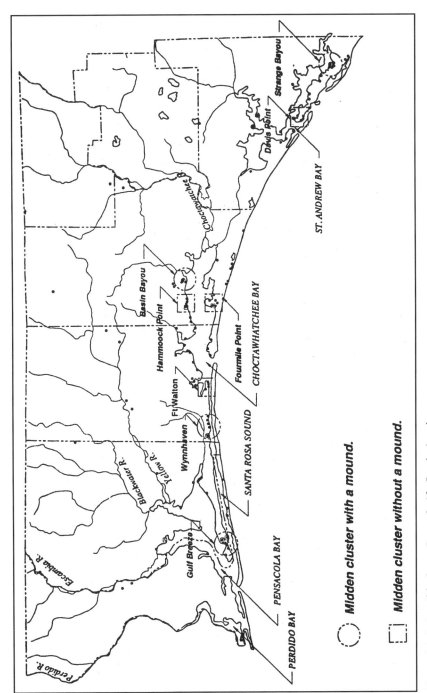

Figure 14-4. Possible Santa Rosa–Swift Creek site clusters.

It is reasonable to question the reality of these suggested eight Santa Rosa–Swift Creek clusters. As very little of the area has been systematically surveyed, the clusters could be just the result of surveys having been conducted in those areas. This possibility has been tested on only one of the proposed site clusters in the Santa Rosa–Swift Creek culture area, the Basin Bayou cluster on the northern shore of Choctawhatchee Bay. In their survey of Eglin Air Force Base, Thomas and Campbell (1992) documented this cluster and then intensively surveyed the adjacent coast and stream drainages to the east and west. Only one small Santa Rosa–Swift Creek midden was found between the Basin Bayou cluster and the Hammock Point site cluster to the west, and none was found to the east on the military property. From this limited survey, it appears that the Basin Bayou site cluster is not likely a product of unsystematic surveys. Of course, other systematic surveys will be necessary to validate other site clusters and the general site cluster pattern proposed here.

Bernath Place:
A Santa Rosa–Swift Creek Ring Midden near Pensacola

The Bernath site is located at the head of Escambia Bay in the Pensacola Bay system, 32 kilometers from the mouth of the bay at the Gulf of Mexico (Figure 14-1). The site is situated on well-drained sandy soil at the confluence of Mulatto Bayou and a small spring-fed tidal creek. Survey, testing, and data recovery investigations were conducted at the Bernath site between 1991 and 1994 by University of West Florida archaeology staff and students (Bense 1992, 1993, 1994; Chapman 1994; Stringfield 1994; Quitmyer 1994). Six radiocarbon dates from six features indicate that the site was occupied between A.D. 300 and 670. Ceramic studies have documented that the major occupation at this site was by groups of the Middle Woodland Santa Rosa–Swift Creek culture. There is a small scatter of shell-tempered Mississippian Pensacola ceramics in the plow zone, which indicates the site was visited after A.D. 1200. The ceramic assemblage and radiocarbon dates indicate that the site was occupied at least intermittently throughout the four centuries of the Santa Rosa–Swift Creek period (Chapman 1994). Initial floral and faunal studies have indicated that the site was occupied at least during the summer and fall seasons (Quitmyer 1994).

Bernath is a ring midden site composed primarily of a dark midden about 30 centimeters thick with submidden refuse pits and piles of shell midden. The midden was deposited in a crescent-shaped ring outside a well-defined central area or plaza, shown in Figure 14-5, which contains many human burials (Bense 1994; Chapman 1994; Stringfield 1994).

The plaza covers about 35 × 25 meters (875 square meters). The sediment in this area is a light yellowish-brown sand with little organic staining and no midden and sparse cultural material. The perimeter of the plaza is well defined by the surrounding contrasting dark-brown shell midden with abundant artifacts and areas of dense shells (Figures 14-5 and 14-6). Plaza features include pits, a hearth, and burials. Refuse pits were encountered along the northern and southern plaza perimeter. Two large refuse pits along the northern edge of the plaza were excavated. Both pits are more than 2 meters wide and more than a meter deep and contained shell midden domestic refuse (Tables 14-8 and 14-9). Dates of A.D. 670 ± 60 and A.D. 430 ± 50 were obtained from these pits. A refuse pit was encountered along the shoreline edge of the plaza. Also along the shoreline was a large, flat, basin-shaped dark brown stain approximately 8 meters wide and 50 centimeters thick. This could be a large basin-shaped pit and, given its location in the plaza, it may have had a nonutilitarian special function. In the center of the plaza a feature containing several pieces of burned sandstone was encountered, which could have been the base of a hearth.

The most abundant features in the central plaza are human burials. Their discovery was quite unexpected, as there is no precedent to my knowledge in the Southeast for burials in the plaza of a ring midden of any age. Two block units were opened in the plaza, respectively 5 × 6 meters and 4 × 4 meters in size. Burials were encountered almost everywhere in the two units, and exposure was halted before either unit had been completely examined. A total of seventeen burials was exposed in the two blocks. Human remains are restricted to the midden-free plaza and are present throughout it. Of the seventeen burials documented, only one is extended and facing east. The other sixteen are flexed with no discernible orientation. It is possible that some of the flexed burials are actually secondary bundle burials, but further work must be done to confirm this suspicion. All burials are within 5 to 10 centimeters of the surface in or at the base of the plow zone, and all burials had been disturbed to some degree by plowing. It is thought that the burials

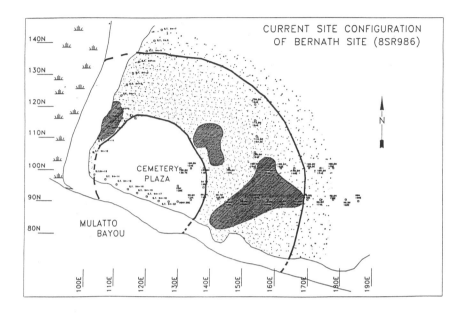

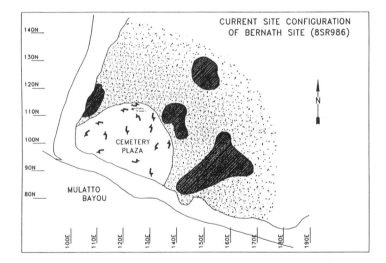

Figure 14-5. Base map of the Bernath Place site, a Santa Rosa–Swift Creek shell midden.

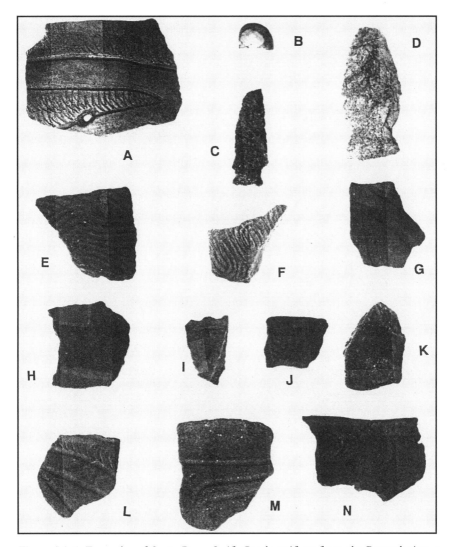

Figure 14-6. Examples of Santa Rosa–Swift Creek artifacts from the Bernath site: *a* and *l*, Alligator Bayou Stamped; *b*, split quartzite pebble; *c* and *d*, chipped-stone points (quartzite); *e, f, h, i,* and *j*, Swift Creek Complicated Stamped; *i*, crenelated rim; *j*, straight rim; *g* and *m*, Basin Bayou Incised; *n*, Santa Rosa Stamped; *k*, plain podal support.

Table 14-8. Ceramics from a Large Refuse Pit, Feature 8, at the Bernath Site

Ceramics	Number	Percent
Sand tempered, plain	364	91.92
Swift Creek Complicated Stamped	10	2.53
Santa Rosa Stamped	0	0.00
Santa Rosa Punctated	0	0.00
Alligator Bayou Stamped	3	0.76
Basin Bayou Incised	10	2.53
Porter Zone Incised	1	0.25
Unidentified incised/punctated	6	1.51
Eroded check stamped	1	0.25
Podal supports	1	0.25
Unidentified stamped	0	0.00
Total	396	100.00

Table 14-9. Ceramics from a Large Refuse Pit, Feature 14, at the Bernath Site

Ceramics	Number	Percent
Sand tempered, plain	316	87.78
Swift Creek Complicated Stamped	3	0.83
Santa Rosa Stamped	6	1.67
Santa Rosa Punctated	1	0.28
Alligator Bayou Stamped	18	5.00
Basin Bayou Incised	8	2.22
Porter Zone Incised	0	0.00
Unidentified Incised/Punctated	4	1.11
Eroded check stamped	0	0.00
Podal supports	1	0.28
Unidentified stamped	3	0.83
Total	360	100.00

originally were farther below the surface and that deflation from plowing and runoff has brought them closer to the present surface. Despite the shallow burials, dark brown stains were very visible around the burials. From the limited work conducted in the plaza, it could not be determined whether the burials had been placed as individuals or groups in pits or on the plaza surface and covered. The dark stains surrounding the burials could be from pit fill and/or from decomposition. Two clusters of three and four burials have been tentatively identified. The others appear to have been interred individually. It is quite possible that all the burials were interred at the same time, as there are no intersecting burials. Very few artifacts were recovered around the burials, and it is difficult to associate artifacts with a specific burial because of their shallowness and plowing disturbance. However, three items appear to have been placed with burials. A large shell from a cardium, a species that inhabits the Gulf shore, and a sandstone nutting stone are associated with one burial and another had a piece of red ocher near the cranium. The burial density in the two excavation blocks averaged 2.9 square meters per burial. If this density is uniform for the entire 875-square-meter plaza, there could be as many as 302 burials.

The shape of the plaza today is semicircular. As Stringfield (1994) reports, the outside plaza perimeter is well defined by color and texture from the surrounding midden band. However, the shoreline is actively eroding and the original shape of the plaza cannot be absolutely determined. The presence of a high number of burials in the plaza stands out as the most unusual aspect of the plaza; however, the central hearth-like feature and perimeter pit features may be important elements.

The midden ring consists of the naturally occurring sandy soil, which has been stained dark brown from organic matter and charcoal, and has an average thickness of only about 30 centimeters. The midden deposit is thickest nearest the plaza (30 to 40 centimeters) and decreases in thickness toward the outside perimeter. The midden matrix contains very little shellfish. Dense shells are directly associated with refuse pits containing shell midden. The midden ring is not a shell midden; rather, it is an earth midden with scattered shell. The midden contains much cultural material, especially pottery, animal bones, charred plant material, and shell. In all areas of the midden investigated, refuse-filled pits have been encountered. The pits range from 50 centimeters to 2 meters in diameter and 50 to 100 centimeters in depth and extend well below the midden. Refuse pits occur singly and in clusters and are more numerous on the inside of the midden band. Plowing has disturbed the upper portion of the shell midden refuse pits, which has created areas of thick shell midden on the present surface.

The overall shape of the midden deposit at the Bernath site is an asymmetrical horseshoe or crescent-shaped ring. The width ranges from 30 to 41 meters on the north and east to 5 to 11 meters on the west. The most clear edge of the ring is the interior boundary between the dark midden and yellow-brown midden-free plaza. Because the shoreline is actively eroding, it is possible that the original shape of the midden ring was a more symmetrical horseshoe or a circular ring. The outside perimeter of the midden ring is less well defined because of both the thinness of the midden in the periphery and disturbance from cultivation and borrowing. Oral reports from the Bernath family relate that this field was heavily farmed because of the richness of the midden soil and that some shell midden was removed for road fill. While the tractor used in cultivation was small and the shell midden was removed by hand and wagon, the impact on the midden could have been severe because of its shallowness. However, some of the midden is still intact below the plow zone.

The current surface of the midden ring, and the site in general, has a gentle slope of 1 meter in 30 to 40 linear meters from the toe of a low ridge on the northern part of the site to the surrounding wetlands. There is no evidence that a deep midden deposit has been removed as is often revealed in pedestaled trees or stumps or borrow pits. Along the old fence line surrounding the site, the surface is only slightly higher (about 10 to 20 centimeters) than the surface in the area that was regularly cultivated. The surface of the site is smooth with a gentle slope, which is typical of this physiographic position in this area. This smooth surface is one of the main reasons that the presence of a midden ring was not detected earlier in our investigations at the Bernath site. Usually, ring middens are elevated above the surrounding terrain and they are detectable by contour mapping; however, one flat Late Woodland Weeden Island ring midden, 8SR64, has been previously identified in the Pensacola Bay system on the Gulf Breeze peninsula on the Naval Live Oaks section of Gulf Islands National Seashore.

The midden ring appears to have formed by accretion, sheet deposits, and filling of refuse pits. No structural features have been identified anywhere on the site yet such as post mold patterns, pit house floors, or large hearths. It is possible that structures that are difficult to detect could have been located on the midden ring. This is the situation at most sites on the Gulf Coast.

Thus, the Bernath site is a Middle Woodland Santa Rosa–Swift Creek midden ring in the shape of an asymmetrical horseshoe. The central midden-free plaza is 25 × 35 meters in size and has a few pit features along the perimeter and a possible hearth near the center. The primary characteristic of this plaza is the presence of dense burials in all areas investigated. Of these burials, only one is extended, and all others are flexed or bundled. Grave goods are few.

The midden at the Bernath site appears to have been purposefully placed to outline a central, midden-free area. The inside perimeter of the ring is well defined, and the outside edge is more blurred due to plowing disturbance. The shape of the midden ring today is that of an asymmetrical horseshoe, but given the erosion of the shoreline, the ring may have been circular or a more symmetrical horseshoe. The midden is only about 30 centimeters thick and it is composed of dark, organically stained sand with sparse shell and abundant cultural material. Refuse pit features that contain dense shell midden and extend below the midden are located in all areas of the midden ring investigated.

Comparing the Bernath site to what is known about the Santa Rosa–Swift Creek site types and distribution reveals some interesting observations. As stated previously, there are four other ring midden sites in the Santa Rosa–Swift Creek culture area (Figure 14-1). There are two in the Pensacola Bay system, two in the Choctawhatchee Bay system, and one in the St. Andrews Bay system. In the Pensacola Bay system, the Bernath site is about 20 miles from the Third Gulf Breeze ring midden (Doran and Piateck 1985). As shown in Figures 14-2 and 14-5, both sites are horseshoe-shaped and have semicircular plazas that open to the south. However, the Third Gulf Breeze site plaza is much larger (63 percent). Cultural materials are sparse in both plazas, but features and burials have been identified only in the Bernath plaza. It should be noted that there well may be features and burials in the Gulf Breeze ring midden plaza that have not been discovered, as only ten shovel tests at 10-meter intervals have been excavated there. We missed the burials in the Bernath plaza in both the survey and testing phases with thirteen shovel tests.

The midden rings at the Third Gulf Breeze and Bernath sites are similar in shape, but differ in several aspects. The most noticeable difference is in elevation. The Third Gulf Breeze midden ring was built up to between 50 and 80 centimeters above the surrounding area, while there is no measurable elevation of the ring at Bernath. The fact that the Gulf Breeze ring has not been plowed and Bernath has been both plowed and borrowed may account for some of the differences in elevation. Neither midden ring is consistent in width throughout the site. Both rings have quite narrow and wide areas, but the Gulf Breeze ring is wider by 10 meters at its widest point than that at Bernath. The construction material for the two rings is different. At Gulf Breeze, the ring is composed exclusively of dense shell midden. At Bernath, the ring is made of a dark earth midden. In addition, no features have been identified in the Third Gulf Breeze midden ring, while many refuse-pit features have been identified in the Bernath ring.

A significant difference between the midden rings is the presence of a wide black-earth midden surrounding the perimeter of the ring at Gulf Breeze that is buried 15 to 20 centimeters below the present-day surface. This midden is irregular in shape, varying between 10 and 60 meters in width, and is 25 to 30 centimeters thick. Doran and Piateck (1985) documented that this flat, surrounding midden is primarily organically stained soil with sparse or little shell.

In reviewing the range of features of the two documented Middle Woodland Santa Rosa–Swift Creek midden rings in the Pensacola Bay system, we now know that the plaza is much more formally defined than the surrounding midden rings. Plazas are semicircular, opening to the southern or adjacent shore. The plazas were consciously kept free of midden, and perimeter features and abundant burials can be present. There is much more variation in the surrounding midden ring. While the rings at both sites discussed are generally horseshoe-shaped, they vary in elevation, width, composition, features, and surrounding middens.

Summary, Conclusions, and New Ring Midden Interpretations

The best-known material trait of the Santa Rosa–Swift Creek period is pottery types. While the bulk of the ceramic assemblage is sand-tempered plain, the Santa Rosa and Swift Creek pottery series are consistently present in minor amounts, and they are diagnostic of the period. The Santa Rosa series now has been dated in closed pit features at two sites in the Pensacola Bay system: Hawkshaw (8ES1287), a single-component Early Woodland Deptford site (Bense 1985), and Bernath, a single-component Santa Rosa–Swift Creek site. Three dates between A.D. 1 and A.D. 260 for this ceramic series were obtained at Hawkshaw, where these types were consistently associated with the Deptford ceramic series. The new dates on the Santa Rosa series at Bernath push the use of these types to at least A.D. 590 in the Pensacola area. Most Santa Rosa series vessels at the Hawkshaw site appear to have been serving or eating containers, not cooking vessels, and preliminary results from Bernath indicate that this pattern continued during the following Santa Rosa–Swift Creek period. These vessels also are often clay tempered and probably were imported from the lower Mississippi Valley, but this is yet to be demonstrated.

The earliest dates for the Swift Creek Complicated Stamped series in the Pensacola Bay system are A.D. 160 and 180, and these were also obtained at the Hawkshaw site in association with Deptford ceramic types. The two new dates from the Bernath site indicate that while Swift Creek types appear later than Santa Rosa types, both were used through the Middle Woodland in the Pensacola area. At both the Hawkshaw and Bernath sites, Swift Creek series vessels appear to have been used for cooking activities as indicated by their large size and sooted bases.

The long-suspected coastal preference for the Santa Rosa–Swift Creek population has been fairly well documented. The interior apparently was used on a limited basis. Coastal site types consist of large ring middens, long linear middens, or small midden dumps. Burial mounds were also constructed throughout the culture area. Sites types include middens with a mound and middens without an associated mound. Sites appear to be organized into site clusters characterized by small middens near a large site. Four of the clusters identified have a ring midden as their largest settlement, and four have a burial mound associated with the largest settlement.

If the suspected site cluster pattern is genuine, it would be reflective of the typical Woodland base camp–satellite camp settlement pattern and the egalitarian sociopolitical organization of the Big Man–Big Woman segmented lineage. It is hypothesized that the self-made leader resided at the largest site in each cluster, and that he/she was buried in the burial mounds. Ceramics that may indicate participation in the Hopewell Ceremonial Complex were buried with the dead and in the mounds, but there is a curious absence of the more exotic items found just to the east in the Apalachicola drainage. Ceramics were the only mound and grave goods in the Santa Rosa–Swift Creek culture area.

While subsistence studies are few thus far, it is likely that fish played a large role in the coastal diet, and that deer and nuts were the other dietary mainstays. A wide variety of shellfish, small mammals, birds, and reptiles likely rounded out the diet.

While many questions about Santa Rosa–Swift Creek remain unanswered, there is a large and relatively well-preserved archaeological record in northwestern Florida. In the research to be done in the near future, I will refine the ceramic chronology and assemblage, settlement pattern, and subsistence of the Santa Rosa–Swift Creek culture in northwestern Florida.

After discovering the cemetery plaza at the Bernath site, visiting the Pine Arbor Square Ground of the Florida Creek tribe, and reviewing the concept of what a plaza means, I have developed a new interpretation of ring middens sites—one that views the sites from the perspective of the plaza. The plaza could well be the key feature of these site types. Keeping the plaza free of refuse took considerable effort, which could imply that this was a very special area where important activities occurred. It must have been swept of debris at regular intervals and the well-defined perimeter must have been a clear boundary between two areas that were perceived and treated quite differently.

The practice of designating a special space or plaza that is free of midden is well documented in Southeastern Indian prehistory and history from the Late Archaic stage shell midden rings along the Georgia coast and Poverty Point sites in the lower Mississippi Valley and Gulf Coast through the Woodland, Mississippian, and historic-period mound centers (Bense 1994). The practice continues to the present at square grounds in historic and modern traditional Muskogean cultures. For example, the archaeological deposits and site-formation processes at the Pine Arbor Square Ground of the Florida Creek tribe near Blounstown on the Apalachicola River are forming a modern "ring midden" with segregation of space into a central circular plaza kept free of refuse where special rituals and dances are conducted and a band of midden with features along the perimeter of the plaza. The plaza has a central hearth.

The long tradition of a segregated, special central plaza area surrounded by midden debris in Southeastern Indian culture leads me to theorize that the ring midden sites are the precursors and equivalents of the better-known mound-and-plaza centers. I suggest that the plazas of ring middens are precursors of the square ground still in use by traditional Muskogee people today and that they were used in a similar manner. The local political leader resided at these sites and the central plaza was used for special events and kept clean of everyday refuse.

The presence of burials in the plaza at the Bernath ring midden on Escambia Bay near Pensacola may be the result of a local preference for cemeteries over mound burials, which has been documented in the Pensacola Bay system for all time periods. Several cemeteries for both the elite and commoners have been documented in the Mississippian Pensacola culture area, and no mounds have been located. The cemetery in the Bernath ring midden may be an early indicator of this long local tradition.

Thus, I theorize that ring midden sites were where special ritual and ceremonial activities were conducted and very likely where the local leadership family resided. Given the presence of dense burials in the Bernath site plaza, it is possible that the other ring middens without an associated burial mound could also have a cemetery in the plaza, while those with an associated burial mound do not. This model of ring midden sites can be tested by a reexamination of the results of previous investigations at ring middens and by new investigations in plaza areas of others.

Swift Creek in
a Regional Perspective

David G. Anderson

During the few centuries around and immediately after the time of Christ, as suggested by evidence in the form of shared artifacts and iconography, a diverse range of societies across eastern North America were tied together in some way: this behavior has come to be subsumed under the rubric of Middle Woodland period Hopewellian interaction. The existence of a broadly shared ideology is inferred by the presence of similar decorative motifs, material goods, and mortuary practices over large areas, albeit locally expressed and no doubt locally interpreted as well. As we see from the chapters in this volume, the Swift Creek culture was a major participant in this regionally extensive exchange and ritual-based interaction network. Appreciable evidence for direct contact between Swift Creek and other areas has been found; the interaction appears to have followed major communications arteries, such as along the Gulf Coast and up the major drainages of the Mid-South, such as the Chattahoochee, Mississippi, Tennessee, and Tombigbee, and along overland trails, encompassing the midwestern heartland of Hopewell in Ohio, Indiana, and Illinois. In areas of the East away from these seemingly favored lines of communication, in contrast, evidence for direct exchange or contact tends to be more tenuous. Understanding what is occurring on Swift Creek sites in the South Appalachian area, accordingly, requires familiarity with events and processes occurring elsewhere in the region during the Middle Woodland period.

What Is Swift Creek Culture?

Before we explore what is occurring elsewhere in the region, it will be helpful to address what Swift Creek is, how sites are recognized, and where they are located. As we have seen from the various chapters of this volume, Swift Creek is a Middle Woodland period archaeological culture located in Georgia and northern Florida and extending short distances into adjoining states. Named after the type site, a single platform mound and associated village area excavated near Macon, Georgia, during the Works Progress Administration (Kelly and Smith 1975), Swift Creek components are identified by elaborate curvilinear complicated stamped ceramics that often display animal or cosmological motifs. As Williams and Elliott observed (Chapter 1), it is the uniquely stamped pottery that distinguishes this culture. Loosely speaking, then, Swift Creek sites are considered to be those in the general Georgia/northern Florida area yielding more than incidental amounts of Swift Creek Complicated Stamped pottery. Swift Creek Complicated Stamped pottery has been found in appreciable quantity as far away as the Mann site in southern Indiana; however, at many sites in the so-called Georgia/northern Florida "heartland" it is a decided minority ware. As a result, there are both quantitative and geographic aspects to assigning components to the culture.

The Swift Creek culture area, accordingly, consists of those sites in the South Appalachian area that were in more or less regular interaction with one another and shared (at varying levels of intensity) a common, diagnostic complicated stamped ceramic tradition. The core area has been variously defined but, in general, minimally encompasses the Coastal Plain and lower Piedmont of Georgia into immediately adjacent portions of Alabama and South Carolina and the northern part of Florida from roughly Pensacola Bay to the Suwannee River system; Elliott (Chapter 3) argues that it is restricted to within the Alabama, Apalachicola, and Altamaha river systems. As the various chapters in this volume also demonstrate, however, what we think of as Swift Creek culture encompasses appreciable variation in settlement patterning, organizational complexity, and ceremonial behavior. Rather than being a monolithic entity, Swift Creek clearly represents a number of distinct societies. This is, however, also the case with other well-known subregional

Middle Woodland archaeological cultures, such as Ohio Hopewell, Havana Hopewell, and Marksville. Their distinctive character is no doubt a result of a high degree of internal interaction, which helps set them apart on the prehistoric landscape.

Swift Creek is an integral part of the South Appalachian ceramic and cultural tradition, a concept originally proposed by William Henry Holmes (1903:130–33), who noted that the ceramics from the general Georgia–South Carolina area, or what he called the "South Appalachian" area, were characterized by a distinctive, stamped exterior finish; this suggested a common cultural background. The existence of a South Appalachian cultural province characterized by a distinctive ceramic tradition, and covering the area described by Holmes, is now universally accepted. The South Appalachian geographic variant of Mississippian culture, for example, has been the subject of extensive analysis and synthesis (Ferguson 1971; Griffin 1967:185).

Widespread use of carved wooden paddles to finish pottery first occurred in the South Appalachian area in the Early Woodland period, shortly after 1000 B.C., with the appearance of dentate, check-stamped, and simple stamped ceramics variously classified into series such as Refuge, Deptford, and Cartersville. Some continuity is indicated with Late Archaic Stallings and Thom's Creek ceramics, on which simple stamping occasionally occurred; check and dentate stamping may have been a conscious attempt to imitate earlier drag-and-jab and separate punctated decorations. Complicated stamping, the application of elaborate curvilinear and rectilinear designs, appears around 100 B.C. or shortly thereafter, with the Swift Creek series, and continues unabated through the South Appalachian area until well into the historic period; major later series in northern and central Georgia include Napier, Etowah, Savannah/Wilbanks, Lamar, and Qualla. Some of the most elaborate design motifs, including representations of animals and cosmological themes, occur early, on Swift Creek ceramics. Subsequent designs are typically less complex geometric arrangements and comprise variations on circles, ovals, triangles, and spirals. Throughout the Woodland and Mississippian periods, similar motifs tend to occur almost contemporaneously across much of the South Appalachian area, indicating an appreciable degree of interaction among the local societies. As we have seen, this interaction was particularly extensive during the Swift Creek period and, through the kinds of analyses described in this volume (in particular the work recounted in Chapters 6 through 10), the interaction can be documented to a degree that is most unusual by archaeological standards.

In the "heartland" area, Swift Creek (and St. Andrews) Complicated Stamped ceramics replaced the plain, check-stamped, and simple stamped ceramics of the Deptford series in northern Florida and southern Georgia around 100 B.C. and were in turn replaced by Weeden Island ceramics and culture around A.D. 400. In central and northern Georgia, Swift Creek ceramics appeared about the same time (circa 100 B.C. to A.D. 100) but coexisted with rather than replaced the Deptford, Cartersville, and Connestee series for several centuries. Swift Creek ceramics in this area, in fact, continued in use until as late as A.D. 750, after which Late Woodland Napier and Woodstock series appeared. At many sites in northern Georgia and immediately adjoining areas, therefore, Swift Creek ceramics are found (typically as a minority ware) with Deptford, Cartersville, and Connestee-like ceramics (see Elliott, Chapter 3 herein). A late continuation for Swift Creek is also evident in eastern Alabama (see Chase, Chapter 5 herein).

Classic Early Swift Creek designs are usually simple curvilinear motifs based on concentric circles and ovals; rims are typically notched or scalloped, and tetrapods are common. Late Swift Creek assemblages, postdating circa A.D. 500, are characterized by an increase in the incidence of plain pottery and folded rims, a decline in the incidence of notched and scalloped rims, and (usually) more complex complicated stamped designs with some zoned stamping. Some design motifs and rim treatments have proved to be highly sensitive temporal markers, and some clearly come from specific sites (see Snow, Chapter 6 herein; Snow and Stephenson, Chapter 7 herein). A fine-lined variant of Swift Creek, called B-Complex to differentiate it from classic southern and central Georgia materials, is found in the northern and eastern Georgia Piedmont and appears to be transitional between Swift Creek and Napier (Wood et al. 1986:340–41). Middle Woodland sites in extreme eastern Georgia and South Carolina are largely dominated by Deptford and Cartersville ceramics and are almost completely devoid of Swift Creek influence, although occasional complicated stamped sherds are found; a similar situation occurs in western North Carolina, where assemblages are dominated by Connestee-like ceramics.

Factors Shaping the Location of Swift Creek Sites

The Location of Major Centers

The area of the Southeast centered on Georgia and northern Florida, the heartland of Swift Creek, clearly played a major role in the Middle Woodland panregional interaction network. Swift Creek, Connestee, and other contemporary South Appalachian area ceramics, or at least designs, are found at sites as far removed as Pinson in western Tennessee, Mann in southern Indiana, and Rutherford in southern Illinois and at a number of the major centers in Ohio, including Hopewell, Harness, McGraw, Mound City, Tremper, Turner, and Seip (Chapman and Keel 1979:160; Fowler 1957:11; Kellar 1979:103–4; Mainfort 1988:139; Prufer 1968; Rein 1974; Smith 1979:186). Besides pottery, other locally derived materials such as mica, greenstone, steatite, and galena saw widespread distribution throughout the East, and it is possible that perishables such as feathers, carved masks, or other objects or unusual foods (e.g., leaves from *Ilex vomitoria,* used to make the Black Drink) were also moving outward (Goad 1979; Walthall et al. 1979). As the editors of this book suggest in Chapter 1, the wood-carving skills revealed on elaborate Swift Creek paddles may well have been employed to produce a wide range of items. Swift Creek wooden products such as bowls, clubs, stools, or masks, accordingly, rather than or in addition to paddles, could well have wound up in the Midwest. The potential range and quality of such goods has been demonstrated at a number of wet sites in Florida (Purdy 1991), and some day such finds may be made from Swift Creek culture contexts.

The preeminent product coming from the South Appalachian/Swift Creek culture area, at least in terms of archaeological visibility, was conch or whelk shell. Exact source areas for the vast quantities of shell found at Middle Woodland centers in the Midwest are not well documented, although available evidence (i.e., the location of Middle Woodland centers along probable trade routes/communications arteries) points to the northern and western Gulf coast of Florida and, less likely, the lower Atlantic seaboard (that Marksville-related cultures may have exerted some control over shell sources from the western Gulf is also probable, an inference supported by the strong similarities between Santa Rosa and Marksville ceramics).

The wealth of items found at major and to a lesser extent minor centers in the Swift Creek area, I suggest, derived at least in part from control of the gathering and movement into the interior of shell and, no doubt, other valuable local commodities. Shell was likely a major source of wealth at centers near source areas, such as Block-Sterns in northwestern Florida (Jones, Penton, and Tesar, Chapter 13 herein), while sites such as Mandeville and Kolomoki might have achieved some of their preeminence by controlling the movement of shell, that is, by acting as middlemen (although we must also consider other possible resources these sites may have more directly harvested). Even the location of comparatively minor settlements may have been affected by the shell trade. The analyses of Bense (1993, Chapter 14 herein) document a pronounced coastal orientation to northwestern Florida Santa Rosa–Swift Creek sites, which may be related, in part, to the collecting of shell for exchange, over and above the obvious ecological richness of the area. Unfortunately, while shell is one readily identifiable commodity known to have moved widely over the region, major shell-processing loci are not presently known; these would, almost certainly, occur in or close to coastal areas.

The distribution of Swift Creek sites and centers across Georgia and beyond, I suggest, was to some extent shaped by the panregional demand for shell and by physiographic conditions constraining the routes by which this commodity could pass into the interior. Fluctuations in demand for shell by societies located elsewhere in the region, reflecting changes in the political fortunes of these societies, and fluctuations in the availability of the resource itself no doubt also played important roles in shaping Swift Creek settlement and interaction. The major Middle Woodland settlements along or near the Chattahoochee at Mandeville and Kolomoki in southern Georgia (Sears 1956; B. A. Smith 1979, Chapter 8 herein; Steinen, Chapter 11 herein) and in the northwestern part of the state at Shaw near Cartersville (Waring 1945) and Tunnacunahee near the Tennessee border (Jefferies 1976), for example, likely served as way stations along a north-south trading axis leading to the Tennessee River and from there downstream into the heart of the Midwest, perhaps via sites such as Savannah, Pinson, and Mann (Jefferies 1976:49–50). That these possible communication routes correspond to the locations of major historic Indian trails, which likely had considerable antiquity, has, of course, been noted by a number of authors (Anderson 1994b; Goad 1979:244–45; Jefferies 1976:49–50; Snow and Stephenson, Chapter 7 herein).

The Chattahoochee River valley may have served as a main trade and

communications artery linking societies of the Mid-South and upper Midwest with those in the South Appalachian area. From the upper Chattahoochee "gap," exchange appears to have followed the Tennessee to the Mississippi and Ohio rivers. The Mann site, located near the mouths of the Wabash,
Tennessee, and Cumberland rivers in southern Indiana, may have been a gate-
way community or way station on one of the primary routes linking the
lower Southeast with the Midwest (Brose 1985:73; Chase, Chapter 5 herein;
Kellar 1979:100). Pottery with classic Swift Creek Complicated Stamped design motifs comprises an impressive 2 to 3 percent of the ceramic assemblage
in most areas of the site (Kellar 1979:103), a figure that is higher than that
observed at many contemporaneous Swift Creek sites in the South Appalachian area. These ceramics were made locally, however, on a clay-tempered
paste, indicating that Swift Creek paddles (and/or people knowing how to
use or carve them) rather than vessels were what was transported. The massive Middle Woodland Pinson and Savannah mound complexes in west-cen-
tral and south-central Tennessee are likely other such way stations/trading
communities, as well as major subregional ceremonial centers in their own
right; the latter lies along the Tennessee River while the former is perhaps
more isolated, lying along the South Fork of the Forked Deer River (Mainfort 1988:144). The location and occupational histories of at least some
Middle Woodland sites in the Swift Creek heartland, particularly those of
the major centers, I believe, were strongly shaped by patterns of interaction
occurring over the larger region.

The Location of Minor Centers and Other Sites

What shaped the distribution of Swift Creek sites that occur at some
distance from northwestern Florida/Gulf coastal shellfish sources and those
well away from the major north-south trade artery running roughly up the
Georgia-Alabama line? Williams and Freer (Chapter 4 herein) have noted an
apparent regular spacing (on the order of 30 kilometers) of Middle Woodland mound centers in the Piedmont of northern Georgia, and these data
suggest that populations were distributed widely over this area, although
population density appears to have been quite low. The distribution of these
centers extends to the Savannah River and little farther, indicating this drainage marks the western margin of Swift Creek culture, which is a supposition
supported by artifact distributional analyses (Anderson 1990; Elliott, Chap-

ter 3 herein). The location of these shrines/small centers may be more indicative of a spillover of Hopewellian/Swift Creek ideology than a reflection
of resource control (i.e., collection and exchange) strategies and networks.
Minor resource processing loci have, however, been identified or inferred at
two small centers in the Georgia Piedmont. The reduction of quartz crystals
is indicated at the Little River site (Williams and Shapiro 1990:118–32), and
limonite nodules, a probable source of pigment, have been found at and near
the Fortson mound site (Williams 1992; Williams and Freer, Chapter 4
herein).

Given the absence of large sites and centers along the Savannah, this river
does not appear to have served as a trade and communications artery comparable to the Chattahoochee or even the Altamaha-Ocmulgee-Oconee. The
presence of Hopewellian design motifs (classified as Deptford Zoned Incised
Punctate) at sites such as Deptford on the coast and G. S. Lewis below the
Fall Line on the Savannah (Elliott, Chapter 3 herein; Sassaman et al. 1990),
however, and the presence of a number of Swift Creek sites and centers in the
Georgia Piedmont in the upper Ocmulgee and Oconee drainages (Rudolph
1986, 1991; Williams and Freer, Chapter 4 herein) offer at least the possibility that Atlantic coastal commodities (e.g., shell, shark's teeth, perishable
goods) could have been moving up these rivers and entering into the larger
regional interaction network. The Swift Creek sites and interaction patterns
observed in southeastern Georgia (i.e., Saunders, Chapter 10 herein; Snow
1977, Chapter 6 herein; Snow and Stephenson, Chapter 7 herein) may reflect
the exploitation of Atlantic coastal resources, although this remains purely
speculative. Only when northern Georgia data are examined with the use of
procedures like those Snow (1977, Chapter 6 herein; Snow and Stephenson,
Chapter 7 herein) has developed in south-central Georgia will we begin to
better understand the nature of trade, communication, and interaction over
the whole of the Swift Creek heartland.

At least some Swift Creek settlements may have been located to control
the procurement and subsequent distribution or movement of what were
perceived to be key resources. Swift Creek ceramics are sometimes seen in
western North Carolina, in the Connestee area (Keel 1976), which may be
related to the mica and other mineral resources that are found in that area
and that are known to have been highly prized by Hopewellian populations.
The upper Savannah is the only part of the drainage where appreciable Swift

Creek ceramics have been found (Elliott, Chapter 3 herein); this settlement may have been prompted or facilitated by a desire to obtain or control access to products from nearby areas, such as mica from western North Carolina. Evidence for Middle Woodland/Hopewellian interaction is minimal to the east of the Savannah River in the Coastal Plain and Piedmont of South Carolina, where only occasional Swift Creek materials are found (see Elliott, Chapter 3 herein). The Appalachians may have been something of a cultural barrier, since evidence for Hopewellian interaction is rare in the Middle Atlantic area; the existence of desirable resources elsewhere in the Southeast and East along more easily traveled communications arteries may have precluded the need for such interaction.

Swift Creek Settlement and Subsistence

As the chapters in this volume demonstrate, a great deal of variation in settlement and subsistence practices occurs within what we think of as the Swift Creek culture area; sites and assemblages in the Georgia Piedmont are appreciably different from those in coastal Florida, and we must avoid thinking of the culture as a monolithic entity. Our knowledge of these settlement systems, however, is only beginning to accumulate. The spectacular nature of Middle Woodland ceremonial architecture and interments has meant that until quite recently most research attention across the East, including within the Swift Creek area, was directed to mounds and earthworks rather than habitation areas. Diversifying research interests and cultural resource management–based mandates directing work to a wide range of locales are helping to change this picture, but much remains to be accomplished.

One means of exploring Swift Creek settlement and demography that has proved quite effective locally entails simple distributional analyses that examine the locations and environmental associations of sites with Swift Creek diagnostics. At the present Swift Creek settlement data are perhaps most detailed for the Santa Rosa–Swift Creek area of western Florida, where a series of site clusters made up of base camps and satellite camps have been recognized (Bense, Chapter 14 herein). Other examples of detailed reconstructions of Swift Creek settlement/adaptational systems include Ashley's (Chapter 12 herein) analysis of site variation in northeastern Florida and Snow and Stephenson's work in south-central Georgia (Snow 1977; Snow and Stephenson, Chapter 7 herein). At the 1993 Swift Creek workshop held at Ocmulgee that resulted in this volume, the participants estimated that on the order of 1,000 sites yielding Swift Creek ceramics had already been found in Georgia and northern Florida (although fewer than half were tagged as such in the two states' computerized site files). When updated and examined, this distributional information is likely to tell us a great deal about local settlement systems and interaction pathways.

Excavation data on Middle Woodland settlements and community organization are extremely limited in the Swift Creek area. House plans are few and far between in the Georgia area and, as we have seen, little evidence for domestic architecture has been found at the major centers such as Kolomoki, Mandeville, and Swift Creek (Anderson 1985; Smith and Kelly 1975; Steinen, Chapter 11 herein). The only reasonably complete Middle Woodland age village excavated in Georgia is unreported and unfortunately, given the apparent absence of surviving records, is likely unreportable (Kelly 1973). On the larger, regional scale, Middle Woodland structures have been found in a number of areas of the Mid-South/lower Midwest, yielding data that Bruce Smith (1992a) has admirably synthesized. A fairly common theme in the Middle Woodland world appears to have been one of dispersed populations, living in scattered isolated households or fairly small unfortified villages, that came together periodically at centers (in areas where these were present). The size of these scattered populations is largely unknown, although documenting them is a question of appreciable interest to researchers in the Midwest and Southeast alike.

All of the available evidence collected to date indicates populations throughout the Swift Creek area subsisted almost exclusively on wild plant and animal foods; evidence for the use of agricultural domesticates is minimal and, when found, tends to date fairly late. Detailed zooarchaeological analyses of Swift Creek assemblages are comparatively rare and tend to occur in coastal areas where well-preserved faunal remains are sometimes found in shell midden assemblages. Some of this work is quite innovative; it has been used to document fish-capturing techniques, as well as to improve recovery and analysis procedures (e.g., Byrd 1995; Quitmyer 1995). Byrd (1995), in a comparison of zooarchaeological materials from four coastal Deptford and Swift Creek sites, used size data to suggest the use of focused capture techniques (i.e., weirs, spears, lines) in the Apalachee Bay area, where large specimens are typical, as opposed to the use of mass-capture techniques (i.e., the use of nets, poisoning) on the Atlantic coast and in Pensacola Bay, where a much wider size array was found. Byrd's analysis also indicated that fillets rather than whole fish were being transported, something also indicated at the Block-Sterns site (Jones, Penton, and Tesar, Chapter 13 herein). Whether dried fish could have served as a bulk trade item is unknown. Analyses such as these that make use of marine/estuarine resources may prove to be as valuable a source of information as analyses of terrestrial resources have been in the recognition of status differentiation and hierarchies and provisioning strategies (e.g., Jackson and Scott 1995).

There is a major increase in the occurrence of agricultural domesticates in the archaeological record of the Eastern Woodlands after circa 250 B.C., but this pattern is restricted to the middle part of the continent from about 30 to 40 degrees north latitude (Smith 1992b:272–74). It is becoming clear that at least some Middle Woodland populations in the lower Midwest were intensive agriculturalists, producing extensive harvests of highly nutritional crops such as chenopodium, sunflower, marsh elder, and squash (*Chenopodium, Helianthus, Iva,* and *Cucurbita*). Harvest yields on the order of 500 to 1000 kilograms per hectare have been demonstrated for eastern North American domesticates (Smith 1992b:274), and this productivity likely contributed to the growth of the population and Hopewellian ceremonialism in the Midwest. Maize did not constitute an important part of this complex, however, although it was present. Stable carbon isotope analyses of midwestern Middle Woodland human skeletal series indicate the dietary contribution of maize was minimal (Bender et al. 1981; Van der Merwe and Vogel 1978). Accelerator mass spectrometer (AMS) dates on maize kernels and cupules from the Icehouse Bottom (A.D. 175 ± 110) and Edwin Harness (A.D. 220 ± 105) sites have been assessed as "the most reasonable current estimate of the initial appearance of corn in the prehistoric East" (B. D. Smith 1992a:202–3). Intensive maize-based agriculture does not, however, appear to have been practiced anywhere in the Eastern Woodlands until the Late Woodland era (Lynott et al. 1986; Smith 1992b, 1992c).

Little evidence for agricultural food production has been found on Swift Creek sites (Smith 1992b:270, 273, 1992c; Wagner 1995; Yarnell and Black 1985), although it must be noted that flotation processing has been rare until quite recently. No evidence for native eastern domesticates such as chenopodium, sunflower, or marsh elder has been found, even though appreciable evidence for their cultivation exists in the Midwest. Maize and squash have been reported, but in trace amounts and usually quite late. The earliest secure date for maize utilization in the Swift Creek area comes from a late Cartersville component at the Rush site near Rome, Georgia, where an AMS date on one of two maize cupules found yielded a date of 1290 ± 100 B.P., or A.D. 660 (Wood and Ledbetter 1988:135–36). Other evidence for agriculture is more equivocal. At the Cane Island site in the central Georgia Piedmont, excavated during the Wallace Reservoir project, two corn cupules were found in a post hole located near a well-defined structure, and three grains of corn pollen were found amid a rock cluster located against an inside wall of the same structure (Wood 1981:85, 87). The assemblage was dominated by Cartersville check-stamped pottery and hence likely dates within the latter part of the Early Woodland or the initial part of the Middle Woodland period; the Cartersville assemblage itself has been dated to A.D. 245 ± 95, 115 ± 85, and 80 ± 60 (Wood and Bowen 1995:79). Direct AMS dating of the cupules should determine the accuracy of this association and dating. At the Simpsons Field site on the upper Savannah River a carbonized squash rind fragment, two pollen grains of a *Cucurbita*-like plant, and one grain of maize pollen were found in features attributed to the Late Swift Creek occupation, from circa A.D. 600 to 750; the site was also occupied in the Mississippian period, however, rendering the Swift Creek association open to challenge (Gardner 1986:390; Sheehan 1986:394; Wood et al. 1986:106–7). No evidence for maize was found at the Block-Sterns site in northwestern Florida, despite extensive recovery efforts (Chapter 13 herein).

Given this review of evidence for Middle Woodland agriculture in general, and its minimal presence in the Swift Creek area, Steinen's arguments (Chapter 11 herein) about the importance of maize-based agriculture in the Mandeville and Kolomoki area must be regarded as highly unlikely, although flotation, palynological, phytolith, and human skeletal (i.e., stable carbon and nitrogen isotope) analyses will need to be conducted to conclusively resolve this point. I agree with Steinen that the location of Kolomoki was likely important—not for its agricultural potential, however, but for the rich wild plant and animal resources that were available in the area, as he describes in detail. Agriculture is not a prerequisite for complex organizational forms (e.g., Price and Brown 1985).

Swift Creek Ceremonial Architecture
and Organizational Complexity

Appreciable variability characterizes Middle Woodland ceremonialism and architecture across the East, and the Swift Creek area is no different. The character of the preeminent ceremonial centers in the Swift Creek area, however, is appreciably different from that of centers in the heartland of Ohio Hopewell. No earthwork enclosures forming octagons, circles, or squares or linear causeways such as those observed at a number of major Ohio River valley centers are present. The closest major centers in the Deep South with comparable enclosures occur at Pinson and Savannah in western Tennessee and Marksville in Louisiana (Mainfort 1988; Thunen 1988:106); platform mound architecture of Middle Woodland age is also present at Pinson. Conversely, platform mounds are present at Mandeville and Kolomoki but are, to the best of my knowledge, unknown in the Midwest.

How the kinds of structures that were constructed was related to the organizational forms present in each area is unknown. Enclosures appear to be structures appropriate to collective ceremony by large numbers of people, whereas platform mounds, with their comparatively small summit area, suggest activities restricted to segments of society. It is tempting to suggest that the organizational structure of societies with enclosures was *group-oriented* and somewhat egalitarian, while that of societies represented by platform mounds was *individualizing* or more socially differentiated. These categories are taken from Renfrew's (1974) taxonomy for early European chiefdoms and are meant to suggest possible differences in organization and ceremonialism that may have been present over the region; that these Middle Woodland societies were chiefdoms such as those present in the later Mississippian era, however, is not to be inferred.

In many parts of the region, including at many of the sites where large enclosures are found, elaborate and in some cases spectacular individual burials are also present, indicating the existence of appreciable status differentiation. Middle Woodland social life in many areas appears to have included collective ceremonialism involving most or all segments of society, as well as activities involving only a privileged few. Nowhere in the region, however, did more than a few apical elites wind up in log-lined tombs under elaborately constructed conical burial mounds. Determining how Swift Creek (and indeed all) Middle Woodland centers and ceremonial/communal facilities were formed and used is critical to understanding the organization of these societies.

Variability is clearly evident in the shape, construction, and function of Swift Creek "monumental" architecture, although we have little real understanding of what this variability means. It is reasonable to assume, however, that the social organization of Middle Woodland societies throughout most of the South Appalachian area was qualitatively different and less complex than that present at the major centers such as Mandeville, Kolomoki, and Block-Sterns. In many areas, in fact, either simple shrines or collective burial mounds are present, or no monumental architecture at all has been reported. It is tempting to suggest that those who used the platform mounds at sites such as Kolomoki were incipient elites; the duration of these centers, furthermore, suggests there may have been a hereditary character to the organization. That is, while Middle Woodland societies are typically described as "Big Man" or "Big Woman" societies (after Sahlins 1963; see also Bense, Chapter 14 herein), it is difficult to reconcile the comparatively fragile and ephemeral nature of the ethnographic examples that are known with the scale and apparent duration of the larger Middle Woodland centers.

Accordingly, Sears's ideas about Kolomoki's level of organizational complexity and sphere of influence need to be reconsidered. While hardly a priest state, it could have had characteristics of a chiefdom, perhaps with power residing in a clan or lineage rather than in the person of a single individual and, hence, lasting more than a single lifetime. The major centers of the Swift Creek world may have exercised power not so much through overt or physical control, furthermore, but through the maintenance of an ideological hegemony. By being major players in the Hopewellian world, the principals at these centers could have been perceived as having esoteric knowledge and possibly powers, and this, plus their control of desirable wealth items, may have inspired people to their service over wide areas and at the same time led to their sanctification (*sensu* Clark and Blake 1994; Friedman and Rowlands 1977; Helms 1979; Pauketat and Emerson 1996).

Why did some societies participate more than others in complex Middle Woodland ceremonialism? Partially because of their location: people who lived in sites along potential major trade/exchange routes had greater likelihood of being exposed to Hopewellian ideas and to receiving esoteric goods and knowledge. The power of competitive emulation, specifically the desire to control esoteric knowledge, of which prestige goods are a tangible symbol, appears to be an important force in cultural evolution (Clark and Blake 1994). As Williams and Elliott humorously note in their introduction (in a parallel with today's computer users), greed rather than need may have initially motivated local participation. Those who had something to contribute to Hopewellian exchange, however, could have quickly become locked in to the exchange/ritual/display network.

We thus need to at least consider the possibility that the people responsible for the construction and maintenance of the Mandeville and Kolomoki centers (and other such Middle Woodland centers) quite probably inspired and hence harnessed the gathering or production of resources such as shell, carved wooden products, or other goods from across large areas. Such roles may have included the ideological domination of other centers, a form of control that may have been just as effective as the use of force. Could centers such as Block-Sterns, for example, have served in an ideologically subsidiary role to Mandeville and Kolomoki? We need to explore location, size, and spacing of major and minor centers in the Swift Creek culture area (and indeed over the larger region) with the goal of reconstructing an ideological geography of the Middle Woodland era, much as we now routinely examine the political geography of the Mississippian world.

Williams and Freer's (Chapter 4 herein) interpretation of many of the small mound centers in northern and eastern Georgia as shrines for individual rather than corporate ritual activity—perhaps where offerings to spirit guardians occurred—suggests that their role in regional interaction, ideological domination, or religious activity, or even as a focus for political maneuvering, was comparatively minor. It is probable, however, that these sites served as foci for communal or lineage-centered feasting or mortuary activities. These sites are often found on small tributaries away from major drainages, with little evidence for associated residential areas, a much different pattern from that in the Mississippian era, when ceremonial facilities were often located along the larger drainages and within large villages or towns.

The relation of these smaller centers to historic trail locations is unclear; some seem to be on or near known trails while others are well out of the way. Local considerations, such as a need to maintain adequate subsistence resource appropriation zones, rather than macro-regional interaction, may have shaped their occurrence over the landscape. Williams and Freer note that the spacing of the northern Georgia Middle Woodland centers is circa 30 kilometers apart, which is somewhat less than the circa 40 kilometers observed between many Mississippian administrative centers in the same area (Hally 1993). This may reflect a lower base population and hence the use of a smaller resource procurement zone. The spacing of these centers may indicate the size of local Middle Woodland group hunting territories; in the absence of any evidence for warfare (although our skeletal samples are small), these areas may represent the peacefully delimited precursors of later Mississippian conflict-maintained buffer zones.

Ashley (Chapter 12 herein) documents the accretional character of burial mounds in the St. Johns area and offers the suggestion that they were the facilities of specific lineages occupying the surrounding area. Mounds built in stages require of necessity large-scale communal activity and the cooperative interaction of fairly large numbers of people, while accretional burial mounds do not require such activity. The subregional distribution of public facilities by type (i.e., platform mounds, burial mounds with elaborate tombs, accretional burial mounds) should give us a pretty fair picture of the variation in societal complexity over the Swift Creek area. In coastal areas, ring middens such as Bernath in northwestern Florida may be roughly equivalent to the mound centers in the interior. Settlement size, or at least the extent of monumental construction at Swift Creek sites, and no doubt societal organizational complexity thus appear to be closely tied to proximity to regional trading and communications routes. Major mound centers or sites with impressive mortuary remains in the Swift Creek area such as Mandeville, Kolomoki, and Tunnacunahee typically occur along or near these routes, while mound construction is less extensive or absent in areas farther away from them, as is evidence for elaborate Hopewellian-related mortuary ritual.

Swift Creek Platform Mounds

In recent years it has become apparent that Middle Woodland populations in many parts of the Southeast, including in the heartland of the Swift Creek area, built platform mounds (Brown 1993; Mainfort 1988; Steinen, Chapter 11 herein). Swift Creek sites with platform mounds, besides the type site itself, include Mandeville, Kolomoki, Annewakee Creek, and Cold Springs in Georgia; Garden Creek in western North Carolina, a Connestee occupation but one with some associated Swift Creek sherds; and McKeithen and possibly Block-Sterns in northern Florida (Fish and Jefferies 1983; Jones, Penton, and Tesar, Chapter 13 herein). The construction and use of platform mounds (on the basis of data reported from those that have been excavated) appear tied to mortuary ritual in some cases, to public consumption/feasting activities in others, and at some sites to both forms of behavior.

Platform mounds were, I believe, built and maintained by successful practitioners of Middle Woodland ritual and exchange and used to display their wealth and largess to the greatest public effect. The maintenance and use of these structures may have been controlled by specific families or lineages and may have shifted among such groups. We have little evidence for this theory at present, however. It is likely that these platforms were important arenas whereon competition between individuals and lineages occurred; as noted previously, the small size of the summit area may have meant that access to such ceremonies or competitive displays was restricted to a small segment of society. Competitive feasting atop these mounds would have been one means by which enhanced social status was achieved and proclaimed. At most of the smaller sites mound use and construction may have been under the direction and control of individual families or lineages achieving temporary control over these locations, while at the largest sites, as at centers in the later Woodland and Mississippian periods, control was likely increasingly centered in the hands of dominant lineages whose position was determined through heredity, ideology, and power. Over time the platforms/mounds that hosted the public displays and were the burial areas of the leaders of these (presumably) more or less egalitarian Middle Woodland societies came to serve as the residences and mortuary temples of the victors of this process, the hereditary elites of the Mississippian world. This was not an invariant unilineal progression, however, since much of the Hopewell world collapsed by the middle of the first millennium.

Swift Creek Iconography as a Means of Exploring World View and Cosmology

Swift Creek Complicated Stamped pottery, which is characterized by elaborate design motifs richly imbued with symbolism, offers an almost un-

paralleled opportunity to explore questions of Middle Woodland social organization, interaction, world view, and cosmology, primarily because the
artifact category is so common. The important pioneering contributions of
Bettye Broyles deserve our acknowledgment and appreciation (see in particular the comments on this work by Williams and Elliott, Chapter 1 herein,
and Smith, Chapter 8 herein). Elaborate carved designs, ubiquitous in ceramic assemblages of this culture, are what most of us think of when we
think of Swift Creek. These ceramics were not a specialized elite or burial
pottery but were widespread, so this rich symbolism was an integral part of
the everyday life of the people. Snow's (1977, Chapter 6 herein) analyses
have documented that both animal motifs and cosmological themes (i.e.,
symbolic divisions of the world) are found in Swift Creek ceramic design
motifs. Some of these motifs may have served as individual or lineage/com-
munity guardian spirits (some perhaps intended to signal and reinforce group
or community identity), while others were representations of more general
forces of the cosmos, such as the sky and Under World (Penny 1985:184–
89). The relationship between Swift Creek and other Middle Woodland iconography has received comparatively less attention, although given the pan-
eastern nature of Hopewellian interaction, this should be a profitable area
for study. Hopewellian avian images, for example, often include raptors and
ducks, which is thought to reflect a dichotomy between the separate domains
of the sky and the watery underworld. These representations, fairly common
on classic Ohio, Havana, and Marksville vessels, are less commonly seen
among Swift Creek designs, suggesting the latter may reflect a less ordered
or more casual and diversified view of the natural world and cosmos.

Examination of Swift Creek iconography documents an appreciable antiquity to a number of southeastern Indian motifs and no doubt beliefs.
Some motifs are precursors of classic later Mississippian Southeastern Ceremonial Complex images, such as the sun and eye and the long-nosed god
mask (Snow, Chapter 6 herein). We must look at entire designs and not just
sherds, although Saunders's analysis (Chapter 10) demonstrates much useful
information can come from looking at attributes. The existence of a hierarchy of designs—from cosmological to communal—is an important concept
to explore on Swift Creek and other Middle Woodland pottery. The idea that
particular designs may have been the symbols or signatures (guardian spirits?) of specific communities or kin groups, furthermore, is an inference that
should see increased testing given the level of analytical sophistication now

being brought to Swift Creek stylistic analyses. Saunders and Snow have made important advances in breaking down the components of the designs into those signaling local group affiliation, those indicative of a larger social sphere, and, finally, motifs representing cosmological concepts.

Swift Creek and the Diachronic Exploration of Hopewellian Interaction

Archaeologists are beginning to recognize and explore patterns of change and interaction over time in the Middle Woodland. It is becoming increasingly apparent, for example, that major centers evolved over time, experiencing major periods of growth, interregional or intraregional interaction, and abandonment or decline. The use of the center at Pinson, for example, occurs over a period of several centuries, from circa A.D. 1 to 500, but most of the large mounds and earthworks there were erected in the first two centuries A.D. (Mainfort 1988). Similar patterns appear to characterize the use of major centers of Ohio Hopewell in the Scioto and nearby river valleys, which were alternately used and then abandoned (Greber 1979). Organizational fluctuations like these, particularly at the perceived midwestern centers of the distribution network, may have had ripple effects over much larger areas. There is some evidence, for example, to suggest that interaction between the Southeast and the Midwest increased after A.D. 150 (Brose 1985:76–77). Copena great pipes of steatite from the Tennessee River valley of northern Alabama were exported throughout the upper Midwest in the third and fourth centuries A.D. (Brose 1985:77; Walthall 1980:116–31). Mainfort (1988:145), in contrast, has suggested that much of the interaction likely occurred during the first three centuries A.D. Our chronological resolution of these phenomena, however, is less precise than perhaps it could be.

Organizational fluctuations clearly characterize Middle Woodland societies in the Swift Creek area, as Steinen (Chapter 11 herein) has illustrated through his study of the successive Mandeville, Kolomoki, and Cemochechobee centers along the lower Chattahoochee. The Swift Creek world is an ideal area to explore organizational change and interaction. The variability evident in Swift Creek ceramics, notably in complicated stamp designs and in rim treatment, is comparable to that observed in later Mississippian assemblages from across the South Appalachian area, and the variations are likely equally sensitive temporal markers, offering the possibility of chronological resolution at perhaps fifty- to seventy-five-year intervals or less. Analyses of Swift Creek designs like those described by Snow (1977, Chapter 6 herein; Snow and Stephenson, Chapter 7 herein), accordingly, offer the opportunity not only to explore interaction but also to develop highly detailed chronologies. Such chronological resolution will be essential if we are to successfully explore Hopewellian interaction in the East. Fortunately, many Swift Creek sites, unlike their midwestern analogs, have remained comparatively unplundered and even unrecognized; broken sherds are all that is necessary to conduct these analyses, and looters tend to leave these artifact types behind.

A critically important contribution of this volume is that it presents a series of explicit analytical methods for exploring interaction in the Swift Creek world. Design-matching analyses like those advanced by Snow and Saunders, when conducted over a much larger scale—wherever Swift Creek ceramics occur, even as far away as midwestern centers—should lead to marked insight into Middle Woodland exchange, both within the South Appalachian area and beyond. Both authors document the specific procedures by which designs can be recovered (i.e., lighting conditions, rubbing procedures, orientation studies, comparison with compilations of design elements and motifs), ensuring their work will be emulated. Design-element analysis is a complementary approach to total design-motif analysis and one appropriate to assemblages in which (typically) only small sherds are present.

Smith (Chapter 8 herein) and Stoltman and Snow (Chapter 9 herein) offer complementary petrographic and trace-element analyses by which imports/foreign vessels can be recognized within site assemblages. Stoltman's analyses demonstrate that both pots and paddles were moving over the landscape, and both analyses offer clues about the extent to which materials may have moved. Smith's conclusion that one of the figurines from Mandeville appears to be extralocal in origin, and that it resembles those of the Knight mound area of Illinois and thus may derive from there, is particularly intriguing, since it represents a tie to a part of the midwestern Hopewellian world where Swift Creek interaction is not particularly noted.

Snow and Stephenson's study (Chapter 7 herein) is one of the finest examples of the use of ceramics in the analysis of prehistoric interaction that I know of anywhere. The effort directed to the reconstruction and interpretation of Swift Creek design motifs, the collection and analysis of ceramics samples, the resolution of direct evidence for interaction by the identification of paddle flaws, and the tracing of this interaction all over southern and central Georgia rank this as a singularly important piece of scholarship. Snow's years of careful, quiet, and often unsung research are beginning to result in an impressive research payoff, highlighting the importance of careful, long-term scholarship.

We need to consider how interaction was structured and reasons for the distributions that are observed (e.g., the occurrence over wide areas of designs produced by the same paddle). Snow and Stephenson suggest that, in at least some cases, patterns of settlement expansion are being monitored—the spread of people outward (or, more typically, up or downstream) from a center. Does, as seems likely, much greater design variability (i.e., designs from over a much larger area) occur at the larger centers than at the smaller ones and, if so, does this imply that a political/ideological hierarchy is in place? How does interaction operate at different levels, that is, between roughly equal communities, between small communities and larger centers, and between large centers within the regional Hopewellian Interaction Network? Obviously, the partners at each level in the exchange hold different status positions and have different expectations.

Close-interval design dating should be useful for monitoring such a spread and, by documenting component contemporaneity or lack thereof, patterns of settlement and interaction. There are a great many questions that remain to be answered, of course. What causes both paddles and vessels to move about, and why does one category move in some cases and not the other? Did vessels move because they contained special products whereas the movement of paddles represented the movement of people such as brides or craft specialists (i.e., potters/wood carvers)? What are the sizes of the interaction networks for different site categories? Snow and Stephenson, for example, demonstrate that the Hartford site's sphere of influence or interaction extended over tens of thousands of square kilometers, encompassing almost one quarter of the Georgia Coastal Plain. How does this compare with sites such as Kolomoki or Block-Sterns? Do Renfrew and Cherry's (1986) ideas about peer-polity interaction networks apply to Swift Creek/Hopewell?

As a number of analyses in this volume demonstrate, interaction within the Swift Creek world shifted in directionality and intensity over time. Ashley (Chapter 12 herein) demonstrates that interaction by people in the

St. Johns area appears to have shifted from northwestern Florida to the lower Georgia coast from early to later Swift Creek times. Snow (Chapter 6) suggests that Swift Creek designs become more elaborate over time at least through the middle part of the Swift Creek era, until about A.D. 500, which may indicate that interaction itself was becoming more pronounced. The apparent reduction in intricacy of Late Swift Creek designs that he suggests (e.g., Sears 1952:103; Willey 1949:431) may, in contrast, be tied to a breakdown in interaction, paralleling developments across much of the East at this time.

We need to examine the ties between the Swift Creek world and other major Middle Woodland areas; that is, are influences from, for example, Marksville, Havana Hopewell, and Ohio Hopewell more prevalent in some parts of the Swift Creek area than in others? Why, for example, are classic Hopewellian ceramics rare in the lower Southeast (particularly since panpipes, effigy/platform pipes, and other elaborate materials of likely midwestern origin are found at some centers)? Were these vessels too bulky and fragile to move great distances in quantity? Related to this, how do changes in monumental construction and interaction in midwestern Hopewell and Mississippi Valley Marksville societies tie in with similar changes observed in the Swift Creek world? Extensive western Gulf/Marksville interaction is indicated in the Santa Rosa area, where many classic Santa Rosa vessels are clay tempered and may well be imported from Porter/Marksville cultures farther to the west (Bense, Chapter 14 herein). Why did vessels move along the Gulf but not overland? Is water transport indicated? Santa Rosa–Swift Creek in western Florida, clearly, is an interface or zone of interaction between Swift Creek societies to the east and Porter (and ultimately Marksville) societies to the west. Accordingly, did as much or more shell from the Santa Rosa area move along the Marksville/Mississippi River axis than along the Kolomoki/Chattahoochee?

Warfare, Changes in Regional Power Centers, and the Hopewellian Collapse

Swift Creek centers evolved over time, experiencing major periods of growth, interregional or intraregional interaction, and decline and abandonment, organizational fluctuations that also appear to characterize major Ohio

Hopewell centers. Disruptions at any point in the distribution network may have had ripple effects over much larger areas, and at some times interaction may have been much greater than during others. This process of organizational change at the level of individual societies and centers is similar to that observed in the later Mississippian era and may have occurred for at least some of the same reasons, such as prestige-based competition, changes in leadership ability, climatic factors, and changes in the regional political/ideological landscape (Anderson 1990, 1994a). Differential success in manipulating external relations (i.e., centered perhaps on trade and ritual) by otherwise (potentially) more or less equivalent individuals or lineages likely caused many of the observed Middle Woodland organizational fluctuations, however, rather than the outright and unrestrained competition for power between hereditary elite factions or even different societies that characterizes Mississippian social dynamics. There appears to be little doubt, however, that events at great distances shaped conditions in the Swift Creek world.

The period from the end of the Middle Woodland to the initial Mississippian is a period of apparent religious decline and possibly turmoil across much of the East. The seemingly panregional Hopewellian iconographic/religious complex, with its emphasis on avian images, smoking ritual, and elaborate (albeit varied) mortuary behavior, disappears from many areas, most notably the Midwest, although elements of this complex continue to occur in some parts of the lower Southeast well into the Late Woodland (Brose 1985:83, 89; Penny 1985). These dramatic shifts in iconography appear ultimately to be caused by the increasing importance of agricultural food production in everyday life. The solar disk increasingly replaces avian representations as a central icon, which is thought to reflect the gradual replacement of a highly individualistic and egalitarian animal-centered hunting/guardian spirit–based ceremonialism and ritual—with roots no doubt stretching deep into the Archaic—by a more collective, elite-directed communal ceremonialism centered on agricultural productivity and reinforcing the sacred and hereditary position of the leadership (e.g., Penny 1985). Individualistic expression during this latter period appears to have been channeled from more traditional emphases on hunting to success in warfare and militarism. The iconography of the region thus mirrors the dramatic changes in status and social agendas that were occurring, from achieved prestige through the manipulation of foreign objects to the hereditary dominance of lineages and societies over other such groups. In contrast, changes in underlying cosmology, such as views on the quartering or layered nature of the world, appear to have been less pronounced.

The decline of the Hopewellian world roughly coincides with the appearance of the bow and arrow, which apparently was adopted about the end of the Middle Woodland period in many parts of the East. The introduction of this technology, when coupled with increasing regional populations, may have brought about conditions in which raiding or warfare became more prevalent than trade and ritual as a means of achieving social objectives. What other factors may have contributed to the Hopewell collapse? Agricultural surpluses of native eastern domesticates, I believe, fueled midwestern Middle Woodland ceremonialism and a general absence of warfare. Over time, however, population growth overwhelmed the abilities of this form of provisioning system, leading to its breakdown and to dispersion and warfare over the Eastern Woodlands in the Late Woodland period, which in turn helped prompt the shift to intensive maize-based agriculture and new hierarchical organizational strategies. Middle Woodland may thus be seen, in part, as the triumphant product of the eastern agricultural complex. The chaos of the Late Woodland period was the inevitable result, however, as population levels grew too large. The Early Mississippian era witnessed a new agricultural revolution that could have led to a new era of peaceful conditions, but it unfortunately followed a period when warfare had become ingrained in many areas, which resulted in the continuation of conflict even when such may not have been necessary.

While this picture is admittedly simplistic and overgeneralized, the collapse of the Hopewellian world provides strong evidence that intensive agriculture employing native domesticates and prestige-based exchange and competitive feasting, even at the levels seen in Middle Woodland societies such as those in the Scioto Valley, were not enough to produce social stratification. The appearance of intensive maize-based agriculture and resulting higher population densities appear to have been the necessary thresholds to stratification in many areas.

In the centuries just prior to the introduction of intensive maize-based agriculture across the region, a shift in the location of the primary centers of power or political dominance appears to have occurred, from the upper Midwest to the lower Mississippi Valley and along the Gulf Coast. The Coles

Creek and Weeden Island societies of the Deep South appear to evolve without interruption from the preceding Middle Woodland Marksville/Troyville and Santa Rosa–Swift Creek cultures. The later Woodland Weeden Island societies of the lower southeastern Gulf coastal region were particularly vibrant during this time. This seeming unabated evolution of cultural complexity proceeded in the absence of intensive maize-based agriculture, although once such a cropping strategy appeared in the lower Midwest after circa A.D. 800 power relations shifted again, this time to the central Mississippi Valley from northeastern Arkansas to the American Bottom. Karl Steinen (Chapter 11 herein) discusses this long-term cycle of centralization and decentralization in relation to events in the lower Chattahoochee River valley from the Middle Woodland through Mississippian periods, corresponding to Swift Creek, Weeden Island, and Mississippian cultures. Why centers and cultures rise and fall is one of the many exciting questions that can be addressed by modern archaeological research.

While panregional interaction declined markedly after A.D. 400 or so, Swift Creek culture itself either continued or transformed itself locally, with no evidence for an appreciable break in continuity. Swift Creek ceramics, as indicated by stratigraphic excavations and appreciable numbers of radiocarbon dates, continued in use in the interior of the South Appalachian area for several centuries after the abandonment of the centers in the upper Midwest (Elliott, Chapter 3 herein; Chase, Chapter 5 herein; Steinen, Chapter 11 herein). No evidence currently exists for the presence of the bow and arrow on Swift Creek sites, save perhaps very late (after A.D. 600–750). Most Swift Creek point types, such as Bakers Creek or Swift Creek "spikes," appear to have been used on darts or with atlatls. Only with the terminal Late Woodland Woodstock culture does evidence for fortifications and the use of the bow and arrow appear in the Georgia area (Caldwell 1958).

Conclusions

A number of important questions have been raised here that will require considerable research to answer satisfactorily. Did midwestern demand for shell or other local products, for example, shape southeastern Middle Woodland patterns of settlement and intraregional interaction? Did changes in the prominence and dominance of centers in various areas have a similar effect?

Did changes in mortuary ritual, resulting in greater or lesser quantities of prestige goods being removed from circulation, likewise affect regional patterns of trade and settlement? Can Swift Creek ceramic attributes (i.e., stamp designs, rim decorations) be used to develop fine-grained chronologies? What changes in world view, ideology, and cosmology are reflected by diachronic changes in Swift Creek (and post–Swift Creek) ceramic and other assemblages? To explore these questions we will need to focus empirically based research at specific sites on specific subjects such as design variability or distribution (e.g., Snow, Chapter 6 herein; Saunders, Chapter 10 herein), as well as initiate more areally extensive distributional analyses (e.g., Bense, Chapter 14 herein; Chase, Chapter 5 herein; Elliott, Chapter 3 herein; Snow and Stephenson, Chapter 7 herein). The chapters in this volume provide a good synthesis of research efforts to date and indicate the directions we need to take.

We need good theoretical models to help us explain what is occurring in the Swift Creek area and to guide and inform our data collection and analysis efforts. We always need more fieldwork to augment the primary data all of our efforts are based on. The archaeologist community must be able to effectively salvage critical sites when these are threatened. The Block-Sterns investigations demonstrate the importance of having such capabilities; we now have massive quantities of information from this site—thanks to the work of Jones, Penton, and Tesar and their colleagues and supporting organizations—where we would have otherwise had nothing. Ideally, of course, we must work to see that such efforts are not needed, by striving to preserve sites wherever possible.

For many years Swift Creek culture was something of a gray area archaeologically. In Griffin's classic 1967 synthesis of eastern prehistory, for example, on the map illustrating Middle Woodland sites and interaction, much of the South Appalachian area was blank, although arrows were present indicating movement from mica sources in the mountains and along the Chattahoochee River into the Gulf coastal Santa Rosa–Swift Creek area. As we have seen, this picture is now dramatically different. Swift Creek culture consisted of a range of vibrant societies, with differing levels of organizational complexity, whose adaptations to surrounding societies and resources both in and outside of the region differed in various ways that we look forward to discovering.

Acknowledgments

I wish to thank Mark Williams and Dan Elliott for their invitation to participate in the original Swift Creek workshop at Ocmulgee and for their advice and help in preparing this contribution. I also wish to thank all those people who have kept me informed of their research through reprints, draft manuscripts, and personal correspondence.

References Cited

Adams, William Hampton, ed.

1985 *Aboriginal Subsistence and Settlement Archaeology of the Kings Bay Locality,* Vol. 1. University of Florida, Department of Anthropology, Reports of Investigations 1. Gainesville.

Adams, William R.

1956 Archaeozoology at Kolomoki. In *Excavations at Kolomoki: Final Report,* edited by W. H. Sears, pp. 104–5. University of Georgia Press, University of Georgia Series in Anthropology 5. Athens.

Anderson, David G.

1985 Middle Woodland Societies on the Lower South Atlantic Slope: A View from Georgia and South Carolina. *Early Georgia* 13:29–66.

1990 *Political Change in Chiefdom Societies: Cycling in the Late Prehistoric Southeastern United States.* Ph.D. Dissertation, Department of Anthropology, University of Michigan, Ann Arbor.

1994a *The Savannah River Chiefdoms: Political Change in the Late Prehistoric Southeast.* University of Alabama Press, Tuscaloosa.

1994b Exploring the Antiquity of Interaction Networks in the East. Paper presented at the 51st Annual Meeting of the Southeastern Archaeological Conference, Lexington, Kentucky.

Anderson, David G., Christopher Amer, and Rita F. Elliott

1992 *Archeological Survey along the Upper Savannah River, 1990: Including Underwater Investigations at the Rembert Mound Group.* Interagency Archeological Services Division, National Park Service, Atlanta, Georgia.

Anderson, David G., and Joseph W. Joseph

1988 *Prehistory and History along the Upper Savannah River: Technical Synthesis of Cultural Resource Investigations, Richard B. Russell Multiple Resource Area.* Interagency Archeological Services, U.S. National Park Service, Russell Papers. Atlanta, Georgia.

Anderson, David G., and Joseph Schuldenrein
    1985 *Prehistoric Human Ecology along the Upper Savannah River: Excavations at the Rucker's Bottom, Abbeville, and Bullard Site Groups,* Vols. I and II. Interagency Archeological Services, National Park Service, Russell Papers. Atlanta, Georgia.

Anonymous
    1939 Swift Creek Complicated Stamp. *Southeastern Archaeological Conference Newsletter* 1(2):1–2.

Arnold, Dean
    1984 Social Interaction and Design: Community-Wide Correlates in Quinua, Peru. In *Pots and Potters: Current Approaches in Ceramic Archaeology,* edited by P. Rice, pp. 133–61. University of California Press, Los Angeles.

Ashley, Keith H.
    1991 Archeological Testing and Monitoring at the Naval Midden (8DU7458), Mayport Naval Station. Manuscript on file, Florida Archeological Services, Jacksonville.
    1992 Swift Creek Manifestations along the Lower St. Johns River. *Florida Anthropologist* 45(2):127–38.

Ashley, Keith H., and Robert E. Johnson
    1990 An Archeological Reconnaissance Survey of the Western Portion of the St. Johns Bluff Study Area. Manuscript on file, Florida Archeological Services, Jacksonville.

Ashley, Keith H., and Bob Richter
    1993 Excavation of the Dent Mound (8DU68), Duval County, Florida. Manuscript on file, Jacksonville Museum of Science and History, Jacksonville, Florida.

Ashley, Keith H., and James A. Wheat
    1991 The New Mill Cove Site (8DU5611), Duval County, Florida. Manuscript in possession of the authors.

Ashley, Margaret E.
    1932 A Study of the Ceramic Art of the Etowans. In *Etowah Papers,* edited by W. K. Moorehead, pp. 107–36. Phillips Academy, Andover, Massachusetts.

Belovich, Stephanie, David S. Brose, Russell Weisman, and Nancy M. White
    1983 *Archaeological Survey at George W. Andrews Lake, Alabama and*

Georgia. Cleveland Museum of Natural History, Archaeological Research Report 37.

Bender, Margaret M., David A. Baerreis, and Raymond L. Steventon

1981 Further Light on Carbon Isotopes and Hopewell Agriculture. *American Antiquity* 46:346–53.

Bense, Judith A.

1983 Settlement Pattern, Climate, and Marine Ecosystem Evolution Correlations in the Escambia Bay Drainage System in Northwest Florida. Paper presented at the 40th Annual Meeting of the Southeastern Archaeological Conference, Columbia, South Carolina.

1985 *Hawkshaw: Prehistory and History in an Urban Neighborhood in Pensacola, Florida.* University of West Florida, Office of Cultural and Archaeological Research, Reports of Investigations 7. Pensacola.

1992 Santa Rosa–Swift Creek in Northwest Florida. Paper presented at the 48th Annual Meeting of the Southeastern Archaeological Conference, Little Rock, Arkansas.

1993 Santa Rosa–Swift Creek in Northwest Florida. Manuscript presented at the Lamar Institute Swift Creek Conference, May 28–29, 1993, Ocmulgee National Monument, Macon, Georgia.

1994 Configuration of the Bernath Ring Midden Site (8SR986) near Pensacola, Florida: Introduction of a New Explanation for Ring Midden Sites. Paper presented at the 51st Annual Meeting of the Southeastern Archaeological Conference, Lexington, Kentucky.

Blanton, Dennis

1979 An Archaeological Survey of the Upper Satilla Basin. *Early Georgia* 7(2):43–64.

Brockington, Paul

1971 Preliminary Investigation of an Early Knapping Site in Southeast Georgia. *The Institute of Archaeology and Anthropology Notebook* 3(2):23–46. University of South Carolina, Columbia.

Brooms, Bascom Mack

1977 An Archaeological Inventory of 1PK2 within the Walnut Creek Reservoir. Manuscript on file, Alabama Historical Commission, Montgomery.

Brose, David S.

1979a An Interpretation of Hopewellian Traits in Florida. In *Hopewell*

Archaeology: The Chillicothe Conference, edited by D. S. Brose and N. Greber, pp. 141–49. Kent State University Press, Kent, Ohio.

1979b A Speculative Model of the Role of Exchange in the Prehistory of the Eastern Woodlands. In *Hopewell Archaeology: The Chillicothe Conference,* edited by D. S. Brose and N. Greber, pp. 3–8. Kent State University Press, Kent, Ohio.

1984 Mississippian Cultures in Northwestern Florida. In *Perspectives on Gulf Coast Prehistory,* edited by D. D. Davis, pp. 165–97. The Florida State Museum, Ripley P. Bullen Monographs in Anthropology and History 5. Gainesville.

1985 The Woodland Period. In *Ancient Art of the American Woodland Indians,* edited by D. S. Brose, J. A. Brown, and D. W. Penny, pp. 42–91. Harry N. Abrams, New York.

Brose, David S., and N'omi Greber, eds.

1979 *Hopewell Archaeology: The Chillicothe Conference.* Kent State University Press, Kent, Ohio.

Brose, David S., and George W. Percy

1974 An Outline of Weeden Island Ceremonial Activity in Northwest Florida. Paper presented at the 39th Annual Meeting of the Society for American Archaeology, Washington, D.C.

Brown, Ian W.

1993 Recent Contributions to Woodland Stage Archaeology in the Southeastern U.S. Paper presented in the symposium "Archaeology of the Eastern Woodlands" at the 58th Annual Meeting of the Society for American Archaeology, St. Louis, Missouri.

Broyles, Bettye J.

1968 Reconstructed Designs from Swift Creek Complicated Stamped Sherds. *Southeastern Archaeological Conference Bulletin* 8:49–74. Morgantown, West Virginia.

Buchner, Andrew, and Mitchell Childress

1991 *Phase I Archaeological Reconnaissance Survey of the Smith Bend Development Tract, Rhea County, Tennessee.* Garrow and Associates, Memphis, Tennessee.

Bullen, Ripley P.

1958 *Six Sites near the Chattahoochee River in the Jim Woodruff Reservoir*

Area, Florida. Smithsonian Institution, Bureau of American Ethnology, River Basin Surveys Papers 14. Washington, D.C.

1975 *Guide to the Identification of Florida Projectile Points*. Kendall Books, Gainesville, Florida.

Butler, Brian M.

1979 Hopewellian Contacts in Southern Middle Tennessee. In *Hopewell Archaeology: The Chillicothe Conference,* edited by D. S. Brose and N. Greber, pp. 130–61. Kent State University Press, Kent, Ohio.

Butterfield, Jim, ed.

1973 Division Archaeologists Active throughout Florida. *Archives and History News* 4(4):1–2. Division of Archives, History, and Records Management, Florida Department of State, Tallahassee.

Byrd, John

1995 Differential Subsistence Patterns in the Swift Creek Phase. Paper presented at the 52nd Annual Meeting of the Southeastern Archaeological Conference, Knoxville, Tennessee.

Caldwell, Joseph R.

1953 *The Rembert Mounds, Elbert County, Georgia*. Smithsonian Institution, Bureau of American Ethnology, River Basin Surveys Papers 6. Washington, D.C.

1958 *Trend and Tradition in the Prehistory of the Eastern United States*. American Anthropological Association Memoir 88. Springfield, Illinois.

1964 *Interaction Spheres in the Prehistory of the Eastern United States*. Illinois State Museum, American Anthropological Association Scientific Papers, Vol. X. Springfield.

1978 Report of the Excavations at Fairchild's Landing and Hare's Landing, Seminole County, Georgia. Manuscript on file at the Department of Anthropology, University of Georgia.

Caldwell, Joseph R., and Catherine McCann

1941 *The Irene Mound Site, Chatham County, Georgia*. University of Georgia Press, Athens.

Caldwell, Joseph R., and Antonio J. Waring, Jr.

1939 Some Chatham County Pottery Types and Their Sequence. *Southeastern Archaeological Conference Newsletter* 1(5-6):24.

Cambron, James W., and David C. Hulse

1964 *Handbook of Alabama Archaeology. Part I: Point Types.* Archaeological Research Association of Alabama, Birmingham.

Carr, Christopher

1985 Toward a Synthetic Theory of Artifact Design. Paper presented at the Annual Meeting of the Society for American Archaeology, Denver, Colorado.

1995a A Unified Middle-Range Theory of Artifact Design. In *Style, Society, and Person: Archaeological and Ethnological Perspectives,* edited by C. Carr and J. Neitzel, pp. 171–258. Plenum Press, New York.

1995b Building a Unified Middle-Range Theory of Artifact Design: Historical Perspectives and Tactics. In *Style, Society, and Person: Archaeological and Ethnological Perspectives,* edited by C. Carr and J. Neitzel, pp. 151–70. Plenum Press, New York.

Chapman, Ashley A., II

1994 The Ceramic Assemblage at the Bernath site (8SR986): Temporal and Spatial Evolution of the Ring Midden. Paper presented at the 49th Annual Meeting of the Southeastern Archaeological Conference, Little Rock, Arkansas.

Chapman, Jefferson

1973 *The Icehouse Bottom Site 40MR23.* University of Tennessee, Department of Anthropology, Report of Investigations 13. Knoxville.

Chapman, Jefferson, and Bennie C. Keel

1979 Candy Creek–Connestee Components in Eastern Tennessee and Western North Carolina and Their Relationship with Adena-Hopewell. In *Hopewell Archaeology: The Chillicothe Conference,* edited by D. S. Brose and N. Greber, pp. 157–61. Kent State University Press, Kent, Ohio.

Chartelain, Verne

1935 Letter to Charles C. Harrold, October. Central Classified Files (National Park Service), U.S. National Archives, Washington D.C.

Chase, David W.

1957 The Halloca Creek Site. Manuscript on file, Columbus Museum, Columbus, Georgia.

1966 An Archaic Site in Lowndes County, Alabama. *Florida Anthropologist* 2(3):91–114.

1978 The Harrington Site, 1MT231. Manuscript on file, Auburn University at Montgomery, Alabama.

1991 *Miner's Creek Site, 9DA91.* Report submitted to DeKalb County Parks and Recreation, Decatur, Georgia.

Chase, David W., Harold A. Huscher, and R. Jerald Ledbetter

1994 The Walker Street Site, 9ME60. *Early Georgia* 22(2):1–73.

Clark, John E., and Michael Blake

1994 The Power of Prestige: Competitive Generosity and the Emergence of Rank Societies in Lowland Mesoamerica. In *Factional Competition in the New World,* edited by E. M. Brumfiel and J. W. Fox, pp. 17–30. Cambridge University Press, Cambridge, England.

Clarke, David L.

1968 *Analytical Archaeology.* Methune, London.

Cleland, Charles

1976 The Focal-Diffuse Model: An Evolutionary Perspective on the Prehistoric Cultural Adaptations of the Eastern United States. *Midcontinental Journal of Archaeology* 1(1):59–76.

Cole, Gloria G.

1981 *The Murphy Hill Site (1MS300): The Structural Study of a Copena Mound and Comparative Review of the Copena Mortuary Complex.* University of Alabama, Office of Archaeological Research, Research Series 3. Tuscaloosa.

Conkey, Margaret W., and Christine A. Hastorf, eds.

1990 *The Uses of Style in Archaeology: New Directions in Archaeology.* Cambridge University Press, Cambridge.

Cook, Fred

1979 Kelvin: A Late Woodland Phase on the Southern Georgia Coast. *Early Georgia* 7(2):65–86.

Cordell, Ann S.

1985 Pottery Variability and Site Chronology in the Upper St. Johns River Basin. In *Archaeological Site Types, Distribution, and Preservation within the Upper St. Johns River Basin, Florida,* edited by B. Sigler-Eisenberg, pp. 114–34. Florida State Museum Miscellaneous Project and Report Series 27. Gainesville.

1992 Technological Investigations of Pottery Variability in Southwest

Florida. In *Culture and Environment in the Domain of the Calusa*, edited by W. Marquardt, pp. 105–89. Institute of Archaeology and Paleoenvironmental Studies, Monograph 1. Gainesville, Florida.

1993 Chronological Variability in Ceramic Paste: A Comparison of Deptford and Savannah Period Pottery in the St. Mary's River Region of Northeast Florida and Southeast Georgia. *Southeastern Archaeology* 12(1):33–58.

Cottier, John W.

1968 *Archaeological Investigations in the Miller's Ferry Lock and Dam Reservoir.* Report submitted to the U.S. Department of the Interior, National Park Service, Atlanta, Georgia.

1979 *The Lower Antioch Branch Site, Central Alabama.* Department of Sociology, Auburn University, Auburn, Alabama.

Council, R. Bruce

1989 *The Tennessee Riverpark Excavations. Archaeological Testing at Sites 40HA102 and 40HA233: Chattanooga, Hamilton County, Tennessee.* Jeffrey L. Brown Institute of Archaeology, University of Tennessee, Chattanooga.

Crane, H. R.

1956 University of Michigan Radiocarbon Dates I. *Science* 124(3224):655–72.

David, N., J. Sterner, and K. Gavua

1988 Why Pots Are Decorated. *Current Anthropology* 29(3):365–79.

Deetz, James

1965 *The Dynamics of Stylistic Change in Arikara Ceramics.* University of Illinois Press, Illinois Studies in Anthropology 4. Urbana.

DeFrance, Susan D.

1993 Faunal Material from the Greenfield Site (8DU5543), Duval County, Florida. Report on file at the Florida Museum of Natural History, Gainesville.

DeJarnette, David L., ed.

1975 *Archaeological Salvage in the Walter F. George Basin in the Chattahoochee River in Alabama.* University of Alabama Press, Tuscaloosa.

DePratter, Chester B.

1991 *W.P.A. Archaeological Excavations in Chatham County, Georgia:*

1937–1942. University of Georgia, Department of Anthropology, Laboratory of Archaeology Series Report 29. Athens.

Dickinson, Martin F., and Lucy B. Wayne

1987 *Archaeological Survey and Testing Phase I Development Areas Fairfield Fort George, Fort George Island, Duval County, Florida.* Water and Air Research, Gainesville, Florida.

Doran, Glen H., and Bruce J. Piateck

1985 *Archaeological Investigations at Naval Live Oaks, Studies in Spatial Patterning and Chronology in the Gulf Coast of Florida.* Report submitted to the U.S. National Park Service, Tallahassee, Florida.

Elliott, Daniel T.

1984 *An Archaeological Survey of Selected Timber Stands on the Long Cane Division, Sumter National Forest.* U.S.D.A. National Forest Service, Columbia, South Carolina.

1987 Surface Collections from Five Sites near Brier Creek in Screven County, Georgia. Manuscript on file, Laboratory of Archaeology, University of Georgia, Athens.

1993a *Archaeological Survey of the Dry Creek/Long Cane Creek Area, Abbeville County, South Carolina.* Lamar Institute, Watkinsville, Georgia.

1993b *Chickamauga Reservoir Archaeological Site Inventory: Results of Survey from 1987 to 1993.* Garrow and Associates, Atlanta, Georgia.

1993c *The Clark Hill River Basin Survey.* Lamar Institute and South Carolina Institute of Archaeology and Anthropology, Columbia, South Carolina.

Elliott, Daniel T., and Dennis B. Blanton

1985 *Archaeological Survey of Elbert and Coldwater Creek Recreation Areas, Richard B. Russell Multiple Resource Area, Elbert County, Georgia.* Garrow and Associates, Atlanta, Georgia.

Elliott, Daniel T., and Roy Doyon

1981 *Archaeology and Historical Geography of the Savannah River Floodplain near Augusta, Georgia.* University of Georgia, Department of Anthropology, Laboratory of Archaeology Series Report 22. Athens.

Elliott, Daniel T., and Stephen A. Kowalewski

1989 Fortson Mound, Wilkes County, Georgia. *Early Georgia* 17(1-2):50–75.

Elliott, Daniel T., and Lisa D. O'Steen

1987 Anatomy of the Brier Creek Archaic. Paper presented at the 44th Annual Meeting of the Southeastern Archaeological Conference, Charleston, South Carolina.

Elliott, Daniel T., and Marvin T. Smith

1985 *Final Report on Archaeological Survey of the Fort Howard Paper Company Effingham County Tract.* Garrow and Associates, Atlanta, Georgia.

Elliott, Daniel T., and Jack T. Wynn

1991 The Vining Revival: A Late Simple Stamped Phase in the Central Georgia Piedmont. *Early Georgia* 19(1):1–18.

Emerson, Thomas E.

1989 Water, Serpents, and the Underworld: An Exploration into Cahokian Symbolism. In *The Southeastern Ceremonial Complex: Artifacts and Analysis,* edited by P. Galloway, pp. 45–92. University of Nebraska Press, Lincoln.

Espenshade, Christopher

1992 *Few Visits in Prehistory: Data Recovery Excavations at 9RH18, Randolph County, Georgia.* Report prepared for the Georgia Department of Transportation, Atlanta.

Fairbanks, Charles H.

1940 Memorandum to A. R. Kelly. On file at Ocmulgee National Monument, U.S. National Park Service, Macon, Georgia.

1941 *Archaeological Site Survey on the Kolomoki Mound Groups.* Ocmulgee National Monument, U.S. National Park Service, Macon, Georgia.

1952 Creek and Pre-Creek. In *Archaeology of Eastern United States,* edited by J. B. Griffin, pp. 285–300. University of Chicago Press, Chicago.

Faulkner, Charles H.

1968 A Review of Pottery Types in the Eastern Tennessee Valley. *Proceedings of the 24th Southeastern Archaeological Conference Bulletin* 8:823–35.

Faulkner, Charles, and J. B. Graham

1965 *Excavations in the Nickajack Reservoir: Season I.* Tennessee Archaeological Society, Miscellaneous Paper 7.

1966a *Highway Salvage in the Nickajack Reservoir.* Department of Anthropology, University of Tennessee, Knoxville.

1966b *Westmoreland-Barber Site (40MI11), Nickajack Reservoir: Season II.* Department of Anthropology, University of Tennessee, Knoxville.

Fearn, Miriam L., and Kam-biu Liu
1995 Maize Pollen of 3500 B.P. from Southern Alabama. *American Antiquity* 60(1):109–17.

Fenton, William N.
1940 Masked Medicine Societies of the Iroquois. In *Annual Report of the Smithsonian Institution 1940*, pp. 397–430. Smithsonian Institution, Washington, D.C.

Ferguson, Leland G.
1971 *South Appalachian Mississippian*. Ph.D. Dissertation, Department of Anthropology, University of North Carolina, Chapel Hill.

Fewkes, Vladimir
1938 Irene Mound Excavations, Savannah, Georgia. *Proceedings of the Society for Georgia Archaeology* 1(2):24–31.

Fish, Paul R.
1976 *Patterns of Prehistoric Site Distribution in Effingham and Screven Counties, Georgia*. University of Georgia, Department of Anthropology, Laboratory of Archaeology Series Report 11. Athens.

Fish, Paul R., and Richard W. Jefferies
1978 *Investigation of Two Stone Mound Localities, Monroe County, Georgia*. University of Georgia, Department of Anthropology, Laboratory of Archaeology Series Report 17. Athens.

Fish, Suzanne K.
1978 Preliminary Site Report for Archaeological Salvage Undertaken at 9GE10. Manuscript 228 on file, Laboratory of Archaeology, University of Georgia, Athens.

Fish, Suzanne K., and Richard W. Jefferies
1983 The Site Plan at Cold Springs, 9GE10. *Early Georgia* 11(1-2):61–73.

Florida Archaeological Services
1995 Phase II Archaeological Investigations at Site 8DU5541, 8DU5542, and 8DU5543 at the Queens Harbour Yacht and Country Club. Report on file at the Department of Historical Resources, Tallahassee, Florida.

Fowler, Melvin L.
1957 Rutherford Mound, Hardin County, Illinois. *Illinois State Museum Scientific Papers* 1:1–44.

Friedman, Jonathan, and Michael J. Rowlands
1977 Notes toward an Epigenetic Model of the Evolution of "Civiliza-

tion." In *The Evolution of Social Systems*, edited by J. Friedman and M. J. Rowlands, pp. 201–76. University of Pittsburgh Press, Pittsburgh, Pennsylvania.

Friedrich, Margret H.

1970 Design Structure and Social Interaction: Archaeological Applications of an Ethnographic Analysis. *American Antiquity* 35:332–43.

Galinat, W. C., and J. H. Gunnerson

1963 Spread of Eight-Rowed Maize from the Prehistoric Southwest. *Botanical Museum Leaflet, Harvard University* 20:117–60.

Galloway, Patricia, ed.

1989 *The Southeastern Ceremonial Complex: Artifacts and Analysis*. University of Nebraska Press, Lincoln.

Gardner, Paul S.

1986 Carbonized Plant Remains from Paris Island, South (9EB21); Sara's Ridge (38AN29); and Simpson's Field (38AN8) Sites. In *Prehistory in the Richard B. Russell Reservoir: The Archaic and Woodland Periods of the Upper Savannah River. The Final Report of the Data Recovery at the Anderson and Elbert County Groups: 38AN8, 38AN29, 38AN126, 9EB17, 9EB19 and 9EB21*, edited by W. D. Wood, D. T. Elliott, T. P. Rudolph, and D. B. Blanton, pp. 387–92. Interagency Archeological Services Division, National Park Service, Russell Papers. Atlanta, Georgia.

Garrow, Patrick H.

1975 The Woodland Period North of the Fall Line. *Early Georgia* 3:17–26.

Garrow, Patrick H., ed.

1984 *Cultural Resource Management: Vogtle-Effingham-Thalmann Transmission Line, Burke, Screven, Effingham, Chatham, Bryan, Liberty, Long, McIntosh, and Glynn Counties, Georgia. Resource Inventory II: Final Report*. Submitted to Georgia Power Company by Garrow and Associates, Atlanta, Georgia.

Gilliland, Marion S.

1975 *The Material Culture of Key Marco Florida*. University Presses of Florida, Gainesville.

Glander, Wayne, Gary Barber, and Paul Brockington

1981 *Report of Archeological Testing at Sites 38AB22, 38AB91, and*

38AB288 in the Richard B. Russell Reservoir, Abbeville County, South Carolina. Professional Analysts, Eugene, Oregon.

Goad, Sharon I.
1979 Middle Woodland Exchange in the Prehistoric Southeastern United States. In *Hopewell Archaeology: The Chillicothe Conference,* edited by D. S. Brose and N. Greber, pp. 239–46. Kent State University Press, Kent, Ohio.

Goggin, John M.
1952 *Space and Time Perspective in Northern St. Johns Archaeology, Florida.* Yale University Publications in Anthropology 47. New Haven, Connecticut.

Goodyear, Albert C., William Monteith, and Michael Harmon
1983 *Testing and Evaluation of the 84 Sites and Reconnaissance of the Islands and Cleveland Property, Richard B. Russell Dam and Lake, Savannah River, Georgia and South Carolina.* University of South Carolina, Institute of Archaeology and Anthropology, Research Manuscript Series 189. Columbia.

Graham, J. Bennett
1964 *The Archaeological Investigation of Moccasin Bend (40HA63), Hamilton County, Tennessee.* Department of Anthropology, University of Tennessee, Knoxville.

Graham, Otis L., Jr., and Meghan Robinson Wander, eds.
1985 *Franklin D. Roosevelt: His Life and Times.* G. K. Hall, Boston.

Graves, Michael W.
1981 *Ethnoarchaeology of Kalinga Ceramic Design.* Ph.D. Dissertation, University of Arizona, Tucson.

Greber, N'omi
1979 A Comparative Study of Site Morphology and Burial Patterns at Edwin Harness Mound and Seip Mounds 1 and 2. In *Hopewell Archaeology: The Chillicothe Conference,* edited by D. S. Brose and N. Greber, pp. 27–38. Kent State University Press, Kent, Ohio.

Greenwell, Dale
1984 The Mississippi Gulf Coast. In *Perspectives on Gulf Coast Prehistory,* edited by D. D. Davis, pp. 125–64. University Press of Florida, Gainesville.

Griffin, James B.

1967 Eastern North American Archaeology: A Summary. *Science* 156:175–91.

1984 William H. Sears, Southeastern Archaeologist: A Tribute. *Southeastern Archaeology* 3(2):134–38.

Griffin, John W.

1974 *Investigations in Russell Cave.* National Park Service Publications in Archaeology 13. Washington, D.C.

Griffith, Roberta J.

1981 *Ramey Incised Pottery.* Illinois Archaeological Survey Circular 5. Urbana.

Haag, William G.

1939a Swift Creek Complicated Stamped. *Southeastern Archaeological Conference Newsletter* 1(2):1–2.

1939b Pottery Type Description for Pickwick Complicated Stamped. *Southeastern Archaeological Conference Newsletter* 1(1):20–21.

Hall, Robert L.

1973 The Cahokia Presence Outside of the American Bottom. Paper prepared for the Central State Anthropological Society, St. Louis, Missouri.

1979 In Search of the Ideology of the Adena-Hopewell Climax. In *Hopewell Archaeology: The Chillicothe Conference,* edited by D. S. Brose and N. Greber, pp. 258–65. Kent State University Press, Kent, Ohio.

1980 An Interpretation of the Two-Climax Model of Illinois Prehistory. In *Early Native Americans: Prehistoric Demography, Economy, and Technology,* edited by D. Brownam, pp. 402–62. Moutton, The Hague.

1989 The Cultural Background of Mississippian Symbolism. In *The Southeastern Ceremonial Complex: Artifacts and Analysis,* edited by P. Galloway, pp. 239–78. University of Nebraska Press, Lincoln and London.

Hally, David J.

1993 The Territorial Size of Mississippian Chiefdoms. In *Archaeology of Eastern North America: Papers in Honor of Stephen Williams,* edited by J. B. Stoltman, pp. 143–68. Mississippi Department of Archives and History, Archaeological Report 25. Jackson.

Hanson, Glen T., and Chester B. DePratter

1985 The Early and Middle Woodland Periods in the Savannah River Valley. Paper presented at the 42nd Annual Meeting of the Southeastern Archaeological Conference, Birmingham, Alabama.

Hardin, Margaret Ann

1977 Individual Style in San Jose Pottery Painting: The Role of Deliberate Choice. In *The Individual in Prehistory: Studies of Variability in Style in Prehistoric Technologies,* edited by J. N. Hill and J. Gunn, pp. 109–36. Academic Press, New York.

1984 Models of Decoration. In *The Many Dimensions of Pottery: Ceramics in Archaeology and Anthropology,* edited by S. E. van der Leeuw and A. C. Pritchard, pp. 574–607. University of Amsterdam.

Hardman, Clark, Jr., and Marjorie H. Hardman

1991 Kolomoki: A Prehistoric Linear Solar Observatory and Horizon Calendar. *The Soto States Anthropologist* 1(3):195–227.

Harris, Walter A.

1935 Letter to Demaray, October 19, 1935. Central Classified Files, U.S. National Archives, Washington, D.C.

Heimlich, Marion Dunlevy

1952 *Guntersville Basin Pottery.* Geological Survey of Alabama, Museum Paper 32. University.

Helms, Mary W.

1979 *Ancient Panama: Chiefs in Search of Power.* University of Texas Press, Austin.

Hemmings, E. Thomas

1974 Cades Pond Subsistence, Settlement, and Ceremonialism. Paper presented at the 39th Annual Meeting of the Society for American Archaeology, Washington, D.C.

Hemperly, Marion R.

1989 *Historic Indian Trails of Georgia.* The Garden Club of Georgia.

Hill, James N.

1968 Broken K Pueblo: Patterns of Form and Function. In *New Perspectives in Archaeology,* edited by S. R. Binford and L. R. Binford, pp. 103–42. Aldine, Chicago.

Hill, James N., and Joel Gunn

1977 Introducing the Individual in Prehistory. In *The Individual in Prehistory: Studies of Variability in Style in Prehistoric Technologies,* edited by J. N. Hill and J. Gunn, pp. 1–12. Academic Press, New York.

Hodder, Ian

1977 The Distribution of Material Culture Items in the Baringo District, Western Kenya. *Man* 12(2):239–69.

1979 Economic and Social Stress and Material Culture Patterning. *American Antiquity* 44:446–54.

1982a *Symbols in Action: Ethnoarchaeological Studies of Material Culture.* Cambridge University Press, Cambridge.

1982b *The Present Past.* Pica Press, New York.

Hodler, Thomas W., and Howard A. Schretter

1986 *The Atlas of Georgia.* University of Georgia, The Institute of Community and Area Development. Athens.

Holmes, Michael S.

1975 *The New Deal in Georgia.* Greenwood Press, Westport, Connecticut.

Holmes, William H.

1903 *Aboriginal Pottery of the Eastern United States.* Smithsonian Institution, Bureau of American Ethnology, Annual Report 20. Washington, D.C.

Honerkamp, Nicholas

1983 *Archaeological Survey of the Alvin W. Vogtle Nuclear Plant Property in Burke County, Georgia.* Department of Anthropology, University of Florida, Gainesville.

Houston, Clifton A., and James W. Stoutamire

1982 *The Archaeology of the Naval Live Oaks Reservation, Gulf Islands National Seashore.* Department of Anthropology, Florida State University, Tallahassee.

Hubbell, T. H., A. M. Laessle, and J. C. Dickinson

1956 *The Fling-Chattahoochee-Apalachicola Region and its Environments.* Contributions of the Florida State Museum, Biological Sciences 1:1. Gainesville.

Hudson, Charles

1976 *The Southeastern Indians.* University of Tennessee Press, Knoxville.

1984 *Elements of Southeastern Indian Religion.* State University Groningen, Institute of Religious Iconography, Iconography of Religions X:1. E. J. Brill, Leiden.

Huscher, Harold A.

1959a *Appraisal of the Archaeological Resources of the Columbia Dam and*

Lock Area, Chattahoochee River, Alabama and Georgia. Smithsonian Institution, River Basin Surveys. Washington, D.C.

1959b *Appraisal of the Archaeological Resources of the Walter F. George Reservoir Area, Chattahoochee River, Alabama and Georgia.* Smithsonian Institution, River Basin Surveys. Washington, D.C.

Hutto, Brooks

1970 *Archaeological Survey of the Elbert County, Georgia, Portion of the Proposed Trotters Shoals Reservoir, Savannah River.* University of Georgia, Department of Anthropology, Laboratory of Archaeology Series Report 7. Athens.

Jackson, H. Edwin, and Susan Scott

1995 The Faunal Record of the Southeastern Elite: The Implications of Economy, Social Relations, and Ideology. *Southeastern Archaeology* 14(2):103–19.

Jefferies, Richard W.

1976 *The Tunnacunnhee Site: Evidence of Hopewell Interaction in Northwest Georgia.* Anthropological Papers of the University of Georgia 1. Athens.

Jenkins, Ned

1981 *Gainesville Lake Area Description and Chronology: Archaeological Investigations in the Gainesville Lake Area of the Tennessee-Tombigbee Waterway,* Vol. 2. University of Alabama, Office of Archaeological Investigations, Report of Investigations 12. Tuscaloosa.

1982 *Archaeology of the Gainesville Lake Area: Synthesis,* Vol. 5. University of Alabama, Office of Archaeological Investigations, Report of Investigations 15. Tuscaloosa.

Jenkins, Ned, and Baxter Mann

1985 An Archaeological Study of the Connecuh Drainage. *Florida Anthropologist* 38(1-2):136–43.

Jennings, Jesse D., and Charles H. Fairbanks

1939a Pottery Type Descriptions. *Southeastern Archaeological Conference Newsletter* 1(1).

1939b Pottery Type Description for Swift Creek Complicated Stamped. *Southeastern Archaeological Conference Newsletter* 1(2).

Johannessen, Sissel

1993 Farmers of the Late Woodland. In *Foraging and Farming in the*

Eastern Woodlands, edited by C. M. Scarry, pp. 57–77. University Press of Florida, Gainesville.

Johnson, Robert E.

1988 An Archeological Reconnaissance Survey of the St. Johns Bluff Area of Duval County, Florida. Manuscript on file, Florida Archeological Services, Jacksonville.

Jones, Charles C., Jr.

1873 *Antiquities of the Southern Indians, Particularly of the Georgia Tribes.* D. Appleton, New York.

Jones, Jacqueline

1985 *Labor of Love, Labor of Sorrow.* Basic Books, New York.

Kahler, Herbert

1935a Telegraph to NPS Director, October 30, 1935. Central Classified Files, U.S. National Archives, Washington, D.C.

1935b Letter to NPS Director, November 2, 1935. Central Classified Files, U.S. National Archives, Washington, D.C.

Keel, Bennie

1976 *Cherokee Archaeology: A Study of the Appalachian Summit.* University of Tennessee Press, Knoxville.

Kellar, James H.

1979 The Mann Site and "Hopewell" in the Lower Wabash-Ohio Valley. In *Hopewell Archaeology: The Chillicothe Conference,* edited by D. S. Brose and N. Greber, pp. 100–107. Kent State University Press, Kent, Ohio.

Kellar, James H., Jr., Arthur R. Kelly, and Edward V. McMichael

1962 The Mandeville Site in Southwest Georgia. *American Antiquity* 27(3):336–55.

Kelly, Arthur R.

1938 *Preliminary Report on Archaeological Explorations at Macon, Georgia.* Smithsonian Institution, Bureau of American Ethnology, Bulletin 119. Washington, D.C.

1950 Survey of the Lower Flint and Chattahoochee Rivers. *Early Georgia* 1:27–33.

1956 *The Milamo Site, 9WL1.* University of Georgia, Department of Anthropology, Laboratory of Archaeology Manuscript 19. Athens.

1960 *Weeden Island Burial Mound in Decatur County, Georgia: The Lake*

Douglas Mound, 9DR21. University of Georgia, Department of Anthropology, Laboratory of Archaeology Series Report 1. Athens.

1973 Early Villages on the Chattahoochee River, Georgia. *Archaeology* 26:32–37.

Kelly, Arthur R., and Edward Beam

1956 Exploration of a Stone Mound in Lumpkin County, Georgia. Manuscript 158 on file, Laboratory of Archaeology, University of Georgia, Athens.

Kelly, Arthur R., and Robert S. Neitzel

1961 *The Chauga Site in Oconee County, South Carolina.* University of Georgia, Department of Anthropology, Laboratory of Archaeology Series Report 3. Athens.

Kelly, Arthur R., Richard Nonas, Bettye Broyles, Clemens DeBaillou, David W. Chase, and Frank T. Schnell, Jr.

1962 *Survey of Archaeological Sites in Clay and Quitman Counties, Georgia.* University of Georgia, Department of Anthropology, Laboratory of Archaeology Series Report 5. Athens.

Kelly, Arthur R., and Betty Smith

1975 The Swift Creek Site, 9BI3, Macon, Georgia. Manuscript 333 on file, Laboratory of Archaeology, University of Georgia, Athens.

Kirkland, S. Dwight

1979 Preliminary Investigations on Floyd Creek, Camden County, Georgia. *Early Georgia* 7(2):1–25.

Knight, Vernon James, Jr.

1989 Some Speculations on Mississippian Monsters. In *The Southeastern Ceremonial Complex: Artifacts and Analysis,* edited by P. Galloway, pp. 205–10. University of Nebraska Press, Lincoln.

Knight, Vernon J., and Timothy S. Mistovich

1984 *Walter F. George Lake: Archaeological Survey of Fee Owned Lands, Alabama and Georgia.* University of Alabama Office of Archaeological Research, Report of Investigations 42. Tuscaloosa.

Kohler, Timothy A.

1978 *The Social and Chronological Dimensions of Village Occupation at a North Florida Weeden Island Period Site.* Ph.D. Dissertation, Department of Anthropology, University of Florida, Gainesville.

1991 The Demise of Weeden Island, and Post–Weeden Island Cultural Stability, in Non-Mississippianized North Florida. In *Stability, Transformation and Variation: The Late Woodland Southeast,* edited by M. S. Nassany and C. R. Cobb, pp. 91–110. Plenum Press, New York.

Kosso, Patrick
1991 Method in Archaeology: Middle-Range Theory as Hermeneutics. *American Antiquity* 56(4):621–27.

Larson, Lewis H.
1960 Settlement Distribution during the Mississippi Period. Paper presented at the 27th Southeastern Archaeological Conference, Columbia, South Carolina.

Ledbetter, R. Jerald
1991 *An Inventory of Surface Material: Three Sites in the Theriault Locality, Burke County, Georgia.* Southeastern Archeological Services, Athens, Georgia.

Lee, C., Irvy Quitmyer, Chris Espenshade, and Robert Johnson
1984 *Estuarine Adaptations during the Late Prehistoric Period: Archaeology of Two Shell Midden Sites on the St. Johns River.* University of West Florida, Office of Cultural and Archaeological Research, Report of Investigations 5. Pensacola.

Lewis, Thomas M. N.
n.d. The Prehistory of the Chickamauga Basin. Manuscript on file, Frank H. McClung Museum, Knoxville, Tennessee.

Lewis, Thomas M. N., and Madeline Kneberg
1941 *Prehistory of the Chickamauga Basin in Tennessee: A Preview.* University of Tennessee, Division of Anthropology, Tennessee Anthropological Papers 1. Knoxville.
1946 *Hiwassee Island: An Archaeological Account of Four Tennessee Indian Peoples.* University of Tennessee Press, Knoxville.

Longacre, William A.
1964 Sociological Implications of the Ceramic Analysis. In Chapters in the Prehistory of Arizona, No. 2, by P. S. Martin, J. B. Rinaldo, W. A. Longacre, L. G. Freeman, Jr., J. A. Brown, R. H. Hevly, and M. E. Cooley. *Fieldiana: Anthropology* 55:155–70.
1970 *Archaeology as Anthropology: A Case Study.* University of Arizona Press, Anthropological Papers 17. Tucson.

Lynott, Mark, T. Boutton, Jim Price, and D. Nelson
    1986 Stable Carbon Isotope Evidence for Maize Agriculture in Southeast
    Missouri and Northeast Arkansas. *American Antiquity* 51:51–65.
McIntyre, Lucy B.
    1939 The Use of Negro Women in W.P.A. Work at the Irene Mound,
    Savannah. *Proceedings of the Society for Georgia Archaeology* 2(1):23–26.
McMichael, Edward V.
    1960 *The Anatomy of a Tradition: A Study of Southeastern Stamped Pottery.*
    Ph.D. Dissertation, Department of Anthropology, Indiana University.
McMichael, Edward V., and James H. Kellar
    1960 *Mandeville Site (9CY1), First Season.* Laboratory of Archaeology,
    Department of Anthropology, University of Georgia. Athens.
Mainfort, Robert C., Jr.
    1988 Pinson Mounds: Internal Chronology and External Relationships.
    In *Middle Woodland Settlement and Ceremonialism in the Mid-South and
    Lower Mississippi Valley,* edited by R. C. Mainfort, pp. 132–46. Missis-
    sippi Department of Archives and History, Archaeological Report 22.
    Jackson.
    1990 *Pinson Mounds: A Middle Woodland Ceremonial Center.* Tennessee
    Department of Conservation, Division of Archaeology, Research Series
    7. Nashville.
Mangelsdorf, Paul C.
    1974 *Corn: Its Origin, Evolution and Improvement.* Harvard University
    Press, Cambridge.
Marcus, Joyce, and Kent V. Flannery
    1978 Ethnoscience of the Sixteenth-Century Valley Zapotec. In *The Na-
    ture and Status of Ethnobotany,* edited by R. I. Ford, pp. 51–79. Univer-
    sity of Michigan, Museum of Anthropology, Anthropological Papers
    67. Ann Arbor.
Milanich, Jerald T.
    1971 *The Alachua Tradition of North-Central Florida.* Contributions of
    the Florida State Museum, Anthropology and History 17. Gainesville.
    1974 *Life in a 9th Century Household: A Weeden Island Fall-Winter Site
    in the Upper Apalachicola River, Florida.* Bureau of Historic Sites and
    Properties, Division of Archives, History, and Records Management,
    Bulletin 4. Tallahassee, Florida.

1994 *Archaeology of Precolumbian Florida*. University Press of Florida, Gainesville.

Milanich, Jerald T., Ann S. Cordell, Vernon J. Knight, Jr., Timothy A. Kohler, and Brenda J. Sigler-Lavelle
   1984 *McKeithen Weeden Island: The Culture of Northern Florida*, A.D. *200–900*. Academic Press, New York.

Milanich, Jerald T., and Charles Fairbanks
   1980 *Florida Archaeology*. Academic Press, New York.

Mistovich, Tim S., and Vernon J. Knight
   1986 *Excavations at Four Sites on Walter F. George Lake, Alabama and Georgia*. University of Alabama Office of Archaeological Research, Report of Investigations 49. Tuscaloosa.

Mooney, James
   1900 *Myths of the Cherokee*. Smithsonian Institution, Bureau of American Ethnology, Annual Report 19. Washington, D.C.

Moore, Clarence B.
   1894 Certain Sand Mounds of the St. Johns River, Florida, Parts I and II. *Philadelphia Academy of Natural Sciences Journal* 10:129–246.
   1895 Certain Sand Mounds of Duval County, Florida. *Philadelphia Academy of Natural Sciences Journal* 10:449–502.
   1896 *Mounds of Duval and Clay Counties, Florida: Mound Investigation on the East Coast of Florida*. Philadelphia.
   1902a Certain Aboriginal Remains of the Northwest Florida Coast (Part I). *Journal of the Academy of Natural Sciences of Philadelphia* 11:419–516. Philadelphia.
   1902b Certain Aboriginal Remains of the Northwest Florida Coast (Part II). *Journal of the Academy of Natural Sciences of Philadelphia* 12. Philadelphia.
   1903 Certain Aboriginal Mounds of the Apalachicola River. *Journal of the Academy of Natural Sciences of Philadelphia* 12:440–94. Philadelphia.
   1907 Mounds of the Lower Chattahoochee and Lower Flint Rivers. *Journal of the Academy of Natural Sciences* 12:426–56. Philadelphia.
   1918 The Northwest Florida Coast Revisited. *Journal of the Academy of Natural Sciences (Second Series)* 16:514–81. Philadelphia.

Nance, Roger C.
   1975 Archaeological Survey of the Montgomery Levee Project Area,

Montgomery, Alabama. Report submitted to the U.S. Department of the Interior, National Park Service, Atlanta.

Patrick, Linda
1985 Is There an Archaeological Record? In *Advances in Archaeological Method and Theory,* Vol. 8, edited by M. B. Schiffer, pp. 1–26. Academic Press, New York.

Pauketat, Timothy R., and Thomas Emerson
1996 *Cahokia: Domination and Ideology in the Mississippian World.* University of Nebraska Press, Lincoln.

Peebles, Christopher S.
1971 Moundville and Surrounding Sites: Some Structural Considerations of Mortuary Practices II. In *Approaches to the Social Dimensions of Mortuary Practices,* edited by J. A. Brown, pp. 68–91. Society for American Archaeology Memoir 25, Washington, D.C.

Peebles, Christopher S., and Susan Kus
1977 Some Archaeological Correlates of Ranked Societies. *American Antiquity* 42:421–48.

Penny, David W.
1985 Continuities of Imagery and Symbolism in the Art of the Woodlands. In *Ancient Art of the American Woodland Indians,* edited by D. S. Brose, J. A. Brown, and D. W. Penny, pp. 147–98. Harry N. Abrams, New York.

Penton, Daniel T.
n.d. A Synthesis of the Santa Rosa–Swift Creek Period. Manuscript on file, Bureau of Archaeological Research, Division of Historical Records, Department of State, Tallahassee, Florida.
1974 The Early Swift Creek Phase in Northern Florida: Internal Expressions and External Connections. Paper presented at the Annual Meeting of the Society for American Archaeology, Washington, D.C.

Percy, George W.
1976 *Salvage Investigations at the Scholz Steam Plant Site, a Middle Weeden Island Habitation Site in Jackson County, Florida.* Florida Department of State, Bureau of Historic Sites and Properties, Division of Archives, History, and Records Management, Miscellaneous Project Report Series 95. Tallahassee.

Percy, George W., and David S. Brose
1974 Weeden Island Ecology, Subsistence and Village Life in Northwest

Florida. Paper presented at the 39th Annual Meeting of the Society for American Archaeology, Washington, D.C.

Phelps, David S.

1969 Swift Creek and Santa Rosa in Northwest Florida. *Institute of Archaeology and Anthropology, University of South Carolina Notebook* 1:14–24.

1970 Mesoamerican Glyph Motifs on Southeastern Pottery. *International Congress of Americanists, Thirty-eighth Session, Munich, August 1968, Transactions* 2:89–99.

Plog, Stephen

1978 Social Interaction and Stylistic Similarity: A Reanalysis. In *Advances in Archaeological Method and Theory 1,* edited by M. Schiffer, pp. 143–82. Academic Press, New York.

1983 Analysis of Style in Artifacts. *Annual Review of Anthropology* 12:125–42.

Pluckhahn, Thomas J.

1996 Joseph Caldwell's Summerour Mound (9FO16) and Woodland Platform Mounds in the Southeastern United States. *Southeastern Archaeology* 15(2):191–211.

Pope, Gustavus D.

1956 *Ocmulgee National Monument, Georgia.* National Park Service Historical Series 24, Washington, D.C.

Price, T. Douglas, and James A. Brown, eds.

1985 *Prehistoric Hunter-Gatherers: The Emergence of Cultural Complexity.* Academic Press, New York.

Prufer, Olaf H.

1968 *Ohio Hopewell Ceramics: An Analysis of Extant Collections.* University of Michigan, Museum of Anthropology, Anthropological Papers 33. Ann Arbor.

Purdy, Barbara A.

1991 *The Art and Archaeology of Florida's Wetlands.* CRC Press, Boca Raton, Florida.

Quitmyer, Irvy R.

1985 Aboriginal Subsistence Activities in the Kings Bay Locality. In *Aboriginal Subsistence and Settlement Archaeology of the Kings Bay Locality,* Vol. 2, edited by W. H. Adams, pp. 73–91. University of Florida, Department of Anthropology, Reports of Investigations 2. Gainesville.

1994 The Zooarchaeology of Bernath Place (8SR986), a Santa Rosa–Swift Creek Settlement on Mulatto Bayou, Escambia Bay, Northwest Florida. Report to the University of West Florida. Environmental Archaeology Laboratory, Department of Anthropology, Florida Museum of Natural History, Gainesville.

1995 Swift Creek Subsistence Strategies: Evidence from Three Southeastern Sites. Paper presented at the 52nd Annual Meeting of the Southeastern Archaeological Conference, Knoxville, Tennessee.

Rappleye, Lauralee, and William M. Gardner
1980 *Summary Report. Transect 21: Site Testing Program (Contract No. C-55095-79), Richard B. Russell Multiple Resource Area. Savannah River, Georgia and South Carolina.* Thunderbird Research, Front Royal, Virginia.

Redman, Charles L.
1977 The "Analytical Individual" and Prehistoric Style Variability. In *The Individual in Prehistory: Studies of Variability in Style in Prehistoric Technologies,* edited by J. N. Hill and J. Gunn, pp. 41–54. Academic Press, New York.

1978 Multivariate Artifact Analysis: A Basis for Multidimensional Interpretations. In *Social Archeology: Beyond Subsistence and Dating,* edited by C. L. Redman, M. J. Berman, E. V. Curtin, W. T. Langhorne, Jr., N. M. Versaggi, and J. C. Wanser, pp. 159–92. Academic Press, New York.

Rein, Judith S.
1974 *The Complicated Stamped Pottery of the Mann Site, Posey County, Indiana.* M.A. Thesis, Department of Anthropology, Indiana University, Bloomington.

Reitz, Elizabeth J., and Irvy R. Quitmyer
1988 Faunal Remains from Two Coastal Georgia Swift Creek Sites. *Southeastern Archaeology* 7(2):95–108.

Renfrew, Colin
1974 Beyond a Subsistence Economy: The Evolution of Social Organization in Prehistoric Europe. In *Reconstructing Complex Societies,* edited by C. B. Moore, pp. 69–96. Bulletin of the American Schools of Oriental Research Supplement 20.

Renfrew, Colin, and John F. Cherry, eds.
1986 *Peer Polity Interaction and Socio-Political Change.* Cambridge University Press, Cambridge.

Rice, Prudence M.

   1987 *Pottery Analysis: A Sourcebook.* University of Chicago Press, Chicago.

Richter, Bob

   1993 Surface Collections from 8DU66, the McCormick Site. Manuscript on file with the author.

Rodeffer, Michael J., Stephanie H. Holschlag, and Mary Katherine Davis Cann

   1979 *Greenwood County: An Archaeological Reconnaissance.* Lander College, Greenwood, South Carolina.

Rudolph, Teresa P.

   1980 Testing of Eleven Archaeological Sites in the Vicinity of Proposed Power Plant, Duval County, Florida. Manuscript on file, Florida Division of Archives, History, and Records Management, Tallahassee.

   1985 Late Swift Creek and Napier Settlements in Northern Georgia. Paper presented at the 42nd Annual Meeting of the Southeastern Archaeological Conference, Birmingham, Alabama.

   1986 Regional and Temporal Variability in Swift Creek and Napier Ceramics from North Georgia. Paper presented at the Ocmulgee National Monument 50th Anniversary Conference, Macon, Georgia.

   1991 The Late Woodland "Problem" in North Georgia. In *Stability, Transformation, and Variation: The Late Woodland Southeast,* edited by M. S. Nassaney and C. R. Cobb, pp. 259–83. Plenum Press, New York.

Rudolph, Teresa P., and Thomas H. Gresham

   1980 A Cultural Resource Reconnaissance of a Proposed Coal-Fired Power Plant Site, Duval County, Florida. Manuscript on file, Florida Division of Archives, History, and Records Management, Tallahassee.

Russo, Michael

   1992 Chronologies and Cultures of the St. Marys Region of Northeast Florida and Southeast Georgia. *Florida Anthropologist* 45(2):107–26.

Russo, Michael, Ann S. Cordell, and Donna L. Ruhl

   1993 *The Timucuan Ecological and Historical Preserve Phase III: Final Report.* Southeast Archeological Center, National Park Service, Tallahassee, Florida.

Ryan, Thomas

   1971 *Archeological Resources along the Proposed Route of Interstate 77.* University of South Carolina, Institute of Archaeology and Anthropology, Research Manuscript Series 11. Columbia.

Sahlins, Marshall D.

1957 Land Use and the Extended Family in Moala, Fiji. *American Anthropologist* 59(3):449–62.

1963 Poor Man, Rich Man, Big Man, Chief: Political Types in Melanesia and Polynesia. *Comparative Studies in Society and History* 5(3):285–303.

Sassaman, Kenneth E., Mark J. Brooks, Glen T. Hanson, and David G. Anderson

1990 *Native American Prehistory of the Middle Savannah River Valley: A Synthesis of Archaeological Investigations on the Savannah River Site, Aiken and Barnwell Counties, South Carolina.* University of South Carolina, South Carolina Institute of Archaeology and Anthropology, Occasional Papers of the Savannah River Archaeological Research Program, Savannah River Archaeological Research Papers 1. Columbia.

Saunders, Rebecca

1986a *Attribute Variability in Late Swift Creek Phase Ceramics from King's Bay, Georgia.* M.A. Thesis, Department of Anthropology, University of Florida, Gainesville.

1986b Ceramic Variability during the Swift Creek Phase at Kings Bay, Georgia. In *Ceramic Notes 3*, pp. 145–98. Florida State Museum, Occasional Publications of the Ceramic Technology Laboratory. Gainesville.

1992a *Continuity and Change in Guale Indian Pottery, A.D. 1350–1702.* Ph.D. Dissertation, Department of Anthropology, University of Florida, Gainesville.

1992b Guale Indian Pottery: A Georgia Legacy in Northeast Florida. *Florida Anthropologist* 45(2):139–47.

1994 Swift Creek Design Assemblages on the Georgia Coast. Paper presented at the 51st Annual Meeting of the Southeastern Archaeological Conference, Lexington, Kentucky.

Scarry, C. Margaret, ed.

1993 *Foraging and Farming in the Eastern Woodlands.* University Press of Florida, Gainesville.

Scarry, John

1990 Mississippian Emergence in the Fort Walton Area: The Evolution of the Cayson and Lake Jackson Phases. In *Mississippian Emergence: The Evolution of Ranked Agricultural Societies in Eastern North America,* edited by B. D. Smith, pp. 227–50. Smithsonian Institution Press, Washington.

Scarry, John F., and Claudine Payne

1986 Mississippian Polities in the Fort Walton Area: A Model Generated from the Renfrew-Level XTENT Algorithm. *Southeastern Archaeology* 5(2):79–90.

Schnell, Frank T.

1975 The Woodland Period South of the Fall Line. *Early Georgia* 3(1):27–36.

Schnell, Frank T., Vernon J. Knight, Jr., and Gail Schnell

1981 *Cemochechobee: Archaeology of a Mississippian Ceremonial Center on the Chattahoochee River.* University Press of Florida, Ripley P. Bullen Monographs in Anthropology and History 3. Gainesville.

Schortman, Edward M., and Patricia A. Urban

1992 Current Trends in Interaction Research. In *Resources, Power, and Interregional Interaction,* edited by E. M. Schortman and P. A. Urban, pp. 235–55. Plenum Press, New York.

Schroedl, Gerald

1978 *The Patrick Site, Tellico Reservoir, Tennessee.* University of Tennessee, Department of Anthropology, Report of Investigations 25. Knoxville.

Schroedl, Gerald F., R. P. Stephen Davis, Jr., and C. C. Boyd, Jr.

1985 *Archaeological Contexts and Assemblages at Martin Farm.* University of Tennessee, Department of Anthropology, Report of Investigations 39. Knoxville.

Sears, William H.

1951a *Excavations at Kolomoki. Season I: 1948.* University of Georgia Press, University of Georgia Series in Anthropology 2. Athens.

1951b *Excavations at Kolomoki. Season II: Mound E.* University of Georgia Press, University of Georgia Series in Anthropology 3. Athens.

1952 Ceramic Development in the South Appalachian Province. *American Antiquity* 18(2):101–10.

1953 *Excavations at Kolomoki. Seasons III and IV: Mound D.* University of Georgia Press, University of Georgia Series in Anthropology 4. Athens.

1956 *Excavations at Kolomoki: Final Report.* University of Georgia Press, University of Georgia Series in Anthropology 5. Athens.

1957 *Excavations on Lower St. Johns River, Florida.* Contributions of the Florida State Museum 2. Gainesville.

1958 Burial Mounds on the Gulf Coastal Plain. *American Antiquity* 23:274–83.

1959 *Two Weeden Island Period Burial Mounds, Florida.* Contributions of the Florida State Museum 5. Gainesville.

1962 The Hopewellian Affiliations of Certain Sites on the Gulf Coast of Florida. *American Antiquity* 28:5–18.

1966 Deptford in Florida. *Newsletter of the Southeastern Archaeological Conference* 10(1):3–8.

1967 Review: Excavations at the Mayport Mound, Florida. *American Antiquity* 32(1):120–21.

1968 The State and Settlement Patterns in the New World. In *Settlement Archaeology*, edited by K. C. Chang, pp. 134–53. National Press Books, Palo Alto, California.

1971 Food Production and Village Life in Prehistoric Southeastern United States. *Archaeology* 24:93–102.

1973 The Sacred and the Secular in Prehistoric Ceramics. In *Variations in Anthropology: Essays in Honor of John McGregor*, edited by D. Lathrap and J. Douglas, pp. 31–42. Illinois Archaeological Survey, Urbana.

1977 Prehistoric Culture Areas and Culture Change on the Gulf Coastal Plain. In *For the Director: Research Essays in Honor of James B. Griffin*, edited by C. E. Cleland, pp. 152–85. University of Michigan, Museum of Anthropology, Anthropological Papers 61. Ann Arbor.

1982 *Fort Center: An Archaeological Site in the Lake Okeechobee Basin.* University Presses of Florida, Gainesville.

1992 Mea Culpa. *Southeastern Archaeology* 11(1):66–71.

Shannon, George W., Jr.

1979 *Ceramic Transitions on the Gulf Coastal Plain in the Early Centuries of the Christian Era.* M.A. Thesis, Department of Anthropology, Florida Atlantic University, Boca Raton.

Sheehan, Mark C.

1986 Analyses of Fossil Pollen from 38AN8 and 38AN29. In *Prehistory in the Richard B. Russell Reservoir: The Archaic and Woodland Periods of the Upper Savannah River. The Final Report of the Data Recovery at the Anderson and Elbert County Groups: 38AN8, 38AN29, 38AN126, 9EB17, 9EB19 and 9EB21,* edited by W. D. Wood, D. T. Elliott, T. P. Rudolph, and D. B. Blanton, pp. 393–98. Interagency Archeological Services Division, National Park Service, Russell Papers. Atlanta, Georgia.

Sigler-Lavelle, Brenda

1980 On the Non-Random Distribution of Weeden Island Period Sites in North Florida. *Southeastern Archaeological Conference Bulletin* 22:22–29.

Sitkoff, Harvard

1978 *A New Deal for Blacks.* Oxford University Press, New York.

Smith, Betty A.

1975 *A Re-analysis of the Mandeville Site, 9Cy1, Focusing on its Internal History and External Relations.* Ph.D. Dissertation, Department of Anthropology, University of Georgia, Athens.

1979 The Hopewell Connection in South Georgia. In *Hopewell Archaeology: The Chillicothe Conference,* edited by D. S. Brose and N. Greber, pp. 181–87. Kent State University Press, Kent, Ohio.

Smith, Betty A., and Arthur R. Kelly

1975 *The Swift Creek Site, 9BI3, Macon, Georgia.* University of Georgia, Department of Anthropology, Laboratory of Archaeology. Athens.

Smith, Betty A., John E. Noakes, and James D. Spaulding

1976 Neutron Activation Analysis of Southeastern Ceramics. Paper presented at the 75th Annual Meeting, American Anthropological Association, Washington, D.C.

Smith, Bruce D.

1975 *Middle Mississippi Exploitation of Animal Populations.* University of Michigan, Museum of Anthropology, Anthropological Papers 57. Ann Arbor.

1978 *Prehistoric Patterns of Human Behavior: A Case Study in the Mississippi Valley.* Academic Press, New York.

1992a Hopewellian Farmers of Eastern North America. In *Rivers of Change: Essays on Early Agriculture in Eastern North America,* edited by B. D. Smith, pp. 1–248. Smithsonian Institution Press, Washington.

1992b Origins of Agriculture in Eastern North America. In *Rivers of*

Change: Essays on Early Agriculture in Eastern North America, edited by B. D. Smith, pp. 267–79. Smithsonian Institution Press, Washington.

1992c Prehistoric Plant Husbandry in Eastern North America. In *Rivers of Change: Essays on Early Agriculture in Eastern North America*, edited by B. D. Smith, pp. 281–300. Smithsonian Institution Press, Washington.

Smith, Bruce D., ed.

1978 *Mississippian Settlement Patterns*. Academic Press, New York.

Smith, Marvin T., ed.

1986 *Archaeological Testing of Sixteen Sites on the Fort Howard Tract, Effingham County, Georgia*. Garrow and Associates, Atlanta, Georgia.

Smith, Marvin T., and Stephen Kowalewski

1980 Tentative Identification of a Prehistoric "Province" in Piedmont Georgia. *Early Georgia* 8:1–13.

Smith, Marvin T., and Mark Williams

1994 Mississippian Mound Refuse Disposal Patterns and Implications for Archaeological Research. *Southeastern Archaeology* 13(1):27–35.

Smith, Marvin T., Mark Williams, Chester B. DePratter, Marshall Williams, and Mike Harmon

1988 *Archaeological Investigations at Tomassee (38OC186), a Lower Cherokee Town*. University of South Carolina, Institute of Archaeology and Anthropology, Research Manuscript Series 206. Columbia.

Smith, Philip

1962 *Aboriginal Stone Constructions in the Southern Piedmont*. University of Georgia, Department of Anthropology, Laboratory of Archaeology Series Report 4. Athens.

Smith, Robin L., R. Bruce Council, and Rebecca Saunders

1985 Three Sites on Sandy Run: Phase II Evaluation of Sites 9CM183, 184, 185 at Kings Bay, Georgia. Report submitted to the U.S. Department of the Navy, Kings Bay, Georgia.

Snow, Frankie

n.d. Swift Creek Convenience Paddles and Negative Stamped Ceramics. Manuscript in possession of the author.

1975 Swift Creek Designs and Distributions: A South Georgia Study. *Early Georgia* 3(2):38–59.

1977 *An Archaeological Survey of the Ocmulgee Big Bend Region*. South Georgia College, Occasional Papers from South Georgia 3. Douglas.

1978 The Detection of an Indian Path? *The Profile* 20:12–13.

1982 Kolomoki and Milamo: Some Synchronic Evidence. *The Profile* 36:7–12.

1990 Pine Barrens Lamar. In *Lamar Archaeology: Mississippian Chiefdoms in the Deep South,* edited by M. Williams and G. Shapiro, pp. 82–93. University of Alabama Press, Tuscaloosa.

1993 Swift Creek Design Investigations: The Hartford Case. Manuscript prepared for the Lamar Institute Swift Creek Conference, May 28–29, 1993, Ocmulgee National Monument, Macon, Georgia.

1994 Swift Creek Art: An Anthropological Tool for Investigating Middle Woodland Society in Southern Georgia. Paper presented at the 51st Annual Meeting of the Southeastern Archaeological Conference, Lexington, Kentucky.

Snow, Frankie, and Keith Stephenson

1990 Hartford: A 4th-Century Swift Creek Mound Site in the Interior Coastal Plain of Georgia. Paper presented at the 47th Annual Meeting of the Southeastern Archaeological Conference, Mobile, Alabama.

1991 Salvage Excavations at Hartford (9PU1): A 4th-Century Swift Creek Site on the Ocmulgee River in Pulaski County, Georgia. Manuscript in possession of the authors.

1993 Swift Creek Designs: A Tool for Monitoring Interaction. Paper presented at the Lamar Institute Swift Creek Conference, May 28–29, 1993, Ocmulgee National Monument, Macon, Georgia.

Speck, Frank

1909 Ethnology of the Yuchi Indians. *University of Pennsylvania Anthropological Publications of the University Museum* 1:1. Philadelphia.

Stanyard, William F., and Thomas R. Baker

1992 Two Hundred Years of Woodstock Occupation in Northwest Georgia: The View from Whitehead Farm 1. *Early Georgia* 20(2):33–70.

Steinen, Karl T.

1976a *The Weeden Island Ceramic Complex: An Analysis of Distribution.* Ph.D. Dissertation, Department of Anthropology, University of Florida, Gainesville.

1976b An Archaeological Reconnaissance in Early County, Georgia: A Model of Settlement Patterning. *Early Georgia* 4(1-2):68–75.

1977 Weeden Island in Southwest Georgia. *Early Georgia* 5(1-2):73–99.

1989 The Balfour Mound and Weeden Island Culture in South Georgia. *Early Georgia* 17(1-2):1–23.

Steinen, Karl T., and Thomas J. Crawford

1990 The Sonny Lee Site: Shifting Sands and Archaeological Site Interpretation on the Gulf Coastal Plain. *Early Georgia* 18(1-2):65–81.

Stephenson, Robert L., and Paul Brockington

1969 A Note on the Bostick Site. *Institute of Archaeology and Anthropology University of South Carolina, Notebook* 1(12):7–8.

Stoltman, James A.

1974 *Groton Plantation: An Archaeological Study of a South Carolina Locality.* Peabody Museum Monographs 1. Cambridge, Massachusetts.

1989 A Quantitative Approach to the Petrographic Analysis of Ceramic Thin Sections. *American Antiquity* 54(1):147–60.

1991 Ceramic Petrography as a Technique for Documenting Cultural Interaction: An Example from the Upper Mississippi Valley. *American Antiquity* 56(1):103–20.

Stringfield, Margo

1994 Refined Shovel Testing as a Technique for Tracking Horizontal Stratigraphy. Paper presented at the 49th Annual Meeting of the Southeastern Archaeological Conference, Little Rock, Arkansas.

Swanton, John R.

1928 *Social Organization and Social Usages of the Indians of the Creek Confederacy.* Bureau of American Ethnology, Annual Report 42. Washington, D.C.

1939 *Final Report of the United States de Soto Expedition Commission.* Seventy-sixth Congress, 1st session, House Document 71. Washington, D.C.

1946 *The Indians of the Southeastern United States.* Bureau of American Ethnology, Bulletin 103. Washington, D.C.

Taylor, Richard, and Marion Smith, assemblers

1978 *The Report of the Intensive Survey of the Richard B. Russell Dam and Lake, Savannah River, Georgia and South Carolina.* University of South Carolina, Institute of Archaeology and Anthropology, Research Manuscript Series 142. Columbia.

Tesar, Louis D.

1980 *The Leon County Bicentennial Survey Report: An Archaeological Sur-*

vey of Selected Portions of Leon County, Florida. Florida Department of State, Bureau of Historic Sites and Properties, Division of Archives, History, and Records Management, Miscellaneous Project Report Series 49. Tallahassee.

1994 *Johnson Sand Pit (8LE73): An Analysis and Comparative Review of a Paleoindian through Early Deptford Base Camp in Leon County, Florida.* Bureau of Archaeological Research, Florida Archaeological Reports 32. Tallahassee.

Thomas, David Hurst

1979 *Archaeology.* Holt, Rhinhart, and Winston. New York.

Thomas, Prentice M., Jr., and L. Janice Campbell

1990 The Santa Rosa Swift Creek Culture on the Northwest Florida Gulf Coast: The Horseshoe Bayou Phase. Paper presented at the 47th Annual Meeting of the Southeastern Archaeological Conference, Mobile, Alabama.

1992 *Eglin Air Force Base Historic Preservation Plan. Technical Synthesis of Cultural Resources Investigations at Eglin: Santa Rosa, Okaloosa, and Walton Counties, Florida.* New World Research, Report of Investigations 192.

Thompson, Timothy A., and William M. Gardner

1982 *An Archeological Survey of Five Islands in the Savannah River: An Impact Assessment for the Richard B. Russell Multiple Resource Area.* Thunderbird Research, Front Royal, Virginia.

Thunen, Robert L.

1988 Geometric Enclosures in the Mid-South: An Architectural Analysis of Enclosure Form. In *Middle Woodland Settlement and Ceremonialism in the Mid-South and Lower Mississippi Valley,* edited by R. C. Mainfort, pp. 99–115. Mississippi Department of Archives and History, Archaeological Report 22. Jackson.

Tippitt, V. Ann, and William H. Marquardt

1984 *The Gregg Shoals and Clyde Gulley Sites: Archaeological and Geological Investigations at Two Piedmont Sites on the Savannah River.* Archeological Services, National Park Service, Russell Papers. Atlanta, Georgia.

Toth, Alan

1979 The Marksville Connection. In *Hopewell Archaeology: The Chillicothe*

Conference, edited by D. S. Brose and N. Greber, pp. 188–99. Kent State University Press, Kent, Ohio.

Van der Merwe, Nikolaas J., and J. C. Vogel

1978 13C Content of Human Collagen as a Measure of Prehistoric Diet in Woodland North America. *Nature* 276:815–16.

Van Doren, Mark, ed.

1955 *Travels of William Bartram.* Dover, New York.

Vernon, Richard

1984 *Northeast Florida Prehistory: A Synthesis and Research Design.* M.A. Thesis, Department of Anthropology, Florida State University, Tallahassee.

Wagner, Gail E.

1995 The Prehistoric Sequence of Plant Utilization in South Carolina. Paper presented at the 52nd Southeastern Archaeological Conference, Knoxville, Tennessee.

Walker, Emma, and Ruby Watson

1991 Interview by Alan Marsh, February 21, 1991. Macon, Georgia.

Walthall, John A.

1980 *Prehistoric Indians of the Southeast: Archaeology of Alabama and the Middle South.* University of Alabama Press, Tuscaloosa.

Walthall, John A., Stephen H. Stow, and Marvin J. Karson

1979 Ohio Hopewell Trade: Galena Procurement and Exchange. In *Hopewell Archaeology: The Chillicothe Conference,* edited by D. S. Brose and N. Greber, pp. 247–53. Kent State University Press, Kent, Ohio.

Ward, Trawick

1965 Correlation of Mississippian Sites and Soil Types. *Southeastern Archaeological Conference Bulletin* 3:42–48.

Waring, Antonio J., Jr.

1945 "Hopewellian" Elements in Northern Georgia. *American Antiquity* 11:119–20.

1968 *The Waring Papers,* edited by S. Williams. Peabody Museum, Harvard University, Cambridge, Massachusetts, and University of Georgia Press, Athens.

Washburn, Dorothy K.

1978 A Symmetry Classification of Pueblo Ceramic Designs. In *Discov-*

ering Behavior in the Archaeology of the American Southwest, edited by P. Grebinger, pp. 101–21. Gordon and Breach Science, New York.

Wauchope, Robert

1966 *Archaeological Survey of Northern Georgia with a Test of Some Cultural Hypotheses.* Society for American Archaeology Memoir 21. Salt Lake City, Utah.

Wayne, Lucy B.

1987 Swift Creek Occupation in the Altamaha Delta. *Early Georgia* 15:46–65.

Webb, Malcolm C.

1989 Functional and Historical Parallelisms between Mesoamerica and Mississippian Cultures. In *The Southeastern Ceremonial Complex: Artifacts and Analysis,* edited by P. Galloway, pp. 279–93. University of Nebraska Press, Lincoln.

Webb, William, and David DeJarnette

1942 *An Archaeological Survey of the Pickwick Basin.* Smithsonian Institution, Bureau of American Ethnology Bulletin 129. Washington, D.C.

Webb, William S., and Charles E. Snow

1945 *The Adena People.* University of Kentucky, Publications of the Department of Anthropology and Archaeology 6. Lexington.

Whallon, Robert

1968 Investigations of Late Prehistoric Social Organization in New York State. In *New Perspectives in Archaeology,* edited by S. Binford and L. Binford, pp. 223–44. Aldine, Chicago.

Wharton, Charles H.

1978 *The Natural Environments of Georgia.* Georgia Department of Natural Resources, Atlanta.

White, Nancy Marie, Stephen Belovich, and David Brose

1981 *Archaeological Survey at Lake Seminole.* Cleveland Museum of Natural History Archaeological Research Report 29. Cleveland, Ohio.

Willey, Gordon R.

1939 Ceramic Stratigraphy in a Georgia Village Site. *American Antiquity* 4:140–47.

1949 *The Archaeology of the Florida Gulf Coast.* Smithsonian Miscellaneous Collections 113. Washington, D.C.

Williams, Mark

1975 *Stubbs Mound in Central Georgia Prehistory.* M.A. Thesis, Department of Anthropology, Florida State University, Tallahassee.

1990 *Archaeological Excavations at Shoulderbone Mounds and Village.* Lamar Institute, Lamar Institute Publication 3. Watkinsville, Georgia.

1992 *Archaeological Investigations of Fortson Mound, Wilkes County, Georgia.* Lamar Institute, Lamar Institute Publication 25. Watkinsville, Georgia.

Williams, Mark, and Gary Shapiro

1987 The Changing Contexts of Oconee Valley Political Power. Paper presented at the 44th Annual Meeting of the Southeastern Archaeological Conference, Charleston, South Carolina.

1990 *Archaeological Excavations at Little River (9Mg46), 1984 and 1987.* Lamar Institute, Lamar Institute Publication 2. Watkinsville, Georgia.

Williams, Marshall W., and Carolyn "Liz" Branch

1978 The Tugalo Site, 9ST1. *Early Georgia* 6:32–37.

Williams, Stephen

1958 Review of "Excavations at Kolomoki: Final Report" by W. H. Sears, University of Georgia Series in Anthropology, Athens. *American Antiquity* 23(3):321–23.

Willoughby, Charles C.

1916 *The Art of the Great Earthwork Builders of Ohio.* Annual Report of the Smithsonian Institution 1916. Washington, D.C.

Wilson, Rex L.

1965 *Excavations at the Mayport Mound, Florida.* Contributions of the Florida State Museum 13. Gainesville.

Wimberly, Steve B.

1960 *Indian Pottery from Clarke County and Mobile County, Southern Alabama.* Alabama Museum of Natural History Museum Paper 36. Tuscaloosa.

Wobst, H. Martin

1977 Stylistic Behavior and Information Exchange. In *Papers for the Director: Research Essays in Honor of James B. Griffin,* edited by C. E. Cleland, pp. 317–42. University of Michigan, Museum of Anthropology, Anthropological Papers 61. Ann Arbor.

Wood, W. Dean

  1981 *An Analysis of Two Early Woodland Households from the Cane Island Site, 9PM209.* M.A. Thesis, Department of Anthropology, University of Georgia, Athens.

Wood, W. Dean, and W. Rowe Bowen

  1995 *Woodland Period Archaeology of Northern Georgia.* University of Georgia, Department of Anthropology, Laboratory of Archaeology Series Report 33. Athens.

Wood, W. Dean, Daniel T. Elliott, Teresa P. Rudolph, and Dennis B. Blanton

  1986 *Prehistory in the Richard B. Russell Reservoir: The Archaic and Woodland Periods of the Upper Savannah River.* Archeological Services Branch, National Park Service, Russell Papers. Atlanta, Georgia.

Wood, W. Dean, and R. Jerald Ledbetter

  1988 *Rush: An Early Woodland Period Site in Northwest Georgia.* Southeastern Archeological Services, Athens, Georgia.

Wood, W. Dean, and Charlotte Smith

  1988 *Archeological Evaluation of the Anthony Shoals Site, 9WS51.* Southeastern Archeological Services, Athens, Georgia.

Yarnell, Richard, and M. Jean Black

  1985 Temporal Trends Indicated by a Survey of Archaic and Woodland Plant Food Remains from Southeastern North America. *Southeastern Archaeology* 4:93–106.

Contributors

David G. Anderson (Ph.D., University of Michigan) is an archaeologist with the Southeast Archeological Center of the National Park Service in Tallahassee. His technical interests include cultural resource management, modeling prehistoric population distributions, synthesizing extant archaeological research on locality to regional scales, and exploring the cultural complexity in eastern North America. He has published many books and papers along these lines in recent years.

Keith H. Ashley is an archaeologist living in Jacksonville, Florida. He received his M.A. degree in anthropology from Florida State University in 1988. His research interests include coastal aboriginal adaptations and the archaeology of northeastern Florida.

Judith A. Bense is a Professor of Anthropology and Director of the Archaeology Institute at the University of West Florida in Pensacola. She founded the archaeology program there in 1980 and conducts research in the lower southeastern U.S. in the Woodland, Archaic, and Historic Colonial periods. She has studied the Swift Creek culture since the 1960s and has excavated four shell midden rings of this period on the northern Gulf Coast.

David W. Chase has some fifty years of archaeology experience in Georgia and Alabama. He conducted seminal excavations in the Columbus, Georgia, and central Alabama areas in the 1940s through the 1970s. Most recently he has lived in Stone Mountain, Georgia, and conducted important excavations at the Middle Woodland Miner's Creek site.

Daniel T. Elliott (M.A., University of Georgia, 1980) is a native Georgian and an archaeologist with research interests in the southeastern U.S. and the Caribbean. Trained as a prehistorian with specialization in the Late Archaic period, his current interests span the spectrum of human occupation in the

New World from the Paleoindian period to the early nineteenth century. He currently serves as the Archaeologist for the colonial town of New Ebenezer, near Savannah, Georgia, and as the Secretary for the Lamar Institute, Inc.

Jennifer Freer Harris received her M.A. in anthropology at the University of Georgia, focusing on prehistoric settlement patterns in the southeastern U.S. Jennifer spent several years as a project coordinator in the Zooarchaeology Lab at the UGA Museum of Natural History and as a project director for Southeastern Archeological Services in Athens. For the past several years she has directed an international service project that brings together young Americans and Israelis to work in undeveloped communities in the former Soviet Union.

B. Calvin Jones, a native Texan, received his B.A. (1961) and M.A. (1968) in anthropology from the University of Oklahoma. From his 1968 arrival in Florida as an archaeologist for the state, until his untimely death in early 1998, his reputation grew as a master site sleuth, renowned archaeologist, and friend to everyone. Jones's tremendous contributions to Florida archaeology will stand as his legacy for years to come.

Alan Marsh received a B.A. in history from the University of Georgia in 1983, and an M.A. in history from Georgia College in 1985. He has been employed by the U.S. National Park Service since 1985 as a Park Ranger and a Historian. Alan has a lifelong interest in American Indian cultures, worked seven years at Ocmulgee National Monument, and has written many articles and manuscripts concerning Ocmulgee and Southeastern Indians.

Daniel T. Penton received his M.A. (1970) in anthropology from Florida State University. His long-standing research interest has been in the Middle Woodland of northwestern Florida. Dan lives in Tallahassee where he works as an archaeologist.

Rebecca Saunders is Curator of Anthropology at the Museum of Natural Science at Louisiana State University. She began studying Swift Creek complicated stamped pottery for her M.A. degree and continued researching pottery technology and design information for her Ph.D. work at the University of Florida. More recently, she has extended this type of research to southern Louisiana.

Betty A. Smith (M.A. and Ph.D. in anthropology from the University of Georgia) is Professor of Anthropology at Kennesaw State University. Her research interests include Middle Woodland in the Southeast U.S. and nineteenth-century archaeology in Georgia. Smith wrote her Ph.D. dissertation on the famous Mandeville site, an important Swift Creek center.

Frankie Snow, a native southern Georgian, has spent decades studying the region's cultural and natural history. His archaeological investigations have dealt primarily with revealing the wealth of information about Swift Creek culture as seen through the artwork available on its distinctive pottery. Frankie has discovered and recorded the majority of the known archaeological sites in south-central Georgia.

Karl T. Steinen received his B.A. in anthropology from SUNY Oswego, an M.A. in anthropology from Florida Atlantic University, and a Ph.D. in anthropology from the University of Florida. His main research interests revolve around southern Georgia and the development of political organization during the Woodland period. Steinen is currently a Professor of Anthropology at the State University of West Georgia.

Keith Stephenson received a M.A. in anthropology from the University of Georgia and is a doctoral student at the University of Kentucky. His research area includes the interior Coastal Plain of Georgia and South Carolina. Stephenson's archaeological interests focus on the social structure and political organization of Woodland period societies.

James B. Stoltman was educated at the University of Minnesota (B.A., geology; M.A., anthropology) and at Harvard University (Ph.D., anthropology, 1966). He is Professor of Anthropology at the University of Wisconsin-Madison, where he has taught since 1966. His main research interests are in the prehistory of eastern North America, with a special interest in the application of geological approaches, especially ceramic petrography, to archaeological problems.

Louis D. Tesar received his B.A. (1968) and M.A. (1973) in anthropology from Florida State University. He has been employed by the State of Florida for most of his career and has maintained research interests in many time periods. A font of information about Florida archaeology, Tesar was the editor of *Florida Anthropologist* for many years.

Mark Williams received his B.A. from the University of Georgia (1970), his M.A. from Florida State University (1975), and his Ph.D. (1983) also from the University of Georgia. He is Curator of Archaeology within the University of Georgia Museum of Natural History, Lecturer within the Department of Anthropology, and President of the Lamar Institute, Inc. His research interests and publications are diverse, mostly centering on the Woodland through Mississippian periods in Georgia.

Index